MANDATORY AND DEFAULT RULES IN CONTRACT AND COMMERCIAL LAW

This collection explores the nature and justification of mandatory rules (which are non-excludable) and default rules (which can be modified or excluded by the parties) in contract and commercial law. The collection distinguishes between different kinds of mandatory and default rules that govern commercial transactions. It also explores the choice of rule in various situations. Which rules are mandatory, and are there clearly understood and convincing reasons for parties to be denied choice? In the case of default rules, on what basis is the default position selected? The collection also explores the fundamentally important relationship between default rules and interpretation, and, relatedly, between default rules and contractual risk allocation. The collection will be of interest to academics and practitioners working across the field of commercial law.

Volume 59 in the series Hart Studies in Private Law

Hart Studies in Private Law

This monograph series brings together in one place two types of book: works which examine in-depth the fundamental doctrines and principles of private law, and works which engage with the theoretical underpinnings of private law. The series thus aims to contribute to ever-evolving debates about the nature of private law such as problems of classification and taxonomy, remedies, the relationship with public law and the boundaries of private law generally.

The series includes, but is not confined to, works on contract, tort, unjust enrichment, equity, property and the conflict of laws, welcoming work which intersects with other fields of study to enable a deeper understanding of private law theory and practice.

Mandatory and Default Rules in Contract and Commercial Law

Edited by
Katy Barnett
William Day
Jonathan Morgan
and
Andrew Robertson

•HART•
OXFORD • LONDON • NEW YORK • NEW DELHI • SYDNEY

HART PUBLISHING

Bloomsbury Publishing Plc

Kemp House, Chawley Park, Cumnor Hill, Oxford, OX2 9PH, UK

1385 Broadway, New York, NY 10018, USA

Bloomsbury Publishing Ireland Limited, 29 Earlsfort Terrace, Dublin 2, D02 AY28, Ireland

HART PUBLISHING, the Hart/Stag logo, BLOOMSBURY and the Diana logo are trademarks of Bloomsbury Publishing Plc

First published in Great Britain 2026

A catalogue record for this book is available from the British Library.

A catalogue record for this book is available from the Library of Congress.

Library of Congress Control Number: 2025949140

ISBN: HB: 978-1-50997-120-6
ePDF: 978-1-50997-122-0
ePub: 978-1-50997-121-3

Typeset by Compuscript Ltd, Shannon

For product safety related questions contact productsafety@bloomsbury.com

To find out more about our authors and books visit www.hartpublishing.co.uk. Here you will find extracts, author information, details of forthcoming events and the option to sign up for our newsletters.

ACKNOWLEDGEMENTS

This collection has its origins in papers delivered at five online workshops jointly hosted by Cambridge Private Law Centre and the Melbourne Obligations Group in April and May 2024. We are grateful to the presenters, chairs and other participants in those workshops. The project was organised under the umbrella of the Melbourne Law School – Cambridge Law Faculty Research Partnership, the support from which we gratefully acknowledge. We also express our thanks to Hart for agreeing to publish the output from those workshops in its *Hart Studies in Private Law* series.

Katy Barnett
Andrew Robertson
Melbourne

William Day
Jonathan Morgan
Cambridge

16 May 2025

CONTENTS

CONTRIBUTORS

Devon Airey is a Barrister at 3 Verulam Buildings, London and Bye-Fellow of Wolfson College, Cambridge.

Katy Barnett is Professor of Law at Melbourne Law School.

Ryan Catterwell is a Barrister at Howard Zelling Chambers, Adelaide and Adjunct Senior Lecturer at the TC Beirne School of Law, University of Queensland.

William Day is Fellow of Downing College, Cambridge and a Barrister at 3 Verulam Buildings, London.

David Foxton is a Lord Justice of Appeal in the Court of Appeal of England and Wales.

Rory Gregson is Associate Professor of Law and Fellow of Merton College, Oxford.

Louise Gullifer is Rouse Ball Professor of English Law and Fellow of Gonville and Caius College, Cambridge.

Ying Khai Liew is Professor of Law at Melbourne Law School.

Louise Merrett is Professor of International Commercial Law and Vice Master of Trinity College, Cambridge.

Jonathan Morgan is Professor of English Law and Fellow of Corpus Christi College, Cambridge.

Jeannie Marie Paterson is Professor of Law at Melbourne Law School.

Andrew Robertson is Professor of Law and Director of Studies in Private Law at Melbourne Law School.

David Winterton is Associate Professor at the University of Hong Kong.

Man Yip is Professor of Law at Yong Pung How School of Law, Singapore Management University.

TABLE OF CASES

A

B

C

D

E

F

G

H

I

J

K

L

N

O

P

Q

R

S

T

U

V

W

Y

TABLE OF STATUTES

AUSTRALIA

Commonwealth

New South Wales

Victoria

EUROPEAN LEGISLATION

NEW ZEALAND

PORTUGAL

UNITED KINGDOM

Statutes

TABLE OF INTERNATIONAL INSTRUMENTS

1

Mandatory and Default Rules: Issues and Themes

KATY BARNETT, WILLIAM DAY, JONATHAN MORGAN
AND ANDREW ROBERTSON

I. Introduction

Some legal rules governing commercial transactions operate as defaults, which can be modified or excluded by the parties, while others are mandatory, or non-excludable. While the distinction between default and mandatory rules is simple to state in the abstract, in practice the categories are complicated and unstable. The instability of these categories is revealed by the chapters in this collection. In numerous instances it is not clear whether a given rule is mandatory or default: the nature and extent of party autonomy is often unclear. Not all default rules are the same. The nature of some rules may develop over time, with greater recognition given to party autonomy. Justifications are fundamentally important to both mandatory and default rules, and yet often unclear. Where rules are mandatory, are there clearly understood and convincing reasons for parties to be denied choice? In the case of default rules, the justification is also fundamentally important. On what basis is the default position selected?

Scholars of contract and commercial law almost invariably use the expression 'default rules' to refer to rules that operate in default of party modification. The rules operate as defaults for the parties. It became evident in the course of the seminars that gave rise to this collection that some also consider legal rules from which judges can depart as default rules. The idea of judicial default rules has been given impetus by the recent extra-judicial writing of Lord Sales and is discussed in chapter twelve by Rory Gregson, who prefers the description 'rules with exceptions'. Clearly any exercise of choice by judges in the application of legal rules is fundamentally different to the choice exercised by parties in accepting, modifying or excluding default rules. For that reason, it might be better to avoid any confusion between party defaults and judicial defaults by keeping discussion of them totally separate and using entirely different language, as Gregson argues. In any case, the essays in this collection focus almost exclusively on party defaults and rules that are mandatory because they bind parties to commercial transactions.

The exploration of default and mandatory rules in this collection raises four foundational issues: the taxonomy of mandatory and default rules; the relationship between default rules and interpretation; the justifications and normative bases for mandatory and default rules; and the relationship and points of choice between default and mandatory rules. Those issues are considered across a range of topics spanning contract law, unjust enrichment, the law of trusts and fiduciary duties.

II. A Taxonomy of Mandatory and Default Rules

A major theme explored in this collection is the taxonomy of mandatory and default rules, and it receives particular attention in the contributions of David Foxton and Rory Gregson.

In chapter two, Foxton identifies three forms of mandatory rules: facilitative mandatory rules; prohibitory mandatory rules; and consequential mandatory rules. The first category describes those rules which identify necessary pre-conditions in order to achieve a legal outcome, such as meeting the requirements of the doctrine of consideration in order to create a contract, or the three certainties in order to constitute a trust. Most mandatory rules fall into this category, although even here there may be a role for party autonomy. Consideration again furnishes an example: the parties may choose not to take a point on the lack of consideration, even where it is obviously a problem (as is the case for letters of credit), as William Day explores in chapter five.

Foxton himself acknowledges that the third category is a variant on or development of the first. These are rules which dictate a consequence that follows from a legal outcome. If, for example, a contract is induced by fraudulent misrepresentation, the contract is voidable, and certain consequences follow as a matter of law if the victim of the fraud chooses to rescind the contract (namely that the parties are so far as possible restored to their pre-contractual position).

The second 'prohibitory' category of mandatory rule is intended by Foxton to cover those rules which prescribe limits to what parties can agree by contract (or at least on what contractual terms the courts will enforce, if the parties choose to litigate). Examples discussed in this collection include the rule against penalties (discussed by David Winterton in chapter eleven), the rule against trading with the enemy (discussed by Jonathan Morgan in chapter nine) and exclusions of liability (discussed by Devon Airey in chapter seven). This form of mandatory rule presupposes the existence of default rules: the function of such mandatory rules is to police the outer limits of what can be varied by agreement by that default rule.

In chapter twelve, Gregson identifies three forms of default rules: classic default rules; information defaults; and rules with exceptions. The 'classic' default rule is a one which applies unless the parties agree otherwise, which is the concept of a default rule adopted by most chapters in this volume, including Foxton's. An example is the law of frustration, where the parties can agree an allocation of risk under which their obligations continue even if a supervening event renders performance impossible or radically different, or indeed contract by a *force majeure* clause for frustration-like consequences for a supervening event which the law of frustration would not regard as sufficient to discharge the contract. The law of frustration receives significant attention in this collection, including from Jonathan Morgan and Andrew Robertson, and is addressed later in this introduction.

An 'information' default applies in the absence of the provision of information. Gregson suggests that the duty of fair presentation in insurance law could be understood this way: the cover is presumptively voidable unless the relevant information is given. Terms implied by the Sale of Goods Act 1979 (which Gregson includes in his first category) might also be placed in this category, since they require a seller to be upfront about (for example) any defect in the title or quality of goods rather than hiding behind a principle of *caveat emptor*.[1] Section 14(2) of the 1979 Act, for example, requires goods supplied to be of satisfactory quality, but no breach arises by section 14(2C) if the matter making the goods unsatisfactory was drawn to the buyer's attention before the contract was made. Gregson does not shy away from the prospect that these first two categories are not mutually exclusive: he gives the rule in *Hadley v Baxendale* as an example of something which meets both definitions.[2]

As Gregson notes, the third kind of default rule, namely 'rules with exceptions', is a wide enough category to swallow the previous two forms of default rule as well as extend to other situations, where the choice not to apply the rule does not lie with the parties but rather with the court. An example comes from Ying Khai Liew's chapter fourteen, which notes that the rule requiring certainty of intention for the creation of a trust does not apply to *Quistclose* trusts. Gregson doubts whether it is helpful to describe this third category as a category of default rule at all, given the orthodox focus in scholarship on default rules is on party autonomy but, in this context, the *parties* cannot choose whether the rule or its exception applies.

A taxonomy of mandatory and default rules is not therefore straightforward, and is complicated further by the range and different nature of default rules recognised in contract and commercial law.

III. Default Rules and Interpretation

A second topic explored in this collection is the complicated relationship between default rules, interpretation and contractual allocations of risk. Two principal issues or themes in that relationship are explored in this collection.

The first issue stems from the fact that default rules differ from one another in the extent to which they are dependent for their application on the interpretation of the contract terms. One of the questions explored by Andrew Robertson in chapter three is whether default rules can be situated on a spectrum ranging from the most to the least interpretive. At the least interpretive end are simple default rules like the implication of

[1] W Day, *Key Ideas in Commercial Law* (Oxford, Hart Publishing, 2023) 111.

[2] *cf* NJ McBride, 'Remoteness of Damage in Contract' in M Chen-Wishart and P Saprai (eds), *Research Handbook on the Philosophy of Contract Law* (Cheltenham, Edward Elgar, 2025) 542 (suggesting that the rule in *Hadley v Baxendale* is properly characterised as a default rule because the parties can contract out of it, not because its effects can be altered through the provision by one party to another of information relating to the potential consequences of a breach).

terms as a matter of law in particular classes of contract which, in their application to a particular contract, involve very little interpretation. At the opposite end are highly interpretive doctrines such as the implied duty to cooperate. At that end of the spectrum default rules shade into pure exercises in interpretation: the duty to cooperate can be seen as either a default rule with substantive content or as simply an exercise in interpretation. In the middle of the spectrum are doctrines such as frustration and termination for breach, which combine aspects of both. That raises the question whether there is in fact a spectrum or rather a sharp line between default rules and exercises in interpretation.

That brings us to the second issue in the relationship between default rules and interpretation, which is the idea that there are various points of choice in the law of contract between default rules and the identification of implicit allocations of risk as mechanisms for dealing with particular issues. The doctrines at issue here include frustration, common mistake and remoteness of damage. We could frame the choice between default rules and implicit risk allocation as an interpretive issue (ie, a question about the interpretation of the law), which is whether particular legal doctrines are best understood as default rules or as exercises in identifying implicit allocations of risk. Alternatively, the issue could be framed as a normative question, which is whether particular problems are best addressed by way of default rules or through identification of implicit allocations or risk.

The doctrine of frustration, as noted, receives considerable attention in this collection. In chapter nine, Jonathan Morgan begins with the argument that frustration should be divided into two, basically unrelated, doctrines. First, supervening illegality discharges contracts through a *mandatory* rule of law. It necessarily brings the contract automatically to an end, to preserve the consistency of the legal system (or comity between different systems). Parties are not free to contract out of this rule of public policy.[3] By contrast, Morgan argues, all other situations of 'frustration' concern allocation of the risk of changes in circumstances. This is primarily a matter for the parties to decide. Here, by contrast with supervening illegality, the rules are at best defaults. However, the chapter suggests, radically, that there is no need for any 'rules' (not even default rules). The court need only give effect to the explicit, and implicit, contractual allocation of risk (which, importantly, goes way beyond express '*force majeure*', 'hardship', 'interruption' etc clauses, and includes also, eg pricing mechanisms, break and termination clauses).[4] This maximises party autonomy; contrast the inevitable 'stickiness' of a default rule excusing performance, both 'empirical' and 'normative'[5] (the latter owing to 'the courts' tendency to treat state-created rules as presumptively fair [which] often leads to judicial disapproval of efforts to vary standard implied terms by agreement').[6]

[3] *Ertel Bieber & Co v Rio Tinto Co* [1918] AC 260 (HL). On the distinctiveness of frustration by supervening illegality, see also W Day, 'Shades of Frustration' in E Peel and R Probert (eds), *Shaping the Law of Obligations: Essays in Honour of Professor Ewan McKendrick KC* (Oxford, Oxford University Press, 2023).

[4] *Canary Wharf v European Medicines Agency* [2019] EWHC 335 (Ch).

[5] D Foxton, 'Default and Mandatory Rules in Contract and Commercial Law: A Judicial Perspective', this volume, ch 2.

[6] CJ Goetz and RE Scott, 'The Limits of Expanded Choice: An Analysis of the Interactions Between Express and Implied Contract Terms' (1985) 73 *California Law Review* 261, 263.

Morgan's chapter questions the 'presumptive fairness' (or any presumed superiority) of any frustration 'default'. There is no reliable evidence about a stable, standard set of contracting party preferences or expectations on which to ground a 'majoritarian' default doctrine of excuse. The chapter also doubts whether the courts either can or should attempt to justify a frustration doctrine by first, economic efficiency or, second, fairness and justice. Morgan's praise for private ordering and scepticism about default rules should be contrasted with Robertson's chapter, where the difficulty of identifying implicit allocations of risk is emphasised, alongside the advantages of substantive 'defaults' to fill gaps when the parties leave a risk unallocated.

Given the close connection between frustration and the law dealing with common mistake, it is not surprising that there is a similar divergence of views as to whether the problems in common mistake cases are best dealt with by way of a default rule or the identification of an implicit allocation of risk. The idea that a default rule and the identification of implied terms offer competing paradigms for dealing with common mistake problems is discussed by Andrew Robertson in chapter three. Robertson argues that the default rule approach is easier to comprehend and apply, and is likely to lead to more predictable outcomes. Conversely, Jonathan Morgan has argued in earlier writing that the implied terms approach to common mistake is preferable because the default rule approach is not only unsound as a matter of principle, but is also difficult to apply due to the uncertainty that is inherent in the standard of fundamentality.[7] Morgan has argued that there is no 'doctrine of common mistake' and the English courts can and should approach common mistake cases by asking 'whether the contract, on its true construction, was conditional on the existence of the facts which (it turns out) do not exist'.[8]

Whether the remoteness of damage rule in contract (or the rule in *Hadley v Baxendale*[9]) is best understood as a default rule based on fairness or an exercise in identifying implicit allocations or risk has been the subject of a great deal of debate, both before and after the decision of the House of Lords in *The Achilleas*.[10] The issue is touched on in the chapters by Andrew Robertson, Ryan Catterwell and David Winterton, but is not explored in any detail in this collection.

IV. Justifications for Default Rules

A third set of issues considered in this collection relates to the justifications for and normative foundations of default rules. As noted by several authors in this collection,

[7] J Morgan, 'Common Mistake in Contract: Rare Success and Common Misapprehensions' [2018] *CLJ* 559.

[8] ibid 560.

[9] *Hadley v Baxendale* (1854) 9 Ex 341, 156 ER 145.

[10] *Transfield Shipping Inc v Mercator Shipping Inc (The Achilleas)* [2008] UKHL 48, [2009] 1 AC 61. The pre-*Achilleas* literature on the basis of the rule includes A Kramer, 'An Agreement Centred Approach to Remoteness and Contract' in N Cohen and E McKendrick (eds), *Comparative Remedies for Breach of Contract* (Oxford, Hart Publishing, 2005) 249 and A Robertson, 'The Basis of the Remoteness Rule in Contract' (2008) 28 *Legal Studies* 172. The post-*Achilleas* literature includes, relevantly, A Burrows, 'Lord Hoffmann and Remoteness in Contract' in PS Davies and J Pila (eds), *The Jurisprudence of Lord Hoffmann* (Oxford, Hart Publishing, 2015) 251, A Robertson, 'The Limits of Interpretation in the Law of Contract' (2016) 47 *Victoria University of Wellington Law Review* 191 and McBride (n 2).

including Jonathan Morgan in chapter nine and William Day in chapter five, the typical normative justification given for default rules in an American context is economic efficiency.[11] Default rules are said to exist to 'fill the gaps'[12] in incomplete contracts. Under this theory, default rules are not necessarily geared to fill the gaps in a way that the majority of parties would choose. One path to economic efficiency involves the imposition of 'penalty defaults'. Here, the strategy is to incentivise parties to choose a preferred position expressly, by deliberately putting one party at a disadvantage if they leave the default rules intact. This is said to have the benefit of incentivising the parties to share information, and to negotiate contracts more fully, reducing information asymmetry. However, as Morgan and Day also both observe, this theory does not provide a good 'fit' with Anglo-Australian law. Moreover, specifically in the context of frustration, Morgan notes in chapter nine that assessing the optimal allocation of commercial risk is difficult, even for the parties.

Default rules do not necessarily create incentives for parties to share information or to contract around the default. In fact, as is noted by Katy Barnett in chapter ten, the default position may be subject to a 'status quo bias',[13] making parties *less* likely to contract around some default rules. These kinds of default rules have been called 'sticky' default rules.[14]

A 'majoritarian' approach[15] – where the rule aims to reflect what the majority of parties would want – is a better fit with Anglo-Australian law. So, for example, in the recent case of *Barton v Morris*, Lord Leggatt said in the course of his dissenting judgment that 'default rules are generally optimal when they reflect prevailing social norms and expectations and therefore create rights and obligations which reasonable parties would be likely to agree between themselves'.[16] Under this account, default rules are efficient because they reduce transaction costs and increase certainty for parties. Of course, with mandatory rules, typically the parties have no choice as to whether to adopt them. This often reflects concerns of public policy. The rules of formation of contract are commonly thought to be mandatory, but as Day's chapter five illustrates, the situation may be more complex.

The point of default rules is that parties have choice, and as Andrew Robertson argues in chapter three, make decisions on how to allocate risks (or leave default terms to fill the gaps, in instances where they do not turn their minds to it). In this way, default rules could be said to enhance autonomy.[17] They allow parties to make a choice – and in some instances, incentivise them to do so – but provide baseline rules where parties do not make a choice.

Several of the chapters in this volume contemplate a 'spectrum' of rules from heavily default to mandatory, including those of Ryan Catterwell (chapter four) and Gregson

[11] See especially I Ayres and R Gertner, 'Filling Gaps in Incomplete Contracts: An Economic Theory of Default Rules' (1989) 99 *Yale Law Journal* 87.

[12] ibid.

[13] R Korobkin, 'Status Quo Bias and Contract Default Rules' (1998) 83 *Cornell Law Review* 608.

[14] H Dagan and M Heller, 'Autonomy Defaults' (1 February 2025), available at ssrn.com/abstract=4754123 or dx.doi.org/10.2139/ssrn.4754123.

[15] J Morgan, *Contract Law Minimalism: A Formalist Restatement of Commercial Contract Law* (Cambridge, Cambridge University Press, 2013) 92 and 118.

[16] *Barton v Morris* [2023] UKSC 3, [2023] AC 684 [128].

[17] Dagan and Heller (n 14).

(chapter twelve). As Louise Gullifer and Louise Merritt argue in chapter six – by reference to Sale of Goods legislation and the United Nations Convention on Contracts for the International Sale of Goods – default rules also have the benefit of providing legal certainty, coordination and harmonisation. This highlights the fact that the imposition of certain mandatory or default terms often reflects a choice made by the legislature for public policy reasons, particularly in a contexts where parties are subjected to standard terms. This is considered by Jeannie Paterson's chapter eight on the Consumer Rights Act and Devon Airey's chapter seven on the Unfair Contract Terms Act in the UK.

In chapter ten, Barnett argues that default rules may not have a single justification, but that they may reflect a plurality of aims, including efficiency, proper allocation of risks and resources, and maximising social welfare. How these policy considerations are interlaced in a given case depends upon the particular context. Thus, for example, in chapter nine Morgan considers that neither 'efficiency' nor 'justice' can be understood as the basis for the rules of frustration in the common law. Morgan similarly argues that, in the doctrine of frustration, it is necessary to distinguish sharply between mandatory rules of public policy and other kinds of reasons why courts may wish to hold that a contract will be frustrated.

Ryan Catterwell notes in chapter four that defaults can be seen as more extensive if one subscribes to a theory of contract which emphasises the maximization of autonomy. Conversely, the role of default terms can be seen as more limited if one subscribes to a theory of contract which sees contract as more 'facilitative' or as a useful 'institution' or 'form'. Consequently, as Catterwell points out, looking at whether particular rules are default or mandatory may give a clearer picture of the way in which the law should operate and inform the theory of contract law more generally. The difficulties of classification and movement between categories explored in this collection may, however, limit the conclusions that can be drawn.

V. Between Default Rules and Mandatory Rules

Discussions about 'default' and 'mandatory' rules seem to assume a sharp dichotomy between them. But it is more accurate to postulate a spectrum, comprising shades of compulsion / optionality, rather than a clear-cut binary distinction. This is a fourth theme of the collection.

Default rules can be easier or more difficult to displace by agreement ('contract around'). There may be legal restrictions on their alteration (considered below). In addition, numerous extra-legal factors may inhibit contracting-away from the default, as suggested by behavioural and psychological insights.[18] In response to the critique that default rules are essentially an unimportant category given that parties are legally free to alter them at will, Ayres replies: 'defaults matter and the iron law of default inertia

[18] Foxton (n 5) distinguishes 'normative stickiness' (resulting from rules of law) and 'empirical stickiness' (resulting from factors other than legal rules).

prevails'.[19] As noted above, that 'inertia' is often described as the 'stickiness' of default rules.[20]

Sometimes defaults are left to govern the situation through simple ignorance: parties unaware of background law cannot be in a position to alter it. In commercial transactions however, parties will usually be well informed and legally represented: or, at least, the standard forms they use will have been drafted by sophisticated transactional lawyers. (Standard forms are, again, discussed below.) But several reasons have been postulated for the tenacity of default rules between even well-informed parties. First, it is always costly to negotiate an express term. It reduces such 'transaction costs' simply to allow background defaults to operate. Even if the defaults are not the 'first best' ideal option, parties may rationally 'satisfice' to economise on transaction costs. Secondly, a party suggesting an express alternative to the background defaults may be viewed with suspicion. As Bernstein puts it, 'suggesting too many deviations from the [default rules] … might be interpreted as a signal that [the negotiating party] is a less reliable or more contentious trading partner than the average market participant', that is 'more likely … to rely on his legal rights' than to resolve disputes informally and cooperatively.[21] The counter-party may fear that the proposal to deviate from the default 'hides some unknown problem' and may therefore be some kind of 'trick'.[22] Concern to avoid sending poor 'relational or reputational' signals may again, therefore, lead to default rules governing a transaction even though a different rule might be objectively superior for both contracting parties.

Another, psychological, explanation for tenacious defaults is the so-called 'endowment effect'.[23] Those who have something become attached to it, valuing it more highly (because of that fact of initial possession) than someone who might potentially acquire the thing. This has emerged from, eg, the famous 'coffee mug' experiment, when mugs were given at random to half the members of the group; they were asked the price they'd demand to sell the mug, whereas the other (mug-less) half of the experimental group were asked their price for buying the same. A distinctly asymmetric valuation emerged: those who were given mugs instantly valued them significantly more than those who did not have a mug. Applied to the present debate, the implication is that parties initially granted a legal entitlement (say, to a given remedy) by the law's default rules will place a higher value on that entitlement simply due to the fact of that initial (default) allocation.[24] This entails reluctance to agree to deviations from the default position.

With a legal rule rather than (say) a coffee mug, there could be additional reasons to value its initial assignment. As Sunstein suggests, the law's initial (default) allocation

[19] I Ayres, 'Menus Matter' (2006) 73 *University of Chicago Law Review* 3, 5.

[20] O Ben-Shahar and JAE Pottow, 'On the stickiness of default rules' (2006) 33 *Florida State University Law* Review 651.

[21] L Bernstein, 'Social norms and default rules analysis' (1993) 3 *Southern California Interdisciplinary Law Journal* 59, 72, fn 52.

[22] Ben-Shahar and Pottow (n 20) 652.

[23] eg D Kahneman, JL Knetsch and RH Thaler, 'Experimental Tests of the Endowment Effect and the Coase Theorem' (1990) 98 *Journal of Political Economy* 1325.

[24] R Korobkin, 'The Status Quo Bias and Contract Default Rules' (1998) 83 *Cornell Law Review* 608.

of a right could be given *moral* weight, a signal of its legitimate holder.[25] This would reinforce the default rule's potential to shape parties' preferences (ie, about how the matter in question should be governed). On the other hand, Schwartz is sceptical about a conscious attempt to frame preferences by default rules.[26] He suggests it is more likely that parties will 'resent' rules that they do not (initially) prefer, and seek to displace them by disagreement. Thus preference-shaping default rules' 'immediate and possibly only effect would be to raise transaction costs'.[27] Sunstein also accepts that a preference for default rules may have nothing to do with their presumptive moral legitimacy, but is simply a hard-wired trait of human psychology. That trail, viewed economically, might be 'simple confusion' (ie, the assumption that holding fast to the initial entitlement is cost-free, which ignores the 'opportunity cost' of *not* altering the default position when replacing it would be mutually beneficial).

Sometimes, of course, the default rule does represent the optimal solution to a given question. Katy Barnett argues in chapter ten, for example, that the breach date 'rule' for assessment of damages is likely to be 'very sticky' precisely because it embodies a commercially desirable mixture of policies (such as promoting cost-minimising 'reasonable mitigation') and is applied flexibly by the court. The common law rule's suitability, argues Barnett, explains why it is rare in practice that even sophisticated parties attempt to stipulate a different, explicit date on which damages should be assessed.

Standard-form agreements have dominated commercial activity for two centuries.[28] They contain important sets of rules that are not the product of state activity (ie, lawmaking by legislatures or courts). Therefore, the tenacity of standard forms cannot be attributed to *legal* restrictions on contracting-out. Louise Gullifer identifies powerful reasons that nevertheless drive the de facto binding status of standard forms.[29] Commercial transactions are rarely isolated, but take place within market networks (eg, 'string' or 'back-to-back' contracts). Under such market conditions, *transactional harmonisation* is of the first importance. This is particularly so when instruments themselves became tradeable: 'in some markets a standard term contract is "commodified", that is, can be traded among market participants. A contract whose terms deviates from the standard is less likely to be tradeable'.[30] The result is that through 'extreme' market pressure rather than any legal compulsion, contracts such as the Master Agreement of the International Swaps and Derivatives Association (the famous 'ISDA MA') are near-universal in the relevant trade (applying without modification, save where expressly permitted by the form). Gullifer comments: 'Stickiness, here, is often logical and efficient, since it results in the benefits of certainty and coordination being realised'.[31] Some have criticised such enormous powers of 'private lawmaking' being delegated, de facto,

[25] CR Sunstein, 'Switching the default rule' (2002) 77 *New York University Law Review* 106.

[26] A Schwartz, 'The default rule paradigm and the limits of contract law' (1993) 3 *Southern California Interdisciplinary Law Journal* 389.

[27] ibid 414.

[28] C Mitchell, 'Mercantile Usage, Construction of Contracts and the Implication of Terms, 1750–1850' in C Mitchell and S Watterson (eds), *The World of Maritime and Commercial Law: Essays in Honour of Francis Rose* (Oxford, Hart Publishing, 2020).

[29] L Gullifer, 'The Nature and Function of Default Rules in Commercial Law' in B Häcker and J Ungerer (eds), *Default Rules in Private Law* (Oxford, Hart Publishing, forthcoming).

[30] ibid.

[31] ibid.

to those who draft standard form contracts.[32] But in the business-to-business context, ie away from understandable concerns about uncontrolled imposition of terms on powerless consumers,[33] forms drafted by an industry association (such as the ISDA MA) may be sensitive to the understandings and expectations of market participants (here, banks and other financial institutions). Industry-standard contracts may offer the best prospects for truly 'majoritarian' default rules – precisely because they are produced by trade bodies and *not* by government lawmaking (including by the courts).

Default rules are also 'sticky' because of *legal* restrictions on modification. Ayres has coined the term 'altering rules' to denote the category that regulates modification to the law's default position.[34] A number of the chapters in this collection deal with such 'altering' rules. In chapter fourteen, Ying Khai Liew argues that several rules in trusts law that were previously thought 'mandatory' may be modified, but only when the trust beneficiaries are actively involved in bargaining for the trust's terms at its creation. In chapter seven, Devon Airey analyses statutory regulation, in English law, of contractual exclusion clauses: valid only if 'reasonable'.[35] Legislation in the 1970s elevated (inter alia) the longstanding statutory implied terms in sales contracts from default rules into (absolutely) mandatory rules in consumer sales, and an intermediate presumptive / defeasible mandatory status in commercial sales.[36] The law may also set terms governing permissible alterations to default rules. Sunstein notes the US rule that employees may waive the 40-hour maximum working week, but only if they receive time-and-a-half pay (ie, 50 per cent more than their usual hourly rate) for such additional work.[37]

These last two examples concern *statutory* 'altering rules'. They are explicit and relatively clear-cut. By contrast, the position at common law is typically much less clear. As Ayres has commented, 'courts seldom explicitly state [the] necessary conditions' to contract around the law's default rules.[38] In particular, when holding that a given contract's terms are insufficiently explicit to displace the background default, courts 'usually refuse to articulate what contractual language would be sufficient'. This is problematic when, in order to understand a rule properly,

> a lawyer must know not only the content of the rule itself and whether it is merely a default, but the necessary and sufficient conditions for contracting around it. One cannot effectively practice as a transactional lawyer or as a litigator or as a judge unless one can identify the likely legal response to particular opt-out attempts.[39]

[32] WD Slawson, 'Standard Form Contracts and Democratic Control of Lawmaking Power' (1971) 84 *Harvard Law Review* 529.

[33] ibid 560 ('[business's] freedom is inevitably the consumers' compulsion. It then possesses a lawmaking power affecting the public over which the public has no effective control').

[34] I Ayres, 'Regulating opt out: An economic theory of altering rules' (2012) 121 *Yale Law Journal* 2032.

[35] D Airey, 'When it's Mandatory to be 'Reasonable': the Nature and Application of Reasonableness under the Unfair Contract Terms Act 1977', this volume, ch 7.

[36] J Morgan, 'Compulsion, Choice and Statutory Intervention in Contract: Implied Terms of Quality in Sale of Goods' in TT Arvind and J Steele (eds), *Contract Law and the Legislature* (Oxford, Hart Publishing, 2022) 182–84; *cf* 188–89 (an enduring compromise).

[37] Sunstein (n 25) 108.

[38] I Ayres, 'Preliminary thoughts on optimal tailoring of contractual rules' (1993) 3 *Southern California Interdisciplinary Law Journal* 1, 16.

[39] Ayres (n 34) 2115.

Legal restrictions on modifying default rules can render them 'quasi mandatory'. That results either from the 'altering rules' being narrowly defined, or *poorly* defined. Parties' autonomy to modify 'default' rules is inevitably curtailed if they do not know, and cannot easily predict, the means necessary for modification to be legally effective.

Many examples could be given of this tendency. A well-known controversy surrounds the so-called *contra proferentem* presumption, reading down clauses that would alter legal background rules.[40] As Ryan Catterwell notes in chapter four, running contrary to the modern, ordinary-language approach to construction of legal instruments,[41] *contra proferentem* presents a 'significant complicating factor' in interpretation.[42] Catterwell notes the odd timing of the emergence of the principle in its modern form,[43] 'antithetical' to contract law's contemporary development.[44] The strength of the presumption varies, but Catterwell suggests that the protection given to 'some rights to the exclusion of others lacks coherence'. As Catterwell has demonstrated in other work,[45] it is most unclear how explicit a contract needs to be to displace the common law doctrine of frustration, for example. Courts and distinguished commentators state the rules (or presumptions) in very different ways. Catterwell concludes that judicial interpretation in this context is guided by the severity of the consequences (ie, contractual interruption) that emerge ex post facto, as well as by the contract's wording.[46] For a 'catastrophic' and unforeseeable supervening event, 'a strong indicator [and] clear words would be needed' (whereas the court might enforce (merely) implicit allocation of risk, if the interruption were reasonably foreseeable, or its consequences mild).

Remedies are another disputed area. There seem to be at least some legal rules that parties cannot alter by contract. For example, the prohibition on stipulating disproportionate penal sums, designed to deter breach of contract. David Winterton in chapter eleven explores three uncertain questions in this field: (a) the permissibility of excluding all liability to pay damages for breach; (b) the effect of a stated preference for specific relief; and (c) whether contracting parties can opt out of specific relief. Winterton argues that contracting parties can exclude all liability to pay damages for breach without rendering the relevant promise illusory; that an expressed preference for specific relief should be taken into account by the court, but not be determinative; and that a contractual stipulation that one or both parties should be confined to damages should be honoured. The general issue of whether remedies *should* be susceptible to modification has proved

[40] See, eg, S Tofaris, 'Commercial Construction of Exemption Clauses' [2019] *Lloyd's Maritime and Commercial Law Quarterly* 270; D Foxton, 'The Status of the Special Rules of Construction of Exemption Clauses in Commercial Contracts' [2021] *Journal of Business Law* 205.

[41] *Investors Compensation Scheme Ltd v West Bromwich Building Society* [1998] 1 WLR 896 (HL) 912 (Lord Hoffmann) (legal interpretation 'assimilated' with 'common sense principles by which any serious utterance would be interpreted in ordinary life. Almost all the old intellectual baggage of "legal" interpretation has been discarded').

[42] R Catterwell, 'Party Intention, Default Rules and Contract Theory', this volume, ch 4.

[43] *Gilbert-Ash (Northern) Ltd v Modern Engineering (Bristol) Ltd* [1974] AC 689 (HL).

[44] *cf Photo Production Ltd v Securicor Transport Ltd* [1980] AC 827 (HL) 850–51 (Lord Diplock).

[45] R Catterwell, 'Frustration and assumption of risk' [2022] *Journal of Business Law* 76.

[46] Citing eg *Kuwait Supply Co v Oyster Marine Management Inc (The Safeer)* [1994] 1 Lloyd's Rep 637 (QB) 643 (Rix J) ('[It is] possible for a risk to be covered by express provision of the contract, but for the contract to be frustrated when that risk materialises in some overwhelming form').

controversial. Some argue that these rules too should be 'defaults' (and therefore that any restrictions on agreed remedies are unfortunate).[47] Others defend rules that give some degree of immutability to the legally-supplied remedy regime.[48]

In chapter two, David Foxton also notes the sliding scale of modifiability, commenting that '"Normative stickiness" can, in some instances, assume the qualities of a super-glue, at which point the line between mandatory and default rules becomes vanishingly thin'. Catterwell perhaps ultimately approves of the process by which older, stricter canons of construction have been replaced by a weaker presumption that strikes 'a similar but less rigid balance' – another victory for 'legal pragmatism at the expense of formalism' which allows 'different tiers or levels of default rules'. As Ayres comments, there may be a place for conscious stickiness ('impeding altering rules'), deliberately making it harder to contract out for reasons of 'soft paternalism'. That is to say, concerns to protect weaker parties might not be strong enough to justify fully mandatory rules, yet 'lawmakers can still at times manage and ameliorate these concerns by creating sticky defaults'.[49]

Other commentators are more critical. 'Neo-formalists' doubt the capacity of either courts or legislatures to devise appropriate default rules.[50] Here, for example, Morgan questions whether a legally supplied doctrine of frustration can satisfactorily govern interruptions to performance, with the courts struggling to articulate 'efficient', 'fair' or even predictable rules to allocate the risks of unforeseen events.[51] When defaults are of dubious value, the law should make it as easy as possible to contract out of them. For example Triantis argues that since it is difficult to ascertain 'majoritarian' preferences (or otherwise identify optimal defaults) for heterogenous contracting parties, a more sensible approach to freedom of contract would 'focus more on minimizing the cost of contracting away from the default rather than maximizing the proportion of parties who would (hypothetically) choose it'.[52] For such sceptics, default rules should not be praised as 'norms of commerce which have come to be recognised as ordinary incidents of particular types of contract' with the result that 'the court in construing the contract starts from the assumption that in the absence of clear words the parties did not intend the contract to derogate from these normal rights and obligations'.[53] Lord Leggatt's statement exemplifies what Ayres called 'the disturbing tendency of courts to turn default laws into immutable laws' (scathingly attributed by Ayres to 'judicial egoism').[54]

[47] See, eg, S Rowan, 'For the Recognition of Remedial Terms Agreed Inter Partes' (2010) 126 *LQR* 448; J Morgan, 'On the Nature and Function of Remedies for Breach of Contract' in S Worthington and G Virgo (eds), *Commercial Remedies:* Resolving *Controversies* (Cambridge, Cambridge University Press, 2017).

[48] SV Shiffrin, 'Remedial Clauses: The Overprivatization of Private Law' (2016) 67 *Hastings Law Journal* 407.

[49] Ayres (n 34) 2084.

[50] eg A Schwartz and RE Scott, 'Contract Theory and the Limits of Contract Law' (2003) 113 *Yale Law Journal* 541; A Schwartz and RE Scott, 'The Common Law of Contract and the Default Rule Project' (2016) 102 *Virginia Law Review* 1523.

[51] J Morgan, 'Frustration Dissected: Mandatory and Default Rules', this volume, ch 9 (*cf* generally, J Morgan, *Contract Law Minimalism: A Formalist Restatement of Commercial Contract Law* (Cambridge, Cambridge University Press, 2013)).

[52] G Triantis, 'Promissory Autonomy, Imperfect Courts, and the Immorality of the Expectation Damages Default' (2012) 45 *Suffolk University Law Review* 827, 840 (and *cf* 832 'the focus should be placed on protecting promissory autonomy by structuring defaults so that they are loose and promisors can opt out at low cost').

[53] *Triple Point Technology Inc v PTT Public Co Ltd* [2021] UKSC 29, [2021] AC 1148 [108] (Lord Leggatt).

[54] Ayres (n 39) 17.

We return, finally, to the point that mandatory and default rules inhabit a spectrum rather than a simple dichotomy. Analysing issues facing law-makers in designing *mandatory* rules, Zamir and Ayres argue one important choice is 'the degree to which they are immutable'.[55] For example, where a mandatory rule aims to protect poorly informed parties (consumer contracts exemplifying such information asymmetry), the law may stipulate an 'altering rule' that is rationality-enhancing, ie amounts to 'a kind of mandated disclosure that can educate the nondrafter about the substantive provisions of the contract'.[56] But if such 'disclosures' are unlikely to guarantee effective 'education' and 'protection',[57] a fully immutable rule may be required. (Equally, where a mandatory rule is justified by *externality* concerns such as public policy, 'rationality-enhancing interventions are likely to be ineffective when the central goal is to protect people outside the contract').[58] Thus not only the existence of mandatory rules but their strictness (ie, degree of immutability) is informed by the aim pursued. Ultimately, as Zamir and Eyres put it, 'default rules are often quasi-mandatory, and mandatory rules are sometimes quasi-default'.[59]

[55] E Zamir and I Ayres, 'A Theory of Mandatory Rules: Typology, Policy, and Design' (2020) 99 *Texas Law Review* 283, 320–22.

[56] ibid 290.

[57] *cf* ibid 300 ('suppliers regularly employ behavioral insights to take advantage of customers' heuristics and biases').

[58] ibid 291.

[59] ibid 321.

2

Default and Mandatory Rules in Commercial Law: A Judicial Perspective

DAVID FOXTON

I have spent much of my life getting up at an unearthly hour to stare intently at a small screen, transfixed by an Anglo-Australian encounter. Fortunately, the early morning online engagement between Melbourne Law School and the Cambridge Law Faculty, in the conference which preceded the publication of this book, involved none of the trauma for English spectators of Steve Harmison's opening over bowled in the 2006/07 Ashes. Not only were the sides evenly matched, but the five-test series of seminars (over five weeks in April and May 2024) was an exercise in academic collaboration rather than sporting confrontation, the book now fielding a combined First XI from both jurisdictions. It is, therefore, a privilege to have been given the opportunity to contribute to the book in which those papers now become available to a wider audience. The results of the seminar series amply justify the decision to use the contrast between mandatory and default rules as the point of departure for a wide-ranging analysis of doctrines in contract and commercial law. This essay offers a few thoughts on some of the many interesting questions the collection throws up.

The core instances of default and mandatory rules in contract and commercial law are relatively easy to envisage: a mandatory rule controls the effect of a particular contract or contractual term in a way which cannot be contracted out of, and a default rule gives a particular effect to a contract or contract term unless, with a degree of specificity dependent on the context, the parties agree otherwise.[1] However, it soon becomes apparent from the essays which comprise this collection that the position is much more complex.

Taking mandatory rules first, the contributions reveal at least three different types. The first is mandatory rules of the 'if you wish to achieve legal outcome X, you must meet legal requirement Y' type: what might be termed purely facilitative mandatory

[1] eg, I Ayres and R Gertner, 'Filling Gaps in Incomplete Contracts: An Economic Theory of Default Rules' (1989) 99 *Yale Law Journal* 87; RE Barnett, 'The Sound of Silence: Default Rules and Contractual Consent' (1992) 78 *Virginia Law Review* 821 (both of which are cited extensively in the papers which follow).

rules. The doctrine of consideration or, before the Contracts (Rights of Third Parties) Act 1999, privity of contract, are examples of facilitative rules of contract law of this kind. The three certainties of trusts law are another,[2] as are the so-called 'irreducible core' of fiduciary duties,[3] although here the mandatory nature of this minimum requirement might be thought to be of limited impact. Whereas a failure to meet the mandatory facilitative rules of contract will lead to a relationship which is not legally enforceable, the creation of a managerial role which does not meet the core requirements for a fiduciary relationship will simply not be a fiduciary role, but not for that reason alone devoid of any legal effect.

The second category is mandatory rules which are intended to prevent particular types of contracts or contractual term, or those which would have particular consequences, from being legally effective: what might be termed prohibitory mandatory rules. This would include the doctrine of penalties which David Winterton discusses,[4] the doctrine of restraint of trade, the rules against trading with the enemy discussed by Jonathan Morgan,[5] the exclusion of the warranty of title under the Sale of Goods Act 1979,[6] or the public policy rule which precludes a party excluding liability for its own fraudulent statements.[7] A third type – a variant on purely facilitative mandatory rules – is that 'if you do achieve legal outcome X, mandatory legal consequence Y will follow'. The rule in *Saunders v Vautier* may be an example of such a rule,[8] at least to the extent that it is not possible for the trustee unilaterally to exclude its application in relation to vested interests by provisions of the trust instrument postponing the distribution of trust property.[9] However, it does seem to be possible for the beneficiaries to contract not to exercise their *Saunders v Vautier* entitlement.[10]

The extent to which these distinctions map onto the two different types of mandatory rule recognised in the Rome I Regulation,[11] discussed by Louise Gullifer and Louise Merrett,[12] merits discussion. Rome I distinguishes between 'non-derogable provisions' under Article 3(3)[13] and 'overriding mandatory provisions of the law of the forum' under Article 9. The particular significance of this distinction in the Rome I Regulation is that the former are provisions of national law which will apply to any contract which is wholly domestic for the purposes of that legal system, whereas the latter, a narrower

[2] YK Liew, 'From Mandatory to Default Rules: Trusts in the Commercial Context', this volume, ch 14.

[3] Also discussed by Liew (ibid), and by M Yip, 'Equity in Commerce: Why Do We Need Default Rules?', this volume, ch 13.

[4] D Winterton, 'The Express Modification of Contract Law's Default Remedial Rules', this volume, ch 11.

[5] J Morgan, 'Frustration Dissected: Mandatory and Default Rules', this volume, ch 9.

[6] Discussed in L Gullifer and L Merrett, 'Default Terms in Sale of Goods Contracts', this volume, ch 6.

[7] *S Pearson & Son Ltd v Dublin Corporation* [1907] AC 351. By contrast, liability for an agent's fraud would seem to be a normative sticky default: *HIH Casualty and General Insurance Ltd v Chase Manhattan Bank* [2003] UKHL 6, [2003] 1 All ER (Comm) 349 (see text to nn 25–37 for 'normative stickiness').

[8] *Saunders v Vautier* (1841) Cr & Ph 240, 41 ER 482.

[9] See *Lewin on Trusts*, 20th edn (London, Sweet & Maxwell, 2023) [22-016] ('not a rule of construction … [and] may therefore be invoked even though it will defeat the known intentions of the settlor or trustee'). This view is challenged by Liew (n 2).

[10] *N-Krypt International Corp v LeVasseur* [2018] BCCA 20; *Auto Net v Tyler* [2020] NZHC 2459 [127]–[130].

[11] Regulation (EC) No 593/2008.

[12] Gullifer and Merrett (n 6).

[13] 'Where all other elements relevant to the situation at the time of the choice are located in a country other than the country whose law has been chosen, the choice of the parties shall not prejudice the application of provisions of law of that other country which cannot be derogated from by agreement.'

category, are rules capable of being applied by a particular forum whatever the applicable law of the contract or the state affiliations of the contracting parties.

There appears to be an academic consensus that even purely facilitative mandatory rules of English law such as the doctrine of consideration fall within Article 3(3).[14] While acknowledging that consensus, I have judicially queried its correctness,[15] noting that

> the consequence of a rule that all the 'power conferring' requirements under the law of contract in a particular jurisdiction for the creation of contractual obligations binding under that law constitute mandatory rules of law for article 3(3) purposes might be very significant.

The unattractive consequences, for a well-travelled applicable law like English law, of an interpretation of Article 3(3) which would embrace all facilitative mandatory rules, may be one of the reasons why the English courts have adopted a fairly generous approach to the identification of international elements sufficient to take a contract outside the scope of that article.[16]

Rome I apart, are there any other distinctions between these types of mandatory rule? Ying Liew's work would suggest that it is easier for the courts to develop exceptions, either of particular kinds or in particular contexts, to the facilitative mandatory rules of trusts law,[17] and William Day suggests that this is also true of the facilitative mandatory rule of consideration.[18] However, determining which mandatory rules fall into which category is not straightforward. In my tentative judicial foray, I suggested there 'may be scope, in this context, for distinguishing between the pre-requisites to the conclusion of a binding contract under a particular legal order depending on whether or not they exist to serve a particular public policy'.[19] While the public policy basis of the doctrine of consideration is, at least in this day and age, hard to discern, I accept that there are other rules of contract law which are harder to place – for example, the rules on incorporation of terms discussed by Jeannie Marie Paterson.[20]

The various mandatory rules discussed in this book embrace a range of mandatory legal responses. A mandatory rule of English law can be a gateway for the application of a mandatory rule of some other legal system, as in the rule in *Foster v Driscoll*.[21] It can involve an unconditional denial of legal efficacy.[22] Or it can impose an additional requirement for the enforceability of a contractual term. This could be the requirement to demonstrate the reasonableness of a term, imposed on certain types of provision by the Unfair Contract Terms Act 1977. That requirement, and its place on the scale

[14] As W Day notes in 'Default Rules in Contract Formation', this volume, ch 5: 'it is orthodox to treat consideration in contract formation as a mandatory rule that cannot be changed by contrary agreement'.
[15] *Banca Intesa Sanpaolo Spa v Comune di Venezia* [2022] EWHC 2586 (Comm), [2023] Bus LR 384 [354]–[357] (overturned on other grounds [2023] EWCA Civ 1482, [2024] Bus LR 228).
[16] eg, *Banco Santander Totta SA v Companhia Caris de Ferro de Lisboa SA* [2016] EWCA Civ 1267, [2017] 1 WLR 1323.
[17] Liew (n 2) section I, suggesting that 'there is a detectable shift from *mandatory* trusts rules, as traditionally developed in the domestic context, to *default* rules in the "commercial" context'.
[18] Day (n 14).
[19] *Banca Intesa Sanpaolo Spa v Comune di Venezia* [2022] EWHC 2586 (Comm), [2023] Bus LR 384 [357].
[20] JM Paterson, 'Mandatory Statutory Rules, Consumer Contracts and Contractual Interpretation', this volume, ch 8.
[21] *Foster v Driscoll* [1929] 1 KB 470 and see also Rome I Regulation, Art 9(3).
[22] eg those discussed in the text to nn 3–5 above.

between the exercise of judicial discretions and the application of hard-edged rules of law, is discussed by Devon Airey in her chapter.[23] Paterson's consideration of consumer legislation controls addresses similar issues.[24]

The conceptual dividing line between mandatory and default rules is generally treated as being whether or not it is possible to contract out of the relevant rule.[25] But as so often in private law, what initially appears to be a binary divide soon resolves itself into shades on a continuous spectrum. Jonathan Morgan was surely correct to observe elsewhere that there is 'a spectrum rather than a sharp dichotomy between default and immutable rules'.[26] Picking up on language used by, eg, Omri Ben-Shahar and John Pottow,[27] various of the papers use the concept of 'stickiness' to refer to how frequently or readily parties can contract out of the default rule. That adhesive quality generally refers to the practical difficulty of contracting out of the default – either because it would delay the conclusion of the bargain or increase the transaction costs of doing so – or the absence of a sufficient incentive for contracting out to be worth the attempt.[28] We can refer to this as 'empirical stickiness'. However, 'stickiness' might also reflect principles of law (generally those defining the extent of the 'burden of expression'[29] before contracting out can be achieved) which might be described as 'normative stickiness'. In this context, we enter the realms of 'meta-law', with second-order default rules of interpretation being deployed to determine whether first-order default rules as to the terms of a contract have been displaced[30] – most obviously the *contra proferentem* rule and the associated interpretive principle in *Gilbert Ash (Northern) Ltd v Modern Engineering (Bristol) Ltd*.[31] Those 'rules on rules' are themselves default rules, because the contract can exclude both interpretative presumptions or, put another way, the heightened burdens of expression they entail (as distinct from those rules being 'satisfied', rather than disapplied, by words of the requisite clarity).[32]

[23] D Airey, 'When It's Mandatory to be "Reasonable": The Nature and Application of Reasonableness under the Unfair Contract Terms Act 1977', this volume, ch 7.

[24] Paterson (n 20).

[25] eg R Gregson, 'Three Forms of Default Rules (in the Law of Unjust Enrichment)', this volume, ch 12: 'most often lawyers use the phrase [sc. default rules] to describe rules which apply unless the parties agree that a different rule should apply'; K Barnett, 'Date of Breach as a Sticky Default Rule and the Role of the Court in Assessing Reasonable Mitigatory Measures', this volume, ch 10.

[26] J Morgan, 'Compulsion, Choice and Statutory Intervention in Contract: Implied Terms of Quality in Sale of Goods' in TT Arvind and J Steele (eds), *Contract Law and the Legislature: Autonomy, Expectations, and the Making of Legal Doctrine* (Oxford, Hart Publishing, 2020) 177.

[27] O Ben-Shahar and JAE Pottow, 'On the Stickiness of Default Rules' (2006) 33 *Florida State University Law Review* 651.

[28] A good example of this type of 'unstickiness' is the 'breach date rule' discussed by Barnett (n 25). The 'default' position as to the time for assessing loss is not departed from by contracting parties because the default is itself inherently 'unsticky' in its application.

[29] The phrase, at least in English law usage, is Lord Leggatt's: *Barton v Morris* [2023] UKSC 3, [2024] AC 684 [135].

[30] D Foxton, 'The Status of the Special Rules of Construction of Exemption Clauses in Commercial Contracts' [2021] *Journal of Business Law* 205.

[31] [1974] AC 689.

[32] See K Lewison, *The Interpretation of Contracts*, 8th edn (London, Sweet & Maxwell, 2024), ch 4, s 4, and R Catterwell, 'Party Intention, Default Rules and Contract Theory' this volume, ch 4 (giving the example of clauses such as 'This contract is not to be construed against a party because that party drafted the contract'). The so-called Bermuda Form of insurance contract, which is in widespread usage, excludes various normative principles of construction arising under New York law: see R Jacobs, LS Masters and P Stanley, *Liability Insurance in International Arbitration: The Bermuda Form*, 3rd edn (Oxford, Hart Publishing, 2021) [4.01].

'Normative stickiness' can, in some instances, assume the qualities of a super-glue, at which point the line between mandatory and default rules becomes vanishingly thin.[33] There is no doubt that the burden of expression becomes heavier the closer a contractual clause is said to come to excluding the effective performance obligation of the counterparty.[34] There are 'default' obligations in particular contexts which have proved even more difficult to unstick – for example, a shipowner's obligation to deliver cargo only against production of the bill of lading, of which I previously observed that the judicial response to the argument that this obligation had been excluded had been 'so hostile … that one might begin to wonder whether any provision would be found to have achieved this object'.[35] The concern here appears to be the effect which such an exclusion would have on the complex ecosystem of international sales and the carriage of goods by sea, in which the shipowner's strict obligation to deliver cargo only against production of the bill of lading makes it possible to protect the interest of those who have financed sale transactions while enabling cargo to be unloaded from ships, and moved ashore, even when bills are stuck in the banking and sale chains.[36] To the extent that this is a mandatory rule, it is one intended to serve the interests of third parties relying on the ordinary effects of a contract of a relevant type, rather than the result of a desire to constrain contractual autonomy on a purely *inter partes* basis.[37] Another reason why the distinction between mandatory and default rules in contract is not a clear one is that the rules which enhance the stickiness of particular defaults by seeking to increase the quality of contractual consensus required for any alternative, through a heightened burden of expression, have counterparts in some mandatory rules, where the court is more reluctant to find that the mandatory rule is engaged in contracts between parties of equal bargaining power: the law of restraint of trade,[38] and the penalty clause doctrine.[39]

Man Yip discusses default primary obligations arising in the law of fiduciary duties: in particular, the 'no conflict' and 'no profit' rules.[40] A party who does not agree to undertake a role which traditionally carries fiduciary obligations as a matter of law cannot really be said to be contracting out of these default rules (any more than a party who manifests no intention to create legal relations contracts out of the defaults in the law of contract).[41] However, the position of a party whose position is defined in a

[33] Catterwell (n 32) notes that 'some rules are more "sticky" than others'.

[34] Foxton (n 30) 209–10.

[35] D Foxton, 'Why Shipping Law Still Matters' [2021] *Lloyd's Maritime and Commercial Law Quarterly* 440, 448 (relevant authorities are collected in fn 54).

[36] See *Unicredit Bank AV v Euronav (The Sienna)* [2023] EWCA Civ 471, [2023] Bus LR 1391 as discussed in *Rolls-Royce Holdings Plc v Goodrich Corporation* [2023] EWHC 1637 (Comm) [150]–[156].

[37] A similar concern can be seen at work in cases such as *Gator Shipping Corp v Trans-Asiatic Oil SA (The Odenfeld)* [1978] 2 Lloyd's Rep 357 and *De Monchy v Phoenix Insurance Company of Hartford* (1928) 30 Ll L Rep 194.

[38] *A Schroeder Music Publishing Co Ltd v Macaulay* [1974] 1 WLR 1308, 1314–16; *Dwyer (UK) Franchising Ltd v Fredbar Ltd* [2022] EWCA Civ 889, [2023] FSR 4 [77]; *Credico Marketing Ltd v Lambert* [2022] EWCA Civ 864 [46].

[39] *Alfred McAlpine Capital Projects Ltd v Tilebox* [2005] EWHC 281 (TCC), [2005] Build LR 271 [48]; *Makdessi v Cavendish Square Holdings BV* [2015] UKSC 67, [2016] AC 1172 [33], [35]; *Signia Wealth Ltd v Vector Trustees Ltd* [2018] EWHC 1040 (Ch), [653(3)].

[40] Man Yip (n 3).

[41] See the text to nn 49–51 below for this debate.

manner intended to avoid such duties, but who functionally performs a role normally understood as giving rise to them, can be viewed either as someone who has not brought themselves within the scope of the law of fiduciary duties, or as someone who is seeking to disapply those defaults (where a heightened burden of expression will generally apply) and, in a sufficiently extreme case, someone who has sought to avoid the 'irreducible' (and hence arguably mandatory) core of fiduciary obligations which attach to such a role. These distinctions raise a familiar problem for contract lawyers, and one famously discussed by Brian Coote.[42]

The essays reveal different approaches on whether contracting on a basis which does not engage a rule amounts to 'contracting out' of a default rule, or whether this is equally compatible with the ruling being a mandatory rule, or indeed there being no rule at all. In terms of facilitative mandatory rules, Day gives the example of concluding an agreement by deed which has the effect of removing the agreement from the domain of the law of contract.[43] Similarly, a contractual obligation capable of attracting the operation of the prohibitory mandatory rule constituted by the doctrine on penalties, if it arose as a consequence of breach of a primary obligation, might not do so if it was a primary obligation itself, subject to the issue of 'disguised' penalty clauses.[44] It might be said that the rule that a statement in an offer that it will only be open for acceptance for a specific period is not binding without consideration[45] is not properly classified as a default rule, merely because it is possible to make such a statement binding if there *is* consideration for the offeror's promise not to withdraw the offer.[46] Equally, it can be argued that if the outcome which would otherwise have followed in the 'ticket' or 'receipt' cases[47] is avoided by taking steps bringing the nature of the document to the other party's attention, that amounts to taking a case outside the scope of a mandatory rule, not contracting out of a default. The contrary view is expressed by Jeannie Marie Paterson, who argues that 'rules of incorporation operate as default rules' because

> they present a presumption about the scope of the parties' contract, from which the parties may choose to depart. Provided the parties' agreement to make a contract is clearly manifested, the terms that form part of that contract will be found through the application of the incorporation rules unless the parties clearly signal otherwise.[48]

Lack of intention to create legal relations could be regarded as a general 'opting out' of the default rules of contract law,[49] but might better be regarded simply as a fact

[42] B Coote, *Exception Clauses: Some Aspects of the Law Relating to Exception Clauses in Contracts for the Carriage, Bailment and Sale of Goods* (London, Sweet & Maxwell, 1964). See also E Macdonald, 'Exception Clauses: Exclusionary or Definitional? It Depends!' (2012) 29 *Journal of Contract Law* 47.

[43] Day (n 14).

[44] *Makdessi v Cavendish Square Holdings BV* [2015] UKSC 67, [2016] AC 1172, [77], [258].

[45] *Dickinson v Dodds* (1876) 2 Ch D 463, 472.

[46] *cf* Day (n 14) section IV.A, debating whether *Dickinson v Dodds* is 'a sticky default rule' where 'more effort is required by the parties to "switch off" the default', ie by providing consideration.

[47] eg *Parker v South East Railway Co* (1877) 2 CPR 416; *Curtis v Chemical Cleaning and Dyeing Co* [1951] 1 KB 805.

[48] Paterson (n 20).

[49] *cf* Day (n 14).

which renders a particular agreement one to which contractual rules do not apply.[50] By contrast, the presumption that agreements reached in a business context are intended to be binding, and those reached in a social context are not, seems more genuinely a default rule.[51] As Day notes, the two are not all-encompassing, agreements by businessmen in pubs on a night out apparently engaging neither default.[52]

The argument that what are sometimes viewed as contractual 'default' rules are, in reality, exercises in the construction of contracts is a prominent themes of the essays by Andrew Robertson on the allocation of risk in contracts,[53] and Jonathan Morgan on the 'non-illegality' part of the disaggregated doctrine of frustration.[54] Robertson suggests that default rules can be said to lie at one end of a spectrum, with pure exercises of interpretation at the other. He places implied obligations of cooperation or the implication of terms in fact at the interpretative end, with frustration and termination for breach in the middle.[55] Termination for breach can be said to involve a variety of legal processes: interpretative exercises to the extent that the right to terminate depends on a particular term having the status of a condition or requires the court to ascertain whether a particular breach deprives the other party of substantially the whole of benefit of the contract, and default rules that breaches of the relevant kind give a right to terminate.[56] Morgan moves the doctrine of frustration from Robertson's mid-table position to the interpretative end, once it is successfully disaggregated from the doctrine of discharge for supervening illegality. He argues that the latter forms part of the principles addressing illegality in contract rather than a component of a doctrine addressing unforeseen changes in circumstance.[57] Rory Gregson's rejection of the attempt to characterise failure of basis claims in the law(s) of unjust enrichment as the operation of default or mandatory rules adopts a similar approach: in deciding such cases, the court is merely identifying what the condition of enrichment was.[58] Ying Khai Liew's analysis of unit trusts, and how they interrelate with the more traditional requirements of trust law, may be another example.[59]

In the context of contract and commercial law, we most readily conceive of default rules as providing implied primary obligations which form part of particular types of contract unless the parties 'opt out'. This collection of essays reminds us that this type of legal rule has a much wider application. William Day demonstrates in his paper that it can be found in the rules which determine whether a contract has been made at all.[60] Day argues that not all rules about how contracts are made are mandatory – in the facilitative

[50] Catterwell (n 32) notes that the law of contract can be regarded as an opt out from this default, or that language manifesting the absence of such an intent can be regarded as an opt out of a default rule, at least in a commercial contract, that agreements are intended to be binding. This is essentially a 'telescope point'.

[51] See the discussion in Day (n 14).

[52] Day (n 14).

[53] A Robertson, 'Default Rules, Interpretation and Risk Allocation', this volume, ch 3.

[54] Morgan (n 5).

[55] Robertson (n 53).

[56] For innominate terms at least. Opting out of the rule of contract law that breach of a condition gives a right to terminate is really a means of stating that a particular term does not have the status of a condition.

[57] Morgan (n 5).

[58] Gregson (n 25).

[59] Liew (n 2).

[60] Day (n 14).

sense – because a party can, by the terms in which it manifests its willingness to contract, 'opt out' of default rules which would otherwise determine aspects of the legal consequences of that manifestation. He instances an expressed requirement for the acceptance of an offer to be communicated or other prescribed mode of accepting an offer, to be contrasted with the common law 'postal rule'.

The default rules of contract law relating to offer and acceptance which Day discusses involve a *unilateral* opt out.[61] He also considers the question of mandatory and default rules in relation to other requirements for a binding contract. First, whether the parties' agreement contains the minimum terms which the law regards as essential for an enforceable bargain. In theory, this rule is mandatory, in that the parties' agreement cannot alter the identity of those terms 'the law requires as essential for the formation of legally binding relations'.[62] However, its scope of operation is heavily curtailed by the existence of default rules as to the primary obligations implicit in particular types of contract, unless the parties have anticipatorily excluded their operation in their (*ex hypothesi*) non-binding agreement by making it clear that they are reserving the right to agree for themselves the subject-matter of those essential terms.[63] It may also be possible for the parties to exclude this rule by agreeing that a third party will determine the scope of any essential terms, with arbitration agreements having sometimes been held (rather unconvincingly) to achieve that end.[64]

Thus far, I have focused on default rules with a party opt out – what Rory Gregson describes as 'classic defaults'.[65] However, the essays in this collection also discuss default rules where there is a *court* opt-out, or as more conventionally described, rules with exceptions. Once again, this is a broad church. Some 'exceptions' are simply cases where the rule, on its proper articulation, does not apply – Gregson argues that this is true of many 'exceptions' to the principles applied in determining whether a defendant is obliged to reverse an unjust enrichment, which are really cases where the rationale of a particular unjust enrichment rule is absent.[66] Ying Khai Liew looks at court-fashioned exceptions from certain default trust rules which operate in a particular context (the 'commercial trust' or, more specifically, when the court is dealing with 'bargaining beneficiaries').[67] The change in the interests to which the directors of a company must have regard when the company is on the verge of insolvency from those of the shareholders to the creditors is another example of the court's adjusting a rule for a particular context, and was referred to by Lord Reed as a 'modifying rule' for that reason.[68] In

[61] The disclaimer in *Hedley Byrne & Co Ltd v Heller & Partners* [1964] AC 465 can also been seen as a unilateral opt-out from a default rule. The issue of whether there are other examples of unilateral opts out from default rules in the form of so-called 'information defaults' is considered in the text to nn 78–81 below.

[62] *RTS Flexible Systems Ltd v Molkerei Alois Müller GmbH & Co KG* [2010] UKSC 14, [2010] 1 WLR 753 [45]; *Pagnan SpA v Feed Products Ltd* [1987] 2 Lloyd's Rep 601, 619 (proposition (5)).

[63] See Day (n 14) (discussion of *Wells v Devani* [2019] UKSC 4, [2020] AC 129 and *May and Butcher v Rex* [1934] 2 KB 17 (HL)).

[64] D Foxton, '"When Everything Changes": Adapting Contracts to Fundamental Changes in Circumstance' [2025] *Journal of Business Law* 161, 174–75.

[65] Gregson (n 25). See also Catterwell (n 32) section II ('the dominant or perhaps conventional way in which one understands doctrine to be excluded or modified is by reason of a contrary or inconsistent intention on the part of the parties').

[66] Gregson (n 25).

[67] Liew (n 2).

[68] *BTI 2014 LLC v Sequana SA* [2022] UKSC 25, [2024] AC 211 [11]; see Man Yip (n 3).

these contexts, the adjustment of the basic or default rule is not intended to preserve a space for privileging personal autonomy in private law, but is intended to promote other policies of the law which 'trump' the values embedded in the default rule in particular contexts.

Returning to contract terms, the breach date rule is both a classic default – the parties may specify the date at which loss is to be calculated, as certain forms of ISDA Master Agreement do[69] – and a rule with exceptions. However, the exceptions are more in the nature of an 'override': the court can decide that the overriding policies of the law of contract damages – eg, compensation and incentivising the taking of reasonable steps to mitigate loss – justify adopting a different date. Indeed, the ease with which it is possible for courts to depart from this starting point has led to the convincing argument that there is not really a breach date 'rule'.[70] The exception to the 'signature rule' in written contract cases where the contents of the document have been misrepresented is another instance where a default rule is overridden by counter-rule reflecting a stronger legal policy in particular circumstances.[71] In other cases, the default rule is capable of being overridden by the exercise of a judicial discretion, such as when the court awards a fiduciary who must account for a profit made in breach of fiduciary duty a reasonable allowance for the work done to realise the profit.[72]

In addition to default rules relating to the question of when a contract comes into existence, and what primary obligations the contract gives rise to, there are default rules concerning the so-called 'secondary' obligations which define the legal consequences which flow from breaches of the primary obligations. Once again, these comprise both 'party opt out' rules, and rules from which the court has carved out exceptions. A widespread contract provision which 'opts out' of the secondary rules for the assessment of damages is a liquidated damages clause, although the validity of the 'opt out' will itself be subject to the mandatory rule embodied in the doctrine of penalties. David Winterton refers to the interesting example of the rule that non-pecuniary loss is not generally recoverable in contract.[73] That rule is subject to exceptions – or as it is put in *Chitty*, 'qualifications' – and is a 'default' in that sense.[74] Is it, however, also a classic default? The fact that a breach of contract would be capable of causing (otherwise non-compensable) non-pecuniary loss is one reason why a liquidated damages clause would be enforceable. Where, however, the parties enter into a contract whose object is to provide the counterparty with enjoyment, or a pleasurable amenity,[75] or to protect them from distress,[76] they are not contracting out of the 'no recovery for non-pecuniary loss' default, but entering into a type of contract to which the default rule does not apply.

[69] Barnett (n 25).

[70] A Dyson and A Kramer, 'There is no "Breach Date Rule": Mitigation, Difference in Value and Date of Assessment' (2014) 130 *LQR* 259.

[71] Paterson (n 20). There is room for debate as to whether this is best characterised as a mandatory rule with an exception, or a default rule.

[72] Discussed by Man Yip (n 3).

[73] Winterton (n 4).

[74] *Chitty on Contracts*, 35th edn (London, Sweet & Maxwell, 2024) [30-161] states the rule and the exceptions.

[75] *Ruxley Electronics and Construction Ltd v Forsyth* [1996] AC 344; *Farley v Skinner* [2001] UKHL 49, [2002] 2 AC 732.

[76] *Chitty* (n 74) [30-164] ff.

What, however, of the position where the parties take a conventional commercial or employment contract, and include a provision stating that one of the purposes of the contract is to provide a particular contracting party with enjoyment or amenity? If the general rule precluding recovering of non-pecuniary loss is a classic default, this ought to be permit recovery of such damages, and yet it is questionable whether the mere addition of this label would be determinative, any more than a lease becomes a licence by mere say so.[77] If that is right, this would appear to be a mandatory rule of the law relating to secondary obligations in contract, rather than a true default. That is also true of the restrictions on the recovery of legal costs, to the extent that they exceed those awarded on an assessment,[78] one of a number of rules which reflect a public policy control of costs recovery in litigation.[79]

The rule relating to secondary obligations in contract which features particularly prominently in this collection is the rule in *Hadley v Baxendale*.[80] Gregson adopts the description of this rule as an 'information default', because it is a rule which operates unless one party takes the unilateral act of providing information to the other party at the legally relevant time.[81] That characterisation may need to be adjusted to allow for the fact that there may be contexts in which the mere provision of information may not suffice to oust the default rule – for example, the familiar hypothetical of the taxi driver who is told before the cab is hired that the client needs to get to an important business meeting at which a valuable deal is to be done, and who negligently choses a congested route[82] – although that might simply require the information to be given in a legally appropriate context as well as at a legally relevant time. That issue is connected with the debate about where the rule in *Hadley v Baxendale* sits on Andrew Robertson's sliding scale from true defaults to issues of interpretation,[83] and indeed whether modification of the remoteness default should require the heightened burden of expression which usually attaches to departures from default secondary rules.[84]

Hadley v Baxendale apart, other 'information defaults' are hard to find. While non-disclosure of information in the conclusion of a contract of insurance can provide the basis for avoiding the contract, there are added requirements of inducement and the exercise of the right to avoid before the non-disclosure alters the legal position.[85] While the requirement of inducement is less clear when complaint is made of non-disclosure in the conclusion of a contract of guarantee,[86] in both cases, the provision

[77] *cf Street v Mountford* [1985] AC 809.

[78] *Chitty* (n 74) [30-170].

[79] See D Foxton, 'How Contractual is Arbitration Law?' [2022] *Journal of Business Law* 459, 471–72; *Commercial Bank of Dubai PSC v Al Sari and others* [2024] EWHC 3304 (Comm) [86].

[80] (1854) 9 Exch 341, 156 ER 145.

[81] Gregson (n 25).

[82] E Peel, 'Remoteness Revisited' (2009) 125 *LQR* 6, 12.

[83] The latter view having been most famously championed in A Kramer, 'An Agreement Centred Approach to Remoteness and Contract' in N Cohen and E McKendrick (eds), *Comparative Remedies for Breach of Contract* (Oxford, Hart Publishing, 2005) 249, the former by A Robertson, 'The Basis of the Remoteness Rule in Contract' (2008) 28 *Legal Studies* 172.

[84] eg N Venkatesan, 'The Contract Remoteness Rule: Exclusion, Not Assumption of Responsibility' in A Dyson, J Goudkamp and F Wilmot-Smith (eds), *Defences in Contract* (Oxford, Hart Publishing, 2017) 187.

[85] *Pan Atlantic Insurance Co Ltd v Pine Top Insurance Co Ltd* [1999] 1 AC 501.

[86] As I noted in *Barclays Bank Plc v Borkhatria* [2018] EWHC 1326 (Comm) [34], 'the law addressing the limited duty of disclosure in guarantee contracts still awaits its *Pan Atlantic Insurance Co Ltd v Pine Top Ltd* moment'.

of information does not of itself change the operation of a default rule, but prevents the other party having a legal right which, absent such provision, they would have had. Gregson characterises the defence of change of position as an information default rule – because if the party who had transferred the benefit with a putative right to reverse it informs the recipient of that fact before their position changes, the defence is not available.[87] The same might be said of the *bona fide* purchaser for value doctrine. However, in each case, the applicable legal rule requires anyone seeking to avail themselves of it to have a particular state of mind, something they might not have because of information provided by the claimant or a third party, or a sufficiently suspicious disposition coupled with a failure to enquire.[88] An 'information default' analysis focuses on the provision of information by the putative victim, whereas these rules are more naturally concerned with the state of mind of the party wishing to establish the defence.

The rules attaching to the secondary obligations relating to breaches of primary obligations in equity are also default rules, although the distinction between primary and secondary obligations in relation to equitable duties can be more difficult to draw.[89] Liew[90] notes the modifications of principles of causation applicable to claims for breach of trust in a commercial context in *Target Holdings Ltd v Redferns*[91] and *AIB Group (UK) Plc v Mark Redler & Co.*[92] These cases reflect a particularly noteworthy departure from a default secondary rule. Such departures generally depend on a party opt-out achieved by discharging a heightened burden of expression,[93] and yet in this particular context, the court has created a situational exception to the operation of the usual principles.

I will conclude with some brief observations on a discussion of default rules which does not form part of this collection, but which features prominently in many of the papers. Our Twelfth Man is Lord Sales, his paper titled 'Default Rules in the Common Law: Substantive Rules and Precedent'.[94] Lord Sales surveys the role of default rules in the common law across a broad range of topics: classic defaults; rules with exceptions; default rules intended to 'structure' the evaluation of legal issues in which different and conflicting principles are 'in play'; and within the internal rules of the legal system, through the burden of proof and the doctrine of precedent. He identifies various values which the use of 'defaults' serve across this broad field: rules with exceptions allow the court to address the fact that legal disputes can engage incommensurable competing values, presenting *a priori* but flexible prioritisation between them; they can save transaction costs; they inject values into the law; they address rule of law concerns; and they remedy informational asymmetries.

Some of those justifications more obviously resonate with this study of the operation of default rules in contract and commercial law: in particular the saving of transaction costs through 'classic' default rules in making contracts and identifying their terms,

[87] Gregson (n 25).
[88] *Re Smith* [2021] EWHC 1272 (Comm) [424].
[89] *Hotel Portfolio II UK Limited v Ruhan* [2022] EWHC 383 (Comm) [275].
[90] Liew (n 2).
[91] [1996] AC 421.
[92] [2014] UKSC 58, [2015] AC 1503.
[93] Although *cf Transfield Shipping Inc v Mercator Shipping Inc (The Achilleas)* [2008] UKHL 48, [2009] 1 AC 61.
[94] Lord Sales, 'Default Rules in the Common Law: Substantive Rules and Precedent', Presentation at International Workshop on Default Rules in Private Law (Oxford, 24 March 2023), to appear in B Häcker and J Ungerer (eds), *Default Rules in Private Law* (Oxford, Hart Publishing, forthcoming).

and addressing informational asymmetries in the context of 'information' defaults. However, some of the other values identified by Lord Sales are also 'in play'.

Default rules in contract and commercial law also inject values, and this is true of classic defaults as well as rules with exceptions. I have elsewhere drawn an analogy between the *Gilbert Ash* principle of construction,[95] and the canons of statutory construction used to 'give effect to fundamental constitutional principles and universal human values', noting:

> [T]he principles of contractual construction as applicable to the 'law between the parties' are sometimes similarly value-laden, their normative character most clearly on display in the approach traditionally adopted to the construction of exemption clauses.[96]

Just as the government might shrink from using legislative language spelling out the more extreme possibilities of security legislation, so too a bargaining party might conclude that stating 'I would like to exclude the fraud of my agent' might prove an obstacle to a successful negotiation.

Finally, the tension between the inflexibility of clear rules and the formulation of exceptions to them discussed by Lord Sales has long divided private lawyers, along similar lines to the divide between act- and rule-utilitarians, and between 'hedgehogs' and 'foxes'. Critics of attempts to create exceptions to long-established rules point to the loss of certainty this is said to involve. A particularly powerful invocation of this concern was Lord Sumner's unavailing dissent in *Rodriguez v Speyer Brothers* against the creation of an exception to the disability of alien enemies to sue in cases where proceedings were brought for the purpose of winding up a partnership dissolved on the outbreak of war. He observed of the rule:

> It has always been as certain as language could make it, as curt as the Commandments. It has never been doubted. The current of decision has run strong and steady, and always the same way.[97]

There is also the concern that each exception is simply a beachhead in the battle to destroy the rule, with the 'jagged frontier' (discussed by Man Yip) destined to erode in the face of the incoming tide.[98] Lord Woolf MR once complained of 'the natural tendency for the general principle to be eroded, and for exceptions to grow by accretions as the exceptions are applied by analogy to existing cases'.[99] When attempting to summarise the law relating to backwards tracing, I suggested that it involves a general prohibition with narrow and soft-edged exceptions, and that:

> For those who might object that this involves 'break[ing] down the cases into different factual categories' and thereby 'deconstruct[ing] the law into a fissiparous bundle of distinct rules' … it can be said that while this approach might be deprecated when identifying and formulating rules, it is in the very nature of exceptions to an otherwise general rule, and that the recognition of such exceptions should not inexorably require the re-visiting of the rule.[100]

But perhaps those are the impotent railings of a King's Bench Canute.

[95] *Gilbert Ash (Northern) Ltd v Modern Engineering (Bristol) Ltd* [1974] AC 689.
[96] Foxton (n 30) 208.
[97] *Rodriguez v Speyer Brothers* [1919] AC 59, 117.
[98] Man Yip (n 3) (discussing 'ad hoc' recognition of fiduciary relationships).
[99] *R v Legal Aid Board Ex Parte Kaim Todner* [1999] QB 966, 977.
[100] *Serious Fraud Office v Hotel Portfolio II (UK) Ltd* [2021] EWHC 1273 (Comm) [45].

3

Default Rules, Interpretation and Risk Allocation

ANDREW ROBERTSON

I. Introduction

Default rules in the law of contract provide contracting parties with a set of basic rights and obligations which operate in the absence of any express agreement between the parties in relation to the relevant issues. Within the broad category of legal rules in the law of contract, the defining feature of a default rule is the power of the parties to displace the rule in favour of an agreed allocation of the risk in question. Questions of interpretation are always involved in the application of contractual default rules because a court must always determine whether the parties have allocated the risk in question and thus displaced the default rule. Many default rules require interaction with contract terms, and therefore with the construction of contracts, in a more sophisticated way because the application of the default rule requires attention to, and depends upon, the nature and context of the agreement. When we look across the different kinds of default rules in the law of contract, we can see that some are essentially standalone rules which operate in default of contrary stipulation, while others depend for their application on a more thoroughgoing interpretation of the contract. We might therefore situate the default rules of contract law on a spectrum running from the more rule-based to the more interpretive.

At the more rule-based, less interpretive end of the spectrum, the only interpretive issue to be considered is whether there was a default in dealing with the issue in question. The focus here is on express allocation of the risk in question. Terms that have been established by precedent or statute as implied in law in particular classes of contract provide good examples of simple default rules. As we move through the middle of the spectrum (frustration of purpose, termination for breach), the application of the default rule requires closer attention to the nature and terms of the contract. An interesting issue in relation to these doctrines is whether the interpretive questions involved in their application to particular facts are in substance merely questions about the allocation of risk, or whether something more is involved. In other words, in the application of these doctrines are the courts, in different ways, merely identifying the existence of implicit contractual allocations of risk. To the extent that contracts can be understood essentially as mechanisms for allocating risks, we might say that in a broad sense the answer to that question is yes. A more interesting question is whether that is an illuminating way of understanding the interpretive aspects of these default rules or whether the rules are better understood as raising interpretive questions that go beyond the implicit allocation or risk.

At the more interpretive end of the spectrum (the implied duty to cooperate, the implication of terms in fact), the question arises as to whether the doctrines in question can accurately be understood as default rules at all, or whether we are simply in the realm of interpretation. If the doctrines in the middle (frustration of purpose, termination for breach) are only interpretive in their concern to identify implicit allocations or risk, and the doctrines at the interpretive end are not default rules at all, but simply interpretive principles, then there is no spectrum, but rather simply two entirely separate categories: default rules and interpretive doctrines. The focus of section II of this chapter is whether the default rules of contract law can accurately or helpfully be understood to be situated on a spectrum running from the more rule-based to the more interpretive, or whether default rules and interpretive principles are better understood as separate categories.

Section III will consider another issue involved in the relationship between default rules, interpretation and risk allocation in the law of contract. In some areas of contract law, default rules and the identification of implicit allocations of risk by the contracting parties operate as rival or alternative approaches to dealing with particular issues. The example that will be considered here is common mistake, which can be addressed by way of a default rule or, alternatively, by seeking to identify the way in which the relevant risk has implicitly been allocated by the contracting parties.

In the US legal literature, the term 'default rule' is commonly used in the context of analysing what is the optimal legal rule, usually from the perspective of enhancing social welfare or economic efficiency.[1] In this chapter, the idea of a default rule is not approached from a normative perspective, but in order to understand the nature of the legal rules in question and the relationship between the rules of contract law and the interpretation of contractual agreements.

II. Default Rules and Interpretation: Spectrum or Separate Categories?

A. Simple Default Rules

The simplest form of default rule is one whose operation and effect is essentially independent of the contract terms, save only for the requirement that there has been a default by the contracting parties in dealing with the issue in question. In other words, the only interaction between the rule and the express contract terms is that the rule is excluded

[1] Most famously, I Ayres and R Gertner, 'Filling Gaps in Incomplete Contracts: An Economic Theory of Default Rules' (1989) 99 *Yale Law Journal* 87; *cf* R Barnett, 'The Sounds of Silence: Default Rules and Contractual Consent' (1992) 78 *Virginia Law Review* 821 (offering both a justificatory theory and argument as to how default rules should be chosen).

if the risk in question has been allocated by the express terms. The exemplars here are terms implied as a matter of law in a particular class of contract. Terms implied on this basis have been judicially recognised as 'default rules'.[2] When such a term has already been established in the case law or by statute as implied in a particular type of contract, the only interpretive questions that need to be considered are: (a) whether the contract falls into the class in question; and (b) whether the term said to be implied is inconsistent with the express terms. When a term is claimed for the first time to be implied as a matter of law in a particular class of contracts, a more sophisticated inquiry is of course required, but where a term has already been recognised as implied in contracts falling within a particular class, the default rule applies through 'the force of precedent in relation to other contracts of the same type'.[3]

B. More Interpretive Default Rules

i. *Frustration of Purpose*

Two interpretive questions are involved in determining whether a contract has been discharged by frustration of contractual purpose.[4] First, it is necessary to construe the contract in order to determine whether the contract is capable of being frustrated by the change in circumstances that has occurred. This may, depending on the circumstances, require the court to determine whether the continuation of the relevant state of affairs is the foundation or basis of the transaction, or is essential to achieving its commercial object. It may also, relatedly, require a court to consider whether the contract, properly construed, 'is wide enough to apply to the new situation'.[5] Secondly, if the contract is, on its terms, capable of being frustrated by the change of circumstances that has occurred, it is necessary to consider whether the contract terms deal with and allocate the risk in question, thus excluding the application of the doctrine of frustration, or whether there has been a default in addressing the issue.[6]

A close examination of the cases shows that it is not possible to separate the questions 'Is the contract capable of being frustrated by the relevant change of circumstances?' and 'Has the risk been allocated by the contract terms' because the first question is, essentially, a matter of risk allocation. A conclusion that the continuation of a particular state

[2] *Equitable Life Assurance Society v Hyman* [2002] 1 AC 408, 458 (Lord Steyn); *Malik v Bank of Credit and Commerce International SA* [1998] AC 20, 45 (Lord Steyn); *Barton v Morris* [2023] UKSC 3, [2023] AC 684 [209] (Lord Burrows JSC, dissenting).

[3] *Barton v Morris* [2023] UKSC 3, [2023] AC 684 [135] (Lord Leggatt JSC, dissenting).

[4] For the purpose of this chapter, it is necessary to distinguish frustration of purpose from: (a) frustration by supervening illegality, which raises entirely different considerations (see E Peel, *Frustration and Force Majeure*, 4th edn (London, Sweet and Maxwell, 2022) ch 8) and is best regarded as a distinct doctrine involving a mandatory rule (see J Morgan, 'Frustration Dissected: Mandatory and Default Rules', this volume, ch 9); and (b) frustration by supervening impossibility of performance, which raises somewhat different considerations (see Peel, ibid ch 3).

[5] *Davis Contractors Ltd v Fareham Urban District Council* [1956] AC 696, 721 (Lord Reid). The well-known formulation of Lord Radcliffe (ibid 729) is to the same effect: 'There must be as well such a change in the significance of the obligation that the thing undertaken would, if performed, be a different thing from that contracted for.'

[6] As to which, see R Catterwell, 'Frustration and Assumption of Risk' (2022) *Journal of Business Law* 76.

of affairs is the foundation of a contract is a conclusion that neither party implicitly agreed to bear the risk of that state of affairs not continuing. Conversely, a conclusion that a particular state of affairs is not the foundation of a contract amounts to a conclusion that the risk in question was allocated to the party on whom the burden would fall if the relevant state of affairs did not continue. Similarly, a conclusion that the contract is wide enough to apply to the new situation, or that performance in the new circumstances is not something different from that contracted for, is in effect a conclusion that under the contract terms the risk in question fell on the party burdened by the change in circumstances. A conclusion that the contract is not wide enough to apply to the new situation, and that performance in those circumstances is something different from that contracted for is a conclusion that the risk has not been allocated by the contract. And that, of course, is the situation addressed by the doctrine of frustration.

That relationship between the the foundation of the contract and the allocation of risk can be seen in both the cases in which performance has become futile for one of the parties and those where performance has become more onerous for one of the parties. *Krell v Henry* is one of the best-known examples of the former.[7] The central issue in that case was whether the coronation procession was the 'basis', 'foundation' or 'object' of the contract for the hire of rooms.[8] If the court had concluded that the coronation was not the foundation of the contract, and that it was simply a contract for the hire of rooms, then the hirer would implicitly have taken the risk of all changes in circumstances which might render performance futile for him. Those risks would include, for example, the hirer's own illness (which might have prevented him from travelling to central London to view the coronation procession) and of course the King's illness, which prevented the coronation from taking place as expected. The Court's conclusion that the coronation was the foundation of the contract amounted to a conclusion that the contract did not allocate the risk of cancellation of the coronation to the hirer, thus allowing the doctrine of frustration to deal with the unallocated risk.

Cases involving more onerous performance can be understood in the same way. In *Larrinaga & Co Ltd v Société Franco-Américane des Phosphates de Médulla, Paria*,[9] the parties made three contracts which together provided for the carriage, each year from 1913 to 1920, of two consignments of phosphate from Tampa to Dunkirk. The third contract, made in 1913, was in issue. That contract provided for the carriage of consignments in March and November each year from 1918 to 1920. By mutual agreement, the two charters scheduled to take place during the period of the war were cancelled. After hostilities ended in November 1918, the charterers sought to enforce the contract with respect to the final three charters, beginning in November 1919. The shipping company claimed that the contract had been brought to an end by 'the war and its incidents'.[10] Although some merchant ships remained under government requisition, performance in the post-war period remained possible. If the shipping company's own vessels were unavailable, they could charter other vessels to complete the voyages.

[7] *Krell v Henry* [1903] 2 KB 740.
[8] ibid 751, 754.
[9] *Larrinaga & Co Ltd v Société Franco-Américane des Phosphates de Médulla, Paria* (1923) 39 TLR 316 ('*Larrinaga v Société Franco-Américane*').
[10] ibid 318.

The House of Lords held that there was no frustration, either on the basis that the conditions existing at the time of formation did not form the foundation of the contract, or on the basis that the owner bore the risk of more onerous performance in the post-war conditions. Lord Atkinson based his decision on the fact that no relevant state of affairs (such as England not being at war or the company's ships not being requisitioned) formed the foundation of the contract.[11] Viscount Finlay agreed with the arbitrator that the 'alteration in trade conditions in consequence of the war' was one of the risks taken on by the parties in entering into a 'speculative charterparty' which was not to be performed until after five years had elapsed.[12] Viscount Sumner observed that: 'In effect most forward contracts can be regarded as a form of commercial insurance, in which every event is intended to be at the risk of one party or another.'[13] He observed that the charterparty in question was a 'speculative contract' which was 'so obviously liable to be upset … by changes of circumstances of all sorts' that it can be taken to have distributed 'all the risks on one side or another'.[14] We can see from the reasoning in this case that the conclusion that the relevant state of affairs did not constitute the foundation of the contract amounted to a conclusion that that the risk created by a change in that state of affairs had been distributed by the contract to the owner, who bore the burden of more onerous performance in the changed circumstances.

The Eugenia can be understood in the same way.[15] The vessel in that case was chartered for the carriage of goods from the Black Sea to India. In the weeks before the contract was made, the Suez Canal was nationalised by the Egyptian Government, and British and French forces were sent to the region. The parties realised when the contract was made that there was a risk that the Suez Canal might become impassable and both proposed terms to deal with it. They could not reach agreement on how to deal with the eventuality, however, and so the contract was concluded without any special provision. When the Canal was closed mid-voyage, the Court of Appeal held that the charter was not frustrated because the closure of the Canal did not bring about a fundamental change in the circumstances relevant to performance.[16] But the decision could equally be explained on the basis that, because the event was foreseen and not dealt with, the charterer could be understood to have accepted the risk of the closure,[17] or on the basis that the availability of passage through the Canal was not part of the foundation of the contract. Similarly, in *Tsakiroglou & Co Ltd v Noblee Thorl GMBH*[18] the conclusion that shipment via the Suez Canal was not of fundamental importance to a cif contract for the sale of goods customarily shipped via the Canal, and that the closure of the Canal did not fundamentally alter the nature of the contract,[19] was tantamount to a conclusion

[11] ibid 320.
[12] ibid 318.
[13] ibid 322.
[14] ibid.
[15] *Ocean Tramp Tankers Corp v V/O Sovfracht (The Eugenia)* [1964] 2 QB 226.
[16] ibid 240 (Lord Denning MR), 243 (Donovan LJ).
[17] *cf* ibid 239 (Lord Denning MR): 'If the parties did not foresee anything of the kind happening, you can readily infer they have made no provision for it: whereas, if they did foresee it, you would expect them to make provision for it.' See the discussion of 'express absolute contracts' in Peel (n 4) [12-003].
[18] *Tsakiroglou & Co Ltd v Noblee Thorl GMBH* [1962] AC 93.
[19] ibid 115 (Viscount Simonds), 119 (Lord Reid).

that the possibility of slower, costlier shipment via the Cape of Good Hope was one of the risks allocated by the contract terms to the seller.[20]

There are several ways in which contracting parties can communicate a contractual allocation of the risk arising from the supervening event in question and thereby displace the default rule provided by the law of frustration.[21] Most obviously, contracting parties can do so by way of a *force majeure* or similar clause which, eg, provides for the suspension of the parties' obligations in the circumstances in question. They may also do so by providing for variation (such as sharing of wasted expenditure) or renegotiation on the occurrence of an event of the kind that has arisen.[22]

Contract terms may also indicate, directly or indirectly, that the risk in question has been allocated to the party for whom the changed circumstance have made performance futile or more onerous. An example of a direct allocation of the risk to the party affected is a situation in which the contract terms expressly stipulate that the obligations of one or both parties are 'absolute and unconditional irrespective of any contingency whatsoever'.[23] *Larrinaga v Société Franco-Américane*, which was discussed above,[24] can be seen as an example of an indirect allocation of the risk to the party affected. And without any indication in the express terms, extrinsic evidence may show that the parties foresaw the possibility of the changed circumstances, or that the event was so highly foreseeable as to justify an inference of risk assumption.[25] As *The Eugenia* shows, the failure of the parties to make provision dealing with a foreseen risk may justify a court in concluding that the risk has been allocated to the party on whom it falls. Similarly, the failure of the frustration claim in *Davis Contractors Ltd v Fareham Urban District Council* can equally well be explained on the basis that the change of circumstances did not render the 'job of a different kind from that contemplated in the contract',[26] or on the basis that the risk in question was 'before their eyes' and 'was not any new state of things which the parties could not reasonably be thought to have foreseen'.[27]

Since the fact that an event has been foreseen and not expressly dealt with provides only an indication that the risk has been allocated by the contract terms, there can clearly be no universal rule even in relation to foreseen events. In *WJ Tatem Ltd v Gamboa*,[28] a time charter (to the Spanish Republican Government for the evacuation of refugees) was held to have been frustrated by the seizure of the ship (by nationalists during the

[20] Lord Guest's conclusion (ibid 133) that 'there was no change of circumstances to justify the application of the doctrine' of frustration is to the same effect.

[21] See Catterwell (n 6) (analysing different approaches to the level of textual support required before a court will conclude that a risk has been allocated, and arguing that stronger textual support might be required in cases where the event is more seriously disruptive of performance and in cases where the event is more difficult to foresee).

[22] Peel (n 4) [12-006]–[12-007].

[23] *ACG Acquisition XX LLC v Olympic Airlines SA (in liq)* [2012] EWHC 1070 (Comm), in which the quoted provision was one of the reasons given by Teare J at [181]–[185] for rejecting an argument that the aircraft lease in question had been frustrated by the indefinite suspension of the aircraft's airworthiness certificate.

[24] Text to nn 8–13 above.

[25] As to the latter, see Peel (n 4) [13-014]–[13-016].

[26] *Davis Contractors Ltd v Fareham Urban District Council* [1956] AC 696, 724 (Lord Reid).

[27] ibid 731 (Lord Radcliffe).

[28] *WJ Tatem Ltd v Gamboa* [1939] 1 KB 132.

Spanish Civil War) and its detention for several weeks. That was so even assuming that the parties had contemplated seizure and detention of the ship.[29] The charter was for a specific vessel, for a short period, within a narrow geographical area, and for a specific purpose, and the foundation of the contract was destroyed by the seizure.[30] It could not therefore be said that the charterer had accepted the risk of seizure and detention, and the charterer was not therefore liable to pay hire up to the date of redelivery.

One could, therefore, draw the conclusion that, at a fundamental level, the interpretive aspects of the doctrine of frustration of purpose are concerned with the identification of implicit allocations of risk.[31] The default rule does not apply if the risk that has eventuated is one that was implicitly allocated by the contract to one of the parties, either because the contract is wide enough to cover the situation that has arisen, the foundation or basis of the contract has not been destroyed, the commercial purpose can still be fulfilled, or the risk of the supervening event and its consequences were foreseen or foreseeable in circumstances justifying an inference of risk assumption. If the risk was not in that way implicitly allocated by the contract terms, then the default rule applies, and the contract automatically comes to an end. In relation to its interaction with contractual allocations of risk, therefore, the interpretive aspects of the doctrine of frustration of purpose are essentially confined to determining whether the risk in question was allocated to one of the contracting parties. Identifying implicit contractual allocations of risk is, however, a difficult task. The identification of the foundation, nature, width and commercial object of a contract are important interpretive tools which assist the court in determining whether the risk in question has been allocated by the contract terms to one of the contracting parties and the doctrine of frustration of purpose thereby excluded.

While interpretation plays a fundamentally important role in determining whether the risk in question has been allocated by the contract terms to one of the parties, it must be emphasised that contractual risk allocation determines only whether the default rule applies. The default rule itself (ie, the rule that a contract comes to an end automatically when the supervening event occurs) is a rule of law and not an interpretive doctrine. The contract terminates '*by operation of law* on the emergence of a fundamentally different situation'[32] and not because the contract implicitly provided that it should terminate in such circumstances. Some judges and scholars argue that frustration of purpose is not an independent doctrine and the cases can be rationalised on the basis of implied terms.[33] In *Davis Contractors Ltd v Fareham Urban District Council*,[34] Lord Reid famously dismissed the implied term theory of frustration as artificial. While it may be possible to rationalise some frustration decisions as based on implied terms, not all can

[29] ibid 136.

[30] ibid 140.

[31] Catterwell (n 6) 96 reaches a similar conclusion about the overlap between the 'radical change in obligation' test and the assumption of risk question.

[32] *Davis Contractors Ltd v Fareham Urban District Council* [1956] AC 696, 723 (Lord Reid).

[33] eg, *FA Tamplin Steamship Co Ltd v Anglo-Mexican Petroleum Products Co Ltd* [1916] 2 AC 397, 404; W Day, 'Shades of Frustration' in E Peel and R Probert (eds), *Shaping the Law of Obligations: Essays in Honour of Professor Ewan McKendrick KC* (Oxford, Oxford University Press, 2023); Morgan (n 4).

[34] *Davis Contractors Ltd v Fareham Urban District Council* [1956] AC 696.

be explained this way, as Lord Reid pointed out.[35] That is because the requirements for implied terms are in significant respects stricter. While contracts to which the frustration of purpose doctrine has been applied commonly lack business efficacy, it cannot always be said in all such cases that it is 'so obvious that it goes without saying' that the contract automatically comes to an end on the occurrence of the supervening event. In order for a term to be implied in fact, it is necessary that there is a singularly appropriate solution to the problem that has arisen.[36]

That the doctrine of frustration can operate when this requirement is not met is illustrated by *Codelfa Construction Pty Ltd v State Rail Authority (NSW)*,[37] in which the High Court of Australia held that no term could be implied, but that the contract was nevertheless frustrated. The parties in that case contracted on the assumption that the tunnelling work to be performed by the contractor could be carried out on a continuous basis six days a week. The contract was made on the basis of legal advice to the effect that the contractor would enjoy the immunity conferred by statute on the State Rail Authority. Local residents were nevertheless able to obtain an injunction imposing significant restrictions on the hours of work. No term could be implied because there were multiple reasonable solutions to the problem created by the grant of the injunction. Mason J said:

> [T]here remains an insurmountable problem in saying that 'it goes without saying' that had the parties contemplated the possibility that their legal advice was incorrect and that an injunction might be granted to restrain noise or other nuisance, they would have settled upon the term implied by the Court of Appeal or that implied by the Arbitrator and by Ash J at first instance. I doubt whether the fiction of treating the parties as reasonable and fair makes the problem any the less difficult. This is not a case in which an obvious provision was overlooked by the parties and omitted from the contract. Rather it was a case in which the parties made a common assumption which masked the need to explore what provision should be made to cover the event which occurred. In ordinary circumstances negotiation about that matter might have yielded any one of a number of alternative provisions, each being regarded as a reasonable solution.[38]

The High Court held, however, that the contract was frustrated. Mason J said:

> There is, of course, no inconsistency between the conclusion that a term cannot be implied and the conclusion that events have occurred which have brought about a frustration of the contract. I find it impossible to imply a term because I am not satisfied that in the circumstances of this case the term sought to be implied was one which parties in that situation would necessarily have agreed upon as an appropriate provision to cover the eventuality which has arisen. On the other hand I find it much easier to come to the conclusion that the performance of the contract in the events which have occurred is radically different from performance of the contract in the circumstances which it, construed in the light of surrounding circumstances, contemplated.[39]

[35] ibid 720.
[36] A Robertson, 'Purposive Contractual Interpretation' (2019) 39 *Legal Studies* 230, 243–45.
[37] *Codelfa Construction Pty Ltd v State Rail Authority (NSW)* (1982) 149 CLR 337.
[38] ibid 355–56.
[39] ibid 363.

ii. Termination for Breach

Like frustration of purpose, the common law power to terminate a contract for breach is a default rule that is routinely supplemented or modified by express contractual provision. Also like frustration, termination for breach is a default rule that is heavily dependent on context and interpretation for its application. The common law power to terminate can be excluded or modified by contractual provision, but whether the rule has been excluded or modified is not the most important interpretive question in most termination cases. The main interpretive questions are whether a term that has been breached is a condition and whether a breach would deprive the innocent party of substantially the whole benefit of the contract. If the explanation offered by Diplock LJ in *Hongkong Fir Shipping Co Ltd v Kawasaki Kisen Kaisha Ltd*[40] is accurate, then the interpretive issue in relation to termination for breach should be essentially the same as that for frustration. Diplock LJ said that the test for identifying an event which relieves a party of the obligation to perform ('whether or not the event occurs as a result of the default of one of the parties'):

> [H]as been stated in a number of metaphors all of which I think amount to the same thing: does the occurrence of the event deprive the party who has further undertakings still to perform of substantially the whole benefit which it was the intention of the parties as expressed in the contract that he should obtain as the consideration for performing those undertakings?[41]

The default rule in relation to termination for breach is essentially that a party can terminate a contract for any breach of a term which has the status of a condition, for a breach of an intermediate term which has the effect of substantially depriving the innocent party of the benefit of the contract, or for repudiation of the contract.

Whether a term has the status of a condition depends primarily on: (a) whether the parties have designated it as such; and, if not, (b) whether 'failure to perform it would render the performance of the rest of the contract a thing different in substance from what the defendant had stipulated for'.[42] If the parties have designated a term as a condition then one could say without artificiality that the parties have determined that the party not in breach should not bear the risk that they might be required to perform their obligations in the face of non-performance of the term in question, but instead should have the option of terminating the contract in such a situation. By specifying a term as a condition, the parties are agreeing that, if the term in question is breached, the innocent party will have the option of terminating the contract and avoiding the burden of future performance in the face of the breach. Conversely, if the parties have designated a term as non-essential then one can similarly conclude that the parties have determined that the party not in breach will bear the risk that they might be required to perform their obligations in the face of non-performance of the term in question.

In the absence of specification of a term as either essential or inessential, whether a term is a condition depends on whether performance in the new circumstances gives the innocent party something different in substance from that which they were intended

[40] *Hongkong Fir Shipping Co Ltd v Kawasaki Kisen Kaisha Ltd* [1962] 2 QB 26, 65–66.
[41] ibid 66.
[42] *Bettini v Gye* (1876) 1 QBD 183, 188 (Blackburn J).

to receive. Termination for breach of an intermediate term involves – once the classificatory hurdle has been cleared – essentially the same core question, which is whether the breach has given 'rise to an event which will deprive the party not in default of substantially the whole benefit which it was intended that he should obtain from the contract'.[43] If, notwithstanding the breach, the innocent party stands to receive substantially what they contracted for then the contract effectively allocates to that party the risk of having to perform in those circumstances.

Conversely, if the innocent party will not receive substantially what they were intended to receive then the risk is unallocated and the default rule – that the innocent party has power to terminate – can apply. As with frustration, therefore, we can see the core questions involved in termination for breach as essentially concerned with risk allocation.

Termination for repudiation or renunciation stands on a different footing from termination for actual breach and may be seen as a default rule of a different kind. In the application of the default rule providing a power to terminate for repudiation, the main question is whether the party in question has manifested an unwillingness or inability to perform the contract according to its terms. That often requires an interpretation of the terms in question and sometimes requires a court to determine whether a term that has been repudiated was a condition. For the most part, however, it focuses on an interpretation of the conduct of the party said to have repudiated the contract.

The rationale of the doctrine of repudiation is controversial but, unlike termination for actual breach, it seems unlikely to have any relationship with any implicit allocation of risk. It has been suggested that the justification for the innocent party's entitlement to terminate is that each party is under an implied obligation not to repudiate their obligations. If that were a plausible explanation, it would ground the doctrine in an implicit allocation of risk (neither party having accepted the risk of having to perform in the face of a renunciation by the other), but the idea that such a promise is implied in every contract may be considered fictional.[44] A more plausible explanation is that the doctrine is founded on 'considerations of convenience' and the desirability of allowing the innocent party an early opportunity to mitigate their loss and enter into other contractual relationships.[45]

The application of the default rules relating to frustration and termination for breach involve difficult questions of interpretation and complex factual inquiries. To the extent that the courts are concerned to interpret the contract terms, it is possible to rationalise the core interpretive questions as essentially concerned with identifying express or implicit allocations of risk. Like frustration, however, the power of a party to terminate for breach comes from the default rule. Parties who expressly stipulate that a particular term is a condition are, in effect, opting into the default rule and implicitly stipulating that the innocent party will be entitled to terminate for any breach of that term. In the case of termination for breaches of terms construed as conditions but not specified as such, and also in the case of serious breaches of intermediate terms, the connection with party risk allocation is more tenuous. In the case of termination for repudiation,

[43] *Hongkong Fir Shipping Co Ltd v Kawasaki Kisen Kaisha Ltd* [1962] 2 QB 26, 70 (Diplock LJ).

[44] A Burrows, *A Restatement of the English Law of Contract* (Oxford, Oxford University Press, 2016) 117.

[45] *Woodar Investment Development Ltd v Wimpey Construction UK Ltd* [1980] 1 WLR 277, 296–97 (Lord Keith of Kinkel).

the power to terminate is largely independent of party risk allocation and more clearly grounded in considerations of justice and commercial convenience.

C. Highly Interpretive Default Rules

i. The Duty to Cooperate

As we move from frustration and termination for breach to the implied duty to cooperate, views will differ as to whether we are moving towards the more interpretive end of the spectrum of default rules or leaving the category of default rules behind and moving into the realm of interpretation. In English law the consensus seems to be that the duty to cooperate is not implied in all contracts, but rather is a term or type of term that may be implied in some contracts.[46] In the Scottish case of *Mackay v Dick*, Lord Blackburn famously articulated a duty to cooperate in general terms, but framed it as a principle of construction:

> I think I may safely say, as a general rule, that where in a written contract it appears that both parties have agreed that something shall be done, which cannot effectually be done unless both concur in doing it, the construction of the contract is that each agrees to do all that is necessary to be done on his part for the carrying out of that thing, though there may be no express words to that effect. What is the part of each must depend on circumstances.[47]

In Australian law, on the other hand, there is much stronger support for the view that the duty to cooperate is a term implied by law in all contracts. The authors of the Australian edition of *Cheshire and Fifoot's Law of Contract*, for example, claim (under the heading 'Universal terms') that: 'A strong current of authority establishes *a general obligation implied in every contract* that has been labelled the duty of co-operation.'[48] That is supported by judicial statements at the highest level. In *Commonwealth Bank of Australia v Barker*, for example, French CJ, Bell and Keane JJ referred to the duty to cooperate as an example of a 'universal' implication in law, which is implied in all contracts because it is necessary for the 'effective performance … of contracts generally'.[49] Others see the position in Australian law as far less clear.[50] As Jeannie Paterson observes, the duty to cooperate has been treated in some cases as a term that may be implied in fact to give business efficacy to a contract, in others as 'an independent duty implied in law in all contracts' and in others still as 'a general rule of construction'.[51] In *Commonwealth Bank of Australia v Barker*, French CJ, Bell and Keane JJ referred to the debate on this issue and suggested that it involves 'taxonomical distinctions which do not necessarily

[46] eg: HG Beale (ed), *Chitty on Contracts*, 25th edn (London, Sweet & Maxwell, 2023) 17-207; G McMeel, *McMeel on the Construction of Contracts: Interpretation, Implication, and Rectification*, 3rd edn (Oxford, Oxford University Press, 2017) 9.56.

[47] *Mackay v Dick* (1881) 6 App Cas 251, 263.

[48] NC Seddon and RA Bigwood, *Cheshire and Fifoot's Law of Contract*, 12th edn (Sydney, LexisNexis, 2023) 10.14.

[49] *Commonwealth Bank of Australia v Barker* [2014] HCA 32; (2014) 253 CLR 169 [29].

[50] See eg JD Heydon, *Heydon on Contract* (Sydney, LawBook Co, 2019) 21.370.

[51] JM Paterson, 'Good Faith Duties in Contract Performance' (2014) 14 *Oxford University Commonwealth Law Journal* 283, 293.

yield practical differences'.[52] Whatever its basis, all agree that the content of the duty to cooperate in any given contract is to a significant extent shaped by the contract terms.[53]

The duty to cooperate can therefore be seen either to mark the dividing line between default rules and the principles of contractual interpretation, or as a powerful illustration of the fact that some default rules are more interpretive than others. In English law the duty to cooperate is best seen as an interpretive principle if it does not simply apply in default of contrary agreement, but must in each case be established as an implication arising from the terms of the contract in question. The case of *Ridgebury November LLC v King Crude Carriers SA*, which is currently before the UK Supreme Court, is unlikely to shed direct light on this question because the relevant party in that case was obliged by an express term to cooperate in doing the thing in question.[54] The case is not, therefore, concerned with the existence of a duty to cooperate, but with the consequences of a failure to cooperate which prevents a debt accruing. The principle applied by the Court of Appeal was that:

> [A]n obligor is not permitted to rely upon the non-fulfilment of a condition precedent to its debt obligation where it has caused such non-fulfilment by its own breach of contract, at least where such condition is not the performance of a principal obligation by the obligee nor one which it is necessary for the obligee to plead and prove as an ingredient of its cause of action.[55]

That principle was justified on the basis that 'it represents the presumed contractual intentions of the parties'.[56] It effectively operates as a default rule which applies where certain circumstances exist (namely the accrual of a debt is subject to the fulfilment of a condition precedent and the obligor has expressly or impliedly agreed not to do the thing that has prevented the condition from being fulfilled), but will not apply where 'a contrary intention is sufficiently clearly expressed or can be implied from the circumstances of the case'.[57]

In Australian law, the duty to cooperate may be best seen as a default rule, but one that is at the interpretive end of the spectrum of default rules. If the implication is made as a matter of law in all contracts unless excluded by the contract terms, then it can be seen as a default rule. Although the precise content and application of the rule is context-specific and highly dependent on the nature and express terms of the agreement, the duty to cooperate can nevertheless be understood as a default rule. That is because, unlike the implication of terms ad hoc on the basis of business efficacy or obviousness, the duty to cooperate does itself have substantive content and is not merely a mechanism for determining what was implicitly agreed.[58] That substantive content consists, as Ryan Catterwell has explained, of a performance duty (to 'perform acts reasonably necessary to achieve contractual objectives'), the prevention principle (an

[52] *Commonwealth Bank of Australia v Barker* [2014] HCA 32, (2014) 253 CLR 169 [24].

[53] Beale (n 46); McMeel (n 46) 347; Heydon (n 50); Paterson (n 51) 294.

[54] See *King Crude Carriers SA v Ridgebury November LLC* [2024] EWCA Civ 719, [2025] 2 WLR 181 [81]. Permission to Appeal was granted in October 2024.

[55] ibid [77].

[56] ibid [81]. As J English, 'The Principle in Mackay v Dick' (2025) 141 *LQR* 48, 51 has noted: 'This justification relies upon a particularly capacious notion of agreement.'

[57] *King Crude Carriers SA v Ridgebury November LLC* [2024] EWCA Civ 719, [2025] 2 WLR 181 [81], [83].

[58] As to the substantive content of the duty to cooperate, see R Catterwell, 'Co-operation and Prevention in Contract Law' (2023) 47 *Melbourne University Law Review* 114; Paterson (n 51) 293–98.

obligation not to 'prevent or delay the other party in performing the contract'), a benefit duty ('to do all that is reasonably necessary to ensure that the other party enjoys the benefit of the contract') and a negative covenant (not to 'hinder or prevent fulfilment of the purpose of any express promise that the party has made').[59] Although the precise content of those duties is shaped in significant and often decisive ways by the contract terms, as illustrated by the two cases discussed immediately below, the duty to cooperate has identifiable and distinctive content.

The relationship between the duty to cooperate rule and the terms of a contract to which it applies is illustrated by the influential distinction drawn by Mason J in *Secured Income Real Estate (Aust) Ltd v St Martins Investments Pty Ltd* between: (a) cooperation in the doing of acts necessary for the performance of fundamental obligations under the contract; and (b) cooperation in the doing of acts which are 'necessary to entitle the other contracting party to a benefit under the contract but are not essential to the performance of that party's obligations and are not fundamental to the contract'.[60] While it is easy to imply the former, Mason J said, the latter depends 'on the intention of the parties manifested by the contract itself'.[61] In the *Secured Income* case, the 'general tenor of the provisions of [a] contract' for the sale of an office building supported the existence of an obligation on the part of the purchaser 'to do all things reasonably necessary to enable leases to be granted'.[62] That was so even when, in the situation that arose, it was in the purchaser's interests not to grant a lease because the aggregate rental payable affected the purchaser's obligation to pay a final instalment of the purchase price.

By way of contrast, the benefit aspect of the duty to cooperate was given a narrower scope in light of the contract terms in *Jireh International Pty Ltd v Western Exports Services Inc*.[63] In a letter agreement made in 1995, Western Exports (WES) agreed to help Jireh to become the master franchisee for Gloria Jeans Coffee stores in Australia. Part of the remuneration to be paid to WES was a commission of five per cent of the wholesale price of certain products sold by Jireh International Pty Ltd to Gloria Jeans franchisees. In 2004, for apparently legitimate commercial reasons, sales of relevant products to franchisees began to be made by other companies in the Jireh group, thus depriving WES of commission. WES claimed, inter alia, that a duty to cooperate required Jireh not to do anything that would cause Jireh to be deprived it its commission. The New South Wales Court of Appeal rejected that argument on the basis that any obligation to do what was necessary to entitle WES to a benefit under the contract was dependent on what was promised.[64] The commission was just one of a number of different types of remuneration to be provided to WES. The agreement imposed no obligation on Jireh to make any sales to franchisees, did not specify any minimum level of sales, and did not communicate any intention to prohibit sales to franchisees by any associated entities (at least for bona fide commercial reasons). The express terms thus governed the scope and operation of the duty to cooperate, which did not require Jireh to take steps necessary to ensure that WES received the benefit of the commission.

[59] Catterwell (n 58) 121.
[60] *Secured Income Real Estate (Aust) Ltd v St Martins Investments Pty Ltd* (1979) 144 CLR 596, 607.
[61] ibid 607–08.
[62] ibid 608.
[63] *Jireh International Pty Ltd v Western Exports Services Inc* [2011] NSWCA 137.
[64] ibid [68]–[87].

It is not possible or necessary for the purpose of this chapter to offer a definitive justification of the duty to cooperate, but it might nevertheless be helpful to provide a rough indication of what such an explanation might look like. Combining and building on the explanations offered by Elizabeth Peden[65] and Ryan Catterwell, the substantive content of the duty to cooperate, and the standard or standards of conduct required of it, might perhaps be justified on the following basis. The institution of contract gives legal effect to bargains, which are exercises in cooperation to achieve mutually agreed ends. Parties who invoke the institution of contract can fairly be assumed to intend the bargain they have made to be legally and practically effective.[66] That assumption in turn justifies the recognition that inherent in the institution of contract is a duty requiring such cooperation from each party as is needed to make the bargain effective.[67] Not only is such a duty subject to any indication to the contrary in the agreed terms, but in any given contract it is shaped by the contract terms.

ii. Terms Implied in Fact

If default rules do sit on a spectrum running from the least to the most dependent on the interpretation of the contract the parties have made, one might place at the far interpretive end those terms implied ad hoc on the basis that they are 'obvious' or necessary to give business efficacy to a contract. It is possible to formulate the relevant principle as a rule, and that rule operates in default of an express stipulation dealing with the issue in question.[68] Because the rule has no substantive content, however, it is best understood as an interpretive device rather than a default rule. It is, in other words, best understood as a mechanism for determining how a risk was implicitly allocated than as a default rule for allocating the risk in the absence of allocation by the contracting parties. The identification of implied terms in fact is now widely recognised as an interpretive exercise, the aim of which is to identify what a reasonable person would understand the contract to mean.[69] Although the identification of terms implied in fact is a 'different and altogether more ambitious undertaking' than the orthodox interpretation of express terms,[70] it is not helpfully understood as a default rule.[71]

[65] E Peden, '"Cooperation" in English Contract Law: To Construe or Imply' (2000) 16 *Journal of Contract Law* 56.

[66] ibid 56.

[67] To expand on the explanations of Peden (ibid) and Catterwell (n 58) 120.

[68] See eg *BP Refinery (Westernport) Pty Ltd v Shire of Hastings* (1977) 180 CLR 266 (PC) 283 (Lord Simon); *Marks and Spencer plc v BNP Paribas Securities Services Trust Company (Jersey) Ltd* [2015] UKSC 72, [2016] AC 742 [21] (Lord Neuberger JSC).

[69] *Codelfa Construction Pty Ltd v State Rail Authority of NSW* (1982) 149 CLR 337, 345 (Mason J); *Attorney General of Belize v Belize Telecom Ltd* [2009] UKPC 10, [2009] 1 WLR 1988 [21]; *Marks and Spencer plc v BNP Paribas Securities Services Trust Company (Jersey) Ltd* [2015] UKSC 72, [2016] AC 742 [26] (Lord Neuberger PSC, with whom Lord Sumption and Lord Hodge JJSC agreed); *Commonwealth Bank of Australia v Barker* [2014] HCA 32, (2014) 253 CLR 169 [22]; *Realestate.com.au Pty Ltd v Hardingham* [2022] HCA 39, (2022) 277 CLR 115.

[70] *Philips Electronique Grand Public SA v British Sky Broadcasting* [1995] EMLR 472l, 481 (Lord Bingham MR), quoted with approval in *Marks and Spencer plc v BNP Paribas Securities Services Trust Company (Jersey) Ltd* [2015] UKSC 72, [2016] AC 742 [29].

[71] See further Robertson (n 36) 242–46 (arguing that the identification of terms implied in fact is an exercise in purposive interpretation).

Nor is the implication of terms in fact helpfully understood as an exercise in gap-filling. In *Equitable Life Assurance Society v Hyman*, Lord Steyn characterised terms implied in fact as 'ad hoc gap fillers'.[72] While the identification of an implied term does fill a gap in the express terms, if the exercise is essentially one of interpretation, and its aim is to identify what a reasonable person would understand the contract to mean,[73] then it is inaccurate to characterise implied terms of this type as 'gap fillers'. If a term is implied in fact then there is no gap in relation to the issue in question. The identification of an implied term is an exercise in construction in the sense in which that word was used by Francis Lieber:[74] it involves 'the drawing of conclusions respecting subjects, that lie beyond the direct expression of the text, from elements known from and given in the text – conclusions which are in the spirit, though not within the letter of the text.'[75]

III. Default Rule and Contractual Risk Allocation as Competing Paradigms

While in many areas of contract law default rules are intertwined with questions about contractual allocations of risk, in some areas default rules and the identification of contractual allocations of risk constitute rival approaches to resolving particular problems. A well-known – and in recent years much discussed – example of that rivalry is in relation to remoteness of damage.[76] Another example, at least in Australian law, is in relation to common mistake as to the subject matter of a contract. The rule in English law is that a mistake that is shared by contracting parties will render a contract void if the mistake is 'so fundamental that it makes the "contractual adventure" impossible, or makes performance essentially different to what the parties anticipated', provided neither was responsible for the state of affairs and neither took the risk of 'the situation being as it really is'.[77] That is a default rule because it operates only if the risk in question has not been allocated by the contract. If a party expressly or impliedly warrants that the subject matter exists or performance is possible, then the rule will not apply.[78] The relevant provision in the American Law Institute's *Second Restatement of Contracts* has

[72] *Equitable Life Assurance Society v Hyman* [2002] 1 AC 408, 458.

[73] As I have argued (n 36) 242–46, with particular reference to the decision in *Equitable Life Assurance Society v Hyman* (ibid 244). See also the fuller discussion of that decision in A Robertson, 'The Foundations of Implied Terms: Logic, Efficacy and Purpose' in S Degeling, J Edelman and J Goudkamp (eds), *Contract in Commercial Law* (Sydney, LawBook Co, 2016) 143, 157–59.

[74] F Lieber, *Legal and Political Hermeneutics* (Boston, Little and Brown 1839) 56.

[75] ibid. See further Robertson (n 73) and Robertson (n 36).

[76] See *Transfield Shipping Inc v Mercator Shipping Inc (The Achilleas)* [2008] UKHL 48, [2009] 1 AC 61 and, eg, A Robertson, 'The Basis of the Remoteness Rule in Contract' (2008) 28 *Legal Studies* 172 and A Robertson, 'The Limits of Interpretation in the Law of Contract' (2016) 47 *Victoria University of Wellington Law Review* 191, 200–07.

[77] Beale (n 46) 9-015; *cf* J Morgan, 'Common Mistake in Contract: Rare Success and Common Misapprehensions' [2018] *CLJ* 559 (arguing that there is no 'doctrine of common mistake' and the English courts can and should approach common mistake cases by asking 'whether the contract, on its true construction, was conditional on the existence of the facts which (it turns out) do not exist' (at 560).

[78] *Great Peace Shipping Ltd v Tsavliris (International) Ltd (The Great Peace)* [2002] EWCA Civ 1407, [2003] QB 679 [75] (Lord Phillips MR for the Court).

a similar relationship to the contractual allocation of risk. A mistake of both parties as to a basic assumption that has a material effect on the agreed exchange of performances renders a contract voidable by the adversely affected party unless that party bears the risk of the mistake.[79] A party bears the risk of a mistake if the risk is allocated to that party by the agreement, the party made the contract notwithstanding an awareness that their knowledge of the relevant facts was limited, or the court allocates the risk to that party on the ground that it is reasonable in the circumstances to do so.[80]

The two principal interpretive questions in a common mistake case are: first, whether the mistake relates to 'the existence, or a vital attribute, of the consideration to be provided or circumstances which must subsist if performance of the contractual adventure is to be possible';[81] and, secondly, whether the contract terms allocate the risk of the mistake to one or other of the contracting parties.[82] Lord Atkin observed in *Bell v Lever Brothers* that the first question is essentially the same as the test for frustration, but applied to present facts rather than future facts:

> We therefore get a common standard for mutual mistake, and implied conditions whether as to existing or as to future facts. Does the state of the new facts destroy the identity of the subject-matter as it was in the original state of facts?[83]

The second question is also essentially the same as the risk allocation question in frustration: was the risk of the relevant assumption not being correct allocated by the contract terms to one of the contracting parties? Most commonly, that risk allocation will take the form of an express or implied promise by one of the parties that the relevant assumption is correct, such as a promise that the subject matter exists. If the mistake is fundamental and the risk was not allocated by the contract terms, then under English law the contract is void by virtue of a legal rule.[84]

In *McRae v Commonwealth Disposals Commission*, Dixon and Fullagar JJ preferred to deal with common mistake on a constructionist basis, by asking whether the promisor promised to perform in all events, 'or only subject to the mutually contemplated original or continued existence of a particular subject matter?'.[85] In that case the Commonwealth invited tenders for, and then purported to sell, a non-existent tanker said to be lying on a reef, apparently acting on rumours as to its existence. The Commonwealth then attempted to avoid liability in contract for the costs incurred by the buyers in mounting a futile salvage expedition on the basis, inter alia, that the contract was void for common mistake. Dixon and Fullagar JJ found that the correct construction of the contract was that the Commission promised that there was a tanker in the location specified.[86] Alternatively, they said, if there is a common law doctrine rendering contracts void

[79] American Law Institute, *Restatement (Second) of Contracts* (1981) § 152.
[80] ibid § 154.
[81] *Great Peace Shipping Ltd v Tsavliris Salvage (International) Ltd (The Great Peace)* [2002] EWCA Civ 1407, [2003] QB 679 [76].
[82] ibid [80] (quoting with approval *Associated Japanese Bank (International) Ltd v Crédit du Nord SA* [1989] 1 WLR 255, 268 (Steyn J).
[83] *Bell v Lever Brothers Ltd* [1932] AC 161, 226–27.
[84] *The Great Peace* [2002] EWCA Civ 1407, [2003] QB 679 [73].
[85] *McRae v Commonwealth Disposals Commission* (1951) 84 CLR 377, 407–08.
[86] ibid 410.

for fundamental common mistakes, the Commission could not rely on it because the mistake was induced by its own fault.[87]

In *The Great Peace*, Lord Phillips MR, influenced by the rejection of the implied term theory of frustration, observed that it is unrealistic to ask whether the parties impliedly agreed that a contract would not be binding if a fundamental assumption proves to be mistaken.[88] Rather, he said:

> The avoidance of a contract on the ground of common mistake results from a rule of law under which, if it transpires that one or both of the parties have agreed to do something which it is impossible to perform, no obligation arises out of that agreement.[89]

In *Bell v Lever Brothers*, Lord Atkin was also sceptical about the capacity of the courts to deal adequately with mistake cases on the basis of an inferred or implied contractual condition that the relevant assumption is correct. There is, he said, no clear basis on which to make such an implication and a great danger in judges allowing themselves to remake contracts by 'importing implications' to make them more just.[90] Any implication, he said, must be necessary to give business efficacy to the transaction.[91]

If, as Lord Atkin suggests, the business efficacy standard is strictly adhered to before any implication is made, then constructionist and default rule approaches are likely to produce different results. If a mistake is such as to render performance of the contractual venture impossible, then the contract will clearly be inefficacious in a business sense without an implication that the contract is subject to the existence of the assumed state of affairs. There is a slight awkwardness in applying the test to the mistake context, however, because the implication of the condition will not make the contract efficacious (in the literal sense of being capable of fulfilling its purpose), but instead will prevent the contract from coming into existence. If we take the idea of an implication to give business efficacy to a contract seriously, then the test does not really work in this situation. If, however, 'obviousness' is accepted as an alternative to business efficacy as a basis for implication, as suggested by Lord Neuberger in *Marks and Spencer plc v BNP Paribas Securities Services Trust Company (Jersey) Ltd*,[92] then outcomes will be far more difficult to predict. As I have argued elsewhere, since there is no reasoning process by which it can be determined whether a term is 'obvious' or not, it cannot be applied as a legal standard and operates as a *deus ex machina*.[93] The default rule recognised in *Bell v Lever Brothers* and *The Great Peace* may therefore be considered preferable to the implied term approach because it is more predictable. In any case it offers a simpler solution that is easier to comprehend and apply.[94]

[87] ibid.

[88] *The Great Peace* [2002] EWCA Civ 1407, [2003] QB 679 [73].

[89] ibid.

[90] *Bell v Lever Brothers* [1932] AC 161, 226.

[91] ibid.

[92] *Marks and Spencer plc v BNP Paribas Securities Services Trust Company (Jersey) Ltd* [2015] UKSC 72, [2016] AC 742 [21] (Lord Neuberger JSC).

[93] Robertson (n 36) 244–46. The requirement of obviousness in the *BP Refinery (Westernport) Pty Ltd v Shire of Hastings* (1977) 180 CLR 266, 283 criteria is best understood as a requirement that the proposed solution is singularly apt: see Robertson (n 36) 243–44, Robertson (n 73) 161–64, Robertson (2016) (n 76) 199.

[94] *contra* Morgan (n 77), arguing that the 'doctrine of common mistake' is not only unsound as a matter of principle, but is also difficult to apply due to the uncertainty that is inherent in the standard of fundamentality.

A choice between an interpretive approach and a default rule approach can also be seen in relation to the question whether the party who is affected by the mistake and seeks to avoid the contract entered into the contract with incomplete knowledge and with the intention of taking a speculative risk. As noted above, the approach reflected in the Second Restatement of Contracts in the US is to treat that party as one who 'bears the risk of a mistake'.[95] The preferred solution of Steyn J in *Associated Japanese Bank (International) Ltd v Crédit du Nord SA* was to adopt a rule that 'a party cannot be allowed to rely on a common mistake where the mistake consists of a belief which is entertained by him without any reasonable grounds for such belief'.[96] That rule was not, he said, based on negligence or estoppel (or, one might add, any implicit assumption or allocation of risk) but operates 'simply because policy and good sense dictate that the positive rules regarding common mistake should be so qualified'.[97]

IV. Conclusion

The application of default rules in the law of contract is inextricably linked with interpretive questions. Close scrutiny of the contract terms is always necessary because a default rule can have no application if the risk in question has been allocated by those terms. Some default rules appear to raise deeper interpretive questions because the rules themselves require inquiries about the nature of the contract that the parties have made. In the case of some doctrines, it may be possible to rationalise those interpretive questions as inquiries into risk allocation. Other doctrines may be rationalised as purely interpretive and not default rules at all. There is therefore room for debate as to whether we see in the law of contract a spectrum of default rules (running from the less to the more interpretive) or simply two different types of doctrine: default rules (which operate in default of explicit or implicit risk allocation); and interpretive doctrines (which are best understood as techniques or tools of interpretation).

It does matter which understanding we adopt. In recognising the existence of a default rules, we are acknowledging that there is a principle of justice in operation. Contractual allocations of risk are of overwhelming importance in the law of contract because the law of contract is a mechanism for risk allocation. Attempting to identify the existence of a contractual allocation of risk must, therefore, always be the starting point in the resolution of a contract problem. Because the law of contract generally favours default rules over mandatory rules, in most cases a contractual allocation of risk will be determinative when it can be identified. It is, however, important to recognise the existence of default rules in order to remain conscious of the fact that that there is an underlying principle which will govern in the absence of a contractual allocation of risk. Judges need to recognise the existence of those principles in order to develop them. Scholars need to recognise the existence of those principles in order to scrutinise and

[95] American Law Institute (n 79) § 154.
[96] *Associated Japanese Bank (International) Ltd v Crédit du Nord SA* [1989] 1 WLR 255, 268.
[97] ibid.

(where necessary) critique them, to enhance understanding of them, and to enhance broader understanding of the nature of the common law of contract.

The situations in which the identification of an implicit allocation of risk is understood to provide an alternative to a default rule raise related issues. There is a well-recognised risk that, because implicit allocations of risk can be elusive, problem-solving on that basis can produce inconsistent or unpredictable results. Where the issue is narrow and a clear path of reasoning can be specified, it may be possible for an allocation of risk approach to produce similar outcomes to a default rule approach. But the broader and more open-ended the inquiry, the more unreliable it becomes to try to solve problems by identifying implicit allocations of risk. Just because contracting parties *can* allocate risks, and just because risks *can* be allocated implicitly, that does not mean that all risks *have* been allocated or that it is always possible, if we look hard enough, to determine how a risk has been allocated. It is essential to recognise that sometimes risks have not been allocated by contracting parties and that default rules have an important role to play in dealing with those unallocated risks.

4

Party Intention, Default Rules and Contract Theory

RYAN CATTERWELL

I. Introduction

Almost every contract dispute involves a question of intention or a question regarding what the parties agreed. That is to say, to apply contract doctrine, one usually needs to answer a question of construction, interpretation or intention. This chapter approaches the topic of default rules in the common law of contract by focusing on the relationship between doctrine and party intention.[1] It seeks to answer the question: in what circumstances does intention impact doctrine in such a way that the doctrine is considered to operate by 'default'? Or, to put it differently, what is necessary in terms of excluding or modifying a rule for the rule to be considered defeasible? In answering this question, the chapter draws on normative justification and contract theory. It analyses the impact of intention on doctrine through a theoretical prism and thereby distils what it means for a doctrine to operate by 'default' (or at least what it means for someone to say that it does).

The thesis of this chapter is that the way in which one justifies contract law has an impact upon how one perceives default rules in contract. At the extremes, the whole of contract law can be regarded as default or only a very small part of it can be regarded that way. The more orthodox position appears to lie somewhere in the middle: doctrine regarding formation and vitiation is not default, but the rest of contract law may or may not operate in such a way. The extent to which it does is shaped in large part by particular principles, preferences and presumptions relating to the construction of contracts.

There are three limbs to this argument. The first is that the concept of rules being default is elastic. Whether a doctrine operates by default turns on how the doctrine is impacted by intention, and intention impacts doctrine in a variety of ways. Hence, one can take either a narrow or a broad view of what constitutes a default rule in contract law by adopting a particular position regarding what is necessary to exclude or modify a rule. Default rules may be limited to those doctrines the application of which are conditional upon there

[1] For a similar approach to the question of default rules, see A Robertson, 'Default Rules, Interpretation and Risk Allocation', this volume, ch 3.

being no contrary intention. On other hand, default rules may also include all doctrines the application of which simply involve a determination of intention. Or, to take the broadest view possible, the whole of contract law can be seen as operating by default because the application of contract law to an agreement depends upon a positive determination regarding intention to contract.

The second limb to the thesis advanced in this chapter is that theoretical perspectives regarding contract law lean towards particular perceptions of default rules. In broad terms, autonomy-based theories lead to a more expansive view of how much of the common law of contract operates by default. By comparison, institutional perspectives give intention a more limited role in contract law and so default rules are narrower in scope. The middle ground appears to be that, if contract is conceptualised as a matter of consent or assumption (or something similar), the institutional rules governing formation and vitiation are mandatory in the sense of not operating by default. But the remainder of contract doctrine – those rules and principles dealing with terms, performance, discharge, remedies and so on – may operate by default.

The third limb to the argument put forward in this chapter is that the nature of default rules in contract is shaped by particular principles, preferences and presumptions. In particular, the scope to infer intention, thereby overriding a default rule, is dictated by the principles guiding construction and related techniques. These principles evolve over time. This can be seen most vividly by analysing the relationship between the modern and flexible approach to construction and the presumption in favour of common law (and statutory) rights and remedies, which requires clear words to override particular default rules.

This chapter consists of four substantive sections. Section II analyses the nature of contract doctrine. In particular, it draws an important distinction between deductive rules and guiding principles in contract doctrine. Section III examines how party intention impacts doctrine and what this means in terms of conceptualising default rules in contract. Section IV demonstrates that theoretical perspectives regarding the nature of contract law naturally tend towards either an expansive or narrow view regarding the nature of default rules in contract. And section V examines how contract law principles, preferences and presumptions shape default rules in contract.

II. Contract Doctrine: Rules and Principles

To understand the nature of default rules in the common law of contract, it is important to understand contract doctrine and its composition. Contract doctrine consists of the rules and principles developed by precedent in relation to contractual bargains. These doctrines were synthesised in part by judges and in part by notable scholars, particularly during the eighteenth and nineteenth centuries.[2] Contract doctrine covers a vast array of matters that determine contractual rights and obligations. It dictates formation of a contract, what constitutes the terms of a contract, consequences for breach of contract,

[2] See generally W Swain, *The Law of Contract 1670–1870* (Cambridge, Cambridge University Press, 2015) ch 8.

and the circumstances in which a contract is terminated or vitiated. Doctrine also influences how contract terms are interpreted, which terms are implied, whether a contract has been performed, and so on.

Contract doctrine consists of a combination of norms that take different forms. While it is not possible to dissect and distinguish the different norms in precise terms, it is possible to draw at least one key distinction. The foundational aspects of contract doctrine (relating to, eg, formation, terms, termination, vitiation and remedies) are most accurately understood as 'rules'. That is to say, the norms in these areas usually resemble deductive rules in the form of 'if p, then q'.[3] Hence, for example, if we look at contract formation, a contract is formed if there is agreement, certainty and completeness, intention and consideration. Likewise, written terms form part of a contract if they constitute an offer that is accepted or if they are incorporated by signature, notice or course of dealing. And a contract is terminated at common law if a party repudiates the contract or commits a substantial breach and the other party elects to terminate.

By contrast with the deductive 'rules' that make up part of contract doctrine, there are other norms in the common law of contract that take the form of flexible 'principles'. The distinction can be understood as one between a 'rules-based approach' and 'an approach concerned with a flexible balancing of particular factors'.[4] It is a distinction between 'rules as specific prescriptions' and 'principles as unspecific or vague prescriptions'.[5] It is the difference between broad guidelines of flexible application and 'hard and fast rules'.[6] Rules are 'applicable in an all-or-nothing fashion' and dictate consequences.[7] By contrast, principles may simple state 'a reason that argues in one direction, but does not necessitate a particular decision', such as the principle that no person should profit from their own wrong.[8]

In the context of contract law, the distinction between rules and principles can be understood by contrasting the deductive rules for establishing contract formation with the principles that guide the modern approach to interpretation. A contract is formed if certain criteria are met: agreement, certainty and completeness, intention and consideration. By contrast, when interpreting a contract, the court ascertains the reasonable person's understanding by considering a range of factors, namely, the meaning of the words, background, contractual purpose, commercial consequences and normative factors, such as business commonsense.[9] The court may also take into

[3] See further N MacCormick, *Legal Reasoning and Legal Theory* (Oxford, Oxford University Publishing, 1994) 45.

[4] Borrowed from A Burrows, 'Form and Substance: Fictions and Judicial Power' in A Robertson and J Goudkamp (eds), *Form and Substance in the Law of Obligations* (Oxford, Hart Publishing, 2019) 17, 18 (discussing the distinction between form and substance).

[5] J Braithwaite, 'Rules and Principles: A Theory of Legal Certainty' (2002) 27 *Australian Journal of Legal Philosophy* 47, 47.

[6] *Peppers Hotel Management Pty Ltd v Hotel Capital Partners Ltd* [2004] NSWCA 114, (2004) 12 BPR 22,879, 22,893 [73] (McColl JA) (rejecting such 'rules' in the law of interpretation). See also *Bank of Credit and Commerce International SA v Ali* [2001] UKHL 8, [2002] 1 AC 251 [55] (Lord Hoffmann), [79] (Lord Clyde).

[7] R Dworkin, 'The Model of Rules' (1967) 35 *University of Chicago Law Review* 14, 25.

[8] ibid 26.

[9] See eg, *Arnold v Britton* [2015] UKSC 36, [2015] AC 1619 [15] (Lord Neuberger, Lord Sumption and Lord Hughes agreeing at [1] and Lord Hodge agreeing at [66]).

account a number of bespoke maxims, presumptions or preferences.[10] The principles that guide the interpretive process are flexible. On one view at least, the reasoning involves a balancing of considerations to reach a conclusion as a matter of probable inference;[11] interpretation is 'an iterative process by which each suggested interpretation is checked against the provisions of the contract and its commercial consequences are investigated'.[12] A similar approach arguably applies when implying a term in fact and in resolving questions of intention otherwise than through interpretation.[13]

The distinction between rules and principles in contract law, as defined above, poses two challenges for this chapter. The first is substantive. On one view, the focus on default rules in this chapter is a focus on the deductive rules that make up the essential bodies of law in the common law of contract, such as the rules regarding formation and termination. However, many, if not most, of the principles that feature in contract law are directed to how one ascertains party intention. Hence, if the nature of default rules is dictated by the relationship between doctrine and intention (as posited in this chapter), the principles are instructive in understanding which rules are default because the principles guide how one ascertains intention. Further, the principles themselves can also be considered to be default in that they can be excluded or modified.[14]

The second challenge is one of nomenclature. This chapter (and indeed all the chapters in this book) consider 'default rules'. Hence, in line with most other contributions in this book, this chapter uses the term 'default rules' to refer to the collection of rules and principles in the common law of contract that can be regarded as operating by default.

III. Doctrine and Intention: The Elasticity of Default Rules

Many, if not most, contract doctrines require input from the parties; that is to say, the application of doctrine often depends upon the resolution of questions of intention (usually questions of objective intention). For example, the question might be whether an offer was objectively intended, whether a party intended to accept an offer, whether parties intended to create legal relations or intended to be immediately bound by a preliminary agreement, whether performance was to be entire or divisible, whether substantial or exact performance was required, whether a term was meant to be essential, whether a particular risk was assumed by one party or another, and so on. Contract doctrine is littered with these sorts of questions. Contract law principles, in particular those governing interpretation, are often applied to resolve these questions by guiding how one ascertains intention.

[10] For example, the traditional Latin maxims, such as *expressio unius* and *contra proferentem*, are occasionally applied in modern cases. There are also principles that apply to specific types of clauses and contracts, such as those applicable to exclusion clauses, notices and guarantees. There are also idiosyncratic preferences or presumptions, such as the preference in favour of upholding contracts and the preference against construing a contract so that a party can take advantage of its own wrong: see R Catterwell, *A Unified Approach to Contract Interpretation* (Oxford, Hart Publishing, 2020) [3-33]–[3-45].

[11] See generally, ibid ch 6.

[12] *Wood v Capita Insurance Services Ltd* [2017] UKSC 24, [2017] AC 1173 [11]–[12] (Lord Hodge).

[13] See Catterwell (n 10) ch 7.

[14] For example, parties regularly exclude the contra proferentem maxim by use of a specific 'interpretation' clause, such as 'This contract is not to be construed against a party because that party drafted the contract'.

The relationship between doctrine and party intention is a natural starting place for an analysis of the nature of default rules in the common law of contract. This is because, in its essence, a rule is 'default' if it can be excluded or modified and, under contract law, the dominant or perhaps conventional way in which one understands doctrine to be excluded or modified is by reason of a contrary or inconsistent intention on the part of the parties.[15] Further, the relationship between doctrine and intention offers fertile ground for analysing the nature of default rules because intention impacts doctrine in a variety of ways. Hence, we can conceptualise what constitutes a 'default' rule by reference to the way (or ways) in which intention must impact the application of a rule in order for the rule to be considered default. The impact of intention on doctrine can be framed on a sliding scale. As a consequence, default rules can be cast in either broad or narrow terms.

On a very narrow view, the only default rules in contract law are the terms that are implied into contracts unless the parties positively exclude them. In fact, this is often what people understand by the term 'default rules' in contract.[16] Conventionally, these terms are understood as terms implied in law as an incident of a class of contract. The terms that are implied into employment contracts,[17] leases,[18] contracts for professional services,[19] and contracts for works and materials[20] are illustrative examples. These terms were described by Lord Steyn in *Equitable Life Assurance Society v Hyman*[21] as 'standardised implied terms operat[ing] as general default rules'.[22] They are often regarded as terms implied based on public policy.[23] They are, in essence, terms that are implied into contracts of a relevant category 'unless the parties have expressly excluded [them]'.[24]

Taking a more expansive approach, a rule is default if it constitutes a presumption or preference because, inherently, the application of the rule can be excluded or modified by an express or implied intention. Many doctrinal rules in contract regarding formation and performance can be understood in this way. For example, in contract formation, there is a presumption that parties in a commercial setting intend to create legal relations,[25] which can be overridden, for example, by the use of an 'honour' clause'.[26] Likewise, with respect to performance, there is a presumption that substantial

[15] *cf* R Craswell, 'Contract Law, Default Rules, and the Philosophy of Promising' (1989) 88 *Michigan Law Review* 489, 489–90 (default rules in contract are those that can be excluded or varied); J Morgan, 'Contract Remedies as Default Rules' in R Halson and D Campbell, *Research Handbook on Remedies in Private Law* (Cheltenham, Edward Elgar, 2019) 472, 472.

[16] CA Riley, 'Designing Default Rules in Contract Law: Consent, Conventionalism, and Efficiency' (2000) 20 *OJLS* 367, 367.

[17] See, eg, *Wessex Dairies Ltd v Smith* [1935] 2 KB 80 (CA); *Malik v Bank of Credit and Commerce International SA* [1998] AC 20 (HL).

[18] *Liverpool City Council v Irwin* [1977] AC 239 (HL).

[19] *Henderson v Merrett Syndicates Ltd* [1995] 2 AC 145 (HL).

[20] *GH Myers & Co v Brent Cross Service Co* [1934] 1 KB 46 (DC).

[21] *Equitable Life Assurance Society v Hyman* [2002] 1 AC 408 (HL).

[22] *Equitable Life Assurance Society v Hyman* [2002] 1 AC 408, 458 (Lord Steyn). See also *Commonwealth Bank of Australia v Barker* [2014] HCA 32, (2014) 253 CLR 169 [113] (Gageler J).

[23] See, eg, G McMeel, *McMeel on the Construction of Contracts: Interpretation, Implication and Rectification*, 3rd edn (Oxford, Oxford University Press, 2017) [1.23].

[24] *Geys v Societe General* [2012] UKSC 63, [2013] 1 AC 523 [55] (Baroness Hale).

[25] *Edwards v Skyways* [1964] 1 WLR 349 (QB). But note, under Australian law, that the role of presumptions has been questioned: *Ermogenous v Greek Orthodox Community of SA Inc* (2002) 209 CLR 95 [26] (Gaudron, McHugh, Hayne and Callinan JJ).

[26] *Rose & Frank Co v JR Crompton & Bros Ltd* [1925] AC 445 (HL).

(rather than exact) performance is sufficient.[27] In each of these circumstances, a default position applies, by reason of a presumption, which may be excluded or modified by a contrary intention.

Under a slightly broader view of what constitutes a default rule, there are those rules or principles that can be excluded or modified by an express or implied intention but not because the rule or principle takes the form of a preference or presumption. One can view doctrine dealing with terms and interpretation in this manner. For example, the parol evidence rule[28] and the principles regarding pre-contractual statements[29] are regularly in effect overridden by the parties through an entire agreement clause. And, although rare, even the ordinary approach to the interpretation of contracts can be modified by a contrary intention. For example, the parties can expressly require that the contract be construed literally or that it not be construed in such a way.[30]

Adopting a more expansive position regarding the nature of default rules, a rule is also default if application of the rule can be excluded or modified, but only by clear words. Doctrinal rules dealing with termination and remedies usually fall into this category. This is because of the presumption in favour of common law (and statutory) rights and remedies. The presumption is a focus of the final section of this chapter because the nature of the presumption and its relationship to construction illustrates the way in which default rules are shaped by contract law principles.

Applying an even broader view, a rule operates by default simply if its application requires and therefore turns on the determination of a question of intention. For example, the rules regarding termination for breach at common law could be viewed as default because they require a determination regarding whether or not a term is essential. Perhaps more convincingly, the doctrines that require the resolution of questions expressed in terms of assumption or allocation of risk can be understood as operating by default. Whether a contract is frustrated turns on whether either party assumed the risk of occurrence of the relevant supervening event.[31] Likewise, the question of remoteness of loss involves a determination whether one party or another had assumed risk of the particular loss.[32] And whether a contract is vitiated by common mistake requires a determination regarding whether one party or the other should bear the risk of imperfect or altered performance.[33]

[27] *Hoenig v Isaacs* [1952] 2 All ER 176 (CA) 180 (Denning LJ).

[28] To the extent it is still a feature of the common law: Law Commission for England and Wales, *Law of Contract – The Parol Evidence Rule* (Law Com No 154, January 1986); McMeel (n 23) [15.03], [15.46]; *Chartbrook Ltd v Persimmon Homes Ltd* [2009] UKHL 38, [2009] 1 AC 1101 [99] (Baroness Hale) ('no real content').

[29] See, eg, *Oscar Chess v Williams* [1957] 1 WLR 370 (CA); *Dick Bentley Productions Ltd v Harold Smith (Motors) Ltd* [1965] 1 WLR 623 (CA).

[30] See, eg, JW Carter, *The Construction of Commercial Contracts* (Oxford, Hart Publishing, 2013) [15-15], citing *Home and Overseas Insurance Co Ltd v Mentor Insurance Co (UK) Ltd* [1990] 1 WLR 153 (CA) 161–62 (Parker LJ) (clause requiring that contract not be construed literally). For a detailed analysis of frustration in the context of default rules, see J Morgan, 'Frustration Dissected: Mandatory and Default Rules', this volume, ch 9.

[31] *Edwinton Commercial Corp v Tsavliris Russ (Worldwide Salvage & Towage) Ltd (The Sea Angel)* [2007] EWCA Civ 547, [2007] 2 Lloyd's Rep 517 [111] (Rix LJ); G Treitel, *Frustration and Force Majeure*, 3rd edn (London, Sweet & Maxwell, 2014) [12-002].

[32] *Transfield Shipping Inc v Mercator Shipping Inc (The Achilleas)* [2008] UKHL 48, [2009] 1 AC 61.

[33] *Lehman Brothers International (Europe) (In Administration) v Exotix Partners LLP* [2019] EWHC 2380 (Ch) [195] (Hildyard J). See also *Great Peace Shipping Ltd v Tsavliris Salvage (International) Ltd (The Great Peace)* [2002] EWCA Civ 1407, [2003] QB 679 [76] (Lord Phillips, for the Court).

These questions of risk allocation are, at least on one view, questions of intention. Hence, the relevant doctrinal rules are impacted by intention in their application. On this basis, the rules can be regarded as default if one takes a broad approach to the concept.

Taking a still wider view of what constitute default rules in contract, all doctrines in contract law can be regarded as default other than those doctrines which, once contract law is taken to apply, cannot be excluded or modified by the parties under any circumstances. The doctrines in contract law that cannot be excluded or modified are quite narrow in compass. They include the doctrine regarding penalties[34] and the doctrine regarding restraints of trade.[35] Vitiating factors can also be understood in this way. Whether vitiating factors create a power to rescind or simply negate contract formation,[36] the rules permitting rescission for undue influence, duress, unconscionability, misrepresentation and so on cannot be excluded by express agreement. Beyond these narrow categories of doctrinal rules that cannot be excluded or modified, on a broad view of what constitutes a default rule, the rest of contract law is defeasible.

Finally, the whole of the common law of contract can be viewed as default on the basis that the application of contract law depends upon a positive determination regarding the collective intention of the parties. To establish a contract, one must find that the parties reached an agreement. This finding turns on a determination regarding what was objectively intended by the parties' communications, namely, was there offer and acceptance[37] or a mutual manifestation of assent.[38] Likewise, an agreement is only binding as a contract if the parties objectively intend to create legal relations. The agreement must be 'reasonably intended to be enforceable in the courts'.[39] Even in the case of a commercial arrangement, the parties can effectively exclude the application of contract law to their agreement.[40] Hence, on a very broad view of what constitutes a default rule, contract law in its totality is defeasible because it can be ousted by express agreement.

IV. Contract Theory and Default Rules

Because the concept of default rules is elastic, the scope of default rules in the common law of contract is influenced by one's theoretical perspective. Contract law is, of course, conceptualised in a variety of ways. At one end of the spectrum, contract is about giving effect to party autonomy; contract is promise,[41] agreement,[42] consent,[43] assumption[44] or

[34] *Cavendish Square Holdings BV v Makdessi* [2015] UKSC 67, [2016] AC 1172.

[35] *Harcus Sinclair LLP v Your Lawyers Ltd (Parker, third party)* [2021] UKSC 32, [2021] 3 WLR 598.

[36] See M Chen-Wishart, 'The Nature of Vitiating Factors in Contract Law' in G Klass, G Letsas and P Saprai (eds), *Philosophical Foundations of Contract Law* (Oxford, Oxford University Press, 2014) 294, 295–96.

[37] *Carlill v Carbolic Smoke Ball Co* [1893] 1 QB 256 (CA).

[38] *Branir Pty Ltd v Owston Nominees (No 2) Pty Ltd* [2001] FCA 1833, (2001) 117 FCR 424 (FCAFC) [329] (Allsop J); *cf New Zealand Shipping Co Ltd v AM Satterthwaite & Co Ltd* [1975] AC 154 (HL) 167 (Lord Wilberforce).

[39] *Blue v Ashley (No 2)* [2017] EWHC 1928 [55] (Leggatt J).

[40] *Rose & Frank Co v JR Crompton & Bros Ltd* [1925] AC 445 (HL).

[41] See generally C Fried, *Contract as Promise* (Cambridge, MA, Harvard University Press, 1981).

[42] See J Penner, 'Voluntary Obligations and the Scope of the Law of Contract' (1996) 2 *Legal Theory* 325.

[43] See RE Barnett, 'A Consent Theory of Contract' (1986) 86 *Columbia Law Review* 269.

[44] See B Coote, *Contract as Assumption: Essays on a Theme* (Oxford, Hart Publishing, 2010).

expectation.[45] If one views contract in this way, one may tend to take an expansive view of default rules in contract. By contrast, at the other end of spectrum, contract law is an 'institution';[46] it is a 'facility'[47] through which contractual relationships are governed according to shifting societal values.[48] On this view, one may tend to adopt the position that much of contract law is mandatory; there are fewer default rules.

Supporters of autonomy-based theories of contract often view the principle of 'freedom of contract' as paramount. In its most rudimentary form, the principle of freedom of contract simply denotes the idea that, through contract, private individuals can 'effect changes … in their legal relations'[49] and 'create rights between [them] … that did not exist before'.[50] For this reason, it is perhaps better conceptualised as a 'power to contract', rather than a 'freedom'.[51] Contract facilitates the giving of effect to rights, obligations, liabilities and so on that the parties chose to create.[52] If one views the common law of contract through this prism, the whole of contract law can be viewed as default. Contract is about choice; the parties can choose whether or not the law of contract applies; and hence, the law of contract is by its nature defeasible in its entirety.

Of course, many theorists and scholars view the principle of freedom of contract not simply as a matter of choice, but as a matter of voluntariness and freedom. Parties must have 'the utmost liberty of contracting' in the sense that agreements must be enforced 'when entered into freely and voluntarily'.[53] Hence, the orthodox view of 'freedom of contract' is 'the idea that … the obligations *voluntarily undertaken by the parties* are enforced by the courts'.[54] If one perceives contract law as underpinned by freedom of contract in this sense, all of the rules and principles that make up contract doctrine can be regarded as default. Indeed, this appears to be the view taken by Lord Leggatt in *Barton v Morris*,[55] where his Lordship remarked:

> The idea of freedom of contract is that contractual obligations should be freely chosen. But that does not mean that the choice to be bound by an obligation must be expressly stated. If it

[45] See A Smith, *Lectures on Jurisprudence*, RL Meek, DD Raphael and PG Stein (eds) (Oxford, Oxford University Press, 1978) 87, 92.

[46] See B Coote, 'The Essence of Contract Part II' (1988) 1 *Journal of Contract Law* 183, 203; Lord Hoffmann, 'The Intolerable Wrestle with Words and Meanings' (1997) 114 *South African Law Journal* 656, 664; Carter (n 30) [2-06]; BJ Reiter, 'The Control of Contract Power' (1981) 1 *OJLS* 347, 348.

[47] Coote (n 46) 201.

[48] *cf* H Dagan and M Heller, *The Choice Theory of Contracts* (Cambridge, Cambridge University Press, 2017) 43.

[49] L Fuller, 'Consideration as Form' (1941) 41 *Columbia Law Review* 799, 806 (describing 'the principle of private autonomy'). See also P Benson, 'Contracts' in D Patterson (ed), *A Companion to Philosophy of Law and Legal Theory*, 2nd edn (Oxford, Blackwell Publishing, 2010) 29, 37.

[50] R Stevens, 'Binding Our Future Selves' in PS Davies and M Raczynska (eds), *Contents of Commercial Contracts: Terms Affecting Freedoms* (Oxford, Hart Publishing, 2020) 13, 13 (explaining 'freedom of contract').

[51] ibid 13.

[52] Dagan and Heller (n 48) 41–42.

[53] *Printing and Numerical Registering Co v Sampson* (1875) LR 19 Eq 462 (Ch) 465 (Jessel MR).

[54] M Raczynska and PS Davies, 'Freedom of Contract and Terms Affecting Freedoms' in PS Davies and M Raczynska (eds), *Contents of Commercial Contracts: Terms Affecting Freedoms* (Oxford, Hart Publishing, 2020) 1, 1 (emphasis added).

[55] *Barton v Morris* [2023] UKSC 3, [2023] AC 684.

> did, there would be very little to the law of contract. *A principal function of contract law is to provide a framework of rules which apply to contractual relationships unless the parties expressly opt out of them.*[56]

In the alternative, one may view contract as a matter of voluntarily undertaken obligations, but take the position that certain rules and doctrines are mandatory and not defeasible, such as those doctrines permitting vitiation of the contract in the case of misrepresentation, duress, undue influence and so on.

Turning to the opposite end of the spectrum, if contract is taken to serve particular social or moral objectives beyond simply giving effect to party autonomy, then there is a greater inclination to view default rules in contract in a restrictive way. For example, if one conceptualises contract as a tool to implement distributive justice,[57] then default rules should be narrow in scope; one should not be able to readily contract out of rules designed to redistribute wealth and property.[58]

The sensible middle ground appears to be one based on the conceptualisation of contract as a matter of consent or assumption. The making of a contract is an '"institutional" act' with legal consequences.[59] By entering into a contract, the parties consent to regulation in accordance with prevailing norms.[60] To put it differently, by satisfying the formal requirements for contract formation – namely, agreement, intention, consideration, and certainty and completeness – the parties assume obligations arising under the law of contract.[61] They enter a contract knowing full well and very much intending the legal consequences that follow; they voluntarily assume obligations imposed upon them by law. On this view, the rules dealing with contract formation are mandatory and not defeasible.[62] It is the satisfaction of these rules that render the parties bound to contract doctrine.[63] They are, to put it loosely, entry requirements. Likewise, the rules providing for vitiation of particular clauses (ie, agreed damages clauses or restraints of trade) or vitiation of the contract itself are also mandatory.[64] With respect to the latter, they cannot be default if contract is about consent and assumption, at least insofar as rules regarding contract vitiation are premised on the notion that a party's entry into the contract was not free and voluntary. That said, how much of the rest of the law of contract operates by default, and in what way, is an open question. It is dictated by the scope and effect of contract law principles, presumptions and preferences.

[56] ibid [126] (Lord Leggatt) (dissenting on the facts) (emphasis added).

[57] See, eg, AT Kronman, 'Contract Law and Distributive Justice' (1980) 89 *Yale Law Journal* 472.

[58] Beyond the common law, legislative regulation of unfair contract terms and related statutory intervention has had the effect of creating what can be understood as a mandatory welfarist regime for regulating contracts: *cf* H Collins, *Regulating Contracts* (Oxford, Oxford University Press, 2002) 8.

[59] A De Moor, 'Are Contracts Promises?' in J Eekelaar and J Bell (eds), *Oxford Essays in Jurisprudence: Third Series* (Oxford, Clarendon Press, 1987) 103, 105.

[60] See generally Barnett (n 43). See also Carter (n 30) [2-06] (entry into a contract signifies assent to the contract institution).

[61] See Coote (n 46) 195.

[62] For a persuasive argument regarding why some formation rules should be regarded as default, see W Day, 'Default Rules in Contract Formation', this volume, ch 5.

[63] See Craswell (n 15) 503 ('agreement rules').

[64] See ibid ('background rules').

V. Defining Default Rules: Principles, Preferences and Presumptions

The concept of default rules is elastic. It is shaped by theoretical perspectives regarding contract law. However, the middle ground appears to be one in which doctrine regarding formation and vitiation is mandatory, but the rest of the common law of contract may operate by default. If one adopts this view, the remaining controversy about default rules in contract law can be understood as a controversy regarding particular contract law principles, presumptions and preferences. This is because it is ultimately these principles that dictate the relationship between intention and the deductive rules that make up essential contract doctrine; it is these principles that shape the nature of default rules in contract. The principles evolve and adapt over time. This can be seen by analysing the tension between, on the one hand, the modern and liberal approach to interpretation and, on the other, the presumption in favour of common law (and statutory) rights and remedies.

The modern approach to interpretation is one through which the court ascertains the reasonable person's understanding of what was meant by the words in a contract.[65] This approach facilitates (among other things) the resolution of ambiguity, the reconciliation of inconsistency, and the correction of obvious error through construction.[66] The law regarding interpretation has shifted away from reliance on bespoke and specific maxims tied to linguistic formulations; it has shifted from focus on 'special "rules" of interpretation' to an 'emphasis on context and objective meaning'.[67] A key influence on the evolution in principles of interpretation over the last century has been an emphasis on particular normative elements in the construction process. This focus emerged in the middle of the twentieth century in the form of what can be understood as preferences, in particular, the preference in favour of giving effect to contractual intent and the preference in favour of construing commercial contracts in a flexible and broad way. As was famously stated in *Hillas & Co Ltd v Arcos Ltd*,[68] the law should avoid 'incur[ring] the reproach of being the destroyer of bargains';[69] commercial contracts should be construed 'fairly and broadly, without being too astute or subtle in finding defects'.[70] The normative focus in contract interpretation later crystallised into an emphasis on commercial purpose and practical consequences and the recognition that 'business common sense' was a relevant (and often significant) factor in the construction of a commercial contract.[71] Hence, in an oft-quoted remark from *Antaios Compania Naviera*

[65] See, eg, *Arnold v Britton* [2015] UKSC 36, [2015] AC 1619 [15] (Lord Neuberger, Lord Sumption and Lord Hughes agreeing at [1] and Lord Hodge agreeing at [66]).

[66] *cf* McMeel (n 23) [1.03]–[1.06] (there are several 'sources of construction disputes', including 'incompleteness', 'ambiguity', 'error' and 'deliberate equivocation').

[67] *cf Triple Point Technology Inc v PTT Public Co Ltd* [2021] UKSC 29, [2021] AC 1148 [107] (Lord Leggatt, Lord Burrows agreeing at [73]) ('*Triple Point*').

[68] *Hillas & Co Ltd v Arcos Ltd* (1932) 43 Lloyd's Rep 359.

[69] ibid 364 (Lord Tomlin).

[70] ibid 367 (Lord Wright).

[71] See, eg, *Prenn v Simmonds* [1971] 1 WLR 1381 (HL) 1383 (Lord Wilberforce, Lord Reid and Lord Donovan agreeing at 1383, Lord Pearson and Lord Diplock agreeing at 1390); *Reardon Smith Line Ltd v Yngvar Hansen-Tangen* [1976] 1 WLR 989 (HL) 995–96 (Lord Wilberforce, Viscount Dilhorne agreeing at 1000, Lord Simon and Lord Kilbrandon agreeing at 1001).

SA v Salen Rederierna AB (The Antaois),[72] Lord Diplock stated: 'If detailed semantic and syntactical analysis of words in a commercial contract is going to lead to a conclusion that flouts business commonsense, it must be made to yield to business commonsense.'[73]

The liberal approach to construction is best understood by looking at some of the more extreme examples of what is possible. In *Rainy Sky SA v Kookmin Bank*,[74] a refund guarantee issued in relation to a shipbuilding contract was construed as being responsive in the event of the shipbuilder's insolvency even though the guarantee did not specify (or at least did not clearly specify) that event as a basis triggering its application.[75] In *Mannai Investment Co Ltd v Eagle Star Life Assurance Co Ltd*,[76] a termination notice expressed to terminate a set of two leases on '12 January' was read as terminating the lease in accordance with the relevant break clause, that is, on 13 January.[77] And, perhaps most controversially, in *Investors Compensation Scheme Ltd v West Bromwich Building Society*,[78] an assignment of claims by investors to a compensation fund, which excluded 'any claim (whether sounding in rescission for undue influence or otherwise)' against a particular lender, was nonetheless construed as assigning claims for damages against that lender.[79]

Despite what the preceding examples suggest, the scope to construe contracts in a broad and flexible way is of course not limitless. In fact, in recent years, there has been a tempering of this normative influence on construction and a reinstated emphasis on textual analysis. In particular, in *Arnold v Britton*,[80] Lord Neuberger remarked: 'Reliance on commercial common sense and surrounding circumstances … should not be invoked to undervalue the importance of the language of the provision which is to be construed.'[81] The facts of that case also demonstrate the limits of the liberal approach. A covenant to pay expenses in 99-year leases of holiday homes was, in the case of most of the leases, construed as obliging the lessees to pay an indexed sum increasing by 10 per cent per annum rather than a proportionate part of actual expenses. This is what the clause said on its apparent meaning.[82] It was also justified by conceptualising the covenant as a bilateral gamble on inflation, considering that inflation was at ten per cent per annum or thereabouts at the time of entry into the leases.[83] The lessees were being

[72] *Antaios Compania Naviera SA v Salen Rederierna AB (The Antaois)* [1985] AC 191 (HL).

[73] ibid 201 (Lord Diplock, Lord Keith agreeing at 207, Lord Scarman agreeing at 207–08, Lord Roskill agreeing at 208–09 and Lord Brandon agreeing at 209).

[74] *Rainy Sky SA v Kookmin Bank* [2011] UKSC 50, [2011] 1 WLR 2900 ('*Rainy Sky*').

[75] The guarantee did not list insolvency of the builder as one of the circumstances in which the purchaser was entitled to a refund under the shipbuilding contract, even though insolvency was included as a basis for a refund under the shipbuilding contract itself.

[76] *Mannai Investment Co Ltd v Eagle Star Life Assurance Co Ltd* [1997] AC 749 (HL).

[77] Because this is how a reasonable recipient would have read the notice: see ibid 774–75 (Lord Hoffmann).

[78] [1998] 1 WLR 896 (HL) ('*ICS*').

[79] The parenthesised words were themselves suggestive of error. Further, as a matter of background and purpose, the lenders in question were the primary targets of the scheme: see further Catterwell (n 11) [6-98]–[6-99].

[80] *Arnold v Britton* [2015] UKSC 36, [2015] AC 1619.

[81] ibid [15] (Lord Neuberger, Lord Sumption and Lord Hughes agreeing at [1] and Lord Hodge agreeing at [66]).

[82] The clause stated: 'The lessee hereby covenants … To pay to the lessors … as a proportionate part of the expenses and outgoings incurred … the yearly sum of £90 and VAT (if any) for the first year of the term hereby granted increasing thereafter by ten pounds per hundred for every subsequent year or part thereof.'

[83] *Arnold v Britton* [2015] UKSC 36, [2015] AC 1619 [36] (Lord Neuberger).

asked to pay significant sums: for some, in 2015, the figure was £2,500, and, by 2072, it would exceed £550,000.[84] Nonetheless, business commonsense and a consideration of the commercial consequences was an insufficient basis to depart from the clear meaning of the words agreed.

In light of the above, one can conceptualise modern construction as a process through which the courts strike a balance between loyalty to the text and a focus on flexibility and commercial common sense. This flexibility inherent in modern construction makes one think that default rules in contract are not particularly difficult to dislodge. That is to say, it is at least easier in theory to exclude or modify a default rule under the modern approach than under a strict or literal approach to construction. If '12 January' can be taken to mean '13 January' and 'any claim' can be construed so as not to encompass claims for damages, then parties can more readily override default rules. A loose indication by the parties should be sufficient.

However, of course, it is not that simple. A significant complicating factor is that there is a well-established presumption in contract law to the effect that clear words are needed to abrogate common law (and statutory) rights and remedies. The presumption is a complicating factor because it makes it harder to exclude or modify particular rules.[85] The focus of the remainder of this chapter is exploring the tension between this presumption and the modern approach, and analysing what it means in terms of understanding default rules in the common law of contract.

The presumption in favour of common law rights and remedies was originally formulated, at least as a feature of the modern law of contract, by Lord Diplock in *Gilbert-Ash (Northern) Ltd v Modern Engineering (Bristol) Ltd*.[86] In that case, his Lordship stated:

> [O]ne starts with the presumption that neither party intends to abandon any remedies for [breach of contract] arising by operation of law, and clear express words must be used in order to rebut this presumption.[87]

Gilbert-Ash was a building case in which common law and statutory rights of set-off were held not to be excluded under the contract in question. Lord Diplock's statement of principle was later quoted with approval by Lord Hoffmann in *Beaufort Developments (NI) Ltd v Gilbert-Ash (NI) Ltd*.[88] The presumption has since been discussed and applied in numerous other cases.[89]

The presumption was most recently considered in detail by the Supreme Court of the United Kingdom in *Triple Point Technology Inc v PTT Public Co Ltd*.[90] In that case,

[84] ibid [30] (Lord Neuberger).

[85] But note the rejection by Moore-Bick LJ in *Stocznia Gdynia SA v Gearbulk Holdings Ltd* [2010] QB 27 (CA) (at [23]) of the notion that there are 'two competing approaches struggling for supremacy: one requiring clear express words, the other favouring the natural meaning of the words used'.

[86] *Gilbert-Ash (Northern) Ltd v Modern Engineering (Bristol) Ltd* [1974] AC 689 (HL).

[87] ibid 717 (Lord Diplock).

[88] *Beaufort Developments (NI) Ltd v Gilbert-Ash (NI) Ltd* [1999] 1 AC 266 (HL) 279–80 (Lord Hoffmann, Lord Goff agreeing).

[89] See the cases cited and discussed in Lord Justice Lewison, *The Interpretation of Contracts*, 8th edn (London, Sweet & Maxwell, 2023) [12.24]–[12.41].

[90] *Triple Point* [2021] UKSC 29, [2021] AC 1148.

Lord Leggatt couched the presumption in the context of the approach to interpretation as follows:

> The modern view is accordingly to recognise that commercial parties are free to make their own bargains and allocate risks as they think fit, and that the task of the court is to interpret the words used fairly applying the ordinary methods of contractual interpretation. It also remains necessary, however, to recognise that a vital part of the setting in which parties' contract is a framework of rights and obligations established by the common law (and often now codified in statute).[91]

Triple Point involved a software supply contract. One focus of the dispute was the construction of a cap on liability which was expressed not to apply to liability resulting from, among other things, 'negligence'. A key question was whether the exclusion from the cap was limited to liability in the tort of negligence or whether it also applied to liability for breach of an implied contractual duty of care.[92] By majority, the Court held that the carve out applied to both tortious and contractual liability for negligence; hence, the cap did not limit liability for breach of the implied duty. For Lord Leggatt and Lord Burrows, the presumption played a role. Rather than exclude the implied term, the parties 'positively reinforced it'[93] by including an express obligation to exercise reasonable care and skill. Further, the ordinary legal meaning of the term 'negligence' included both tortious and contractual negligence; it denoted negligence in the performance of the services under the contract. It followed that to construe the cap as applying to liability for breach of the implied term 'would involve a substantial departure from the obligations implied by law in a contract of the present kind'.[94] Clear words were needed to limit liability for breach of the implied term and they had not been used.

On one view, the effect of the presumption is that some default rules in contract cannot be rebutted by mere interpretive 'inference',[95] that is, the sort of flexible interpretive inference evident in *Rainy Sky*, *ICS* and similar cases. To put it differently, some rules are more 'sticky' than others.[96] It is not possible to merely *infer* a common objective intention displacing some default rules because those rules underpin common law or statutory rights and remedies, and hence, clear words are necessary.[97] To put it crudely, default rules in the common law of contract 'vary in strength'[98] with the strength of a particular rule depending on the extent to which the presumption (or another rule) requires clear words to override it.

[91] ibid [108] (Lord Leggatt, Lord Burrows agreeing at [73]). See also *Herculito Maritime Ltd v Gunvor International BV* [2024] UKSC 2, [2024] Bus LR 580 [57] (Lord Hamblen, Lord Hodge, Lord Leggatt, Lady Rose and Lord Richards agreeing).

[92] The implied duty is an implication in law 'originally at common law and now by section 13 of the Supply of Goods and Services Act 1982': *Triple Point* [2021] AC 1148 [112] (Lord Leggatt, Lord Burrows agreeing at [73]).

[93] ibid [113] (Lord Leggatt, Lord Burrows agreeing at [73]).

[94] ibid [112] (Lord Leggatt, Lord Burrows agreeing at [73]).

[95] *cf* JW Carter and W Courtney, 'Unexpressed Intention and Contract Construction' (2017) 37 *OJLS* 326, 353–54.

[96] See generally H Dagan and M Heller, 'The Autonomy Default Paradigm in Contract Law' (3 February 2025), available at papers.ssrn.com/sol3/papers.cfm?abstract_id=4754123. See also K Barnett, 'Date of Breach as a Sticky Default Rule and the Role of the Court in Assessing Reasonable Mitigatory Measure', this volume, ch 10 (discussing the date of breach rule).

[97] *cf* Carter and Courtney (n 95) 353–54.

[98] *cf* ibid, 353–54 (conceptualising default rules as 'presumptions of intention').

One difficulty with the presumption is that its scope is not entirely clear. As originally outlined by Lord Diplock, the presumption was one in favour of 'remedies for … breach arising by operation of law'[99] and 'implied primary and secondary obligations'.[100] It is now defined in largely the same terms as being limited to the protection of remedies, rights and obligations arising at common law or under statute. According to Lord Leggatt in *Triple Point*, the presumption protects 'the framework of rights and obligations established by the common law (and often now codified in statute)';[101] it has the effect that 'clear words are necessary before the court will hold that a contract has taken away valuable rights or remedies which one of the parties to it would have had at common law (or pursuant to statute)'.[102]

The presumption has been applied so as to require clear words in excluding or modifying rights to damages for breach at common law and under statute,[103] including the right to loss of bargain damages upon termination.[104] It has also been applied with respect to the exclusion of common law powers of termination,[105] obligations implied by law,[106] the right to recover debts accrued prior to termination,[107] and common law and statutory set-off rights.[108] And recent cases have seen the presumption extended to rights far removed from those ordinarily connected with contract law, such as common law maritime rights[109] and the right to adduce evidence.[110]

The effect of the presumption has also been expressed in various ways. For example, it has been said that the 'strength [of the presumption] will vary according to the circumstances of the case',[111] that '[t]he more valuable the right, the clearer the language will need to be'[112] and that the exclusion of some rights would require 'very clear language'.[113] That is to say, 'the strength of the presumption is reduced in proportion to the degree of derogation from the common law position'.[114]

[99] *Gilbert-Ash (Northern) Ltd v Modern Engineering (Bristol) Ltd* [1974] AC 689 (HL) 717 (Lord Diplock).
[100] *Photo Production Ltd v Securicor Transport Ltd* [1980] AC 827 (HL) 851 (Lord Diplock).
[101] *Triple Point* [2021] UKSC 29, [2021] AC 1148 [108] (Lord Leggatt, Lord Burrows agreeing at [73]).
[102] ibid [106] (Lord Leggatt, Lord Burrows agreeing at [73]).
[103] See, eg, *Bem Dis a Turk Ticaret S/A TR v International Agri Trade Co Ltd (The Selda)* [1999] 1 Lloyd's Rep 729, 731–32 (CA) (damages at common law and under the Sale of Goods Act 1979).
[104] *Stocznia Gdynia SA v Gearbulk Holdings Ltd* [2009] EWCA Civ 75, [2010] QB 27 [22]–[23] (Moore-Bick LJ).
[105] *Concut Pty Ltd v Worrell* [2000] HCA 64, (2000) 176 ALR 693 [23] (Gleeson CJ, Gaudron and Gummow JJ).
[106] *Triple Point* [2021] UKSC 29, [2021] AC 1148 [112] (Lord Leggatt, Lord Burrows agreeing at [73]).
[107] *Stocznia Gdanska SA v Latvian Shipping Co* [1998] 1 WLR 574 (HL) 585 (Lord Goff, Lord Hoffmann, Lord Hope and Lord Hutton agreeing at 603), 597 (Lord Lloyd) (payments accrued due under a contract prior to discharge).
[108] See, eg, *Gilbert-Ash (Northern) Ltd v Modern Engineering (Bristol) Ltd* [1974] AC 689 (HL).
[109] *Herculito Maritime Ltd v Gunvor International BV ('The Polar')* [2024] UKSC 2, [2024] Bus LR 580 [57] (Lord Hamblen, Lord Hodge, Lord Leggatt, Lady Rose and Lord Richards agreeing at [1]) (the right of 'general average').
[110] *Battersea Project Phase 2 Development Co Ltd v QFS Scaffolding Ltd* [2024] EWHC 591 (TCC) [45] (Nissen KC) (conclusive evidence clause).
[111] *Triple Point* [2021] UKSC 29, [2021] AC 1148 [108] (Lord Leggatt, Lord Burrows agreeing).
[112] *Stocznia Gdynia SA v Gearbulk Holdings Ltd* [2009] EWCA Civ 75, [2010] QB 27 [23] (Moore-Bick LJ).
[113] *Stocznia Gdanska SA v Latvian Shipping Co* [1998] 1 WLR 574 (HL) 597 (Lord Lloyd).
[114] *Scottish Power UK Plc v BP Exploration Operating Company Ltd* [2016] EWCA Civ 1043 [30] (Christopher Clarke LJ).

Our focus is the extent to which the presumption impacts our understanding of default rules in the common law of contract. In this regard, the impact of the presumption appears to be that rules dealing with remedies, termination and implied rights and obligations are protected; it is harder to displace those rules than it is to displace other rules in relation to which clear words are not required. However, the scope of the presumption is awkward, if not incoherent, in at least two respects.

First, while the presumption requires clear words to exclude particular rules (in particular, those regarding remedies and termination), the rules themselves often turn upon interpretive inference and hence can effectively be excluded or displaced without clear words. For example, under the presumption, clear words are needed to exclude a right to common law damages. However, to exclude a particular loss as being recoverable, on the basis that one party or another has assumed risk of the loss, a mere assumption of risk is sufficient. This is a matter of interpretation[115] or at least a question of presumed intention.[116] Clear words are (arguably) not required.[117] Similarly, by reason of the presumption, common law powers of termination can only be excluded by clear words. Yet whether a term is essential, which determines whether or not any breach gives rise to a power to terminate, can be established by 'necessary implication'.[118]

Second, the protection of some rights to the exclusion of others arguably lacks coherence. Rights to damages, powers of termination and rights to sue in debt are protected. Clear words are needed. Yet there is no similar requirement insofar as a party seeks to establish an assumption of risk displacing a finding of frustration[119] or common mistake.[120] Presumably there is no common law 'right' to claim frustration or common mistake. Yet the same could be said of powers of termination. This is particularly so considering that termination powers are arguably underpinned by similar normative justification to that justifying the doctrines of frustration and common mistake, namely, the notion that a party should not be bound by an altered state of affairs (in the case of termination, brought about by reason of breach or repudiation).[121]

In seeking to understand the nature of the presumption and its impact on default rules, it is worthwhile tracing its development. The emergence of the presumption can be regarded as antithetical with the development of the common law of contract at the time. Traditionally, exclusion and limitation clauses had been strictly construed; for example, they were construed *contra proferentem*,[122] as not applicable in the case of fundamental breach,[123] and as not excluding liability for conduct not authorised by the contract.[124] In *Photo Production Ltd v Securicor Transport Ltd*,[125] Lord Diplock famously rejected this

[115] See *The Achilleas* [2009] 1 AC 61 [25] (Lord Hoffmann).

[116] See ibid [25], [36] (Lord Hope). See also ibid [78] (Lord Walker) ('a question of what the contracting parties must be taken to have had in mind').

[117] But see Carter and Courtney (n 95) 353–54.

[118] *Bunge Corp New York v Tradax Export SA Panama* [1981] 1 WLR 711 (HL) 717 (Lord Roskill).

[119] See above n 30.

[120] See above n 32.

[121] See F Wilmot-Smith, 'Termination After Breach' (2018) 134 *LQR* 307, 314.

[122] See, eg, *Wallis, Son & Wells v Pratt & Haynes* [1911] AC 394 (HL).

[123] See, eg, *Suisse Atlantique Societe d Armement Maritime SA v NV Rotterdamsche Kolen Centrale* [1967] 1 AC 361 (HL).

[124] See, eg, *Sydney City Council v West* (1965) 114 CLR 481 (HCA).

[125] [1980] AC 827 (HL).

approach, reasoning that recently enacted legislative protections had rendered such paternalism unnecessary.[126] Broadly speaking, exclusion clauses should be construed like any other contractual provision.[127] This development was in line with general developments in the common law of contract during this period which saw courts shy away from welfarist objectives and give prominence to party autonomy. That is to say, the expansion of statutory protections arguably led to courts more freely giving effect to party intention in contract matters.[128] Hence, it is curious that the presumption emerged at the time that it did.

One explanation for the recognition and development of the presumption is that it aligns with the rise of legal pragmatism at the expense of formalism in the common law.[129] On one view, the presumption is a diminished form of the strict approach to the interpretation of exclusion or limitation clauses. However, the alternative view is that the presumption emerged as a broad and flexible replacement; a principle that accounts for the various discrete rules dealing with exclusion or limitation clauses,[130] including in particular the *Canada Steamship* rules regarding the exclusion of liability for negligence.[131] The principle was recognised at a time when outdated maxims and rules, such as those associated with the strict or literal approach, had given way to modern principles and preferences that strike a similar but less rigid balance.

The presumption is usually justified in terms of presumed intention. Clear words are needed to exclude or modify common law (or statutory) rights and remedies because it is presumed that parties would not lightly intend such rights to be abrogated. Parties are taken to know of their common law and statutory rights.[132] Hence, the presumption is said to be a matter of 'common sense'; 'parties do not normally give up valuable rights without making it clear that they intend to do so'.[133] One could criticise this justification as lacking a firm foundation, empirical or otherwise. What it effectively does is elevate the desire to preserve common law rights and remedies above other desires, such as the desire to avoid the imposition of obligations or even the desire to divest rights. For example, the guarantee in *Rainy Sky* was given a broad construction even though it was amenable to 'two meanings';[134] clear words were not required to impose an obligation on the bank to refund payments in the event of the shipbuilder's insolvency.[135] Clear words were also not needed in *ICS* to exclude

[126] *Photo Production Ltd v Securicor Transport Ltd* [1980] AC 827, 850–51 (Lord Diplock).

[127] See, eg, *Darlington Futures Ltd v Delco Australia Pty Ltd* (1986) 161 CLR 500, 510 (the Court).

[128] See R Catterwell, 'Autonomy and Institutionalism in the Law of Contract' (2022) 42 *OJLS* 1067.

[129] *cf* A Burrows, 'Form and Substance: Fictions and Judicial Power' in A Robertson and J Goudkamp (eds), *Form and Substance in the Law of Obligations* (Oxford, Hart Publishing, 2019) 17, 18 (a shift from 'a rule-based approach' to 'an approach concerned with a flexible balancing of particular factors').

[130] *Triple Point* [2021] UKSC 29, [2021] AC 1148 [111] (Lord Leggatt, Lord Burrows agreeing at [73]).

[131] See *Canada Steamship Lines Ltd v The King* [1952] AC 192 (PC).

[132] But note the rejection by Moore-Bick LJ in *Stocznia Gdynia SA v Gearbulk Holdings Ltd* [2010] QB 27 (CA) (at [23]) of the notion that there are 'two competing approaches struggling for supremacy: one requiring clear express words, the other favouring the natural meaning of the words used'.

[133] *Seadrill Management Services Ltd v OAO Gazprom* [2010] EWCA Civ 691 [29] (Moore-Bick LJ).

[134] *Rainy Sky* [2011] UKSC 50, [2011] 1 WLR 2900 [40] (Lord Clarke, Lord Phillips, Lord Mance, Lord Kerr and Lord Wilson agreeing at [1]).

[135] Contrast *Trafalgar House Construction (Regions) Ltd v General Surety & Guarantee Co Ltd* [1996] AC 199, 208 (Lord Jauncey) (clear words are needed to 'exclude any one or more of the normal incidents of suretyship'). The result in *Rainy Sky* is surprising considering the numerous authorities in which it has been said

claims for damages from the assignment. Yet a party that enters into a contract of a particular type, such as a contract for services, can rely on the presumption that clear words are needed to exclude implied obligations under statute.

The broad and perhaps crude effect of the presumption on the nature of default rules in contract is that contract rules exist in a hierarchy. At the top are rules regarding formation and vitiation that, by their institutional nature, cannot be overridden. Then there are rules regarding remedies, termination and implied rights and obligations which require clear words to be displaced. And then, loosely speaking, there is the rest. Clear words are not needed to displace these rules.

It may be that the nature of the presumption – or, to put it more accurately, the nature of the principle that clear words are required to exclude or modify a rule – is simply a matter of balance. That is to say, in line with the thesis of this chapter, the scope of the presumption is a matter of theoretical preference. Those who support autonomy-based theories of contract will be more inclined to view the presumption as being narrow in scope. By contrast, those who view contract as fundamentally serving institutional objectives will tend to view the presumption as broader in its application.

However, there may be a more theoretically rigorous way to justify the presumption and its apparent impact on the schema of default rules in contract. If one takes the position that contract law is about consent or assumption, then the scope of the presumption can be justified in terms of what that consent or assumption means. Parties enter into a contract by satisfying formation requirements and thereby consent to being regulated in accordance with the contract institution. They are free to override most rules, but not those regarding vitiation. And, since common law (and statutory) remedies are critical to a party in entering into a contract, they are taken to have consented to the imposition of those remedies unless clear words are used.

The elevation of rules regarding remedies is also justified if one analyses the core features of contract law.[136] A contract is formed through an exchange or bargain.[137] Hence, no matter one's theoretical bent, it is hard to deny that a key goal of the law of contract is protecting that exchange. Contract seeks to enforce each party's 'performance interest', that is, the interest of each party 'in getting that which the other party has to offer', being 'the other party's performance [of the contract]'.[138] The imposition of damages upon breach, as a monetary substitute for performance, is a key protection of that interest.[139] On this basis, one can justify the presumption: clear words are required to exclude or modify rules regarding remedies because it is those rules that protect and give effect to the bargain or exchange at the heart of contractual obligation.

that guarantees must be construed *strictissimi juris* in favour of the surety in the event of ambiguity: see, eg, *Bacon v Chesney* (1816) 1 Stark 192, 193; 171 ER 443, 443–44 (Lord Ellenborough); *Ankar Pty Ltd v National Westminster Finance (Australia) Ltd* (1987) 162 CLR 549, 561 (Mason ACJ, Wilson, Brennan and Dawson JJ).

[136] Many of the most significant works on the theory of contract law have focused on the question of damages: see, eg, LL Fuller and WR Perdue, 'The Reliance Interest in Contract Damages: 1' (1936) 46 *Yale Law Journal* 52.

[137] *Currie v Misa* (1875) LR 10 Ex 153, 162 (Lush J); *Australian Woollen Mills Pty Ltd v Commonwealth* (1954) 92 CLR 424, 456–57 (Dixon CJ, Williams, Webb, Fullagar and Kitto JJ).

[138] D Friedmann, 'The Performance Interest in Contract Damages' (1995) 111 *LQR* 628, 629.

[139] B Coote, 'Contract Damages, *Ruxley*, and the Performance Interest' (1997) 56 *CLJ* 537, 541–43; D Winterton, *Money Awards in Contract Law* (Oxford, Hart Publishing, 2015).

One can see from the preceding analysis that the nature of default rules in contract law is shaped by the principles and presumptions that feature in it. While all rules other than those regarding formation and vitiation are often regarded as defeasible, the presumption in favour of common law rights and remedies makes it more difficult to exclude or modify certain rules. It creates different tiers or levels of default rules in contract law.

VI. Conclusion

A discussion regarding default rules in contract may be thought to be an esoteric exercise. However, as this chapter has shown, an analysis of what constitutes a default rule in the common law of contract illuminates particular features of the law and assists in understanding how the law works and how it is perceived. In particular, such analysis highlights that the common law of contract is ultimately a somewhat messy combination of deductive rules and flexible principles, with the latter often serving to establish whether the former are satisfied by guiding the process through which one arrives at party intention. Investigating default rules also shows that certain doctrines are in effect elevated above others, namely, doctrine regarding formation and vitiation (which cannot be overridden) and doctrine regarding remedies and termination (which can only be excluded or modified by clear words). This makes one wonder why contract law is composed in such a way.

On the question of theory, as outlined in this article, how one views the nature of contract law may impact how one perceives default rules. But, looking at the question the other way around, an examination of default rules in contract throws up significant clues in terms of overarching theoretical justification for the law of contract. It certainly speaks to one of the more entrenched controversies in contract law, namely, the nature and rationale for contract law damages. It paints a particular picture of contract where formation requirements and rules regarding vitiation are effectively gateways, with enforcement of the bargain (usually through an award of damages for expectation loss) sitting at the core of contract. Most of the rest of the rules that make up contract are auxiliary and merely serve as guidelines that can be overridden.

Any theory of contract needs to account for this doctrinal landscape. For example, if contract is about consent or assumption, then one can conceptualise these features within that framework. By satisfying formation requirements, parties consent to or assume the imposition of rights and obligations. One of the formation requirements is that the relevant agreement constitutes a bargain or exchange of value. Hence, parties are taken to consent to or assume not only the imposition of remedies designed to give effect to their bargain, but also the requirement that clear words are necessary to abrogate rules dealing with remedies. That is to say, the structure of default rules in contract and the impact required of party intention on those rules can be justified as a matter of contract theory.

5

Default Rules in Contract Formation

WILLIAM DAY*

I. Introduction

Contracts are agreements; if there is no agreement, there is no contract. That much is a rule of recognition which the parties cannot change. The central thesis of this chapter is that, beyond that irreducible core, much of the law on contract formation consists of default rules. Many of the principles relating to offer and acceptance are best conceptualised as default rules that can be disapplied through the parties' expression of contrary intention. Default rules also operate to fill gaps in unspoken aspects of agreements to ensure that they are sufficiently complete to be valid. A distinction between mandatory and default rules is also relevant in understanding the rules that filter between those agreements that are legally binding and those that are not. While consideration is still formally a mandatory requirement for contract formation, at least on an orthodox analysis, much of the law on intent to create legal relations is concerned with default or presumptive rules as to the intent of parties in particular contexts, which can be disapplied by expression of contrary common intent. Likewise, most of the rules governing authority to enter into agreements on behalf of others are defaults, since parties can impose terms that modify or disapply the normal operation of actual and apparent authority.

It is suggested in this chapter that drawing a distinction between mandatory and default rules is useful in shedding new light on old problems: not just in terms of understanding and explaining the operation of contract formation, but also in using doctrinal examples to demonstrate the *variety* of ways in which default rules can operate across contract law. So, for example, terms of offers that are implied in fact have to be positively communicated (even though not expressed) whereas terms implied in law act as defaults which have to be negatived by express or other implied terms if not to apply to the offer. Some rules, such as the communication rule for acceptances and intention to create legal relations, are defaults which can only be weakened but not strengthened. Further, while some defaults are readily overridden by the terms of an offer, in other

* In addition to the assistance I received from discussion of a draft of this paper at the workshop, I am particularly grateful to Rory Gregson and Jonathan Morgan for pre-workshop comments on an earlier draft and to Andrew Robertson and Peter Radan for comments from an Australian law perspective.

cases the parties' choice to disapply a presumptive common law rule must be supported by clear words, consideration, or even longstanding commercial practice or convention.

II. Are Formation Rules Necessarily Mandatory?

In US scholarship, two principal justifications have been identified for the existence of default rules. The first is a law and economic theory that defaults can act as penalties that encourage parties to reduce information asymmetries in their bargaining positions.[1] In contrast to the US, however, law and economics analyses have singularly failed to influence the development of English law. English law has been more receptive to 'majoritarian'[2] theory, which seeks to explain default rules in a manner consistent with promissory or agreement-centric theories of contract law. The most prominent and recent endorser of this approach as explaining English contract law is Lord Leggatt in *Barton v Morris*, where he said in the course of his dissenting judgment: 'default rules are generally optimal when they reflect prevailing social norms and expectations and therefore create rights and obligations which reasonable parties would be likely to agree between themselves'.[3]

From a majoritarian viewpoint, an argument that formation rules can be defaults rather than mandatory may appear initially to be incongruous. When dividing contract law into mandatory and default rules, there is a natural tendency to pigeonhole rules on contract formation into the former rather than the latter category. That follows from the definition of a default rule as being something which governs in the absence of any agreement to the contrary.[4] Since contract formation rules are concerned with whether there is any contract at all, these can be seen as mandatory rules of recognition that must be satisfied in order to recognise a contract that is capable of overriding default rules. A distinction is therefore drawn by some scholars between default or 'background' rules and formation or 'agreement rules specifying the conditions and procedures the parties must satisfy in order to change an otherwise applicable background rule'.[5] On this analysis, rules concerned with contract formation by definition cannot be default rules.[6] That dichotomy becomes particularly pronounced in scholarship focused on implied terms where such default rules are characterised as 'gap filling' measures, and the existence of

[1] Most closely associated with I Ayres and R Gertner, 'Filling Gaps in Incomplete Contracts: An Economic Theory of Default Rules' (1989) 99 *Yale Law Journal* 87.

[2] This is Jonathan Morgan's label: see J Morgan, *Contract Law Minimalism: A Formalist Restatement of Commercial Contract Law* (Cambridge, Cambridge University Press, 2013) 92 and 118.

[3] *Barton v Morris* [2023] UKSC 3, [2023] AC 684 [128].

[4] A definition adopted by law and economics and majoritarian advocates alike. See, eg, Ayres and Gertner (n 1) 87: 'rules that parties can contract around by prior agreement'; RE Barnett, 'The Sound of Silence: Default Rules and Contractual Consent' (1992) 78 *Virginia Law Review* 821, 825: 'default rules are binding in the absence of manifested assent to the contrary'; Morgan (n 2) 91: 'a rule that will govern in the absence of any agreement to the contrary'.

[5] R Craswell, 'Contract Law, Default Rules, and the Philosophy of Promising' (1989) 88 *Michigan Law Review* 489, 503.

[6] See, eg, EA Posner, 'There are no Penalty Default Rules in Contract Law' (2006) 33 *Florida State University Law Review* 563, 565: 'Rules cited by Ayres … as examples of penalty default rules are not default rules but instead are contract formation rules'.

the gap can be taken to presuppose the existence of a valid agreement with a gap to fill. As Randy Barnett has put it, 'We can speak in gaps in a contract that must be filled by default rules only if a contract can first be shown to exist.'[7]

However, other commentators have recognised that certain formation rules can be characterised as default rules. Indeed, in their seminal 1989 article on default rules, one of the main examples deployed by Ian Ayres and Robert Gertner is the provision in the US Uniform Commercial Code (UCC) that a contractual offer for a sale can be accepted in any reasonable form 'Unless otherwise unambiguously indicated by the language or circumstances'.[8] Ayres and Gertner are far from alone amongst US scholars in extending the default rules project to contract formation.[9] The aim of this chapter is to contribute to this debate by showing not only that many formation rules in contract law are default not mandatory in nature but also to demonstrate variety and differences within formation rules that can be characterised as defaults. Although the inspiration comes from US scholarship, the focus is on English law, albeit with some cross-references to the position in Australian law.

III. Agreements

A. The Requirement that Agreements be Complete

An agreement can only become a valid contract if it is complete. Alan Schwartz and Robert Scott argue that the rule that an incomplete contract is void is a default rule: 'the common law presumed that the failure to reach an agreement on material terms, where no terms could be objectively supplied, implied an intention not to be legally bound'.[10] But this cannot fit with English law. If it were only a default, an 'agreement to agree' should oust such a rule and be treated as a valid and binding. However, it is well established since *May and Butcher v R* that such an agreement does not have contractual effect.[11] It might be argued that agreements to agree are a special category because they are a contradiction in terms and really there is no agreement at all. That may be true in some cases, such as where there is an agreement to agree a sale, but the parties have yet to agree the subject matter or the price, and so there really is nothing agreed at all. However, in other cases, the parties have reached a good deal of consensus

[7] Barnett (n 4) 860, also 862 and 865. See also, eg, WD Slawson, 'The Futile Search for Principles for Default Rules' (1993) 3 *Southern California Interdisciplinary Law Journal* 29, 29–30 and 32; DK Hart, 'Contract Formation and the Entrenchment of Power' (2009) 41 *Loyola University Chicago Law Journal* 175, 201.

[8] Ayres and Gertner (n 1) 105–06 discussing UCC §2-206 and *Leftowitz v Great Minneapolis Surplus Store In* 251 Minn 188, 86 NW 2d 689 (1957).

[9] See, eg, BA Eisler, 'Default Rules of Contract Formation by Promise and the Need for Revision of the Mailbox Rule' (1990) 79 *Kentucky Law Journal* 557; O Ben-Shahar and JAE Pottow, 'On the Stickiness of Default Rules' (2006) 33 *Florida State University Law Review* 651, 670–75; A Schwartz and RE Scott, 'The Common Law of Contract and the Default Rule Project' (2016) 102 *Virginia Law Review* 1523, 1535.

[10] Schwartz and Scott (n 9) 1542, fn 79.

[11] *May and Butcher v R* [1934] 2 KB 17 (HL). In English law, an agreement to negotiate in good faith is also void, but Australian law is more receptive to such an agreement. Contrast *Walford v Miles* [1992] 2 AC 128 (HL) with, eg, *Coal Cliff Collieries Pty Ltd v Sijehama Pty Ltd* (1991) 24 NSWLR 1 (NSWCA) and *United Group Rail Services Ltd v Rail Corporation New South Wales* [2009] NSWCA 177, (2009) 74 NSWLR 618.

and have only deferred certain (albeit important) points. So, for example, in *May and Butcher* itself the subject matter was settled but the agreement was nonetheless insufficiently complete because the parties had expressly agreed to defer negotiation of the amount and date of payment. But they were not entitled to treat the requirement that their agreement be complete to take contractual effect as a default which could be overruled. This demonstrates that the requirement that the agreement must be complete is part of the irreducible core of mandatory rules as to the recognition of agreements.

The question as to whether an agreement is sufficiently complete is answered by reference to certainty: the terms of the agreement must be certain enough to be enforceable. In *May and Butcher*, Lord Dunedin said that a concluded contract is 'one which settles everything that is necessary to be settled and leaves nothing to be settled'.[12] But the modern approach emphasises the first part of that dictum and not the second. As Lord Clarke recognised in *RTS Flexible Systems Ltd v Molkerei Alois Müller GmbH & Co KG*, certainty is only required on 'the terms which [the parties] regarded or the law requires as *essential* for the formation of legally binding relations'.[13] However, even with that lowered threshold for reaching sufficient agreement to conclude a contract, there will still be cases where the parties may not have expressly said anything about an essential element of the agreement. Implied terms – which can be seen as the paradigm default rule in contract law – are relevant in determining whether an agreement on the 'essential' elements has indeed been formed. The irony of *May and Butcher* is that, if the parties had simply stayed silent in respect of the points on which they wanted to defer discussion, the contract would have been sufficiently complete: the law would have provided by way of default implied terms to pay a reasonable price within reasonable time. The case is therefore a salutary example of 'less is more'.

B. The Use of Defaults to Complete Agreements

The use of defaults provided by implied terms in contract formation was the central issue in *Wells v Devani*.[14] Mr Wells built a block of flats in Hackney in east London which he then struggled to sell. During a telephone call an estate agent called Mr Devani offered his services at commission of two per cent of the purchase price plus VAT, which Mr Wells accepted, but they did not discuss what event would trigger payment of that commission.[15] A short time later, Mr Devani introduced a housing trust which acquired the flats for £2.1 million. Mr Wells disputed any liability to pay commission on the basis

[12] *May and Butcher* (ibid) 21. See similarly *Scammell and Nephew Ltd v Ouston* [1941] AC 251 (HL) 255 (Viscount Maugham): 'In order to constitute a valid contract the parties must so express themselves that their meaning can be determined with a reasonable degree of certainty.'

[13] *RTS Flexible Systems Ltd v Molkerei Alois Müller GmbH & Co KG* [2010] UKSC 14, [2010] 3 All ER 1 [45] (Lord Clarke) (*RTS*) (emphasis added). The approach in Australian law is essentially the same: *Australian Goldfields NL (in liquidation) v North Australian Diamonds* (2009) 40 WAR 191 (WACA) 199 (McClure JA): 'A contract (or a term thereof) is void for uncertainty if … all the *essential and critical* terms of the bargain have not been agreed upon' (emphasis added).

[14] *Wells v Devani* [2019] UKSC 4, [2020] AC 129.

[15] Mr Devani later provided written terms that stipulated that the commission would be triggered by exchange of contracts, but this post-dated the introduction and so could not be relied upon: ibid [7]–[8].

that, in the absence of an express term dealing with when the payment obligation would be triggered, the agreement was too incomplete and uncertain to give rise to a contract.

The trial judge rejected Mr Wells' argument by implying a term in fact that the commission was payable on completion of the purchase. In the Court of Appeal, Lewison LJ held that this was wrong in principle. His analysis has (possibly unconscious) resonances of Barnett's scholarship as to the conceptual limits on default rules:[16]

> It is of course the case that the court may imply terms into a concluded contract. But that assumes that there is a concluded contract into which terms can be implied. It is not legitimate, under the guise of implying terms, to make a contract for the parties. That is to put the cart before the horse. … it is wrong in principle to turn an incomplete bargain into a legally binding contract by adding expressly agreed terms and implied terms together. In my judgment that is what the judge did in this case.

In the Supreme Court, however, the agreement was held to have contractual effect. Lord Kitchin in effect adopted Arden LJ's dissenting analysis in the Court of Appeal that the discussion on the telephone call could be interpreted to find agreement that completion of purchase of the flats was the triggering event for the payment of commission.[17] There are real problems with that interpretative analysis because there was no relevant express term to interpret.[18] This part of the decision in *Wells v Devani* could be understood as unprincipled but pragmatic: a product of the court's instinct to not 'throw its hands in the air' and treat the contract as being void for uncertainty,[19] especially given that there had been performance by Mr Devani when he introduced Mr Wells to the housing trust that then purchased the flats.[20]

Lord Leggatt sought to put the Supreme Court's decision on interpretation in *Wells v Devani* (a case in which he was not on the panel) on a more principled footing in his dissenting judgment in *Barton v Morris*.[21] Emphasising that parties are to be taken as contracting against the background of implied terms that act as default rules,[22] Lord Leggatt then drew the following distinction:[23]

> [T]here is a difference in who bears what may be called the burden of expression … A contract is presumed to include any term implied in law as a standard incident of a contract of that type, unless such a term is expressly excluded … By contrast, a party contending that a term is to be implied in fact has to overcome a presumption that, at any rate where the parties have entered into a detailed written contract, they have expressed all the terms particular to their individual bargain.

[16] *Wells v Devani* [2016] EWCA Civ 1106, [2017] QB 959 [19] and [24], and see text to n 7 above.

[17] *Wells v Devani* [2019] UKSC 4, [2020] AC 129 [17]–[19], see also [59]–[61] (Lord Briggs); *Wells v Devani* [2016] EWCA Civ 1106, [2017] QB 959 [90]–[94] and [109]–[111] (Arden LJ).

[18] PS Davies 'Interpretation and Implication in the Supreme Court' (2019) 78 *CLJ* 267, 268. Other commentators – including Rory Gregson, who presented on this paper at the workshop where it was discussed – take a different view, and contend that the case fairly can be regarded as an example of the courts giving meaning to the words used by the parties rather than using an implied term.

[19] That being a 'last resort' or a 'counsel of despair': *Astor Management AG v Atalaya Mining plc* [2017] EWHC 425 (Comm), [2018] 1 All ER (Comm) 547 [64] (Leggatt J).

[20] See, eg, *G Percy Trentham Ltd v Archital Luxfer Ltd* [1993] 1 Lloyd's Rep 25 (CA) 27 (Steyn LJ).

[21] *Barton v Morris* [2023] UKSC 3, [2023] AC 684.

[22] ibid [126]–[133].

[23] ibid [135] adopting EA Farnsworth, 'Disputes over Omission in Contracts' (1968) 68 *Columbia Law Review* 860, 884.

Lord Leggatt considered that the finding in *Wells v Devani* that the 'usual terms' or 'commercial norm' in estate agent contracts would be to pay commission on completion of the purchase was critical in explaining the outcome of the case.[24] This gave rise to a default rule in the form of a term implied in law, which had not been excluded by the express terms agreed on the telephone call.[25]

This re-analysis of *Wells v Devani* further emphasises the role which default rules can play in contract formation. It brings English law closer to the claims made by Ayres and Gertner as to the extent to which default rules operate throughout contract law. As they put it, the

> question of when a contract is complete is identical to the question of what is sufficient to contract around a default. A court's holding that the parties' attempt to contract around a given default is insufficient is identical to a holding that there is still a gap in the contract.[26]

Thus, on this view, Mr Wells failed to contract around the default position which entitled Mr Devani to commission on completion of the purchase or, put another way, left the contract with a gap to be filled by that default position.

Notwithstanding Lord Leggatt's dissenting judgment in *Barton v Morris*, however, it is important not to forget that *Wells v Devani* was actually concerned with terms implied in fact, not law. On that issue Lord Kitchin made clear that Lewison LJ was wrong to hold that, where the obviousness or business efficacy tests are otherwise satisfied, a term can nonetheless not be implied if the contract is insufficiently complete on its express terms. While Lewison LJ had relied on the reasoning in *Scancarriers A/S v Aotearoa International Ltd* in support of that proposition,[27] Lord Kitchin emphasised that the facts of that case were 'unusual',[28] and did not support:[29]

> [A]ny general rule that it is not possible to imply a term into an agreement to render it sufficiently certain or complete to constitute a binding contract. Indeed, it seems to me that it is possible to imply something that is so obvious that it goes without saying into anything, including something the law regards as no more than an offer. If the offer is accepted, the contract is made on the terms of the words used and what those words imply.

If the words used on the telephone call between Mr Wells and Mr Devani could not be construed to pinpoint the triggering event, Lord Kitchin would have implied a term in fact that payment be on completion of the purchase.[30] Paul Davies has called Lord Kitchin's reasoning on this point a return to 'orthodoxy',[31] noting that it is no different to the frequent implication of a term that a reasonable price be paid where the parties have not expressly agreed the price.[32] The latter is a default provided by the law in the

[24] *Wells v Devani* [2019] UKSC 4, [2020] AC 129 [23].
[25] *Barton v Morris* [2023] UKSC 3, [2023] AC 684 [156]–[157].
[26] Ayres and Gertner (n 1) 120. And see also D Patterson, 'The Pseudo-Debate over Default Rules in Contract Law (1993) 3 *Southern California Interdisciplinary Law Journal* 235, 242–52 who ties the issue of gap-filling to solving issues of contractual incompleteness on formation from a different perspective.
[27] *Scancarriers A/S v Aotearoa International Ltd* [1985] 2 Lloyd's Rep 419 (PC) 422 (Lord Roskill).
[28] *Wells v Devani* [2019] UKSC 4, [2020] AC 129 [31].
[29] ibid [33].
[30] ibid [29].
[31] Davies (n 18) 267. See similarly T Pilkington and J Eldridge, 'Implied Terms and Contract Formation' (2019) 135 *LQR* 526, 530.
[32] See, eg, Sale of Goods Act 1979, s 8(2).

absence of expressed contrary intention from the parties, whereas *Wells v Devani* (on its face) concerned a default arising from the facts of the case as being the court's best guess as to the (un-expressed) intention of the parties given the circumstances in which they contracted. There is a normative difference between these two different forms of default rule,[33] although exploration of that difference is beyond the scope of this chapter. The effect of Lord Kitchin's judgment is that to confirm that both forms of default rules are available to complete an agreement in contract formation, even if (as Lord Leggatt emphasises) their effect during the formation process may differ.

IV. Identifying Agreements

Offer and acceptance are analytical tools to be deployed where the parties dispute whether they have reached an agreement. The New South Wales Court of Appeal has said that offer and acceptance is 'neither sufficient to explain all cases nor necessary to explain all cases' and 'does not work well in various circumstances'.[34] However, in the vast majority of cases, the question of formation can be (and is) looked at through the prism of offer and acceptance. These are objective concepts which assist with the application of the irreducible core of the law on the recognition of contracts, and the parties cannot agree that an offer is an offer, when it is not, and likewise with acceptances. An offer is an objective expression of willingness to be bound by certain terms, and an acceptance is an objective and unqualified expression of assent to those terms.[35] They are also supplemented by a range of default rules. On the alternative analysis in *Wells v Devani*, and Lord Leggatt's approach in *Barton v Morris*, the existence of default rules provide context to parties' words and conduct and so should influence whether they are to be taken to have made, or accepted, an offer (and on what terms, express or implied).

A. Duration and Revocability of an Offer

Default rules governing offers (and their disapplication) can be overridden by the express and implied terms of the offer itself. But not all default rules are equal: while some can be overridden simply by the terms of the offer, others are 'sticky' and something more is required before the default falls away.[36] An example of this is the rule

[33] Some might say, as Rory Gregson did at the workshop, that the latter is not a default at all or is simply the court giving effect to what the parties have agreed. This is really a debate about how broadly to define the concept of default rules in contract law, and it is fair to say that this chapter adopts a fairly broad definition in that regard.

[34] *Brambles Holdings Ltd v Bathurst City Council* [2001] NSWCA 61, 53 NSWLR 153 [71] (Mason P, Heydon JA and Ipp AJA). See also K Barnett, 'Accepting Offer and Acceptance? Implied or Inferred Contracts' in PG Willis (ed), *Binding Authority: 150 Years of Authorised Law Reporting in Victoria* (Melbourne, Little William Bourke, 2024). A similar approach has been taken in English law: see, eg, *Finmoon Ltd v Baltic Reefers Management Ltd* [2012] EWHC 920 (Comm) [22] (Eder J).

[35] See, eg, *Chitty on Contracts*, 35th edn (London, Sweet & Maxwell, 2023) paras 4-003 and 4-032.

[36] On stickiness in default rules generally see Ben-Shahar and Pottow (n 9).

providing for the revocability of offers. The UCC provides, in effect, that this is a default rule that can be disapplied by the terms of the offer:[37]

> An offer by a merchant to buy or sell goods in a signed writing which by its terms gives assurance that it will be held open is not revocable, for lack of consideration, during the time stated or if no time is stated for a reasonable time, but in no event may such period of irrevocability exceed three months; but any such term of assurance on a form supplied by the offeree must be separately signed by the offeror.

In contrast, in English and Australian law, a bare promise of irrevocability in an offer is not normally enforceable.[38] To take legal effect, the promise of irrevocability must be made not in contract, but may be a deed or otherwise be in exchange for money or some other form of consideration. That includes in the case of some unilateral offers, if the circumstances permit the implication in fact of a term not to revoke the offer, consideration in the form of the counterparty commencing performance even though not yet complete.[39] This could be described as providing a mandatory rule either that gratuitous offers are revocable or that consideration is required to render the offer irrevocable.[40] Another description would be that this is a sticky default rule: an offer can be made irrevocable, but more effort is required by the parties to 'switch off' the default in English and Australian law than under the UCC.

Conversely, offers are 'implicitly open for acceptance only within a reasonable period',[41] unless the offer states otherwise.[42] This is not a sticky default rule. Where the offer states otherwise (eg 'open for acceptance by the end of Friday') that does not need to be supported by consideration to take contractual effect: the default is disapplied simply by the terms of the offer. Buckley J suggested in *Manchester Diocesan Council for Education v Commercial & General Investments Ltd* that the simplest explanation for the general rule that offers are open for a reasonable length of time is that a failure to respond within reasonable time amounts to a rejection.[43] Put another way, it is an implied term of the offer that it is accepted within reasonable period: that is the natural understanding to be given to an offer in the absence of contrary intention.[44] That explains why the express contractual terms on offer can not only provide colour as to what constitutes a reasonable period,[45] but also provide for some other deadline (unreasonable or otherwise).

[37] UCC §2-205. For discussion see Ben-Shahar and Pottow (n 9) 670–75.

[38] See, eg, *Dickinson v Dodds* [1876] 2 Ch D 463 (CA); *Goldsbrough Mort & Co v Quinn* (1910) 10 CLR 674 (HCA). There appears to be an exception in the insurance context: see text to n 84 below.

[39] Although it is controversial to call this consideration or to treat this as sufficient in all cases. Contrast *Errington v Errington* [1952] 1 KB 290 (CA) with *Luxor (Eastbourne) Ltd v Cooper* [1941] AC 108 (HL).

[40] *cf Varty v British South Africa Co* [1965] Ch 508 (CA) 523 (Diplock LJ): 'juristically a contradiction in terms'.

[41] *LJ Korbetis v Transgrain Shipping BV* [2005] EWHC 1345 [18] (Toulson J) ('*Korbetis*').

[42] See, eg, *Grant v Bragg* [2009] EWCA Civ 1228 [25] (Lord Neuberger MR).

[43] *Manchester Diocesan Council for Education v Commercial & General Investments Ltd* [1970] 1 WLR 241 (Ch) 247–48 ('*Manchester Diocesan Council*').

[44] See similarly J Cartwright, *Formation and Variation of Contract*, 2nd edn (London, Sweet & Maxwell, 2021) para 3-33.

[45] As in *Korbetis* [2005] EWHC 1346 [18] where the word 'forthwith' in the offer was held to 'connote[] some urgency'. Other examples where a reasonable period may be shortened include offers in respect of the sale of perishable goods or for assets which are price sensitive: *Chitty* (n 35) para 4-127.

B. The Requirement to Communicate Acceptance

The terms of the offer – even when not supported by consideration – may also override default rules relating to the communication of acceptances. The requirement that acceptance must be communicated to the offeror is only a starting point which can be expressly or impliedly disapplied by the terms of an offer.[46] This is best explained on majoritarian grounds: it reflects the likely intentions of most offerors.[47]

The default nature of the communication rule is seen most obviously with unilateral contracts,[48] where the terms of the offer typically envisage acceptance by action not communication and so communication is not required. Thus, in *Carlill v Carbolic Smoke Ball Co*,[49] an advertisement stated that £100 from £1,000 already deposited at the bank would be paid to anyone who used the Carbolic Smoke Ball three times a day for two weeks and still caught influenza. It was enough that Mrs Carlill had accepted by using the Ball in the way prescribed; the terms did not contemplate communication by the offeree, and so the default 'communication rule' was disapplied. As Bowen LJ put it, 'as notification of acceptance is required for the benefit of the person who makes the offer, the person who makes the offer may dispense with notice to himself if he thinks it desirable to do so'.[50]

Similarly, in *Argo Fund Ltd v Essar Steel Ltd*,[51] a borrower disputed the validity of a transfer of its debt from one creditor to another. Aikens J held that the novation took effect through a unilateral contract set up by way of a 'standing offer' in the terms of the facility agreement from the borrower to terminate the facility with the old lender and conclude a new facility (on the same terms) with the new lender, which could be accepted by way of agreement between the old and new lenders.[52] Aikens J noted that the facility agreement did

> not require that the Borrower be notified of the transfer, although in fact it is accepted that Essar [the borrower] did have notice of each transfer. However, a party can waive the right to be notified of an acceptance and perhaps that is the correct analysis of the position under this Agreement.[53]

It is therefore hard to see how the earlier case of *Felthouse v Bindley* would be decided the same way today.[54] That concerned negotiation between uncle and nephew over the

[46] *Chitty* (n 35) para 4-058. The position is the same in Australian law: *Latec Finance Pty Ltd v Knight* [1969] 2 NSWR 79 (NSWCA) 81 (Jacobs JA).

[47] But for US law and economics scholarship on this topic, see, eg, A Katz, 'The Strategic Structure of Offer and Acceptance: Game Theory and the Law of Contract Formation' (1990) 89 *Michigan Law Review* 215, 249–72.

[48] But not limited to unilateral contracts. For an example in the bilateral contract context, in the insurance market 'Assuming that there is nothing in the insurer's offer which requires notification of acceptance, reliance by the assured upon the policy – or at least a failure to object to its terms – is generally all that is required': *Colinvaux's Law of Insurance*, (13th edn, London, Sweet & Maxwell, 2022) para 1-050.

[49] *Carlill v Carbolic Smoke Ball Co* [1893] 1 QB 256 (CA) ('*Carlill*'). See also Schwartz and Scott (n 9) 1535, fn 39.

[50] *Carlill* (ibid) 269.

[51] *Argo Fund Ltd v Essar Steel Ltd* [2005] EWHC 600 (Comm), [2006] 1 All ER (Comm) 56.

[52] ibid [51]–[52].

[53] ibid [53]. The point did not arise for determination on the appeal: [2006] EWCA Civ 241, [2006] 2 All ER (Comm) 104.

[54] *Felthouse v Bindley* (1862) 11 CB (NS) 869, 142 ER 1037.

price of a horse. There had been an earlier oral agreement for sale, but there was a difference of opinion as to what the price was to be so the uncle wrote to the nephew splitting the difference, stipulating that the price would be £30 15s unless he heard otherwise. The evidence suggested that the nephew accepted that price, as he then told the auctioneer to mark the horse as sold, which the auctioneer failed to do, but the contract was held invalid and so the auctioneer escaped liability for selling the horse to a third party, Willes J holding that the uncle 'had no right to impose upon the nephew a sale of his horse for £30 15s, unless he chose to comply with the condition of writing to repudiate the offer'.[55] This conflates the question of whether the nephew had accepted the offer (part of the irreducible core of an agreement) with the question of whether it needed to be communicated (a default requirement that can be waived by the terms of the offer). As the nephew had objectively accepted the offer, the contract should not have been invalidated because the uncle had – in order to cut short a continuing argument about the price – disapplied his default entitlement to receive a communication confirming acceptance of his offer to split the difference.

C. The Postal Rule

A further example of a default rule in the context of acceptances is the 'postal rule'.[56] This provides that acceptance of an offer is complete when the letter of acceptance is posted rather than when the letter is received.[57] The original reasoning in the nineteenth-century case law that the postal service was agent for the offeror has been comprehensively demolished.[58] But it can nonetheless be understood as a default rule. The postal rule simply takes the position that the communication rule is itself not immutable further by providing a default disapplication of the latter rule in circumstances where the offeror reasonably contemplates (or, in the agency analysis of the old cases, authorises)[59] that the offeree will communicate any acceptance by post.[60] And, even in those circumstances, the postal rule is itself not mandatory. It too is a default that can then be negatived by the terms of the proposed offer. In *Holwell Securities Ltd v Hughes*,[61] for example, a six-month option was granted to purchase property which was to be exercised (ie that offer accepted) by notice in writing. Russell LJ held that, even though the parties 'contemplated that the postal service might be used to communicate acceptance of the offer … that is not and cannot be the end of the matter'.[62] The requirement for notice in writing was thus construed as requiring receipt of acceptance,

[55] ibid 875; 1040.

[56] For an analysis of the equivalent issue in the US through the prism of default rules, see Eisler (n 9).

[57] *Adams v Lindsell* (1818) 1 B & Ald 681. See also Schwartz and Scott (n 9) 1535, fn 39.

[58] See, eg, D Marshall Evans, 'The Anglo-American Postal Rule: Some Problems of Offer and Acceptance in Contracts by Correspondence' (1966) 15 *International & Comparative Law Quarterly* 553, 558–59.

[59] *Henthorn v Fraser* [1892] 2 Ch 27 (CA) 32–33 (Lord Herschell).

[60] In Australia, the postal rule may have been retained in narrower form as against its English ancestor, requiring not just *contemplation* of posted acceptance but an *intention* that this should be so: *Tallerman & Co Pty v Nathan's Merchandise (Vic) Pty Ltd* (1957) 98 CLR 93 (HCA) 111–12 (Dixon CJ and Fullagar J).

[61] *Holwell Securities Ltd v Hughes* [1974] 1 WLR 155 (CA).

[62] ibid 157–58.

disapplying the default that simply posting the notice would suffice, and in effect reimposing the communication rule.[63]

The majoritarian approach to default rules helps to explain both why the postal rule came into existence in the first place, and why it should now be abolished. Simon Gardner has shown that the rule is a product of its time, likely linked to contemporaneous perceptions and expectations of the postal service as it developed in the nineteenth century.[64] In that context the invention of the postal rule as a default made some sense; but the perception that 'a letter takes effect on posting'[65] has long since gone, and the default rule which it created should likewise be jettisoned. As Beth Eisler has put it (in her analysis of US law),[66] 'The dispatch or mailbox rule departs from the parties' expectations and from a more logical rule which would be in keeping with modern communications technology', namely that acceptances usually take effect when communicated. The Scottish Law Commission has also taken the same view, and recommended the abolition of the postal rule, noting an unanimity from responses to its consultation that the postal rule was outdated and did not reflect 'modern conditions'.[67] Two different default rules applying to the communication of acceptances, depending on whether or not the offeror objectively contemplates a posted acceptance at the time of making the offer, is overly complicated and a recipe for unnecessary and avoidable argument.

D. Prescribed Modes of Communicating Acceptance

So far the analysis has focused on the *weakening* of the communication rule. It is not, however, clear whether the communication rule can also be *strengthened* by the terms of an offer so as to limit the form of communication required for acceptance. The UCC recognises this possibility.[68] That would also fit with the requirement in English law that acceptance should be an unqualified expression of assent to all terms of the offer:[69] if one term is that the offer must be accepted (for example) by a communication in writing, with a 'wet ink' signature, or in English, then the acceptance is not unqualified if the communication of acceptance is by telephone, with a typed signature, or in Chinese. The High Court of Australia has made clear that 'for an acceptance to be effective, it must comply with the requirements stipulated in the offer'.[70]

John Cartwright has commented that 'this rule is less straightforward in its application than at first appears',[71] and, while *Chitty on Contracts* states that formalities on acceptance must 'generally' be complied with,[72] it is not clear that this is correct. The law appears to have been changed or at least softened in England by the decision of the

[63] For the same approach in Australia, see *Bressan v Squires* [1974] 2 NSWLR 460 (Eq) 462–63 (Bowen CJ).
[64] S Gardner, 'Trashing with Trollope: A Deconstruction of the Postal Rules in Contract' (1992) 12 *OJLS* 170.
[65] ibid 181.
[66] Eisler (n 9) 558.
[67] Scottish Law Commission, *Report on Review of Contract Law: Formation, Interpretation, Remedies for Breach, and Penalty Clauses* (Scot Law Com No 252, 2018) [2.1]–[2.4] and [4.87]–[4.90].
[68] See text to n 37 above.
[69] See text to n 35 above.
[70] *George Hudson Holdings Ltd v Rudder* (1973) 128 CLR 387 (HCA) 395 (Menzies J).
[71] Cartwright (n 44) para 3-41.
[72] *Chitty* (n 35) para 4-083.

Court of Appeal in *Reveille Independent LLC v Anotech International (UK) Ltd*, which suggests that any mandatory formalities stipulated by one party as to the other party's acceptance of an offer (such as by a signature)[73] cannot override a clear acceptance of that offer by equivalent means (such as by starting performance) so long as that other form of acceptance is, in turn, not rejected by the offeror.[74] Cranston J (with whom Elias and Underhill LJJ agreed) emphasised that the court would not strain to find a waiver of the formalities envisaged by the original offer, saying that a 'realistic approach must be taken' which protects 'the reasonable expectations of honest sensible businessmen'.[75] Thus any party retrospectively deciding to stand on the stipulated formalities in their offers will likely not be successful, especially in circumstances where performance has commenced or been completed, as was the case on the facts of *Reveille*.

There is a stark contrast between this development in English law and not only the position in Australia but also the effect now given to no oral modification clauses after *MWB Business Exchange Ltd v Rock Advertising Ltd*.[76] On the other hand, the approach taken in *Reveille* is no different to the proposition recognised in *RTS Flexible Systems* that 'subject to contract' markings on drafts are a factor that weigh against the conclusion of a contract, but are not determinative: the ultimate question in each case is 'whether the parties have nevertheless agreed to enter into contractual relations on particular terms notwithstanding their earlier understanding or agreement'.[77]

V. Agreements that Count as Contracts

Even if an agreement is identified, and is sufficiently complete for contractual purposes, it nonetheless will not constitute a contract if not supported by consideration and in the absence of intention to create legal relations.

A. Consideration

It is orthodox to treat consideration in contract formation as a mandatory rule that cannot be changed by contrary agreement,[78] unless the parties enter into a deed. But there are suggestions in the case law that the requirement for consideration for contracts *can* be overridden in exceptional circumstances where longstanding commercial practices treat agreements as binding even in the absence of consideration. As Gerard

[73] And in some cases the Court may construe a written offer to be accepted by signature (or some other formality) as 'not 'a prescription'' but merely an indication of one way in which the offer can be accepted: see *Maple Leaf Macro Volatility Fund* [2009] EWCA Civ 1334, [2010] 2 All ER (Comm) 788 [16] (Longmore LJ); also *Manchester Diocesan Council* [1970] 1 WLR 241 (Ch) 246 (Buckley J).

[74] *Reveille Independent LLC v Anotech International (UK) Ltd* [2016] EWCA Civ 443 [40]–[41] (Cranston J).

[75] ibid [41]–[42] (Cranston J).

[76] *MWB Business Exchange Ltd v Rock Advertising Ltd* [2018] UKSC 24, [2019] AC 119 ('*MWB*'). See further W Day, 'Variation and Waiver' in W Day and S Worthington (eds), *Challenging Private Law: Lord Sumption on the Supreme Court* (Oxford, Hart Publishing, 2020).

[77] *RTS* [2010] UKSC 14, [2010] 3 All ER 1 [55] (Lord Clarke).

[78] See, eg, Slawson (n 7) 32.

McMeel has put it, in such circumstances it appears that 'Doctrinal certainties yield to pragmatic realities'.[79] Or, in the words of Lord Wilberforce:

> English law, having committed itself to a rather technical and schematic doctrine of contract, in application takes a practical approach, often at the cost of forcing the facts to fit uneasily into the marked slots of offer, acceptance and consideration.[80]

This is not a new trend. Warren Swain has noted that the rules on consideration were 'downgraded in importance' in the early eighteenth century as English law sought to give effect to bills of exchange.[81] The most obvious modern example is the letter of credit, which is a payment mechanism for sales (especially cross-border sales). Opening a credit involves a matrix of contracts. The buyer must secure a credit facility with the bank issuing the credit. The seller likewise has a relationship with its own bank, which either assumes no payment obligations of its own (an 'advising bank') or also promises to pay on receipt of the stipulated trade documents (a 'confirming bank'). Although the seller is the beneficiary under the letter of credit, and can enforce its right to payment on default by the issuing bank from the moment of issuance, the seller provides no consideration to the issuing bank. Despite this, Lord Clarke said in *Taurus Petroleum Ltd v State Oil Marketing Co of the Ministry of Oil, Iraq* that a court would be 'loath to hold, particularly in a commercial context, that a promise which both parties intended should be relied on was unenforceable for want of consideration'.[82]

That example has been followed in the insurance market. As discussed earlier,[83] the general rule in English law is that offers are revocable unless there is a contractual promise to the contrary. However, in *Citadel Insurance Co v Atlantic Union Insurance Co SA*, the Court of Appeal gave contractual effect to a reinsurance arrangement whereby the insurer had an option to 'declare risk' falling within the scope of the reinsurance, by treating the reinsurer as making a 'standing offer' which could not be revoked and which was accepted by each declaration of risk.[84] Kerr LJ said:

> When I say that [the reinsurer] bound themselves, I am using the language of the market, because everyone concerned would regard this as a binding commitment, even though it might be said that the arrangement was not binding, because there was no consideration moving from [the insurer]. They accepted no obligation and suffered no detriment. They had an open option or standing offer available to them. However, in this respect the arrangement is similar, for instance, to that of a bank confirming a letter of credit to a beneficiary, which is always regarded as binding on the bank. Much has been written as to how these ordinary commercial transactions fit in with our doctrine of consideration; but for present purposes it is quite unnecessary to consider these academic problems, since no one suggests that the initialling of the slip did not create any commitment which was binding on the defendants. If any such suggestion were made, let alone litigated, by any reinsurer, he would never again be acceptable to anyone in the market; and no such suggestion is made here.

[79] G McMeel, 'Are there any General Principles of Commercial Law?' in C Mitchell and S Watterson (eds), *The World of Maritime and Commercial Law* (Oxford, Hart Publishing, 2020) 186.

[80] *New Zealand Shipping Co Ltd v AM Satterthwaite & Co Ltd (The Eurymedon)* [1975] AC 154 (PC) 167.

[81] W Swain, *The Law of Contract 1670-1870* (Cambridge, Cambridge University Press, 2015) 56.

[82] *Taurus Petroleum Ltd v State Oil Marketing Co of the Ministry of Oil, Iraq* [2017] UKSC 64, [2018] AC 690 [25] (Lord Clarke) ('*Taurus*'), rather 'breezily' as put by McMeel (n 79) 186.

[83] Text to n 38 above.

[84] *Citadel Insurance Co v Atlantic Union Insurance Co SA* [1982] 2 Lloyd's Rep 543 (CA) 547–48 (Kerr LJ).

Kerr LJ's analysis suggests a 'soft' contract law or convention where participants within a market tacitly agree not to take a point on consideration. This echoes what Donaldson J in an earlier insurance case, where he said that he was 'sure that the market would disdain to take … nice points founded upon the ancient doctrine of consideration'.[85] And perhaps this form of commercial convention explains the letter of credit cases as well. The point appears never to have been raised in modern commercial disputes until *Taurus*, and, even then, the point does not appear to have been pressed hard by the advocate who raised it.[86] The passing comment by Lord Clarke may be sufficient to ensure that the convention in international trade finance not to take a point on consideration is not broken again.

The orthodox approach is to treat these as marginal cases or exceptions to a still-mandatory rule that consideration is otherwise *always* requirement for contract formation.[87] It is hard to imagine that a court would give effect to an agreement which expressly states that the 'creditor accepts this lesser sum in full satisfaction of the debt owed' (and perhaps adding for good measure: 'and the parties agree that the rule in *Foakes v Beer* does not apply').[88] Yet at the same time it is hard to identify a modern English commercial case where a contract has been invalidated for want of consideration.[89] Even when the point is taken, courts are willing to adopt 'very artificial' analyses to uphold the agreement.[90] As Jonathan Morgan has recently noted, 'consideration has rarely proved an obstacle to enforcement of commercial agreements. A near-irrebuttable presumption holds that in business dealings, what appears 'gratuitous' is actually reciprocal'.[91]

The point is particularly acute in contract variation cases, where consideration is essentially invented in the form of a 'practical benefit'.[92] So, for example, in *Williams v Roffey Bros*, a subcontractor was offered a further £10,300 by the contractor to do the carpentry work on time for flats under construction which he had already agreed to do for £20,000. The Court of Appeal held that the contractor had received a practical benefit in avoiding a financial penalty that would have been triggered by late completion.[93]

[85] *Jaglom v Excess Insurance Co Ltd* [1972] 2 QB 250 (Com Ct) 257–58.

[86] Despite raising a fundamental point of contract formation, it was only raised as an alternative submission, and did not need to be resolved given the conclusion reached as to construction if the contract was valid: *Taurus* [2017] UKSC 64, [2018] AC 690 [25] (Lord Clarke). See also *Taurus Petroleum Ltd v State Oil Marketing Co of the Ministry of Oil, Iraq* [2015] EWCA Civ 835, [2015] 2 All ER (Comm) 1037 [13] (Moore-Bick LJ). The advocate was Gordon Pollock QC – not a barrister known for pulling his punches.

[87] See, eg, the treatment of letters of credit in *Chitty* (n 35) para 6-136.

[88] *Foakes v Beer* (1884) 9 App Cas 605 (HL).

[89] Presumably because the requirements of consideration can be met relatively easily by commercial parties (assuming they are alive to the point). There are relatively recent examples of contracts failing in Australia for lack of consideration, however, which Andrew Robertson helpfully drew to my attention after the workshop. See, eg, *Atco Controls Pty Ltd (in liquidation) v Newtronics Pty Ltd* [2009] VSCA 238, (2009) 25 VR 411.

[90] Cartwright (n 44) para 8-41. See also PS Atiyah, 'Consideration: A Restatement' in PS Atiyah, *Essays on Contract* (Oxford, Oxford University Press, 1986) 179 'the conventional account of "the doctrine of consideration" no longer accords with the law actually enforced in the courts'.

[91] J Morgan, 'Judges, Jurists and Style' in J Sampson and S Tofaris (eds), *Essays in Law and History for David Ibbetson: Querella* (Oxford, Hart Publishing, 2024) citing by way of example *Woodhouse AC Israel Cocoa Ltd SA v Nigerian Produce Marketing Co* [1972] AC 741 (HL) 757 (Lord Hailsham).

[92] See further Day (n 76) 32–37.

[93] *Williams v Roffey Bros & Nicholls (Contractors) Ltd* [1991] 1 QB 1 (CA), followed in Australia including in *Musumeci v Winadell Pty Ltd* (1994) 34 NSWLR 723 (NSWCA).

Although there was an attempt to limit that analysis so that it did not apply to the part payment of a debt,[94] that distinction has largely been wiped away (in England at least) by the Court of Appeal's decision in *MWB* v *Rock*,[95] where a part payment of a fee by the licensee of premises was held to discharge the whole, on the basis that the licensor received a practical benefit given the risk of being paid less and from the continued occupation of those premises. On reaching the Supreme Court, the decision was overturned on other grounds,[96] with Lord Sumption saying little on this issue beyond remarking that the rule in *Foakes v Beer* (namely, that variation requires fresh consideration) is 'probably ripe for re-examination'.[97]

Thus, although the doctrine of consideration probably is still a mandatory rule,[98] it is a one that can be ignored by commercial parties by convention and will be ignored where there is a market expectation to do so. And, where not so ignored it can be manipulated by the court or the parties (such as by agreeing a nominal or 'peppercorn' consideration) or skirted around altogether by the parties opting to embody their agreement in a deed. As Warren Swain has perceptively noted, the 'survival of … consideration after 1850 can in a large part be explained by the fact that its role was much diminished'.[99]

B. Intent to Create Legal Relations

The requirement that there be intent to create legal relations is of recent origin compared to the ancient roots of consideration.[100] Its very existence could be taken as confirmation that all other formation rules are default rules in the sense that the parties can agree that an agreement that would otherwise be a contract should nonetheless be treated as not being a contract. But this would be a one-way default rule: parties can use this requirement to 'opt out' of contract law where all other formation requirements are satisfied, but they cannot use it to 'opt in' where other formation requirements have not been satisfied.

The first case to recognise a requirement that there be intent to create legal relations may have been *Carlill v Carbolic Smoke Ball Co*,[101] where the terms of the advertisement – with the reference to the £1,000 bank deposit – were considered by the Court of Appeal to evidence an intention to be bound.[102] But the recognition of this rule is more

[94] *Re Selectmove Ltd* [1995] 1 WLR 474 (CA) 481 (Peter Gibson LJ).

[95] *MWB Business Exchange Ltd v Rock Advertising Ltd* [2016] EWCA Civ 553, [2017] QB 604 [47] (Kitchin LJ). In Australia the authorities are not consistent on this. Contrast *Wolfe v Permanent Custodians Ltd* [2012] VSC 275 and *Amos v Citibank Ltd* [1996] QCA 129.

[96] By enforcement of the party agreed formalities for the variation of contracts: *MWB* [2018] UKSC 24, [2019] AC 119.

[97] ibid [18].

[98] Day (n 76) 34–35.

[99] Swain (n 81) 186.

[100] See, eg, D Ibbetson, *A Historical Introduction to the Law of Obligations* (Oxford, Oxford University Press, 1999) 233.

[101] *Carlill* [1893] 1 QB 256 (CA).

[102] AWB Simpson, 'Quackery and Contract: Carlill v Carbolic Smoke Ball Company (1893) in *Leading Cases on the Common Law* (Oxford, Oxford University Press, 1995) 282: 'Until Mrs Carlill brought her action there was no case which had clearly recognized the requirement of an intention to create legal relations; her case did.'

commonly associated with *Balfour v Balfour*,[103] where the Court of Appeal held that the domestic nature of the relationship between the parties (husband and wife)[104] or of the agreement (maintenance payments)[105] meant that there was no intention to create legal relations.[106] The difference between *Carlill* and *Balfour* is that the former turned on an analysis of the express terms of the agreement whereas the latter focused on what could be implied into the terms of the agreement from the circumstances.

In English law (but no longer to the same extent in Australian law),[107] *Balfour* has been taken as having created a form of default rule as to when contracts do (and do not) come into existence. The earliest expression of this was probably in the Court of Appeal in *Rose & Frank Co v JR Crompton and Bros Ltd*,[108] where Bankes LJ cited *Balfour* and explained it on majoritarian grounds:[109]

> In the case of agreements regulating business relations it follows almost as a matter of course that the parties intend legal consequences to follow. In the case of agreements regulating social engagements it equally follows almost as a matter of course that the parties do not intend legal consequences to follow.

These default rules can be understood as terms implied into the offer when it is made. An offer made in a social setting contains, unless otherwise stated, an implied term that no legally enforceable contract is proposed. Conversely, in commercial cases, the offer implies a contract unless otherwise stated (such as through 'subject to contract' markings). These are best understood as terms implied in law, and so create presumptions for commercial and social settings that alter the burden of expression required to enter into (or avoid entering into) a contract: this reflects the general expectation in commercial contexts that parties are bound to their agreements and the general expectation in domestic contexts that agreements do not generate legal consequences.

Rose & Frank was a commercial case where the presumption was in fact rebutted; the agreement contained a clause stating that it was not a 'legal agreement' but merely a 'pledge of honour',[110] not unlike the modern use of 'subject to contract' markings. Sometimes it not clear whether the offer is made in a social or commercial context, and so whether any presumption arises; the boundaries can become blurred. In *Blue v Ashley*, a financial consultant, Mr Blue, claimed that he was offered £15 million by Sport Direct's founder, Mr Ashley, if the price per Sport Direct share reached £8.[111] But that agreement was reached in a pub after heavy drinking, which Leggatt J considered was 'an unlikely setting in which to negotiate a contractual bonus arrangement',[112] and none

[103] *Balfour v Balfour* [1919] 2 KB 571 (CA).
[104] ibid 575 (Warrington LJ) and 576 (Duke LJ).
[105] ibid 578 (Atkin LJ).
[106] S Hedley, 'Keeping Contract in its Place: Balfour v Balfour and the Enforceability of Informal Agreements' (1985) 5 *OJLS* 391, 393: '*Balfour v Balfour* introduced a new obstacle for plaintiffs which had not been there before'. Also Ibbetson (n 100) 234.
[107] *Ermogenous v Greek Orthodox Community of SA Inc* (2002) 209 CLR 95 (HCA) 106 (Gaudron, McHugh, Hayne and Callinan JJ): 'we doubt the utility of using the language of presumptions in this context'. But in the commercial context contrast, eg, *Ailakis v Olivero (No 2)* [2014] WASCA 127 [91] (Martin CJ).
[108] *Rose & Frank Co v JR Crompton and Bros Ltd* [1923] 2 KB 261 (KBD and CA).
[109] ibid 282. See also 288 (Scrutton LJ) and 293 (Atkin LJ).
[110] See also the decision of the House of Lords: [1925] AC 445 (HL).
[111] *Blue v Ashley* [2017] EWHC 1928 (Comm).
[112] ibid [81].

of the third parties present during the conversion thought that Mr Ashley was 'being serious': it was just 'banter'.[113] There was no reference to presumptions in *Blue v Ashley*, so it is not clear whether the judge considered that this was a commercial agreement where the burden of expression had been discharged by Mr Ashley, or a social setting where Mr Blue had failed to discharge the burden of expression, or whether (as may be most likely) that in such a borderline case, there was no presumption (and so no relevant implied term in the offer) with the burden simply falling on Mr Blue as the party alleging the existence of the contract.

It has been said these presumptions do not arise where the agreement is implied rather than express, at least in the commercial context.[114] It is not clear why this should always disapply the default. It may be a product of the same reluctance to use implied terms in contract formation that led the Court of Appeal astray in *Wells v Devani*.[115] It cannot be true of social interactions where agreements may well be reached without words. In the commercial context, the reasoning appears to be that because the parties could have used words to express their agreement, but have 'chosen not to', 'the court should be slow to find that they have entered into such a contract by conduct'.[116] But that seems like an over-generalisation. It may be true of contexts where commercial parties are dealing at arm's length, and one would expect a degree of formality, but where commercial parties have dealt with each other over a long period of time, that may not be true.[117] The better approach would be to retain the default, but recognise that the absence of any written agreement may be a factor that can rebut the presumption.

The reason for seeking to carve out implied commercial agreements from the default rule may be that, when the presumption is engaged, the 'onus' to rebut it is a 'heavy one'.[118] In other words, this is another sticky default rule. But that stickiness is not seen in the domestic setting, where it is contended that an agreement nonetheless should be given contractual effect. So, for example, separation agreements between husband and wife are given effect, because they 'want everything cut and dried. It may safely be presumed that they intend to create legal relations'.[119] And the same is now true of prenuptial agreements after *Radmacher v Granatino*:[120] with the public policy impediment to such agreements removed, effect is given to be given to such agreements if the parties 'intend that the agreement should be effective'.[121] There is no reason why the opposite presumption in the commercial context should carry greater strength. Although the starting point is that the parties would intend an agreement between them to be binding, if the

[113] ibid [87] and [98].

[114] See, eg, *Baird Textile Holdings Ltd v Marks & Spencer plc* [2001] EWCA Civ 274, [2002] 1 All ER (Comm) 737 [61] (Mance LJ); *Family Finance Ltd v JD Cleverly Ltd* [2010] EWCA Civ 1477 [28] (Tomlinson LJ); *James-Bowen v Commissioner of Police for the Metropolis* [2016] EWCA Civ 1217 [24] (Moore-Bick LJ).

[115] See text to n 16 above.

[116] *James-Bowen* [2016] EWCA Civ 1217 [24] (Moore-Bick LJ).

[117] See eg, *Re MF Global UK Ltd (in special administration)* [2016] EWCA Civ 569, where the court implied a contract between two companies in administration, pursuant to which one company paid the expenses of staff seconded to a second company within the same group.

[118] *Edwards v Skyways Ltd* [1964] 1 WLR 349 (CA) 355 (Megaw J).

[119] *Merritt v Merritt* [1970] 1 WLR 1211 (CA) 1213 (Lord Denning MR) citing *Gould v Gould* [1970] 1 QB 275 (CA) 280 (Lord Denning MR).

[120] *Radmacher v Granatino* [2010] UKSC 42, [2011] 1 AC 534.

[121] ibid [70] and [74] (Lords Phillips, Hope, Rodger, Walker, Brown, Collins and Kerr).

court is satisfied on the balance of probabilities that is not the case, there should be no reluctance to find that the parties have chosen to 'opt out' of contract law.

VI. Authority to Enter into Agreements

The vast majority of contracts in modern commercial life are entered into by companies and so, necessarily, by agents. Principles of actual and apparent authority are therefore important formation rules in most scenarios where parties are contracting.

A. Actual Authority

Actual authority arises from an agreement between agent and principal that the agent can transact with a third party for the principal. The agreement can be express or implied, and the test for the existence and the scope of such an agreement is objective as for any contract.[122] The operation of default rules within actual authority can be illustrated from two perspectives: first, the implication of – or into – agency agreements between agent and principal (the internal aspect of agency) and, second, by the third party's ability to exclude the operation of actual authority by the terms of the contract they enter into with the agent (the external aspect of agency).

i. The Internal Aspect

Like (any other) contractual terms, actual authority can be implied either in law, most obviously in cases of so-called 'usual' authority, or in fact, from the parties' conduct and from the circumstances of the case, and also where further ('incidental') authority needs to be implied to enable the agent to do what they have been tasked to do or achieve. As with implied terms in contract more generally, the type of implied authority at issue should affect who bears Lord Leggatt's 'burden of expression' when the agency agreement is entered into.[123]

So, for example, in *The Unique Mariner*, Brandon J held that a ship's master had implied usual authority (ie authority implied in law) by virtue of that position to engage a salvage tug to rescue the ship, unless expressly restricted by the shipowner. On the facts, however, the shipowner met that 'negative'[124] burden of expression since its instructions limited the master's authority to contract with anyone other than the salvage tug nominated by the shipowner.[125] In contrast, in *SMC Electronics Ltd v Akhter Computers Ltd*,[126] a case on incidental authority, the burden of expression fell on the third party who was seeking to establish authority. The principal manufactured power

[122] See, eg, *Freeman & Lockyer (a firm) v Bucklehurst Park Properties (Mangal) Ltd* [1964] 2 QB 480 (CA) 502 (Diplock LJ) ('*Freeman & Lockyer*').

[123] See text to n 23 above. This is also a feature of authority by custom, where the burden of expression changes depending on whether or not the custom is reasonable: see eg *Robinson v Mollett* (1875) LR 7 HL 802.

[124] The phrase in *Barton v Morris* [2023] UKSC 3, [2023] AC 684 [157] (Lord Leggatt).

[125] *The Unique Mariner* [1978] 1 Lloyd's Rep 438 (Ad) 450–51.

[126] *SMC Electronics Ltd v Akhter Computers Ltd* [2001] 1 BCLC 433 (CA).

supply units and sought to deny that it was bound by a commission contract on the basis that its sales director had not been authorised to enter into it. The Court of Appeal was satisfied that the sales director had such implied authority in fact. Even if not written in terms into the sales director's contract, the positive burden of expression was discharged: entering into commission agreements was incidental to the sales director's task of maximising sales by incentivising sales agents though commission structures to market the power supply units.[127]

In some cases concerned with implied actual authority, it is not clear whether the burden of expression is positive or negative: the courts appear to use authority implied in fact and in law interchangeably. This is seen, for example, in the case law on the implied authority of managing directors. In *Freeman & Lockyer (a firm) v Bucklehurst Park Properties (Mangal) Ltd*, the directors could formally nominate a managing director by board resolution but did not do so; the fact that one of their number, a Mr Kapoor, nonetheless held himself out as managing director (to the knowledge of the others) was not thought sufficient in the circumstances of that case to imply actual authority to engage architects on behalf of the company.[128]

The position was different in *Hely-Hutchinson v Brayhead Ltd*,[129] where the question was whether the managing director, a Mr Richards, had implied actual authority to commit the company to liabilities under a guarantee for a separate company. Lord Wilberforce and Lord Pearson undoubtedly treated the exercise as involving implication in fact. They found that there was implied actual authority because Mr Richards was allowed to take 'general, financial and policy' decisions without consulting board members on each occasion, and also because the guarantee was given in the context where the board had formally authorised a strategy which would see the company becoming a subsidiary of the other company whose liabilities it had guaranteed.[130] Lord Denning MR's judgment was different: he reasoned that Mr Richards had implied authority because he 'was the chief executive who made the final decision on any matter concerning finance'[131] and because he was acting in the 'usual scope of that office'.[132] Although Lord Denning MR thought that he was identifying actual authority by way of implication in fact,[133] in his (operative) reasoning he clearly was engaged in an exercise of implication in law, and he thereby shifted from a positive to negative burden of expression which fell on the company to limit the scope of Mr Richards' usual authority (which it had not). It remains unclear, however, as to which is the correct approach, since commentary identifies uncritically both types of implied terms as arising from the reasoning of *Hely-Hutchinson*.[134]

[127] ibid [20].

[128] There is a suggestion in the judgments that the Court of Appeal might have taken a different view if the trial judge had developed findings on implied actual authority. See, in particular, *Freeman & Lockyer* [1964] 2 QB 480 (CA) 501–02 (Diplock LJ).

[129] *Hely-Hutchinson v Brayhead Ltd* [1968] 1 QB 549 (CA).

[130] ibid 586–88 (Lord Wilberforce) and 592 (Lord Pearson).

[131] ibid 584.

[132] ibid 583.

[133] ibid 583.

[134] See, eg, *Bowstead & Reynolds on Agency*, 23rd edn (London, Sweet & Maxwell, 2023) paras 3.029 and 3-042; and R Munday, *Agency: Law and Principles*, 3rd edn (Oxford, Oxford University Press, 2016) paras 3.16–3.17 and 3.20.

ii. The External Aspect

The operation of default rules can also be seen in the external aspect of actual authority. Ratification – which is actual authority conferred after the event – has retrospective effect in that, by the so-called 'rule in *Bolton Partners v Lambert*',[135] the contract can be treated as having been authorised when first agreed (such that any revocation of the offer prior to ratification is ineffective). This cuts across the default rule in contract law that offers are revocable at any point before acceptance,[136] and the latter rule is intuitively easier to justify on a majoritarian basis. Nonetheless the retrospective effect of ratification itself can be modified by terms of the contract entered into by the third party. If the third party's contract is expressly said to be subject to ratification, ratification is not permitted to have its usual retrospective effect and the third party can withdraw before the principal approves the agent's agreement.[137] Similarly, ratification cannot take place after an agreed time limit has passed.[138] This also suggests – although it appears that there is no authority directly on point – that effect could be given to a term that excluded the prospect of ratification altogether.

The conclusion that parties can contract out of ratification altogether would be also consistent with the well-established ability of the third party to contract out of undisclosed actual authority by the express or implied terms of the contract.[139] As discussed elsewhere,[140] the justification for a default rule permitting undisclosed agency is controversial, and it is certainly difficult to understand how this could be explained as reflecting the position which reasonable parties would be likely agree between themselves if they had turned their minds to it.[141] This is said, in principle, to be a sticky default rule in that it is difficult to override, save with clear words. The law is meant to assume that an ordinary commercial party is 'willing to treat as a party to the contract anyone on whose behalf the agent may have been authorised to contract',[142] and too liberal an approach to the interpretation and implication of contract terms to exclude intervention would 'go far to destroy the beneficial assumption in commercial cases'.[143] Yet this assumption is unsound. Commercial parties do normally care about who their counterparty is: the market exists to enable parties to choose their counterparties, and therefore the risk they are prepared to take on with a transaction.[144] And recent cases suggest that the courts are in practice very ready to imply an exclusion of the default rule even where there is no express exclusion.[145] Even vanilla provisions such as an entire agreement

[135] *Bolton Partners v Lambert* (1889) 41 Ch D 295 (CA).

[136] See text to n 38 above.

[137] See, eg, *Watson v Davies* [1931] 1 Ch 455 (Ch).

[138] This is one explanation for the decision in *Bird v Brown* (1854) 4 Ex 786: see *Presentaciones Musicales SA v Secunda* [1994] Ch 271 (CA) 279 (Dillon LJ).

[139] *Siu Yin Kwan v Eastern Insurance Co Ltd (The Ospery)* [1994] 2 AC 199 (PC) 207 (Lord Lloyd).

[140] W Day, 'Justifications for and Limitations on Interventions by Undisclosed Principals' in PS Davies and Tan CH (eds), *Intermediaries in Commercial Law* (Oxford, Hart Publishing, 2022) 68–77.

[141] For a strongly expressed view to the contrary, see Tan CH, 'Undisclosed Principals and Contract' (2004) 120 *LQR* 480; Tan CH, 'Implied Terms in Undisclosed Agency' (2021) 84 *MLR* 532.

[142] *Teheran-Europe Co Ltd ST Belton (Tractors) Ltd* [1968] 2 QB 545 (CA) 555 (Diplock LJ).

[143] *Siu Yin Kwan* [1994] 2 AC 199 (PC) 207 (Lord Lloyd).

[144] W Day, *Key Ideas in Commercial Law* (Oxford, Hart Publishing, 2023) 62.

[145] This is discussed in greater detail in Day (n 140) 78–82.

clause[146] and exclusion of the Contracts (Rights of Third Parties) Act 1999[147] may be sufficient to displace the default rule that permits a contract to be formed between a third party and an undisclosed principal.

B. Apparent Authority

The doctrine of apparent authority can also be understood as a default rule. It arises, in broad terms, where a principal is responsible for a representation that the agent has authority, the third party relies on that representation, and changes their position accordingly. In those circumstances, the principal is precluded from denying the formation of the contract.[148] This is again a default justified by majoritarian principles, since the scope of the authority dovetails with the representation, and the representation reflects prevailing expectations as to the authority of an agent placed in that position. As Lord Keith said in *The Ocean Frost*, apparent authority can be 'general in character, arising when the principal has placed the agent in a position which in the outside world is generally regarded as carrying authority to enter into transactions of the kind in question'.[149]

It follows that the holding out by the principal of the agent's authority can (and usually does) arise simply from the agent's appointment to a particular position to the effect that the agent is generally able to enter into a certain ('usual') type of transaction for the principal. *Freeman & Lockyer* again provides a good example. Although, as already noted,[150] the de facto managing director Mr Kapoor was found not to have implied actual authority, he was found to have apparent authority. The decision to engage architects was clearly within the ambit of the authority which a managing director would usually have, and since Mr Kapoor had been acting openly and throughout as though he were managing director, with the silent acquiescence of the board, that amounted to a relevant holding out, by persons with the relevant actual authority to make that representation.[151]

Given the requirement for a representation emanating from the principal, this might be thought to be analogous with terms implied in fact, arising from a positive expression from the principal. But this would be a false analogy. The test giving rise to an implied representation as to authority appears to be much weaker than the obviousness and business efficacy tests,[152] and in substance it falls to the principal – having appointed the agent to a position which comes with some prevailing expectations as to the authority of an agent placed in that position – to discharge a negative burden of expression. This weaker test for implication no doubt reflects the information asymmetry which arises

[146] *Kaefer Aislamientos SA de CV v AMS Drilling Mexico SA de CV* [2019] EWCA Civ 10, [2019] 1 WLR 3514 [112] (Green LJ).

[147] *Bell v Ivy Technology Ltd* [2020] EWCA Civ 1563 [28] (Arnold LJ) and [2022] EWHC 1218 (Comm) [503] (Henshaw J).

[148] See the classic statements in *Rama Corp Ltd v Proved Tin and General Investments* [1952] 2 QB 147 (QB) 149–50 (Slade J) and *Freeman & Lockyer* [1964] 2 QB 480 (CA) 503 (Diplock LJ).

[149] *Armagas Ltd v Mundogas SA (The Ocean Frost)* [1986] AC 717 (HL) 777.

[150] Text to n 128 above.

[151] *Freeman & Lockyer* [1964] 2 QB 480 (CA) 503–04 (Diplock LJ).

[152] See, eg, *Bowstead & Reynolds* (n 134) paras 8-014 and 8-027 describing the notion of a representation arising from the mere appointment to a position as being 'tenuous' and 'artificial'.

in such a case: the third party is unlikely to be privy to the actual terms of the mandate conferred by the principal on the agent, in contrast to the principal. This switch in the burden of expression arises in the context of the requirement that reliance on any representation be reasonable, meaning that the default rule is disapplied if the third party has notice of a lack of actual authority. As Lord Leggatt recently explained in *Philipp v Barclays Bank UK plc*,

> the doctrine will not protect a third party which has reason to believe that the agent is acting without authority and fails to make inquiries that a reasonable person would have made in the circumstances to verify that the agent had authority.[153]

A principal can put a third party on notice as to a lack of actual authority by contractual terms that act as a trigger for the third party to make inquiries or lose the protection of apparent authority. This was the position in *Overbrooke Estates Ltd v Glencombe Properties Ltd*.[154]

There, a property was sold by way of auction, and the buyer received the conditions of sale which clearly stated that the auctioneer had no authority to give any representations or warranties in respect of the property. The auctioneer had in fact misled the buyer by telling the buyer that there was no prospect that the property would be subject to any compulsory purchase programme by local government. After entering into the contract at the auction, the buyer discovered that in fact there was a risk that the property could be acquired as part of a slum clearance programme. The buyers sought to rescind the contract for misrepresentation, and the sellers sued for specific performance. Brightman J agreed with the sellers and gave the order for specific performance. The buyer knew or ought to have known from the 'publicised limits' in the conditions of sale for the auction that the auctioneer was not authorised to make representations for the seller.[155] In those circumstances, it was not possible for the buyer to say that it had reasonably relied on any representation as to the auctioneer's authority to make representations in respect of the property on behalf of the seller.

Limits can be publicised to negative the default created through apparent authority by means other than contractual terms. In *East Asia Company Ltd v PT Satria Tirtatama Energindo (Bermuda)*,[156] those means were the company's bye-laws. The dispute concerned the register of shareholders of a Bermudan company, and whether it should be rectified to remove East Asia Company as the sole shareholder and insert instead PT Satria as the sole shareholder. The basis of the claim in rectification was a heads of terms document and a share transfer form signed by the directors of East Asia Company and PT Satria. However, East Asia Company argued that it was not bound by those documents because the executive director ('Chief of General Affairs') who signed it – a Mr Joenoes – lacked authority, and that PT Satria was on notice as to Mr Joenoes's lack of authority. At trial, the judge had found that Mr Joenoes had apparent authority because of the way in which East Asia Company held him out to PT Satria during negotiations. On appeal to the Privy Council, Lord Hodge disagreed on the basis that

[153] *Philipp v Barclays Bank UK plc* [2023] UKSC 25, [2023] 3 WLR 284 [86] (Lord Leggatt).
[154] *Overbrooke Estates Ltd v Glencombe Properties Ltd* [1974] 1 WLR 1335 (Ch).
[155] ibid 1341.
[156] *East Asia Company Ltd v PT Satria Tirtatama Energindo (Bermuda)* [2019] UKPC 30.

PT Satria had conducted due diligence. That had included actually looking at the byelaws of East Asia Company, which made clear that authority for the transaction rested with the board as a whole, not any single director. PT Satria was therefore on notice because it had looked at the very thing which precluded Mr Joenoes from having actual authority, and so had not reasonably relied on any representations as to his wider authority that could give rise to apparent authority.[157]

VII. Conclusion

Contracting parties cannot avoid the need to reach an agreement, and, in principle, consideration also remains a mandatory requirement albeit rarely requiring enforcement. However, implied terms can be used to fill any gaps in the agreement to ensure that it is complete, and, where the agreement falls to be identified through the prism of offer and acceptance, a range of default rules may be engaged including on the revocability of offers and the communication of acceptance. Further, not all default rules are the same. Some default rules are simply provided by the law in the absence of expressed contrary intention from the parties (eg terms implied in law), whereas others arise from the facts of the case as being the court's best guess as to the (un-expressed) intention of the parties given the circumstances in which they contracted (eg terms implied in fact). Default rules also assist in determining whether parties intend their agreements to have legal effect at all, as well as whether contractual intermediaries have authority to conclude agreements. Not all rules of contractual formation are therefore mandatory by their nature. Far from it: very many are not.

[157] ibid [70]–[94]. This was strictly *obiter* since Lord Hodge had concluded that no such representations had been made by East Asia Company in any event: ibid [41]–[69].

6

Default Terms in Sale of Goods Contracts

LOUISE GULLIFER AND LOUISE MERRETT

I. Introduction

This chapter will look at default rules on sale of goods in two systems which can be chosen (or excluded) by parties: English law (and particularly the Sale of Goods Act 1979 (SGA)); and the UNICITRAL Convention on the International Sale of Goods 1980 (CISG). We will compare and contrast the extent to which choice is available, and not available, and the reasons why choices are made. In both contexts, choice takes place on two levels: first, the choice of the system or overall rules (for example, choice of English law or a complete code plus 'background law'); this can be thought of as private international law autonomy. Secondly, the exercise of the ability to contract out of or to modify part of actual default rules themselves, that is contractual or party autonomy.

The focus will be on international non-consumer sales. It is on international sales because in cases involving different jurisdictions there is then much wider scope for and impetus for party choice, and also because the CISG is targeted at international sales. Consumer sales are excluded because they are much more likely to be governed by mandatory statutory rules. We will start by describing private international law autonomy: first considering the rules by which applicable law is determined and secondly how CISG applies to contracts. Secondly, we will consider party autonomy by looking first at default rules in SGA and secondly CISG, looking at the extent to which parties can modify those default rules. Finally, we will consider role of default rules by considering why choices are made. In particular, we will consider the balance between, on the one hand, uniform law with all the advantages that offers, and, on the other hand, party and state autonomy to contract out of the entire system or particular rules.

In the commercial law sphere we will see that very often there is not a single or binary choice, and this is very much the case in relation to sale of goods. In fact, there are multiple layers of default rules, ranging from the general to the specific and emanating from a number of sources. At the state level, there is domestic national law, which can be either in the form of legislation or case law. For example, in the context of sale of goods in English law, there is the SGA, and a large body of case law. At the international level, there is the CISG, which is hard law (a treaty) and which applies via national law; that is, it becomes national law when ratified and implemented by a state. In addition to international hard law, there is also softer law such as model laws and principles produced by international inter-governmental bodies, such as UNIDROIT, UNCITRAL and the Hague Conference. While the CISG remains the main international law instrument on sale of goods contracts, there are a number of other instruments that relate both to its application[1] and to other aspects of sale of goods transactions.[2]

At a more specific level, there are model rules and standard terms produced by international and national trade bodies,[3] such as the International Chamber of Commerce (ICC), which, amongst others, produce the Uniform Customs and Practice for Documentary Credits (UCP) 600 and the INCOTERMS, which set out standard terms for carriage transactions such as fob and cif. More specific trade bodies include the Grain and Feed Trade Association (GAFTA), an international organisation producing standard terms for many varieties of sale contracts, and the Refined Sugar Association.

There is a large jurisprudence about default rules and may theories and arguments about their benefits, their content and their use. In the commercial law field, the dominance of the principle of party autonomy means that mandatory rules are kept to a minimum, at least in areas such as contract law where the parties' freedom to define their own relationship does not impact third parties. Given this freedom, the wide existence of, and use of, default rules shows that there is an added benefit to having default rules rather than a 'blank slate'. The benefit most usually identified is that having default rules reduces transaction costs, and therefore promotes market efficiency, since they set out a 'template' from which the parties only need to deviate by negotiation if they wish. On this view, the closer the default rules reflect what most parties would want, the more efficient the default rules are (this is known as the 'majoritarian' view).[4] In the area of commercial law there are (at least) two other benefits derived from default rules.[5] The first is legal certainty: a set of default rules can become the subject of numerous court decisions on the same wording of a rule, which, providing that the courts decide consistently, provides 'settled' law on which parties can rely.[6] The second is coordination and harmonisation: where there are a number of back-to-back contracts or otherwise related contracts it makes sense for the same rules to apply to all of them, even in an international context. Harmonisation brings the additional benefit of reducing

[1] See, eg, the Hague Conference Principles on Choice of Law In International Commercial Contracts, Art 3, and the UNIDROIT Principles of International Commercial Contracts (first issued 1994, latest version 2016).

[2] See, eg, the UNCITRAL Rules 1978 and Rotterdam Rules 2008 on Transport of Goods.

[3] J Morgan 'Compulsion, Choice and Statutory Intervention in Contract: Implied Terms of Quality in Sale of Goods' in TT Arvind and J Steele (eds), *Contract Law and the Legislature: Autonomy, Expectations, and the Making of Legal Doctrine*, (Oxford, Hart Publishing, 2020) 190 notes that 'private legislation' by standard forms is very common in commodities trading.

[4] See, eg, I Ayres and R Gertner, 'Filling Gaps in Incomplete Contracts: An Economic Theory of Default Rules' (1989) 99 *Yale Law Journal* 87; D Charny, 'Hypothetical Bargains: The Normative Structure of Contract Interpretation' (1991) 89 *Michigan Law Review* 1815, 1841–44; R Korobkin 'Status Quo Bias and Contract Default Rules' (1997–1998) 83 *Cornell Law Review* 608, 611. For a concise judicial statement of the majoritarian position, see *Barton v Morris* [2023] UKSC 3, [2023] AC 684 [126] (Lord Leggatt).

[5] L Gullifer, 'The Nature and Function of Default Rules in Commercial Law' in B Häcker and J Ungerer (eds), *Default Rules in Private Law* (Oxford, Hart Publishing, 2025).

[6] See, eg, *Pioneer Shipping Ltd v BTP Tioxide Ltd (The Nema)* [1982] AC 724 (HL) 730 (Lord Diplock): 'It is only if parties to commercial contracts can rely upon a uniform construction being given to standard terms that they can prudently incorporate them in their contracts without the need for detailed negotiation or discussion.'

transaction costs even in unrelated transactions, in that parties do not need to invest time and money in becoming familiar with many different sets of rules.

This theoretical framework underpins much of the reasoning in the rest of this chapter. The presence of different layers of default rules in the sale of goods context, however, appears to have the effect that the advantages of default rules are perceived differently at different levels. In particular, the certainty that comes from the use of a national law appears, for many parties, to trump the benefits of international harmonisation. In particular, in the international context, parties appear to consider that the greatest benefits come from opting for a national law that has become 'market standard' (in the sale of goods context), namely English law.

II. Private International Law Autonomy

A. Applicable Law in the Courts of England and Wales

The rules which the English court applies to determine what law applies to a contract are contained in Rome I Regulation (RIR),[7] which now applies as assimilated law. Party autonomy is crucial. The court will start by considering whether the parties themselves have made an express or implied choice of law by Article 3. Pursuant to Article 3, parties are free to determine what law governs their contract. Parties to sale of goods contracts often include an express provision stipulating that the contract will be governed by English law. The law does not need to have any connection to the parties or to the contract. Indeed parties in commercial contracts often chose English law as a 'neutral law'.

It is also possible to imply a choice of law under Article 3 where a choice can be 'clearly demonstrated by the terms of the contract or the circumstances of the case'. Most commonly, the choice of exclusive jurisdiction in a particular forum can lead the courts to imply a choice of law in favour of that jurisdiction.[8] Again, parties, commonly choose English jurisdiction, and this choice can lead to the implication that English law should also govern the contract.

If the parties have not expressly or impliedly chosen a particular law to govern the contract, rules are set out in Article 4 to determine the applicable law in the absence of choice. Under Article 4(1)(a) a sale of goods contract will be presumed to be governed by the law of the habitual residence of the seller.[9] If there is a country which is manifestly more closely connected to the sale the presumed applicable law can be displaced in favour of that law under Article 4(3). An English statute (including, for example, the SGA) will apply to a sales contract if the contract is governed by English law, including because the parties have chosen to make it an English law contract. In that way, parties

[7] Regulation (EC) No 593/2008.

[8] See Recital 12: 'An agreement between the parties to confer on one or more courts or tribunals of a Member State exclusive jurisdiction to determine disputes under the contract should be one of the factors to be taken into account in determining whether a choice of law has been clearly demonstrated.'

[9] Which, pursuant to Art 19, in the case of a company will be the place of central administration unless the contract is concluded or performed through a particular branch.

can select the default rules in the SGA by choosing English law. If the contract is not governed by English law, the default terms will not apply.

However, that is only a starting point. There are a number of exceptions whereby the application of the applicable law is either modified or excluded (many of which are particularly relevant in an international context.

i. Non-excludable Rules

Overriding or mandatory rules are rules of a legal system (usually in a statute) which must be applied despite not being part of the law which otherwise applies to the contract. There are two different types of mandatory rule, referred to in the RIR as law which cannot be derogated from by agreement or 'non-derogable provisions' and 'overriding mandatory provisions. The rules are described in Recital 37, which provides:

> Considerations of public interest justify giving the courts of the Member States the possibility, in exceptional circumstances, of applying exceptions based on public policy and overriding mandatory provisions. The concept of 'overriding mandatory provisions' should be distinguished from the expression 'provisions which cannot be derogated from by agreement' and should be construed more restrictively.

A non-excludable rule is a rule which cannot be contracted out of. Non-excludable rules are the subject of Article 3(3) of the RIR, which provides:

> Where all other elements relevant to the situation at the time of the choice are located in a country other than the country whose law has been chosen, the choice of the parties shall not prejudice the application of provisions of the law of that other country which cannot be derogated from by agreement.

Article 3(3) is a compromise between differences of opinion in the working group prior to the adoption of the Rome Convention. On the first view, choice should not be allowed where there is no foreign element. The other view (particularly) of the UK was that there should be no such limitation, particularly because there were many cases with no *apparent* international element in which a choice of a foreign law was justified. Furthermore, given that the prime objective of contract law is to protect the justified expectations of the parties and make it possible for them to predict what their rights and obligations are going to be, that objective is best served by allowing choice of law. In the end the compromise was to respect party autonomy but with limits.[10]

Article 3(3) can operate in two different scenarios, essentially either wholly English or alternatively wholly foreign situations. First, if 'all of the elements relevant' to a sale of goods are located in England, but the parties have chosen, say, New York law, that choice shall not prejudice the application of provisions of English law that cannot be derogated from by agreement. Examples of non-derogable rules in English law are the rule that a contractual penalty clause is unenforceable and the requirement of consideration. Equally, Article 3(3) would apply to the provisions in the SGA and other statutes that cannot be excluded or restricted by reference to a contract term (or can only be excluded under particular conditions) by reason of the provisions of the Unfair Contract Terms

[10] See further *Dicey, Morris & Collins: The Conflict of Laws*, 16th edn (London, Sweet & Maxwell) para 32-226.

Act 1977 (UCTA).[11] Accordingly, *if* all the elements relevant to the sale are English (that is, it is essentially a domestic English contract for the sale of goods) – even if the parties have chosen a different law to govern, for example New York law – non-excludable rules of English law will apply including provisions of SGA if under UCTA the terms are made non-derogable. The opposite case is where all of the elements relevant to a sale of goods are located in a foreign jurisdiction, say New York, but the parties have chosen English law to govern the contract. In that situation English law will apply, but subject to any provisions of New York law that cannot be derogated from by agreement.[12]

In practice, Article 3(3) will rarely apply, particularly to internationals sales of goods. The Court of Appeal in *Banco Santander Totta SA v Companhia Carris de Ferro de Lisboa SA*[13] stressed that the expression 'elements relevant to the situation' was wide and not confined to factors connecting the contract to a particular country in any narrow sense. Account must be taken of elements that point directly from a purely domestic to an international situation. Even though the contracts (for long-term interest rate swaps) were entered into between a Portuguese bank and Portuguese state-owned transport companies; the international nature of the swaps market, the chain of back-to-back contracts all on ISDA terms governed by English law and the reliance of the bank on its Spanish parent for negotiating and concluding the swaps confirmed the international nature of the swaps and meant it was not a purely domestic Portuguese contract. Similarly, in *Caterpillar Financial Service Corp v SNC Passion*,[14] a loan agreement between a Delaware and French company was expressly governed by English law. The fact that the agreement was in English, and was connected to the purchase of a ship being built in Singapore and was with a Delaware company meant that it was not a purely domestic French contract and English law applied in full.

ii. Overriding Mandatory Rules

Non-excludable rules are therefore rules which the parties cannot contract out of by use of a choice of law provision. But non-excludable rules only apply if the contract would otherwise be governed by the relevant law. Overriding mandatory rules are overriding in a more fundamental way in that they apply regardless of what law would otherwise be applicable to the situation. Overriding mandatory rules are defined in Article 9(1) of the RIR as:

> [P]rovisions the respect for which is regarded as crucial by a country for safeguarding its public interests, such as its political, social or economic organisation, to such an extent that

[11] *Chitty on Contracts*, 35th edn (London, Sweet & Maxwell, 2023) para 32-239.

[12] An example of such a foreign rule was at issue in *Banco Santander Totta SA v Companhia Carris de Ferro de Lisboa SA* [2016] EWCA Civ 1267, [2017] 3 All ER 838. On the facts, Art 3(3) did not apply because it was held to be an international contract. But the rule sought to be relied on was Art 437 of the Portuguese Civil Code which provided for modification or termination of the swaps by the court (by allowing termination in the case of 'abnormal change of circumstances', in this case the global financial crisis). At first instance, the Court had concluded that Art 437 was not a rule of law which 'cannot be derogated from by contract' because, under Portuguese law, it could be waived by agreement of the parties. The Court of Appeal held that it was not possible under Portuguese law to exclude beforehand the application of Art 437 to any unidentified risks. An ex post facto agreement not to rely on Art 437, following the occurrence of a particular risk, did not make the rule derogable.

[13] ibid.

[14] *Caterpillar Financial Service Corp v SNC Passion* [2004] EWHC 569 (Comm).

> they are applicable to any situation falling within their scope, irrespective or the law otherwise applicable to the contract under this Regulation.

Article 9(1) differentiates overriding rules from non-excludable rules as they are rules which are applicable 'irrespective of the law otherwise applicable to the contract under this Regulation'. The provision is also restrictive in that to qualify as an overriding mandatory rule under the RIR, such rules must be crucial for safeguarding important public interests.

The RIR contains two different provisions dealing with overriding mandatory provisions. Under Article 9(2) 'Nothing in this Regulation shall restrict the application of the overriding mandatory provisions of the law of *the forum*' (emphasis added). This provision allows the English court to apply English overriding mandatory rules. Most rules in UK law are not overriding. A UK statute, such as the SGA, generally does not apply to a contract unless the governing law of the contract is the law of some part of the UK. Many of the examples which do exist in the UK are in the fields of employment and consumer law. For example, section 204 of the Employment Rights Act 1996 provides 'for the purposes of this Act it is immaterial whether the law which (apart from this Act) governs any person's employment is the law of the United Kingdom, or a part of the United Kingdom, or not'. However, some examples are in the commercial law field, such as *The Hollandia*,[15] where it was held that the Hague-Visby Rules scheduled to the Carriage of Goods by Sea Act 1971 applied if the place of shipment was a UK port, regardless of the governing law (which in this case was Dutch law under an express choice of law agreement).

Article 9(3) provides that:

> Effect may be given to the overriding mandatory provisions of the law of the country where the obligations arising out of the contract have to be or have been performed, in so far as those overriding mandatory provisions render the performance of the contract unlawful. In considering whether to give effect to those provisions, regard shall be had to their nature and purpose and to the consequences of their application or non-application.

Article 9(3) allows for the application of overriding mandatory rules of a *third state*. in the sense that the rules are not rules of English law or the law applicable to the contract. The permissible application of third state rules is much narrower than under Article 7(1) of the Rome Convention,[16] which allowed application of any state's mandatory rules. Article 9(3) appears to be based on cases like *Foster v Driscoll*.[17] In that case, an English court refused to enforce a contract for the sale of whisky to the US as it was illegal according to its place of performance because of US prohibition laws.

iii. Public Policy

Pursuant to Article 21 of the RIR: 'The application of a provision of the law of any country specified by this Regulation may be refused only if such application is manifestly

[15] *Owners of Cargo on Board the Morviken v Owners of the Hollandia (The Hollandia)* [1983] 1 AC 565 (HL).

[16] 1980 Rome Convention on the law applicable to contractual obligations. Art 7(1) provided that when applying under the Convention the laws of a country, effect may be given to the mandatory rules of the law of the country with which the situation had a close connection. The UK exercised its right of reservation under the Convention and opted out of Art 7(1).

[17] *Foster v Driscoll* [1929] 1 KB 470 (CA).

incompatible with the public policy (*order public*) of the forum'. This provision reflects a general principle in conflict of laws which allows domestic courts to preserve fundamental public policy principles of their domestic legal system. The expression in the RIR which requires any inconsistency with domestic policy to be 'manifest' emphasises that the application of public policy must only be used in narrow and exceptional cases. To apply this exception whenever the rule identified by the Regulation differs from English law would be fundamentally to undermine the purpose of conflict of law rules. The narrowness of the public policy doctrine (and the narrow definition of overriding mandatory rules), based on rules of law regarded as essential or fundamental in the domestic legal order, mean that both will rarely apply in commercial cases such as sale of goods. In particular, public policy will not apply simply because a contract valid under its foreign governing law would be invalid according to English law, for example requiring consideration,[18] or relating to penalties. Even if the English rule is 'imperative'[19] that does not mean will be applied to a contract governed by a foreign legal system.

B. Application of CISG to International Sales Contacts

The CISG is, at least on paper, a highly successful transnational law treaty ratified by 97 states.[20] On ratification, and any necessary implementing legislation, it becomes part of the domestic law of the ratifying state. It provides a set of default rules for most issues arising in relation to a contract for the sale of goods, although it does not cover the passing of property in such a transaction. It applies only to sale contracts where the parties have their places of business in different states. If that is the case, unless the CISG has been excluded under Article 6, it applies to displace the otherwise applicable domestic law if either: (a) both states are Contracting States (Article 1(1)(a));[21] or (b) the relevant rules of private international law lead to the applicable law being that of a Contracting State (Article 1(1)(b)). A state, when ratifying, can make a declaration (under Article 95) that it will not be bound by Article 1(1)(b), that is, that the CISG will not apply as a matter of that state's domestic law merely because the law of a Contracting State is the applicable law.[22] In such a state, therefore, the CISG will only apply if the places of business of both parties are in (different) Contracting States.

Additionally, Article 6 states the parties 'may exclude the application of this Convention or … derogate from or vary the effect of any of its provisions'. It enables contracting out on the two levels identified above: the whole CISG can be excluded (in which case the applicable law is either that chosen by the parties or, in the absence of

[18] *cf* W Day, 'Default Rules in Contract Formation', this volume, ch 5.

[19] In the sense that it cannot be excluded by contract: see *Dicey, Morris & Collins* (n 10) para 32-282.

[20] It has therefore been ratified by a very large proportion of trading nations, including common law countries such as the US, Australia, New Zealand and Canada. Notable exceptions are the UK and India.

[21] A Contracting State is one that has ratified the Treaty.

[22] This declaration has been made by Armenia, China, Lao People's Democratic Republic, St Vincent and the Grenadines, Singapore, Slovakia and, importantly, the US. The result of making this declaration gives rise to some complexities, see F. Ferrari, 'Indirect applicability pursuant to article 1(1)(b)', available at www.iicl.law.pace.edu/cisg/page/annotated-text-cisg.

choice, the law to which the rules of private international law lead) or the parties can 'choose' the CISG but derogate from or vary the effect of any of its provisions.[23]

The practical effect of these provisions is that parties to an international sales contract have various choices. If both parties have their places of business in Contracting States, then CISG will apply unless they make a conscious decision to exclude it under Article 6. If they wish to do this, they need to exclude the CISG expressly,[24] and, in addition, to achieve certainty they need to choose an applicable law, as otherwise the law will be that applicable under the private international law rules of the forum. Even if the parties want the CISG to apply, they would be well advised to choose an applicable law, since there are many issues that are not governed by the CISG (including both general contractual issues and also 'gaps')[25] which may need to be determined under a background law.

If only one, or neither, party has its place of business in a Contracting State, then the parties do not need to exclude the CISG if they do not want it to apply. However, they can make a choice which will result in the application of the CISG. First, they can choose an applicable law of a Contracting State, which will automatically bring in the CISG under Article 1(1)(b) unless the forum state has made a declaration under Article 95.[26] It is also possible (though perhaps riskier because the rules of private international law will then determine the 'underlying' applicable law) to choose the CISG as the applicable law. The choice of a non-state law has been possible if disputes are referred to arbitration for some time, and Principle 3 of the Hague Choice of Law Principles now permits this, although the status of such a choice is a matter of some uncertainty.[27]

Another alternative would be to incorporate the provisions of the CISG as terms of the contract. However, this could be open to a number of issues,[28] for example, inconsistency between the interpretation rule of the applicable domestic law and the interpretation rule of the CISG in Article 7, which provides that in 'the interpretation of this Convention, regard is to be had to its international character and to the need to

[23] The sentiment of Art 6 tracks that of Art 3 of the UNIDROIT Uniform Law of International Sales 1964, the predecessor to the CISG, but the wording was changed to the current wording to better reflect the dual purpose of the section as described in the text: see the Report of the Second Session of the Working Group on the International Sale of Goods 7–18 December 1970 (A/CN.9J52) [46].

[24] Art 6 does not prevent an implied exclusion, but subsequent interpretation by the courts establishes that the intention has to be very clearly shown in the absence of an express exclusion, and that merely choosing the law of a Contracting States is not sufficient. Choosing the law of a non-Contracting State (for example, English law) could be sufficient to exclude the CISG, but even then the courts have interpreted this choice narrowly and the CISG could apply if there is a gap in the chosen domestic law, see CP Gillette and SD Walt (eds), *The UN Convention on Contracts for the International Sale of Goods: Theory and Practice* (Cambridge, Cambridge University Press, 2016) 66–69.

[25] Some gaps are, under Art 7(2) of CISG, to be determined in accordance with the 'general principles on which it is based' and only in the absence of such principles does the applicable law apply. However, other matters are just not governed by the CISG at all, and the applicable law applies in any event: see H Gabriel, 'The Misplaced Reliance on Default Rules in International Sales Contracts' (2020) 38 *Journal of Law and Commerce* 333.

[26] For detailed discussion, see F Ragna, 'The CISG and choice of law' (2019) 38 *Journal of Law and Commerce* 245.

[27] B Marshall, 'The Hague Choice of Law Principles, CISG, and PICC: A Hard Look at a Choice of Soft Law' (2018) 66 *American Journal of Comparative Law* 175. Such a choice was also foreshadowed by Art 4 of the UNIDROIT Uniform Law of International Sales 1964, but this provision (originally included in the draft CISG) was removed because of concerns that it could enable parties to choose the CISG in relation to contracts outside its scope, such as consumer contracts, and a proposal to reinstate it with wording to exclude that possibility was rejected at the Diplomatic Conference, see ibid (Marshall) 193.

[28] See, eg, O Toth, *The Lex Mercatoria in Theory and Practice* (Oxford, Oxford University Press, 2017) 34–39.

promote uniformity in its application and the observance of good faith in international trade'. Another potential problem is that the CISG formation rules would not apply to the making of the contract incorporating it.[29] Perhaps more realistically, parties in non-Contracting States who do not want to choose the law of a Contracting State as the applicable law could use the CISG as a 'template' to fashion their own contract. That way the general principles could apply, but the applicable law would be that chosen by the parties (or by private international law rules), which could then be a system with which the parties are familiar, such as English law.

A final permutation is where only one or neither party has its place of business in a Contracting State, and they choose the law of a Contracting State as the applicable law but do not want the CISG to apply. Here, the parties must exclude the CISG, preferably expressly, as otherwise it would, of course, apply unless the forum state has made a declaration under Article 95.

It can be seen that the application of the CISG is not entirely straightforward, even when we look at the binary question of whether it applies or does not apply. As discussed below, its application is excluded extensively (for many reasons, but including concerns on certainty and predictability). However, the CISG also operates as a set of default rules at a more granular level and parties that choose it (or that do not exclude it) can modify it extensively. The only mandatory provision is Article 12, and this only applies if the relevant state has made a declaration under Article 96, namely, that writing is required for the conclusion of a contract of sale (or any step in the formation process) or for the termination of a contract of sale.[30]

The CISG, therefore, is a hard law international instrument designed to aid harmonisation (one of the benefits of default rules), but this benefit will only be realised if, first, many states ratify the treaty (which is the case) and, second, parties actually use it. Arguably, the harmonisation and coordination benefits would be realised even if parties modified its provisions at the granular level reasonably extensively to suit their own situation. However, those benefits are unlikely to be realised if parties exclude the CISG altogether under Article 6.

III. Scope and Nature of the Default Rules which Apply under SGA and CISG

A. Overview

The rules set out in the SGA and CISG are not a complete or comprehensive code. The SGA expressly preserves normal common rules in areas not covered by the statute. Section 62(1) provides that

> the rules of the common law, including the law merchant in so far as they are inconsistent with the provisions of [the Act], and in particular the rules relating to the law of principal and

[29] See B Hayward, B Zeller and CB Andersen, 'The CISG and The United Kingdom: Exploring Coherency and Private International Law' (2018) 67 *International and Comparative Law Quarterly* 607, 616.

[30] Such declarations have been made by Argentina, Armenia, Belarus, Chile, Democratic People's Republic of Korea, Paraguay, Russian Federation, Ukraine and Vietnam.

> agent and the effect of fraud, misrepresentation, duress or coercion, mistake or other invalidating cause, apply to contracts for the sale of goods.[31]

Similarly CISG does not cover these general matters, but also excludes matters such as the passing of property, which is an essential part of a sale of goods transaction. However, both the SGA and CISG contain rules governing most aspects of the sale contract. Sometimes in SGA these rules are expressed as implied terms; in other cases they are described as rules. However, nothing turns on these different formulations since, as explained below, in almost all cases these are default not mandatory rules in that they are subject to party or contractual autonomy.[32] In other words, parties can customise the default rules.

The SGA implies a number of terms into a sale of goods contract.[33] In particular, in relation to the quality of the goods themselves, under section 12 that the seller has the right to sell, under section 13 that the goods will meet their description, under section 14 that the goods will be of satisfactory quality and under section 15 that the goods will correspond with any sample. The rules in Articles 35–36 and 41–42 of the CISG have a similar purpose and content. The rules on passing of risk are also a good example of default rules, often contracted out of by parties (SGA section 20; CISG Articles 68–69), as are the 'rules' on the passing of property (SGA sections 16–20B; passing of property is not covered by the CISG). Other points covered by both SGA and CISG are: delivery obligations (SGA sections 27–32; CISG Articles 30–34), rejection of goods and when the right is lost (SGA sections 34–36; CISG Articles 37–40, 43–44 and 81–84), buyer's remedies for breach (SGA sections 51–53A; CISG Articles 54–52, although some of the CISG rules are not spelt out in the SGA such as the right to terminate the contract for breach), payment of price (SGA sections 8, 27, 49; CISG Articles 54–59) and buyer taking delivery (SGA sections 27, 37, 50; CISG Articles 60–62). There is a lot more in CISG than in SGA on anticipatory breach and fundamental breach and the consequences of it (Articles 71–77). Other default rules (or rules with the same effect) are those dealing with frustration/force majeure/hardship (SGA section 7, though to a limited extent, and CISG Articles 79–80) and the consequences of avoidance (CISG Articles 81–84; there is nothing explicit in SGA).

These terms are default, in the sense that they apply unless the parties provide otherwise. Parties often do so by agreeing their own set of terms and guarantees to replace those set out in the SGA or CISG. For example, in *Air Transworld Ltd v Bombardier Inc*,[34] which concerned the sale of an aircraft, the defendant successfully argued that the implied terms in the SGA had been replaced with the express warranties set out in an agreement between the parties. For example, the seller warranted to the buyer that at

[31] Capacity to buy and sell is also regulated by the general law: SGA, s 3(1).

[32] *Barton v Morris* [2023] UKSC 3, [2023] AC 684 [132] (Lord Leggatt). See also [157] where Lord Leggatt explains such implied terms (whether implied at common law or in a statute) mean that the burden of expression is on the party seeking to avoid the rule.

[33] The evolution of the SGA is described in detail in Morgan (n 3). Lord Leggatt in *Barton v Morris* [2023] UKSC 3, [2023] AC 684 [132] describes sale of goods law as an example of a body of commercial law which developed through usages and norms of commerce such that by the time the law was codified in the Sale of Goods Act 1893 the common law had developed a sophisticated set of rules that apply to this type of contract unless a contrary intention is expressed.

[34] *Air Transworld Ltd v Bombardier Inc* [2012] EWHC 243 (Comm) ('*Air Transworld*').

delivery time and for the warranty periods expressly set out, the aircraft would be free from (for example) defects in material, manufacture and design. In case of any such defect during the warranty periods, the seller's sole obligation was expressly limited to correction by repair, replacement or rework.

In many other cases, parties chose more specific rules established by national or international trade bodes. For example, GAFTA is an international trade association which develops the standard forms of contract on which it is estimated that 80 per cent of the world's trade in grain is shipped. The standard forms contain detailed terms covering all aspects of the international sale of a variety of agricultural goods,[35] including terms on price and destination, shipment, payment, insurance, default as well as provision for arbitration. GAFTA contracts include a choice of law (usually English law) and expressly exclude the CISG.[36] The ICC produces INCOTERMS which are standardised rules relating to carriage for different types of international trade contracts which are usually incorporated into standard trade contracts. While these specific standard term contracts displace the default rules of the SGA (and general contract law) the extent to which they do is always a matter of interpretation of the words of the relevant clause.[37]

B. Party Autonomy in the SGA

i. Terms which cannot be Freely Excluded

In the SGA, the 'default' nature of the rules, or more accurately the ability of parties to contract out of the default terms, is complicated by provisions of UCTA.[38] Under section 6(1) of UCTA, liability for breach of the obligations arising from section 12 of SGA cannot be excluded or restricted by reference to any contract term. Under section 6(1A)(a), liability for breach of the obligations arising from section 13, 14 or 15 of the SGA cannot be excluded or restricted by reference to a contract term except in so far as the term satisfies the requirement of reasonableness.[39]

The provisions of UCTA make what appear to be gap-filling default rules into matters which the parties cannot determine by explicit agreement.[40] However, other

[35] There are different contracts for different types of grain and feedstuffs, and also different contracts for goods from particular jurisdictions or areas of the world: see www.gafta.com/All-Contracts.

[36] The same is true of the model contract from the Refined Sugar Association, which, in particular, includes detailed rules on quantity, packing, weight and quality which refine (but do not supplant) the SGA implied terms.

[37] See, eg, *Bunge SA v Nidera BV* [2015] UKSC 43, [2015] 3 All ER 1082 [27] (Lord Sumption) 'But it is a question of construction whether the mere fact that [the clause] deals with damages means that it must have been intended to do so exhaustively, thereby impliedly excluding any considerations which it has not expressly addressed.'

[38] And also potentially by principles of construction such as contra proferentem and the presumption that neither party intends to abandon any remedies for breach: *Gilbert Ash (Northern Ltd v Modern Engineering (Bristol) Ltd* [1974] AC 689 (HL). The result is a 'spectrum rather than a sharp dichotomy between default and immutable rules': Morgan (n 3) 177.

[39] Under s 6(4), the section applies to any contract of sale of goods not just the business liabilities in standard form contracts defined in s 1(3) but does not apply to consumer contracts. Provision is made for such contracts under s 31 of the Consumer Rights Act 2015.

[40] The provisions do not apply to international supply contracts as defined in s 26.

than in relation to section 12, the parties are free to exclude or modify the provisions of the SGA provided they do so in a way which is reasonable. If the parties replace the terms with their own provisions as to quality etc, these terms may well be considered to be reasonable. A clause which excludes liability altogether is less likely to be reasonable than a clause which provides an alternative remedy.[41] For example, if parties to a contract that would otherwise be determined by English law choose for it to be governed by the CISG, in relation to sections 13, 14 and 15, the answer probably would be that the CISG (as an internationally recognised standard) is reasonable.

Similarly the provisions in a GAFTA standard term are likely to be considered to be reasonable. The parties are not excluding the quality terms implied in SGA; rather they are replacing them with industry-agreed specialist terms. The facts that a term has been set by a neutral body or that it reflects an industry standard agreed by a process involving discussion by representatives from different sides of the industry are factors which can be seen as arguing in favour of reasonableness.[42]

The answer in relation to section 12 would be less straightforward. But even in the case of section 12, the obligations are modified where there appears from the contract or is to be inferred from its circumstances an intention that the seller should transfer only such title as he or a third person may have.

ii. Self-denying Statutes

For the reasons already given, parties who expressly choose English law to govern their sale of goods contract will thereby also chose the default terms set out in that Act. Furthermore, the provisions of UCTA will also apply to a contract governed by English law, which means that in certain circumstances those 'default' rules cannot be excluded or can only be excluded by a term which is reasonable. Parties will then be choosing fixed rather than default terms.

However, UCTA is an unusual example of what is sometimes referred to as a 'self-denying statute'. Section 27(1) provides:

> [W]here the law applicable to a contract is the law of any part of the United Kingdom only by choice of the parties (and apart from that choice would be the law of some country outside the United Kingdom) sections 2 to 7 and 16 to 21 of this Act [exclusion of negligence liability, liability in contract and other controls on exclusion of liability] do not operate as part of the law applicable to the contract.

A self-denying statute is essentially the opposite of an overriding statute in that it does not apply even though the applicable law is English law.[43]

[41] *Chitty* (n 11) para 18-118.

[42] ibid para 18-132 and *Schroeder Music Publishing Co Ltd v Macaulay* [1974] 1 WLR 1308 (HL) 1316 (Lord Diplock). However, the fact that a clause is very widely used means that the party may have little choice but to accept it is recognised in schedule 2(b) as a factor against reasonableness. See on the approach to the assessment of reasonableness D Airey, 'When it's Mandatory to be "Reasonable": the Nature and Application of Reasonableness under the Unfair Contract Terms Act 1977', this volume, ch 7.

[43] *Dicey, Morris & Collins* (n 10) para 1-066.

For example, in *Air Transworld Ltd v Bombardier Inc*,[44] the question was whether the normal implied terms as to quality and description under sections 13 and 14 of SGA were replaced by the provisions of an aircraft purchase agreement. It was held that the wording of the agreement was sufficiently clear to exclude obligations under the SGA which would otherwise be implied. In fact, not only did UCTA not apply here,[45] but section 27(1) applied as English law was the governing law solely as a result of the express choice of law. This meant that the reasonableness test did not apply to the exclusion of the normal default terms.[46]

In *Deutsche Bank (Suisse) SA v Khan*,[47] a facility agreement contained a choice of law clause for English law. But for this express choice, the presumptively applicable law would have been Swiss because the Bank was the characteristic performer whose central of administration was Geneva and therefore section 27(1) applied. Although there was also an English jurisdiction agreement which would usually be a strong factor in favour of implying a choice of English law, in considering whether the presumed applicable Swiss law could be displaced in favour of English law (which would mean that section 27(1) would not apply), the premise of section 27 was to identify the applicable law based on considerations other than the parties' choice.[48]

The idea of a self-denying statute has been subject to criticism. In an article written in response to the Law Commission report which preceded the implementation of UCTA, FA Mann submits that it is almost perverse in character. He says 'it can be suggested without exaggeration that this subsection is unique in the history of the law. Whether English or foreign'. It states in effect that provisions which English law considers fair and reasonable are not available to parties who have chosen English law, when they ought to or might have allowed non-English law to govern.

> If, as one must presume, the Bill expresses such social and legal policy as this country thinks just and proper, it excludes from its benefits persons who, as still seems often to happen, have chosen English law for the very reason that they have faith in its being the embodiment of what is just and reasonable.[49]

If the only legislative policy is the prevention of evasion of statutory provisions, section 27(1) does appear to do the very opposite. If foreign parties choose to have their contract governed by English law they ought to take the rough with the smooth and must be presumed to know what they are doing. It is not for English law to protect them against the folly of their choice or deprive them of the fruits of their wisdom. If default rules are seen in part as being an issue relating to the burden of expression,[50] there does

[44] *Air Transworld* [2012] EWHC 243 (Comm).

[45] The provisions of UCTA were excluded under s 26(4)(b) because it was an international supply contract.

[46] Similarly, in *Wilmington Trust SP Services (Dublin) Ltd v Spicejet Ltd* [2021] EWHC 1117 (Comm) the court held obiter that s 27(1) would have excluded operation of UCTA. But for the express choice of English law, applying Art 4 of RIR there would not have been reason to displace the presumed applicable law. English law was chosen as a neutral law and that choice did not demonstrate any independent connection with England.

[47] *Deutsche Bank (Suisse) SA v Khan* [2013] EWHC 482 (Comm).

[48] ibid [367] (Hamblen J). See also *Surzur Overseas v Ocean Reliance* [1997] CLY 906 (Com Ct).

[49] FA Mann, 'The Proposed New Law of Exemption Clauses and the Conflict of Laws' (1977) 26 *International and Comparative Law Quarterly* 903, 907–09.

[50] See, eg, *Barton v Morris* [2023] UKSC 3, [2023] AC 684 [157] (Lord Leggatt).

not seem to be any reason why parties could not opt into UCTA (by choosing English law plus UCTA without section 27(1)), but the onus would be on the parties to do so. Alternatively, the parties could incorporate the provisions of UCTA as terms of their contract, although for the reasons discussed above in relation to CISG this can cause complications, particularly if the governing law is not English law.

Section 27 does indeed seem contradictory. UCTA is a non-excludable rule of English statute law, precisely because the protection it provides to contracting parties should not be capable of avoidance. But when parties chose English law they are deprived of that protection. Nonetheless, the Law Commission identified an interesting legislative policy behind this provision which goes beyond evasion, expressly based on rule arbitrage. The intention behind section 27(1) was to encourage parties to chose English law (and jurisdiction), including, for example, the default terms in the SGA. However, there is an assumption that commercial parties would prefer the terms to remain default terms, rather than mandatory, and accordingly would prefer not to be subject to the restrictions imposed by UCTA. Thus, the Law Commission report explains:[51]

> The parties to contracts of which the proper law would otherwise be the law of some country other than England and Wales or Scotland often choose English or Scots law as the proper law of their contracts. Sometimes there is an express provision to that effect, more often the choice is made by providing for disputes arising under such contracts to be settled by arbitration in England or Scotland, generally in the City of London. The effect of imposing our proposed controls in relation to those contracts might well be to discourage foreign businessmen from agreeing to arbitrate their disputes in England or Scotland. We see no reason why the controls proposed in this report should apply to such contracts and we therefore consider that it should be provided that the controls over exemption clauses proposed in this report should apply only where, apart from a term that the proper law of the contract should be the law of England and Wales or Scotland the proper law of the contract would be the law of England and Wales or Scotland.
>
> Recommendation
>
> We recommend that provision should be made to ensure that the controls proposed in this report should not apply where, apart from a term that the proper law of the contract should be the law of England and Wales or Scotland, the proper law of the contract would be the law of some other country.

The issue of why parties chose particular default rules is considered further in section IV below.

C. Party Autonomy in CISG

As already mentioned, there are no mandatory provisions in the CISG unless a state has made a declaration under Article 96. It is therefore open to parties to modify it how they wish, although modifications will, of course, be subject to the mandatory rules and public policy of the applicable domestic law. As set out in section IV below, there

[51] Law Commission and Scottish Law Commission, *Exemption Clauses: Second Report* (Law Com No 69; Scot Law Com No 39, 1975) paras 232–33.

is considerable empirical evidence that parties in many countries either exclude it altogether or modify it considerably. This raises the question, however, as to how useful the CISG is as a set of default rules if the criterion for good default rules is the reduction of transaction costs, and the content of default rules is governed by majoritarianism. This question will be addressed below, but several points can be made here about the content of the CISG.

First, like the SGA, the CISG is designed as a general set of rules in relation to sale contracts. It governs a number of different types of situations, for example, one-off sales of single items, repeat sales of single items, commodity sales, string contracts and so on. It also covers may many different types of goods, all of which have their idiosyncrasies. And although it only applies to (international) commercial sales, these can include all types of parties from single entrepreneurs to huge multi-national companies, and parties can either be of equal or very unequal bargaining power. It is therefore to be expected that the CISG does not provide a perfect set of default rules for these disparate transactions.[52] Nonetheless, the CISG does serve a purpose as a framework or template which parties can modify: rather than having to start from scratch they can focus on what needs to be specifically agreed and tailored to their own circumstances. Some provisions of the CISG invite particularisation through their inherent vagueness,[53] a trait it shares with general English contract law, and, to some extent, the SGA. An example is the foreseeability limit on recovery of damages in Article 74, which is often seen as unacceptably uncertain. However, parties can agree on liquidated damages thus removing the uncertainty (subject to the mandatory provisions on penalty clauses in the applicable law).[54]

Second, majoritarian default rules are more easily arrived at in a more particular context than that of the CISG. For example, the requirements of different types of transport of goods can be addressed by the various INCOTERM sets of provisions. These can be incorporated within the CISG easily enough, and because they themselves are standardised, guidance on how to incorporate them has been developed and is available.[55] More broadly, Article 9 of CISG provides that not only are the parties bound by any trade usage they have established between themselves, but also to have impliedly incorporated any well-known international trade usage in the relevant trade.[56] The CISG, therefore, anticipates particularisation and adaptation to specific trades and markets.

[52] See M Cenini and F Parisi, 'An Economic Analysis of the CISG' in A Janssen and O Meyer (eds) CISG Methodology (Munich, Sellier European Law Publisher, 2009) 151 and 154.

[53] This is the case in comparison with, eg, Art 2 of the US Uniform Commercial Code. See, eg, the list of provisions which can be particularised to increase certainty included in H Gabriel, The Misplaced Reliance on Default Rules in International Sales Contracts (2020) 38 *Journal of Law and Commerce* 333, 345–57.

[54] This example is often relied upon as an example of a 'penalty default rule' which encourages parties to reveal information when they bargain round it: see I Ayres and R Gertner, 'Filling Gaps in Incomplete Contracts: An Economic Theory of Default Rules' (1989) 99 *Yale Law Journal* 87. However, here the example is merely that: an example of where a vague rule can be made more certain. Another example is Art 78 of the CISG which gives the seller a right to interest on non-payment of the price but does not specify the rate of interest: the parties can fill in this 'gap'.

[55] See, eg, J Ramberg, 'Incoterms 2000 – The Necessary Link between Contracts of Sale and Contracts of Carriage' (2008) 58 *Collected Papers of Zagreb Law Faculty* 35, 42; J Coetzee, 'The Interplay between Incoterms and the CISG" (2013) 32 *Journal of Law and Commerce* 1.

[56] Art 9(2): 'The parties are considered, unless otherwise agreed, to have impliedly made applicable to their contract or its formation a usage of which the parties knew or ought to have known and which in international

Against this, it can be argued that, without expressly drafted provisions, the extent of the trade usage that applies could be unclear. It is such concerns that lead to standard trade agreements excluding the CISG entirely, and providing their own, more tailored, set of rules which, although in theory default rules, tend to be sticky[57] because of market practice and the benefits of certainty and coordination.[58]

Third, it is often said that the content of the CISG is less than optimal (as default rules) given the fact that it is the product of international negotiation.[59] It is, of course, often the case that international instruments, particularly treaties, end up as a compromise between the views of representative from different states, and (often) from different legal traditions. Often the choice is between compromise (on the one hand) and permitting reservations or declarations (on the other hand), the latter of which jeopardises uniformity; thus, an optimal solution is not available. Therefore, in order to agree a text, the compromise solution is adopted. However, where the resulting text consists of default rules, this may not be fatal to the utility of the text, nor does it necessarily prevent individual rules being optimal. For example, Article 18 providing that silence does not amount to acceptance is likely to be the majoritarian rule,[60] as is the rule that risk passes on delivery (Articles 67 and 69, with Article 68 being a limited exception),[61] in contrast to the SGA default rule in section 20 that risk passes with property, which is almost always contracted out of. Other CISG rules may not be optimal, but they can operate as 'defaults' in that parties reveal information in the course of negotiating the optimal rule for them.[62]

IV. Why do Parties Choose Default Rules and/or to Modify Default Rules?

A. English Law

Currently, English substantive law and an English forum are businesses' prevailing choices in international business transactions.[63] This is the case both in court proceedings

trade is widely known to, and regularly observed by, parties to contracts of the type involved in the particular trade concerned.'

[57] 'Sticky' here is used in the sense it is used in the US jurisprudence on default rules; that is, to describe a situation where parties do not contract out of default rules when, as a matter of the content of the rule, it might seem more efficient for them to do so: see O Ben-Shahar and J Pottow, 'On the Stickiness of Default Rules' (2006) 33 *Florida State University Law Review* 651.

[58] For discussion of the benefits of certainty and coordination, see Gullifer (n 5).

[59] See, eg, CP Gillette and SD Walt, *The UN Convention on Contracts for the International Sale of Goods: Theory and Practice* (Cambridge, Cambridge University Press, 2016) 8.

[60] Cenini and Parisi (n 52) 162.

[61] ibid 164–65. *cf* M Bridge, 'The Transfer of Risk under the UN Sales Convention 1980 (CISG)' in C Andersen and U Schroeter (eds), *Sharing International Commercial Law across Boundaries* (London, Wildy, Simmonds & Hill Publishing 2008) 77, 105 arguing that the CISG rules do not provide a majoritarian solution in commodity string sales.

[62] See text to n 54 above in relation to Art 74 (foreseeability of loss as a limit to damages) and see, in relation to the quality warranty in Art 35, Cenini and Parisi (n 52) 158–64.

[63] See A Sommerfeld and L Merrett, 'Incentives for Choice of Law and Forum in Commercial Contracts: Predicting the Impact of Brexit' (2020) 28 *European Review of Private Law* 627.

and in arbitration. Studies identify a number of factors which influence businesses' choice of contract law. A number of different surveys of practitioners and businesses have been conducted in relation to court proceedings and arbitration. National courts and arbitration bodies also publish reports and statistics which can provide useful data.[64]

First, and perhaps most relevant for the purposes of this chapter, is the content of the substantive law. Specific elements which have been identified as important factors are the possibility of limiting liability, and the absence of any general principle of good faith. Parties also value legal certainty.[65] There is some resonance here with the Law Commission's stated rationale in relation to section 27(1) of UCTA.[66] There is evidence that parties choosing English law would prefer a default set of rules which can be modified by the parties rather than compulsory rules.[67] Businesses also value predictability of outcome which is presumably one of the reasons why they avoid systems of law with broad concepts of good faith and reasonableness, and prefer a well-established common law system with settled rules and case law plus damages as the default remedy rather than specific performance to allow for a clean break.[68] Linked to this is the widespread use of model contracts in international transactions that are mostly drafted in English language.

Another important factor in favour of English law is its impression of neutrality. English law is valued as being neutral in two different but linked ways. First, neutral means the law of a third country not connected to either of the contracting parties. Parties often prefer their own contract law, but failing that a neutral law (ideally with which both parties are familiar). Secondly, some parties associate neutral with a perception of a contract law that is fair and unbiased between contracting partners which is perceived to be a feature of English contract law. The forum itself also influences choice of law. Many parties coordinate choice of forum with choice of law. The popularity of the English Commercial Court as a venue for international litigation accordingly also contributes to parties deciding to choose English law.

All of these factors have contributed historically to the popularity of English law as a chosen applicable law. And having become so widely used, this choice tends to become locked in for a number of reasons. Familiarity with a legal system is attractive for businesses. It enables businesses to be efficient as it saves research and information costs. Once a business has chosen English law there will be an incentive to continue to do so.[69]

Furthermore, network effects occur when the value of a good depends on the quantity of users of the specific or compatible good (for example, use of social networks such as Facebook). Because English law is chosen so regularly, lawyers and employees of a

[64] ibid. See also G Moser, 'Parties' preferences in international sales contracts: an empirical analysis of the choice of law' (2015) 20 *Uniform Law Review* 20 19.

[65] ibid (Moser) questions 1 and 2.

[66] Text to n 51 above.

[67] Moser (n 64) question 2 referring to the importance of freedom of contract; question 3 indicating that mandatory provisions are a factor which discourages the choice of that law; and question 5 identifying the importance of flexibility to design the contract.

[68] ibid question 2.

[69] A different example of very strong path-dependence is Delaware's dominance in seat of incorporation. There were competitor jurisdictions in the nineteenth and early twentieth centuries but, once Delaware came out ahead, its success has become self-perpetuated. More than 50% of all publicly traded companies in the US, including 64% of the Fortune 500, have chosen Delaware as their legal home: see M Hemraj, 'The US corporations' preference to incorporate in Delaware: the search for justification' (2016) *Company Lawyer* 256.

company are familiar with that law and it will reduce transaction costs to continue to choose the same law. This is even more so when a business can use the same contract with multiple parties and in string contracts. This means that a supplier that establishes itself first on the market and establishes a large network has a first mover advantage.

B. CISG

By contrast, the UK has chosen not to implement CISG, partly for reasons of lack of enthusiasm,[70] and partly because of concerns about undermining English law's position in the field of international sales. It appears that the arguments made are either that the CISG is too similar to English law (in function and in some provisions), and will thus detract from the use of English law in international sales, or that it is too different from English law.[71] This latter 'disadvantage' can, of course, be overcome by contracting out of the CISG and into the (background) English law, but the extent that this needs to be done can be seen as a reason for the UK not to ratify the Convention on the grounds of 'if it ain't broke don't fix it'. The counterargument is that the CISG represents the international market standard, and so should be part of English law, if this can be made to work with the needs of international commerce.[72] After all, it has become part of the domestic law of other common law countries including Australia without, seemingly, major problems.

However, the question arises whether the CISG does in fact represent the international market standard has been examined in a number of empirical studies investigating whether, and sometimes why, parties exclude the CISG in its entirety.[73] Many of the studies involve surveys of practitioners and other stakeholders in various jurisdictions, and the answers could be seen as somewhat self-selecting. The most pessimistic study, from the point of view of the use of the CISG, was performed by John Coyle in Canada and the US, where he looked at actual international sale contracts entered into by public companies and concluded that virtually all these contracts expressly excluded the CISG.[74] The two biggest and most global surveys were the Global Sales Law Survey in 2009, carried out with support from UNCITRAL, which produced 640 responses from 88 jurisdictions, and the Global Empirical Survey on Choice of Law carried out by Moser in 2014, which had 228 responses from 93 jurisdictions.[75] Moser's survey included detailed questions on the reasons for choice of law, which inform the following discussion.

The Global Sales Law Survey found that, of lawyers from Contracting States who answered the survey, 13 per cent said they regularly excluded the CISG and 32 per cent

[70] S Moss, 'Why the United Kingdom has not ratified the CISG' (2020) 25 *Journal of Law and Commerce* 483.

[71] For an overview of the arguments, see S Nikolova, 'The UK's ratification of the CISG – an Old Debate or a New Hope for the Economy of the UK in its way out of the Recession: the potential impact of the CISG on UK's SME' (2012) 3 *Pace International Law Review* 69, 85.

[72] Hayward, Zeller and, Andersen (n 28) 607.

[73] See the summary of these studies in I Schwenzer and G Menoz, *Global Sales and Contract Law*, 2nd edn (Oxford, Oxford University Press, 2022) ch 5.

[74] JF Coyle, 'The Role of the CISG in US Contract Practice: An Empirical Study' (2016) 38 *University of Pennsylvania Journal of International Law* 195; JF Coyle, 'The Role of the CISG in Canadian Contract Practice: An Empirical Study' (2019) 38 *Journal of Law and Commerce* 65.

[75] See Moser (n 64).

said they sometimes did so, while those from non-Contracting States (who presumably did not have to exclude the CISG at all unless the law of a Contracting State was chosen to govern the contract) said that 19 per cent always excluded it and around 36 per cent did so sometimes.[76] Moser found that 33 per cent of respondents opted out. Although many gave reasons, 43 per cent did not.

The general view, particularly among US commentators, is that one of the main reasons for excluding the CISG is unfamiliarity with it, as opposed to familiarity with the chosen domestic law. It is assumed that parties (and their lawyers) inherently prefer their own domestic law,[77] and that the effort needed to become familiar with the CISG is seen as too great a transaction cost compared to the benefits.[78] The discussion centres on legal education, and the usefulness of the vis moot in this regard.

While Moser's findings are largely consistent with this, he also lists some other interesting reasons given by respondents, the most frequent and significant are discussed here. First, there was a concern that the CISG did not fit with existing precedents or standard forms. As already discussed, the fact that the CISG is a set of default rules does not necessarily make this a problem, but it would increase transaction costs (at least unless there were enough repeat transactions to make the effort worthwhile) and it could cause uncertainty if a standard form (whether that of a party or a trade association) was based on a particular national law. While Moser does not discuss this, if the standard form is based on English law, this could be a reason for retaining that law, for the reasons already given. Second, there was a concern that even if the CISG applied a background law would be needed as well. This, therefore, militated in favour of a familiar background law applying in its entirety. Third, there was a concern that the CISG, although nominally uniform law, has been interpreted in different ways in different states, and so lacked predictability (compared to litigation in a domestic court). Other studies have reported a 'homeward trend' in the interpretation of the CISG.[79] This point would undermine the 'certainty' advantage of a set of default rules, as well as the harmonisation advantage. Disparate interpretation was less of a concern where disputes were to be arbitrated, since arbitrators who were CISG experts could be chosen.[80]

In contrast the view already set out in relation to English law, the CISG is not necessarily seen as neutral, but as buyer-friendly. Thus Moser found that some respondents

[76] Schwenzer and Menoz (n 73) para 5.19.

[77] Given that the parties are, by definition, from different states, party preference for domestic law does not explain why one domestic law is chosen over another, although the US jurisprudence largely seems to assume that the law of a US state will be chosen to replace the CISG.

[78] See RA Brand, 'The CISG: Applicable Law and Applicable Forums' (2020) 38 *Journal of Law and Commerce* 137, 141; Schwenzer and Menoz (n 73) para 5.14, who suggest that the unfamiliarity is particularly the case in common law countries. For a discussion of surveys on the familiarity of US lawyers with the CISG see C Arlota and B McCall, 'When Federal Law Goes Unnoticed: Assessing the CISG's Applicability Across U.S. Courts Based on an Empirical Research of Decisions from 1988 to 2020' (2023) 60 *American Business Law Journal* 541, 560–64 referring to PL Fitzgerald, 'The International Contracting Practices Survey Project: An Empirical Study of the Value and Utility of the United Nation's Convention on the International Sale of Goods (CISG) and the UNIDROIT Principles of International Commercial Contracts to Practitioners, Jurists, and Legal Academics in the United States' (2009) 27 *Journal of Law and Commerce* 1, 6–25.

[79] Schwenzer and Menoz (n 73) paras 5.50–52 and the cases and literature cited there. The homeward trend is said to be particularly marked in common law countries.

[80] ibid para 5.58. There are two very extensive databases of CISG cases to which experts can have reference, available at www.iicl.law.pace.edu/cisg/cisg and www.cisg-online.org/home.

said that they sometimes chose the CISG when acting for buyers,[81] but most found the buyer-bias to be a reason to exclude it. Again, this 'imbalance' could be redressed by parties by derogating from the provisions of the CISG, but it appears to be seen to be easier to exclude the CISG and apply a national law (perhaps because of familiarity concerns).

Perhaps the most concerning response Moser found (from the point of view of proponents of the CISG) was that clients did not like the CISG because 'people exclude it'.[82] In other words, excluding the CISG has become a market standard and the positive network and reinforcing effect referred to above in relation to English law is not the case in relation to the CISG.

V. Conclusion

International commercial parties want both flexibility and certainty in relation to the law governing their transactions. This could seem contradictory, but in fact both these desires can be seen to be consistent with the existence of default rules. Flexibility is necessary, first, because a basic set of default rules on, for example, sale of goods cannot cover all the possible variations such as between types of goods, types of transactions, and the need for effective means of transporting the goods from seller to buyer. The basic rules can be modified, where necessary, by market standard forms, or by a party's own standard form (the use of the former avoids the 'battle of the forms' problem), and even these can be subject to negotiation. However, the default rules (at both levels) remain the background against which the modifications take place. Certainty, then, is achieved, first, if the applicable law enables the contract to be enforced according to its terms, and second, by the body of existing law governing the default rule background to the transaction.

English law is perceived to provide this desirable mix of flexibility and certainty, and has therefore become the 'sticky'[83] market standard, which would take a lot to displace, even though the English law default rules (the SGA) is itself regularly modified in many respects. The CISG, however, has 'stuck' the other way; that is, it is perceived as regularly excluded. If it is excluded in its entirety, the question of modifying it to deal with the specific situation of the parties (or even to overcome 'deficiencies' in its content) does not arise and so the benefits of it as a set of default rules cannot be realised. CISG optimists take the view that the way forward is to try to overcome the reasons for exclusion that can be tackled, namely, ignorance of parties and inconsistent interpretation, but it is hard to see how this alone can change the underlying perception. Arguably, it does not matter, since the point of default rules is that they can be excluded, and the fact that the CISG is there as an option (and chosen by some market participants) is sufficient to justify its existence.

[81] See also Coyle (2016) (n 74) 80.

[82] Moser (n 64) 51.

[83] Again, used in the sense that parties do not contract out even if the actual rules chosen are not always the most efficient for them; see n 63 above.

7

When it's Mandatory to be 'Reasonable': The Nature and Application of Reasonableness under the Unfair Contract Terms Act 1977

DEVON AIREY

I. Introduction

It is not always easy to determine what is 'reasonable'. What is 'reasonable' on one view may well be considered 'unreasonable' on another. Constructing a mandatory rule in commercial law on the basis of reasonableness, therefore, has its difficulties. Under the Unfair Contract Terms Act 1977 ('the Act' or UCTA), an exclusion clause in a commercial contract formed on a party's standard terms must be reasonable if it is to be relied upon. When a clause is, and is not, reasonable, however, is up for debate. Much has been said in literature and in case law about the various factors the court can (or must)[1] consider in assessing the reasonableness of such clauses. Comparatively little has been written on the underlying approach and rationale courts adopt when applying this mandatory rule. This chapter aims to fill this gap. It places at centre stage decisions of the judiciary surveying prominent cases in the House of Lords, Court of Appeal and High Court. This is for two reasons: first, this approach offers a valuable insight into how reasonableness as a fundamentally evaluative test is applied *in practice*; secondly, from such an assessment it is possible to develop a greater understanding of both the policy and principle underpinning the mandatory rule.

This chapter argues that the starting point for courts in applying reasonableness is to consider whether the parties are of equal bargaining power. Where they are, a 'non-interventionist' policy prevails whereby the courts have shown a reluctance to interfere in the terms negotiated between the parties. However, where the bargaining power is unequal, the courts adopt a 'neutral' approach, weighing up various factors to determine in whose favour the balance falls. Either way, there is no room for the use

[1] Certain factors are mandated by the Act to consider (eg, s 11(4)).

of presumptions on whether a term is reasonable. Further, criticisms that the evaluative nature of the reasonableness test leads to uncertainty are overstated. While courts are to be mindful of the fact-centred nature of the reasonableness test (which limits its precedential value), the wide body of case law developed over the (nearly) 50 years since the Act's enactment makes it possible to reason by analogy in appropriate cases. The application of the test remains one of decision, not discretion.

II. Reasonableness: Common Ground

Many components of reasonableness under the Act are uncontroversial. For example, it is common ground that a contractual term passes the Act's reasonableness test if it was fair and reasonable to include the term in the contract, considering everything the parties knew or should reasonably have contemplated when the contract was made.[2] Reasonableness is therefore assessed at the time the contract is made, not at the time (perhaps much later) when a party is in breach of duty and relies on the clause. It follows that reasonableness is not affected by the nature or seriousness of the loss or damage caused to a party, nor by the way in which the term has in fact operated or been relied on.[3] Further, if a contract term fails to satisfy the requirement of reasonableness in any respect, then it fails in all respects, however immaterial may be the respects in which it is unreasonable to the particular case before the court. This focuses the court's assessment on the potential for unfair use of a contractual term, rather than its actual use.[4] As to the burden of proof, section 11(5) requires the party relying on the contractual term to prove its reasonableness.[5]

The court will consider particular factors in its assessment of a term's reasonableness. Section 11(2) refers to guidelines set out in Schedule 2 of the Act to which a court must have regard when determining whether the term satisfies the requirement of reasonableness for the purposes of sections 6 and 7 of the Act (concerning the exclusion of certain liabilities arising under contracts for sale of goods and hire-purchase, and contracts for the supply of goods, respectively). These include: (i) the relative strength of the bargaining positions between the parties; (ii) whether the customer received an inducement to agree to the term; (iii) whether the customer knew or ought reasonably to have known of the existence and extent of the term; (iv) where the term excludes or restricts any relevant liability if some condition was not complied with, whether it

[2] UCTA, s 11(1). This test is also adopted for the Misrepresentation Act 1967, s 3.

[3] See, eg, *Skipskredittforeningen v Emperor Navigation* [1998] 1 Lloyd's Rep 66 (Com Ct) 75 (Mance J) citing *Stewart Gill Ltd v Horatio Myer & Co Ltd* [1992] QB 600 (CA) 607 (Lord Donaldson MR) ('*Stewart Gill*').

[4] See, eg, *Bacardi-Martini Beverages v Thomas Hardy Packaging Ltd* [2002] EWCA Civ 549 (Comm), [2002] 2 Lloyd's Rep 379 [26] (Tomlinson J); *Balmoral Group Ltd v Borealis (UK) Ltd* [2006] EWHC 1900 (Comm), [2006] 2 Lloyd's Rep 629 [420] (Christopher Clarke J).

[5] See also *AEG (UK) Ltd v Logic Resource Ltd* [1996] CLC 265 (CA) 278 (Hobhouse LJ); *Shah v HSBC Private Bank (UK) Ltd* [2012] EWHC 1283 (QB), [2013] 1 All ER (Comm) 72 [224]–[225] (Supperstone J). Note that this was contrary to the Law Commission's initial recommendation that the burden of proof should lie on a person challenging the reasonableness of a contractual term: Law Commission and Scottish Law Commission, *Exemption Clauses: Second Report* (Law Com No 69; Scot Law Com No 39, 1975) paras 177 and 183. This was proposed in the initial draft of the Unfair Contract Terms Bill but was reversed during its progress through Parliament.

was reasonable at the time of the contract to expect compliance; and (v) whether the goods were manufactured, processed or adapted to the special order of the customer. It is widely acknowledged that the guidelines are of general application to contractual terms subject to the reasonableness test.[6] Further, section 11(4) requires that where a term seeks to restrict liability for a specified sum of money, the court must have regard to the resources the party could expect to have available to meet the liability and how far it was open for the party to cover themselves by insurance. The list of factors is open, and a judge may consider any other factor it considers relevant.[7]

III. The Courts' Approach to Reasonableness

Despite this common ground, courts diverge in how to apply reasonableness under the Act. This is not surprising for a mandatory rule centred on an evaluative, fact-based enquiry. As the Law Commission and Scottish Law Commission's 'Second Report on Exemption Clauses' revealed, the intention was that the test would[8]

> operate flexibly; enabling account to be taken of the great variety of situations to which any general control must apply and without interfering unduly with arrangements which have long operated to the advantage of suppliers and consumers alike.

This is reflected in the general framework of the Act, which affords courts significant leeway in the application of reasonableness. The statutory test prescribes no particular approach by which the court is to assess reasonableness, other than by having regard to certain aforementioned factors (which, as already noted, is not a closed list). It is entirely open, therefore, for a court to select what it considers to be the relevant reasonableness factors, specify what they consider to be the requirements of reasonableness for that factor, in whose favour the reasonableness of a particular factor lies, and how the factors should be weighed and assessed vis-à-vis each other.

Despite this apparent flexibility in how courts may apply reasonableness, however, it is possible to distil policies and principles underpinning its application in any given case. This section examines these policies and principles by references to judgments in the House of Lords,[9] Court of Appeal and High Court.

[6] See, eg, *Flamar Interocean Ltd v Denmac Ltd* [1990] 1 Lloyd's Rep 434 (Com Ct) 438–39 (Potter J); *Stewart Gill* [1992] QB 600 (CA) 608 (Lord Donaldson MR). See also *Singer Co (UK) Ltd v Tees and Hartlepool Port Authority* [1988] 2 Lloyd's Rep 164 (Com Ct) 169 (Steyn J); *Overseas Medical Supplies Ltd v Orient Transport Services Ltd* [1999] 2 Lloyd's Rep 273 (CA) 277 (Potter LJ) ('*Overseas Medical Supplies*'); *Trustees of Ampleforth Abbey Trust v Turner and Townsend Management Ltd* [2012] EWHC 2137 (TCC), [2012] TCLR 8 [199] (HHJ Keyser QC sitting as a Judge of the High Court); *Bates v Post Office Ltd (No 3 Common Issues)* [2019] EWHC 606 (QB) [1089] (Fraser J).

[7] As is frequently cited, Potter LJ listed examples of the additional factors which the courts have considered in *Overseas Medical Supplies* [1999] 2 Lloyd's Rep 273 (CA) 276–77.

[8] *Exemption Clauses: Second Report* (n 5) para 65, specifically in the context of liability for negligence but discussed more generally. Note that contracts with persons 'dealing as consumers' used to fall under the scope of the Act until such provisions were deleted and made inapplicable following the enactment of the Consumer Rights Act 2015.

[9] There have been no decisions of the Supreme Court on the Act's reasonableness test.

A. Reasonableness in the House of Lords

In their 1988 article 'The Unfair Contract Terms Act: a decade of discretion',[10] written 10 years after the enactment of the Act, Adams and Brownsword considered the House of Lords decisions of *George Mitchell (Chesterhall) Ltd v Finney Lock Seeds Ltd*,[11] and *Photo Production Ltd v Securicor Transport Ltd*.[12] These are the only House of Lords judgments which consider the application of reasonableness under the Act and set out two distinct approaches.

In *Photo Production*, a non-interventionist approach was adopted to reasonableness. As Lord Wilberforce stated:[13]

> After this Act, in commercial matters generally, when the parties are not of unequal bargaining power, and when risks are normally borne by insurance, not only is the case for judicial intervention undemonstrated, but there is everything to be said, and this seems to have been Parliament's intention, for leaving the parties free to apportion the risks as they think fit and for respecting their decisions. At the stage of negotiation as to the consequences of a breach, there is everything to be said for allowing the parties to estimate their respective claims according to the contractual provisions they have themselves made … At the judicial stage there is still more to be said for leaving cases to be decided straightforwardly on what the parties have bargained for rather than upon analysis, which becomes progressively more refined, of decisions in other cases leading to inevitable appeals. The learned judge was able to decide this case on normal principles of contractual law within minimal citation of authority. I am sure that most commercial judges have wished to be able to do the same.

In his concurring judgment, Lord Diplock noted:[14]

> As Lord Wilberforce has pointed out, any need for … judicial distortion of the English language has been banished by Parliament having made these kind of contracts subject to the Unfair Contract Terms Act 1977. In commercial contracts negotiated between business-men capable of looking after their own interests and of deciding how risks inherent in the performance of various kinds of contract can be most economically borne (generally by insurance), it is, in my view, wrong to place a strained construction upon words in an exclusion clause which are clearly and fairly susceptible of one meaning only even after due allowance has been made for the presumption in favour of the implied primary and secondary obligations.

Two points arise from these passages. First, in their Lordships' view it was Parliament's intention to leave the parties free to set their own terms, such parties being best placed to allocate risks and look after their own interests. It follows that judges should only rarely strike down commercial exceptions as unreasonable under the Act. For Adams and Brownsword, this approach represents a 'non-intervention philosophy': their Lordships started with an inclination not to intervene in the reasonableness of the term and built from this the argument for the reasonableness of Securicor's exemption clauses by highlighting a particular presentation, on the facts of that case, of the insurance

[10] JA Adams and R Brownsword, 'The Unfair Contract Terms Act: a decade of discretion' (1988) 104 LQR 94, 102.

[11] *George Mitchell (Chesterhall) Ltd v Finney Lock Seeds Ltd* [1983] 2 AC 803 (HL) ('*George Mitchell*').

[12] *Photo Production Ltd v Securicor Transport Ltd* [1980] AC 827 (HL) ('*Photo Production*').

[13] ibid 843.

[14] ibid 851.

situation.[15] The House of Lords in *Photo Production* in effect signalled a presumption in favour of the reasonableness of exclusion clauses in commercial contracts.[16] Secondly, Lord Wilberforce endorsed a restrictive approach to the citation of authority when determining reasonableness under the Act. Trial judges undertaking assessments of reasonableness should do so 'straightforwardly on what the parties have bargained for rather than upon analysis' and with 'minimal citation of authority', thereby reducing the number of appeals.[17] Assessments should focus on determining the parties' intentions at the time of bargaining as opposed to drawing analogies with decided cases.

In *George Mitchell*, however, the House of Lords adopted a different approach to the assessment of reasonableness. As Lord Bridge held:[18]

> [I]n having regard to the various matters to which … section 11 of the Act of 1977 direct[s] attention, the court must entertain the whole range of considerations, put them in the scales on one side or the other and decide at the end of the day on which side the balance comes down. There will sometimes be room for a legitimate difference of judicial opinion as to what the answer should be, where it will be impossible to say that one view is demonstrably wrong and the other demonstrably right. It must follow, in my view, that, when asked to review such a decision on appeal, the appellate court should treat the original decision with the utmost respect and refrain from interference with it unless satisfied that it proceeded on some erroneous principle or was plainly and obviously wrong.

Unlike in *Photo Production*, the House in *George Mitchell* adopted a 'neutral' philosophy.[19] Courts are to undertake a balancing exercise of the various factors for and against reasonableness of the term and determine, ultimately, which side the balance comes down. Accordingly, there is scope for judges to differ on whether a term is or is not reasonable. There is no presumption in favour, or against, reasonableness and nor is the principle of party autonomy given any particular weight. This is borne out in *George Mitchell* itself, where the House considered the arguments for and against reasonableness of a limitation clause as finely balanced. On the one hand, the farmers knew about, and therefore consented to, the relevant terms. The price paid for the seeds was also minimal compared to that of the farmers' claim. This pointed in favour of the reasonableness of the term. On the other hand, the court considered that the seedsmen were at fault and could insure themselves against the farmers' claim, and therefore take on the risk. This pointed against the reasonableness of the term.

As to the approach that appellate courts should take to reviewing first instances decisions on reasonableness, Lord Bridge's judgment in *George Mitchell* adopts a restrictive approach. Appellate courts should treat the decisions of the lower courts with the utmost respect and only interfere if the trial judge proceeded on 'some erroneous principle' or was 'plainly and obviously wrong'.[20] This restricts appellate courts and, in so doing, militates against the overturning of first instance decisions. For Lord Bridge, the restrictive approach is an essential feature of the evaluative and fact-centred nature of

[15] ibid 102.
[16] Adams and Brownsword (n 10) 102.
[17] *Photo Production* [1980] AC 827 (HL) 843.
[18] *George Mitchell* [1983] 2 AC 803 (HL) 815–16.
[19] Adams and Brownsword (n 10) 103.
[20] *George Mitchell* [1983] 2 AC 803 (HL) 816.

the reasonableness test. Judges will differ on whether a contractual term in any given context fulfils the reasonableness requirement, and therefore their decisions are not always capable of being wholly right or wrong.

Thus, on the House of Lords' approach to the assessment of reasonableness: (1) there are a range of reasonableness factors, which reflect ideas explicitly incorporated in the UCTA guidelines and the list is not closed; (2) according to Adams and Brownsword, there is a tension between the non-interventionist philosophy of *Photo Production*, and the neutral philosophy of *George Mitchell*. The House in *Photo Production* signalled a presumption in favour of the reasonableness of exclusions in commercial contracts, whereas in *George Mitchell* the court adopted a 'neutral' philosophy in assessing whether the exclusion clause was reasonable;[21] and (3) appellate courts will only grant themselves a narrow jurisdiction in reviewing trial court rulings under the Act, and given the leeway in identifying, specifying, applying and weighing the reasonableness factors, it is hard to imagine a trial judge going so badly wrong that appellate courts would interfere.

As will be seen, these conclusions have not withstood the test of time. Further, it is doubtful whether Adams and Brownsword's non-interventionist analysis of *Photo Production* is correct. While their Lordships in that case undoubtedly demonstrate a reticence towards intervening in the parties' autonomy to contract, a presumption in favour of reasonableness does not necessarily follow. As both Lord Wilberforce's and Lord Diplock's judgments demonstrate, such a non-interventionist approach arises only if the parties are of equal bargaining power and where risks have been negotiated and allocated, normally by the provision of insurance. All such considerations (bargaining power, knowledge, negotiation of terms and insurance) are factors a court may (or sometimes must) have regard to in the assessment of reasonableness. To this end, the approaches in *Photo Production* and *George Mitchell* are not necessarily at odds. For the *Photo Production* non-interventionist approach to be engaged, the court must first satisfy itself of certain characteristics of the parties' relationship at the time of bargaining. This necessarily requires a weighing up of the merits of certain reasonableness factors, as espoused in *George Mitchell*. On this reading, there is no fundamental difference of approach between the two cases, merely a different outcome which hinges on the particular facts. This view has been recently and helpfully adopted by the Court of Appeal.

B. Reasonableness in the Court of Appeal

The House of Lords did not consider reasonableness under the Act after the 1980s. In contrast, the Court of Appeal has more recently considered the approach to reasonableness under the Act. Two examples are considered here: *Goodlife Foods Ltd v Hall Protection Ltd*;[22] and *Last Bus Ltd v Dawsongroup Bus and Coach*.[23] In the former, the court adopted a non-interventionist approach following *Photo Production* – albeit, the

[21] Adams and Brownsword (n 10) 103.
[22] *Goodlife Foods Ltd v Hall Protection Ltd* [2018] EWCA Civ 1371 ('*Goodlife*').
[23] *Last Bus Ltd v Dawsongroup Bus and Coach Ltd* [2023] EWCA Civ 1297, [2024] 2 All ER 496 ('*Last Bus*').

language of presumptions is thankfully avoided. In the latter, the court (rightly) questions the over-reliance in recent judgments of the Court of Appeal on the so-called 'trend' towards non-intervention arising from *Photo Production*. In the court's view, this analysis omits the importance of the court's assessment as to the relative bargaining power between the parties as the starting point for analysis. Such an approach also fails to consider the '*obvious rationale*' of the Act, which is to control the use of standard terms which, in certain contexts, by their very nature creates disparities in bargaining power and are therefore unreasonable.

i. Goodlife Foods Ltd v Hall Fire Protection Ltd

In *Goodlife*, the defendant (Hall Fire) had 10 years previously supplied a fire suppression system to protect the claimant's factory. Following a fire, the claimant brought a claim in negligence alleging that the system could have operated to stop the fire spreading, but was defective. The defendant relied on an exclusion clause (clause 11) in its standard terms, the reasonableness of which was considered as a preliminary issue. Davies J concluded that clause 11 was reasonable, thereby finding in Hall Fire's favour. The Court of Appeal upheld Davies J's decision, an important factor being that both parties had full insurance (the claim being brought by subrogated insurers).

In so doing, the Court of Appeal unequivocally adopted *George Mitchell* as the correct approach to be taken by appellate courts to first instance decisions: such decisions are to be treated with the utmost respect. Interference should be limited to circumstances where the judge made an error in principle or was plainly wrong.[24] To determine whether Davies J was plainly wrong or erred in principle in finding clause 11 to be reasonable, the 'starting point' for analysis was the judgment of Lord Diplock in *Photo Production*. It was a basic principle of the common law of contract that parties are free to determine for themselves what primary obligations they will accept,[25] as also demonstrated by the Court of Appeal in *Granville Oil & Chemicals Ltd v Davis Turner & Co Ltd*,[26] and *Watford Electronics Ltd v Sanderson CFL Ltd*.[27] The Court of Appeal, cited the judgment of Chadwick LJ in *Watford*, who noted:[28]

> Where experienced businessmen representing substantial companies of equal bargaining power negotiate an agreement, they may be taken to have had regard to matters known to them. They should, in my view, be taken to be the best judge of the commercial fairness of the agreement which they have made; including the fairness of each of the terms in the agreement. They should be taken to be the best judge on the question whether the terms of the agreement are reasonable. The court should not assume that either is likely to commit his company to an agreement which he thinks is unfair, or which he thinks includes unreasonable terms. Unless satisfied that one party has, in effect, taken unfair advantage of the other – or that a term is so unreasonable that it cannot properly have been understood or considered – the court should not interfere.

[24] *Goodlife* [2018] EWCA Civ 1371 [28] (Coulson LJ) and [105]–[106] (Gross LJ).
[25] ibid [61] (Coulson LJ) referring to *Photo Production* [1980] AC 827 (HL) 848 (Lord Diplock).
[26] *Granville Oil & Chemicals Ltd v Davis Turner & Co Ltd* [2003] 2 Lloyd's Rep 356.
[27] *Watford Electronics Ltd v Sanderson CFL Ltd* [2001] EWCA Civ 317 ('*Watford*').
[28] ibid [55] cited in *Goodlife* [2018] EWCA Civ 1371 [63] (Coulson LJ).

The Court of Appeal noted that, following *Photo Production*, there was a trend in UCTA cases to uphold freely agreed exclusion clauses, particularly if the other party could have contracted elsewhere and has, or was warned to obtain, effective insurance cover.[29] It followed that, as Gross LJ noted in his concurring judgment, where reasonableness is considered in the context of commercial contracts between broadly equal bargaining power, principles of party autonomy and freedom of contract 'remain potent'.[30]

The Court of Appeal considered that there was no basis upon which Davies J had erred in principle and he was not plainly wrong in his determination that clause 11 was reasonable. Goodlife could have gone elsewhere and entered into a contract with another supplier but without clause 11 (such a factor being specifically featured at Schedule 2, paragraph (b) of the Act) and the availability of insurance to the parties, which the court considered to be a 'critical factor' in Hall Fire's favour.[31] Further, Davies J had not 'erred in principle'; Goodlife's submission that clause 11 did not satisfy the requirement of reasonableness because it undermined Hall Fire's 'core obligation' under the contract, namely the provision of a proper fire suppression system, ran counter to the tenor of the observations in *Photo Production* that the parties are free to apportion risks and incur obligations, as they think fit (subject only to satisfying the requirement of reasonableness), and therefore was rejected. Overall, this was a commercial contract between parties of broadly equal bargaining power such that 'the Court should be slow to intervene in such a case, all the more so on an appeal'.[32]

Several observations can be made. First, while both *George Mitchell* and *Photo Production* are deemed 'correct approaches' by the Court of Appeal in *Goodlife* to determining the reasonableness of a contractual term, they serve different functions. *George Mitchell* is treated as authority for the restrictive approach appellate courts should adopt to reviewing first instance decisions on reasonableness. Lord Bridge's warning in *George Mitchell* regarding interference with first instance decisions unless the judge is 'plainly wrong' or 'erred in principle' weighs heavily in the judgments of Coulson and Gross LJJ.[33] This left the Court of Appeal very reluctant to interfere with Davies J's judgment unless there was a significant basis for doing so (which it considered there was not).

Secondly, the Court of Appeal considered that *Photo Production* was the correct approach to assessing whether clause 11 was reasonable. The principles arising from it (namely, of not interfering where the parties have agreed freely to the contract's terms) are to be treated as the 'starting point' for analysis.[34] Although a 'presumption' of reasonableness is not expressly referred to, Coulson LJ's reliance in particular on the passage in *Watford* lends weight towards Adams and Brownsword's analysis of *Photo Production*: the parties should be considered to have agreed to reasonable terms unless the evidence

[29] ibid (*Goodlife*) [93] (Coulson LJ).
[30] ibid [103] (Coulson LJ).
[31] ibid [64]–[67] and [76]–[83] (Coulson LJ). As Gross LJ concluded, agreeing with Coulson LJ at [109(v)]: 'on any view, the reference to insurance in clause 11 made Hall Fire's exclusion of liability abundantly plain while leaving it open to Goodlife to obtain its own insurance or contract on a different and more expensive basis if Hall Fire was requested to obtain insurance on Goodlife's behalf'.
[32] ibid [109(vii)] (Gross LJ).
[33] ibid [28], [44] (Coulson LJ) and [105] (Gross LJ).
[34] ibid [61].

suggests that one party took unfair advantage over the other.[35] Such a presumption may also be inferred from Gross LJ's judgment, where *Photo Production* is readily invoked as a reason for dismissing Goodlife's submission that clause 11 was unreasonable because it undermined Hall Fire's 'core obligation' under the contract. Gross LJ considered such a submission to run 'counter to the tenor' of *Photo Production* that parties are free to apportion risks and incur obligations, such principles being 'subject only to' satisfying the reasonableness test.[36]

On the other hand, the Court of Appeal never refers to the use of a presumption, nor (for the reasons already given) does this bear out in its analysis of the reasonableness of clause 11. Despite referring to *Photo Production* as the starting point, Coulson LJ in fact proceeds to consider each of the factors listed in Schedule 2 of the Act and their relevance, if any, to the dispute.[37] For example, the submissions made in favour and against the factor of insurance are carefully balanced.[38] The assessment is neutral like *George Mitchell* and reasonableness is not presumed on the basis of the court's reluctance to interfere with terms agreed between the parties. Further, insofar as the Court of Appeal considers *Photo Production*, it is referred to simply as another relevant factor for consideration, namely the extent to which the terms were freely agreed. As with other factors, the court considers on balance that this supports the finding that clause 11 was reasonable.[39] It is not the starting point from which a non-interventionist approach is adopted or a presumption in favour of reasonableness derives.

The judgment is therefore confusing. On the one hand, it emphasises the (misconceived) trend in the case law that the starting point for analysis is *Photo Production* and its non-interventionist philosophy. On the other hand, the court engages in a detailed analysis of the various reasonableness factors, where the court's reticence to intervene is one factor to be considered in the balance amongst other factors, such as insurance. This is more reflective of the *George Mitchell* neutral philosophy whereby the starting point is in fact to undertake a detailed assessment of various factors, and the weight to be afforded to such factors, in the circumstances of the case.

ii. Last Bus Ltd v Dawsongroup Bus and Coach Ltd

The more recent decision of the Court of Appeal in *Last Bus* departs from the approach adopted in *Goodlife*. In particular, it challenges the reliance placed on *Photo Production* and the view that the court should be slow to interfere. It is a welcome development. It serves to clarify and correct the application of *Photo Production* to determinations of a term's reasonableness. In particular, it emphasises that the relative bargaining position of the parties is a vital first step courts should consider when determining the reasonableness of a contractual term; and, though the question of reasonableness remains one of fact, courts should not shy away from relying on precedent where appropriate to do so and where strong parallels can be drawn.

[35] Text to n 28 above.
[36] *Goodlife* [2018] EWCA Civ 1371 [109].
[37] ibid [73] (Coulson LJ).
[38] ibid [76]–[83] (Coulson LJ).
[39] ibid [88] (Coulson LJ).

The relevant facts are as follows: the claimant (Last Bus) entered into hire purchase agreements with the defendant (Dawson) for coaches. The agreements, on Dawson's standard terms, contained a clause purporting to exclude the statutorily implied term that the hired goods would be of satisfactory quality. Last Bus had also entered into contracts with the supplier of the vehicles, Evobus, which envisaged that Last Bus might finance the purchase through hire purchase and similarly contained exclusion of liability clauses. Subsequently, Last Bus faced issues with the coaches. Four of the coaches suffered fires, and Last Bus alleged that three of those fires were caused by defective cooling systems, amongst other problems. Last Bus commenced proceedings against both Dawson and the supplier, claiming damages and asserting that the exclusion clause in the hire purchase agreements did not satisfy the requirement of reasonableness. Dawson applied for summary judgment, asserting that the claim need not proceed to trial as the exclusion clause was reasonable.

At first instance, Andrew Baker J granted summary judgment. Referring to the Court of Appeal judgments following *Photo Production* including *Goodlife*, Andrew Baker J noted:[40]

> The more recent authorities on UCTA in the Court of Appeal show a marked reluctance to interfere, by concluding that an exclusion clause has not been shown to satisfy the requirement of reasonableness, in substantial transactions entered into by parties of equal bargaining strength …

Having noted this trend, Andrew Baker J held that: (i) there was no inequality of bargaining power between Last Bus and Dawson; (ii) any hire purchase terms available in the market would have come with a similar exclusion; and (iii) Last Bus ought reasonably to have known of the existence and extent of the exclusion clause given previous dealings with Dawson.[41] Given the 'marked reluctance' demonstrated by the case law to interfere, none of the factors raised by Last Bus merited a finding that the exclusion clause was unreasonable. There was therefore no real prospect of Last Bus resisting Dawson's argument that the exclusion clause was fair and reasonable pursuant to the Act.[42]

In rejecting the Andrew Baker J's reasoning, the Court of Appeal directly challenged the trend in cases following *Photo Production* in favour of non-interference. The Court acknowledged Lord Wilberforce's judgment that, in commercial matters where parties are of equal bargaining power, the parties are free to apportion risk as they see fit without judicial intervention, including by way of exclusion clauses.[43] However, the obvious rationale for the Act was that customers contracting with a business on its standard terms were to be considered 'on the face of it, not to be of equal bargaining power, at least in relation to the terms of business which have not been individually negotiated'.[44]

Accordingly, the proper starting point was whether, where the claimant is contracting on the defendant's standard terms of business, the parties are on equal footing as regards those terms. In this respect, the judge's reliance on cases such as *Goodlife* was misplaced;

[40] *Last Bus Ltd v Dawsongroup Bus and Coach Ltd* [2022] EWHC 2971 (Comm) [16].
[41] ibid [35].
[42] ibid [37]–[40].
[43] *Last Bus* [2023] EWCA Civ 1297, [2024] 2 All ER 496 [18] and [45] (Phillips LJ) referring to *Photo Production* [1980] AC 827 (HL) 843.
[44] ibid (*Last Bus*) [46] (Phillips LJ).

there, the parties had negotiated not only as to price, but as to the risks reflected in the specific exclusion clauses. They were therefore cases in which the customer had been proved to be of equal bargaining power after a trial.[45] As the Court of Appeal noted:[46]

> It is perhaps not surprising that cases such as those, where commercial parties were found to be of equal bargaining strength (and particularly where they have insurance), this Court has emphasised that the bargain of the parties should generally prevail and the clause therefore held to be reasonable under UCTA. This is (and can only be) an application of the statutory reasonableness test in the circumstances of the case, with particular regard to Schedule 2(a) of UCTA. It is certainly not, as suggested by Dawson in the conclusion to its submissions, a repudiation of the application of the statute …

It followed that the judge had been wrong to approach the question of reasonableness of the exclusion clause on the basis that the parties were of equal bargaining strength, such that the 'marked reluctance to interfere' was engaged. As regards Dawson's standard terms, the parties had not been on an equal footing given Dawson would not have contracted on any other basis (in other words, without the exclusion clause) and no materially different terms were available in the market.

Further, the exclusion clause was contained in written standard terms and purported to exclude any and all liability for the quality of the coaches supplied to Last Bus, leaving Last Bus without a remedy even if it received no value at all whilst having to pay for the hire. Such clauses are prima facie unreasonable under the Act. Relying upon the judgment of *Lease Management Services Ltd v Purnell Secretarial Services Ltd*,[47] the Court of Appeal concluded that '*Purnell* makes it clear that such clauses [which deny the claimant any other remedy] are prima facie unreasonable under UCTA, an approach adopted in both *Sovereign*[48] and *Danka*[49] and which the judge should have followed in this case'.[50] The absence of evidence, at the summary judgment stage, regarding the insurance positions of the parties was also significant. The Court of Appeal suggested that if Dawson or EvoBus had insurance covering the relevant risks, this could affect the reasonableness assessment.[51]

Finally, on the question of the correct approach by appellate courts to first instance judgments, the Court of Appeal added[52]

> that the warning that this Court should be slow to interfere with a first instance judge's assessment of the reasonableness of a contract term plainly applies where the assessment was made

[45] ibid [47]–[48] (Phillips LJ).
[46] ibid [48] (Phillips LJ).
[47] *Lease Management Services Ltd v Purnell Secretarial Services Ltd* [1993] Tr LR 337 (CA).
[48] In *Sovereign Finance Ltd v Silver Crest Furniture Ltd* (1997) 16 Tr LR 370 (Com Ct) 60 Longmore J regarded himself bound by the decision in *Purnell* that an exclusion clause 'could not reasonably be relied upon by a finance company merely because the finance company had not participated in the pre-contract negotiations and had not themselves inspected the goods'. Longmore J recorded the finance company's agreements, in support of the reasonableness of the clause, that the hirer could have financed the transaction in alternative ways and should be treated as aware of such a term as it had entered other transactions with similar clauses. See also *Last Bus* [2023] EWCA Civ 1297, [2024] 2 All ER 496 [21] (Phillips LJ).
[49] In *Danka Rentals Ltd v Xi Software Ltd* [1998] Tr LR 74 (QB), the approach taken by Longmore J in *Sovereign* to the question of the reasonableness of an exclusion clause in the terms of business of a finance company was followed. See also *Last Bus* [2023] EWCA Civ 1297, [2024] 2 All ER 496 [22] (Phillips LJ).
[50] ibid (*Last Bus*) [51] (Phillips LJ).
[51] ibid [54] (Phillips LJ).
[52] ibid [56] (Phillips LJ).

> at trial on the basis of all the evidence, including oral testimony. I do not consider that it applies with the same force where there has been a summary determination, where this Court has all the materials which were before the Judge, and is asked to review a decision that is not arguable that a contract term is unreasonable. But in any event, my view that the Judge adopted the wrong approach and starting point and did not take into account crucial factors would have justified interfering even after a trial.

The judgment is a welcome clarification of how reasonableness is to apply under the Act. As the Court rightly highlights, the 'marked reluctance to interfere' approach outlined in *Photo Production* is only engaged once it is established that the parties are of equal bargaining power. Insofar as the parties are not of equal bargaining power, it is not engaged. It follows that the starting point is more nuanced. The key question for the Court must, first, be whether the parties are of equal bargaining power. Insofar as the parties are, then the *Photo Production* non-interventionist approach may be appropriate. Nonetheless, where the parties are not of equal bargaining power, it is prudent for the Court to adopt a neutral approach focusing on the various factors between the parties and undertaking a balancing exercise to determine whether the exclusion clause is reasonable or not. In either case, akin to *George Mitchell*, there is no presumption pulling in one particular direction. This approach more readily aligns with the rationale for the reasonableness test, as articulated by the Law Commissions:[53]

> [Arguments that the Act interferes with freedom of contract are] valid only to the extent that there is true freedom of contract to interfere with, and the objection has no validity where there is no real possibility of negotiating contract terms, or where a party is not expected to read a contract carefully or to understand its implications without legal advice. In our view no legislative formula can distinguish between situations where there is genuine freedom of contract and those where there is not. Only individual scrutiny of all the circumstances to take into account the strength of bargaining positions of the parties … can lead to a valid distinction. This is why a test of reasonableness is needed.

That is not to say that the test is entirely a matter of discretion,[54] for which it is difficult for parties to predict whether any given exclusion clause will be deemed reasonable. As *Last Bus* also usefully demonstrates, certain types of exclusion clauses are adopted widely across industries, and (as a matter of consistency) the court should have regard to such decisions when applying the reasonableness test. This was particularly important in *Last Bus* where the exclusion clause in question was markedly similar to that of *Purnell.* In the court's view, the Judge should have followed *Purnell*, where it was held that exclusion clauses in hire-purchase agreements where one party is left entirely without a remedy despite paying for the hire and receiving no value are *prima facie* unequal and therefore likely, without more, to be unreasonable.[55] This view is consistent with Moore-Bick LJ's observations in *Rohlig (UK) Ltd v Rock Unique Ltd* that, while in principle the question of reasonableness must be considered separately in each case because the circumstances surrounding the contract may differ from case to case, it nonetheless remains important for those engaged in commercial activity to

[53] *Exemption Clauses: Second Report* (n 5) para 67.

[54] Adams and Brownsword (n 10) argue that it is. Contrast Lord Bridge in *George Mitchell* [1983] 2 AC 803 (HL) 815: 'It may, therefore, be appropriate to consider how an original decision as to what is 'fair and reasonable' made in the application of any of these provisions should be approached … it would not be accurate to describe such a decision as an exercise of discretion.'

[55] *Last Bus* [2023] EWCA Civ 1297, [2024] 2 All ER 496 [51] (Phillips LJ).

know whether a particular clause will generally be regarded as reasonable in the context of contracts of a routine kind made by commercial parties.[56] Accordingly, while the reasonableness test is by necessity flexible and fact-dependent, it need not be characterised as wholly uncertain.

Finally, the court's observations on the role of appellate courts in reviewing first instance decisions is also worthy of note. In particular, the court draws a distinction between review of summary determinations on reasonableness, and review of determinations made at trial. For the former, Lord Bridge's reservation in *George Mitchell* that appellate courts should be slow to interfere with first instance decisions was deemed not to apply with the same force.[57] This is sensible: if the reasonableness test is principally a fact-centred inquiry of various reasonableness factors, decisions on reasonableness reached through summary determination may require closer review. This is because summary determinations are made necessarily on the basis of limited factual evidence, and the key issue for an appellate court must be whether the issue should have proceeded to trial such that factual evidence as to the reasonableness of the term can be fully considered.

C. Reasonableness in the High Court

The effect of *Last Bus* on first instance decisions on reasonableness is yet to be seen. But it would not be surprising if it is limited. The temptation to adopt a marked reluctance to interfere approach is not a prevalent feature of High Court judgments. By contrast, an assessment of the parties' bargaining strength has long been an important and prevalent factor in determining the reasonableness of a contractual term. In a number of first instance decisions, determinations on the relative bargaining power of the parties has proven influential to determinations on other reasonableness factors (such as whether the terms were consented to) and whether the risks were willingly allocated (such as with insurance). In *Ali v Abbeyfield VE Ltd*, for example, the judge concluded that one party was in a '*far stronger bargaining position*' because the other had not been legally advised and none of the terms were open for negotiation, such that they could 'not possibly have been expected to read through and understand the details of all the provisions'.[58] Accordingly, where there is evidence of inequality of bargaining power, this has on occasion pointed towards the unreasonableness of the term. The reverse is also true. Where the parties are held to have equal bargaining power, this has often pointed in favour of the reasonableness of the term.[59]

In this respect, Adams and Brownsword's analysis on *Photo Production* is not entirely misplaced. Insofar as there is equality in bargaining power, the courts have been more inclined to find the clause to be reasonable. However, this is not a matter of presumption.

[56] *Rohlig (UK) Ltd v Rock Unique Ltd* [2011] EWCA Civ 18, [2011] 2 All ER (Comm) 1161 [23] ('*Rohlig*').

[57] *Last Bus* [2023] EWCA Civ 1297, [2024] 2 All ER 496 [56] (Phillips LJ).

[58] *Ali v Abbeyfield VE Ltd* [2018] EWHC 669 (Ch) [155] (Kelyn Bacon QC sitting as a Deputy High Court Judge). See also *Peart Stevenson Associates Ltd v Holland* [2008] EWHC 1868 (QB) [106] (HHJ Seymour QC sitting as a Judge of the High Court).

[59] See, eg, *JP Morgan Chase Bank v Springwell Navigation Corp* [2008] EWHC 1186 (Comm) [605] (Gloster J) and *Raiffeisen Zentralbank Osterreich AG v Royal Bank of Scotland Plc* [2010] EWHC 1392 (Comm), [2011] 1 Lloyd's Rep 123 [322] (Moore-Bick J).

It is merely a factor weighing in favour of reasonableness. As the judge held in *Horace Holman Group Ltd v Sherwood International Group Ltd*:[60]

> In my judgment the fact that the contract was negotiated between two substantial commercial enterprises with knowledge of its terms is a factor pointing in favour of the reasonableness of the terms. However, it is no more than that. There is clearly no presumption that the terms are reasonable.

For Adams and Brownsword, this causes difficulties in the practical application of reasonableness at first instance. Such an approach, in their view, undermines certainty, which forms a central principle in commercial law.[61] However, this view overstates the issue in several respects.

First, as noted above, while determinations on reasonableness are necessarily context and fact-specific, this does not mean there is no precedential value in reasoning by analogy. Insofar as, for example, standard clauses are commonly adopted across an industry, one court's finding in respect of reasonableness can assist another. Some 50 years after the Act's enactment, and it is becoming increasingly possible to identify types of clauses and contracts for which terms are to be considered reasonable or unreasonable.

Secondly, insofar as the parties' relative bargaining power is a key factor, factors can be distilled from the case law, which point in favour of, or against, the parties having equal bargaining power. For example, mere differences in size are not determinative of the parties' bargaining strength and have been explicitly rejected as a significant factor.[62] More important to the question of the parties' relative bargaining strength is whether negotiation of the term was possible. For example, in *Bates v Post Office Ltd*,[63] the court held that the Post Office and its sub-postmasters were not of equal bargaining power because the Post Office[64]

> occupied a potentially unique position in terms of strength of position … If one wished to become a [sub-postmaster], then it was the Post Office's terms that were available, and those terms alone. There was no negotiation permitted whatsoever. The Post Office is also a sizeable and significant institution. A [sub-postmaster] is a small business person, although some may have more than one branch. The two parties are not remotely equal. In fact, they are almost uniquely unequal.

Accordingly, this pointed against the reasonableness of the term. Such factors invariably assist parties in ascertaining the likelihood on whether certain terms will be found to be reasonable.

Finally, while certainty is undoubtedly an important facet of commercial law, as noted above, the rationale for the Act was not to promote certainty. It was to introduce a legislative control mechanism for the use of standard terms, which by their very

[60] *Horace Holman Group Ltd v Sherwood International Group Ltd* [2001] 2 All ER (D) 83 (TCC).

[61] Adams and Brownsword (n 10) 95.

[62] *Allen Fabrications Ltd v ASD Ltd* [2012] EWHC 2213 (TCC) [73] (HHJ Waksman QC) noting the considerable difference in size of the parties, but observing that 'this is not simply a 'numbers' game. The fact is that both parties were and are substantial commercial entities'; he later considered their relative bargaining power in terms of negotiability as to terms and the importance of the price: ibid [75]. See also *Rohlig* [2011] EWCA Civ 18, [2011] 2 All ER (Comm) 1161 [16] (Moore-Bick LJ).

[63] *Bates v Post Office Ltd* [2019] EWHC 606 (QB).

[64] ibid [1098] (Fraser J).

nature and in certain contexts could lead to unfairness. Reasonableness was adopted as an evaluative standard to exercise that control. It follows that while general principles may be distilled from the courts' application of the test (which in turn assist parties in considering the merits of their particular case), ultimately determinations must centre on the facts before it, and the Court must be given the flexibility to consider and apply all factors deemed relevant.

IV. Concluding Thoughts

This chapter has examined the nature and application of reasonableness as a mandatory rule under the Unfair Contract Terms Act 1977. The following conclusions can be made about the reasonableness test as a mandatory rule:

(1) There is a good deal of common ground as to how the test is to be applied. In particular, it is not controversial that reasonableness is assessed at the time the contract is made and is not affected by the nature or seriousness of the loss or damage actually caused to a party. In determining reasonableness, the court should (and sometimes must) have regard to various factors (provided by the Act and in case law) but the list is not closed.

(2) When applying these factors, the underlying approach or policy to be adopted by the court has not always been clear. The House of Lords decisions in *Photo Production* and *George Mitchell* remain key authorities on the application of the test. Adams and Brownsword consider the cases to be in tension: *Photo Production*, in their view, adopts a non-interventionist philosophy giving rise to a presumption that a term is reasonable. *George Mitchell* asserts a more neutral philosophy of weighing up all the relevant reasonableness factors and determining, on balance, whether an exclusion clause is reasonable.

(3) The view that these cases are in tension, however, is misconceived and proceeds on an incorrect analysis of the judgment in *Photo Production*. In *Photo Production*, non-intervention was only considered appropriate where it was apparent that the parties were of equal bargaining power. On a closer reading of the judgment, it is evident that the correct starting point is to consider whether the parties are of equal bargaining power. Where there is equal bargaining power, a non-interventionist approach may well be appropriate. However, where there is unequal bargaining power, a neutral philosophy is adopted. This view was recently endorsed by the Court of Appeal in *Last Bus* and reflects the intention and provisions of the Act itself. It is also an approach supported by the decisions at first instance.

(4) The application of reasonableness is not one of discretion. Decisions regarding the reasonableness of common standard terms used across industries can (and should, in the view of the court in *Last Bus*) assist courts in applications of the reasonableness test. Further, the vast body of case law on reasonableness now makes it possible to identify particular factors, which assist parties in predicting the likelihood of a clause's reasonableness.

(5) Appellate courts are encouraged to be slow to intervene in first instance decisions on reasonableness, doing so only if they are plainly wrong or where the first instance

court erred in principle. Nonetheless, a distinction is to be made between summary determinations and determinations following a trial. In the former, the court will not have had the benefit of reviewing all the evidence relevant to reasonableness. Accordingly, the arguments in favour of an appellate court's reticence do not apply with the same force; an appellate court should not feel constrained in overturning summary decisions where it considers it to be necessary to have a trial on the issue of reasonableness.

8

Mandatory Statutory Rules, Consumer Contracts and (Default) Incorporation of Terms

JEANNIE MARIE PATERSON

I. Introduction

The foundational contract case law on incorporating terms in standard form contracts commonly involves consumers purchasing everyday services, such as train tickets or dry-cleaning.[1] These cases usefully illustrate the nature and scope of the requirement of consent in assuming contractual obligations. Consent is an immutable requirement of contract, expressing its defining aspirational premise. At least in one sense, the key rules on incorporation (involving signed and unsigned contracts) operate as default rules, providing formal and usually conclusive indicators of consent to contract terms, that the parties may choose not to invoke or to qualify if they do. The rules on incorporation apply to all contracts: they do not vary according to the kind of contract that has been agreed. However, the use of exceptions and qualifications allows the default rules to be adapted to different contracting contexts. In the early classic cases on exclusion clauses, we see courts using these exceptions to adapt the rules to consumer contexts. Thus, in these cases, courts use the requirement of notice in unsigned contracts to protect the expectations of consumers in obtaining the benefit of the bargain they contracted for, or compensation for its loss. More generally, the cases illustrate responses to concerns about the misuse of superior bargaining power and a curtaining of the excesses of freedom of contract, sometimes described as the tension between autonomy and welfare.[2]

The common law rules on incorporating contract terms have now been overlaid by statutory consumer protection regimes. These regimes protect consumers by limiting

[1] See text to n 35 below.

[2] See, eg, JA Adams and R Brownsword, 'The Ideologies of Contract' (1987) 7 *Legal Studies* 205. See also JM Paterson and E Bant, 'Contract and the Challenge of Consumer Protection Legislation' in TT Arvind and J Steele (eds), *Contract Law and the Legislature: Autonomy, Expectations, and the Making of Legal Doctrine* (Oxford, Hart Publishing, 2020).

the use of clauses excluding liability for statutory implied terms[3] and contract terms that are unfair,[4] as well as imposing limits on exclusions in standard form contracts more generally. However, the regimes primarily apply to contract terms.[5] Logically, they follow after the assessment as to incorporation, and thus doctrinal contractual considerations about whether the signature rule applies or whether, in the context, sufficient notice of the terms has been given, remain pertinent.

Unfortunately, questions about the interaction of contract and statute in the incorporation of onerous terms and exclusion clauses rarely come to light in ways that would create new precedent or illustrative case law. The cost of litigation means that consumer disputes do not usually end in court. Moreover, when regulatory enforcement action is brought, courts are often able to rely on legislation without raising difficult or intricate questions of incorporation. These realities lead to a tendency in scholarly discussion and textbooks towards treating consumer contracts as governed by statute, and as not raising significant questions of contract law distinct from the application of the legislation. The main focus is on commercial contracts, and consumer contracts fall in the residual category, along with family arrangements and employment contracts.[6]

However, taken to the extreme, this approach has impacts on both contract law and the application of statute. It risks restricting the scrutinised domain of contract to the law of commercial contracts. The examples used to illustrate the principles and rules of contract law affect how they are understood and applied. A close-to-exclusive focus on commercial, or business-to-business, contracts risks narrowing the understood and discussed domain of contract. It leaves out of contract law those contracts involving ordinary people, which make up by far the largest domain of contract by volume, as opposed to by value. Furthermore, it misses the opportunity to test the adaptivity and ongoing relevance of contract doctrine against changing market practices, of which consumer transactions are often at the forefront.

Conversely, the approach risks neglecting the ongoing relevance of contract law to the proper application of the legislation. As will be seen, these statutory interventions to protect consumers from over-reaching exclusion clauses and other one-sided terms presuppose the existence of a contract with identified terms. The rules of incorporation are a necessary first step in identifying the scope of the contract to be reviewed. The statutory regimes also give rise to new interpretative questions about the scope of the parties' contract, such as in identifying the main subject of the contract or assessing whether a term causes a significant imbalance in the parties' rights and obligations.

This chapter considers these matters with a focus on the default rules for identifying and incorporating contract terms and the mandatory statutory limits on exclusion clauses in consumer contracts. The chapter begins by considering the rules on incorporating

[3] See, eg, Consumer Rights Act 2015 (CRA), ss 31 and 57; Competition and Consumer Act 2010 (Cth) Sch 2 ('Australian Consumer Law') s 64.

[4] See, eg, CRA, Pt 2; Australian Consumer Law Pts 2–3. *cf* Unfair Contract Terms Act 1977, applying to business-to-business contracts where one party deals on the other's written standard terms of business; see D Airey, 'When it's Mandatory to be "Reasonable": the Nature and Application of Reasonableness under the Unfair Contract Terms Act 1977', this volume, ch 7.

[5] The unfair terms protections in the CRA extends to notices (s 61), which presumably must also be prominent to have any binding or probative effect.

[6] *Chitty on Contracts*, 35th edn (London, Sweet & Maxwell, 2023) para 1-070.

terms, their status as default rules and the overlay of mandatory statutory regimes regulating the substantive terms of consumer contracts. It moves to the ongoing interaction between general contract law and the protective statutory regime, considering incorporation, attempts by traders to define the scope of their obligations under a consumer contract, and identifying the main subject matter of the contract for the purposes of applying the unfair terms regime in the UK Consumer Rights Act 2015 (CRA). Finally, the chapter reflects on how contract law might continue properly to include consumer contracts, despite the absence of case law.

II. Setting the Scene: Common Law Doctrine and Intervening Statutory Responses to Exclusion Clauses in Consumer Contracts

The rise in the usage of standard form contracts produced, from at least the mid-nineteenth century, a wealth of case law on core contract principles and rules. The question raised was how to derive consent, the bedrock of contractual liability from prepared forms presented on a 'take it or leave it' basis. This body of case law, often centring around the so-called ticket cases, established rules making signed contracts presumptively binding,[7] while requiring reasonable notice of terms for unsigned contracts,[8] and exceptions from the default rule where the terms of the contract had been misrepresented,[9] or provided only after the contract was made.[10]

A. Identifying and Incorporating Terms

In incorporating contract terms, as with interpretation of those terms, consent to be bound is objective rather than subjective, and, moreover, formal rather than substantive. The key distinction is between signed and unsigned contracts. Parties who sign a standard form consumer contract are bound by the terms presented in that contractual document, regardless of whether they have read or understood those terms,[11] subject to exceptions such as misrepresentation.[12] The signature rule has a normative element. John Spencer suggests that English courts' approach to signature may have been based on a concern about allowing parties to escape the apparent assumption of contractual

[7] *L'Estrange v F Graucob Ltd* [1934] 2 KB 394 (CA) ('*L'Estrange*').

[8] *Parker v South Eastern Railway Co* (1877) 2 CPD 416 (CA) ('*Parker*'). See also *J Spurling Ltd v Bradshaw* [1956] 1 WLR 461 (CA) ('*Spurling*'); *Thornton v Shoe Lane Parking Ltd* [1971] 2 QB 163 (CA) ('*Thornton*').

[9] *Curtis v Chemical Cleaning and Dyeing Co* [1951] 1 KB 805 (CA) 809–10 ('*Curtis*').

[10] *Chapelton v Barry Urban District Council* [1940] 1 KB 532 (CA) ('*Chapelton*'); *Olley v Marlborough Court Hotel* [1949] 1 KB 532 (CA) ('*Olley*').

[11] *L'Estrange* [1934] 2 KB 394 (CA); *Toll (FGCT) Pty v Alphapharm Pty Ltd* [2004] HCA 52, (2004) 219 CLR 165 ('*Toll*'); *Peekay Intermark Ltd v Australia and NZ Banking Group Ltd* [2006] EWCA Civ 386, [2006] 2 Lloyd's Rep 511 [43] ('*Peekay*').

[12] *Curtis* [1951] 1 KB 805 (CA); *Lloyds Bank plc v Waterhouse* [1993] 2 FLR 97 (CA).

obligation by claiming they were unaware of the terms.[13] Thus, in *Blay v Pollard and Morris* Scrutton LJ said:[14]

> It would be very dangerous to allow a man over the age of legal infancy to escape from the legal effect of a document he has, after reading it, signed, in the absence of any express misrepresentation by the other party of that legal effect.

The signature rule also reflects the market-focused pragmatism of the law of contract. The signature rule is based on an approach workable in practice and able to facilitate the needs of commerce. In *Toll* the High Court of Australia explained the rule that signature will bind the party signing to the terms of a written contractual document by reference to the need for certainty in contracting. The Court stated that:[15]

> [I]nstruments of various kinds take their efficacy from signature or execution. Such instruments are often signed by people who have not read and understood all their terms, but who are nevertheless committed to those terms by the act of signature or execution. It is that commitment which enables third parties to assume the legal efficacy of the instrument. To undermine that assumption would cause serious mischief.

In transactions where a contractual document is not signed, the party seeking to incorporate written terms into the contract must do what would be necessary to bring those terms to the attention of a reasonable person.[16] Provided reasonable notice of the terms is given, parties may be held to have consented to those terms regardless of whether they were actually aware of or could have read and understood the terms.[17]

Again, the rule has a pragmatic element. Standard form contracts are so widely used that it would be impractical to require that contracting parties inquire into the circumstances of consent in every case. As Lindsay J explained in *Debenhams Retail plc v Customs and Excise Commissioners*:[18]

> At least as early as the introduction of railways in the second quarter of the 19th century, it became common for suppliers – there the railway companies – to contract with countless members of the public on standard terms as to which, for good and practical reasons it could not be required that the customer should have understood, agreed, read or signed some acknowledgement of them. The courts recognised the impracticality of insistence upon such an informed consensus as idem as to the existence and the language of the terms that one would properly require of an individual contract. Ticket cases were then decided in which it was not so much examined whether the particular complainant has read, understood, agreed to or signed any particular terms but where, on a more objective approach, the existence of the standard terms had been sufficiently brought to the notice of a hypothetical reasonable customer.

The otherwise harsh impact of rigidly applied signature and notice rules is tempered by the presence of exceptions. The main exceptions to these rules arise where the

[13] JR Spencer, 'Signature, Consent, and the Rule in *L'Estrange v Graucob*' (1973) 32 *CLJ* 104, 122, 122.

[14] *Blay v Pollard and Morris* [1930] 1 KB 628 (CA) 633.

[15] *Toll* [2004] HCA 52, (2004) 219 CLR 165 [47].

[16] *Parker* (1877) 2 CPD 416 (CA) 425; *Hood v Anchor Line (Henderson Brothers) Ltd* [1918] AC 837, 842, 844; *Spurling* [1956] 1 WLR 461 (CA); *McCutcheon v David MacBrayne Ltd* [1964] 1 WLR 125, 129; *Thornton* [1971] 2 QB 163, 169–70, 172–73; *Oceanic Sun Line Special Shipping Company Inc v Fay* (1988) 165 CLR 197 (HCA) 228–29 ('*Oceanic*').

[17] See, eg, *Thompson v London, Midland & Scottish Railway Co* [1930] 1 KB 41 (CA) ('*Thompson*'). See also W Barnes, 'The Objective Theory of Contracts' (2008) 76 *University of Cincinnati Law Review* 1119, 1150–54.

[18] *Debenhams Retail plc v Customs and Excise Commissioners* [2004] EWHC 1540 (Ch) [25].

terms of the contract have been misrepresented.[19] Other exceptions arise, in the case of the signature rule, where the terms did not appear to be contained in a contractual document[20] or, in the case of the notice rule, where the terms were provided only after the contract was made.[21] In the UK, it has occasionally been suggested that where a party signs under obvious pressure of time without reading the terms, they may not be bound, at least by unusual or onerous terms of which they were not given notice.[22]

Furthermore, the applicable notice must be proportionate to the significance of the term for the parties to be bound, meaning that more is required to alert the parties to be bound to the presence of unusual or onerous terms.[23] If reasonable notice of the standard terms is given, those terms will be binding, even in circumstances where parties were in fact unaware of the terms, or even where they could not have read or understood those terms. If a trader does not give sufficient notice of the terms it seeks to incorporate into its contracts, those terms will not form part of the contract between the trader and its customers. It is too late after the contract is made to insert terms.[24]

B. Incorporation as Default Rules

William Day, in this volume, has argued persuasively that certain rules of formation should be treated as contract default rules notwithstanding their role in establishing the very existence of a contract.[25] The rules used in identifying terms might also be treated as default rules. Admittedly, they are a unique manifestation of the default rule. Unlike many standard defaults, the rules of incorporation do not fill a gap in the terms of a contract as instead they identify the agreed terms. Nonetheless, they operate in a similar way. They present a presumption about the scope of the parties' contract, from which the parties may choose to depart. Provided the parties' agreement to make a contract is clearly manifested, the terms that form part of that contract will be found through the application of the incorporation rules unless the parties clearly signal otherwise. Parties benefit from the incorporation rules, which provide a relatively clear and certain mechanism for incorporating terms; they allow courts to rely on a formal manifestation of consent rather than inquiring further into the reality of consent by reference to what the actual parties said and did. If the parties do not utilise a recognised form for incorporating terms, then the court will have to consider the parties' conduct to derive their intentions in the circumstances of the case, which may be a more drawn-out process.[26]

[19] *Curtis* [1951] 1 KB 805 (CA) 809–10.

[20] See, eg, *Chapelton* [1940] 1 KB 532 (CA); *Taylor v Glasgow Corp* 1952 SC 440; *Thornton* [1971] 2 QB 163; *Grogan v Meredith Plant Hire* [1996] CLC 1127 (CA).

[21] *Olley* [1949] 1 KB 532 (CA).

[22] *Cargill International Trading Pte Ltd v Uttam Galva Steels Ltd* [2019] EWHC 476 (Comm) [89], referring to *Tilden Rent-a-Car Co v Clendenning* (1978) 83 DLR (3d) 400. See also *Ocean Chemical Transport v Exnor Craggs Ltd* [2000] 1 Lloyds Rep 446 (CA); *Amiri Flight Authority v BAE Systems Plc* [2003] EWCA Civ 1447, [2004] 1 All ER (Comm) 385, 392.

[23] *Interfoto Picture Library Ltd v Stiletto Visual Programmes Ltd* [1989] QB 433 (CA) 438, 439 ('*Interfoto*'); *O'Brien v MGN* [2001] EWCA Civ 1279 [23] ('*O'Brien*').

[24] *Oceanic* (1988) 165 CLR 197 (HCA) 228.

[25] See W Day, 'Default Rules in Contract Formation', this volume, ch 5.

[26] See, on informal contracts, *Realestate.com.au Pty Ltd v Hardingham* [2022] HCA 39, (2022) 277 CLR 115.

On Alan Swartz's taxonomy of default rules, the signature rule would appear to be an efficient problem-solving default.[27] It reduces the costs of transacting by providing a clear rule consistent with the understanding of most parties about the significance of signing a document. The exceptions are also consistent with this approach – there is no efficiency gain where the party signing is acting on incorrect information about the status of the document or the character of the terms, and that misunderstanding is induced by the conduct of the other party. The incorporation by notice rule is an information forcing default.[28] Where a party chooses not to make use of a signed document, which places responsibility for assessing the terms on the party signing, they must do what is reasonable to draw the terms to the notice of that other party.

The attraction of default rules for contracting parties lies primarily in reducing transaction costs,[29] although default rules may also be used for other purposes, such as nudging parties to more effective outcomes.[30] The effectiveness of default rules lies in them being certain so that parties can either accept or contract around them.[31] In this regard, rules have an attraction over standards. Rules have a relatively predetermined operation whereas standards rely on context and give greater interpretative discretion to courts. Default rules fulfil this function best when they are what Schwartz and Robert Scott describes as 'trans contextual'; that is, they apply across different kinds of contracts and associated contexts.[32] The default rules of incorporation meet these requirements, basing the method for incorporating primarily on the binary of signature or notice.[33] The flexibility, and ability to adapt to context, comes through the exceptions to the rules. Some exceptions are rule-based as well, namely the need for a contractual document in the signature rule or notice before formation in the notice rule. The exceptions also draw on more open textured standards, such as misrepresentation or reasonable notice. This combination of defaults and exceptions has allowed courts to use the default rules to promote fair outcomes having regard to the position of the parties.

C. Consumer Contracts and the Incorporation of Terms

Notably, many of the key cases on the incorporation of terms in standard form contracts, and the courts' development of the exceptions, have often worked to the benefit of consumers.[34] Indeed, these outcomes can be seen as courts attempting to mediate the general principle of freedom of contract with concerns about fair allocation of risk and responsibility between consumers and the party drafting the contract.

[27] A Schwartz, 'The Default Rule Paradigm and the Limits of Contract Law' (1993) 3 *Southern California Interdisciplinary Law Journal* 389, 390.

[28] ibid 391.

[29] See I Ayres and R Gertner, 'Filling Gaps in Incomplete Contracts: An Economic Theory of Default Rules' (1989) 99 *Yale Law Journal* 87.

[30] See O Bar-Gill and O Ben-Shahar, 'Rethinking Nudge: An Information-Costs Theory of Default Rules' (2021) 88 *The University of Chicago Law Review* 531; O Ben-Shahar, 'A Bargaining Power Theory of Default Rules' (2009) 109 *Columbia Law Review* 396.

[31] See also J Morgan, *Contract Law Minimalism: A Formalist Restatement of Commercial Contract Law* (Cambridge, Cambridge University Press, 2013) 91 and 99.

[32] A Schwartz and RE Scott, 'The Common Law of Contract and the Default Rule Project' (2016) 102 *Virginia Law Review* 1523, 1527–29.

[33] Terms can also be incorporated by a course of dealings, which is a more contextual assessment.

[34] *George Mitchell (Chesterhall) Ltd v Finney Seeds Ltd* [1983] QB 284 (CA) ('*George Mitchell*').

For example, in *Olley v Marlborough*,[35] a hotel guest had a fur coat taken from her room. The hotel sought to disclaim liability pursuant to a term on the back of the plaintiff's hotel room door: 'The proprietors will not hold themselves responsible for articles lost or stolen, unless handed to the manageress for safe custody.' The court held the term was not part of the contract. The contract was made at the front desk, and the term was therefore disclosed too late to be incorporated.

In *Chapelton v Barry UDC*,[36] Chapelton hired a deck chair from Barry Urban District Council for use on the beach. There was a notice on the beach next to the deck chairs stating that the deck chairs could be hired for three hours. The notice 'respectfully requested' the public to obtain tickets issued by the chair attendants. Chapelton obtained a ticket and put it in his pocket without reading it. The ticket contained a clause purporting to exclude the council's liability for personal injury caused in using the deck chair. Chapelton was injured when he sat on the chair and brought an action against the council. The council was unable to rely on the exclusion of liability. The court held the clause was not incorporated into the contract. A reasonable person would regard the ticket as nothing more than a receipt and would not expect it to contain contractual terms. Additionally, the ticket was provided after the contract was made.

In *Curtis v Chemical Cleaning and Dyeing Co*,[37] Mrs Curtis took a wedding dress to the defendant shop for dry cleaning. She was handed a 'receipt' which she was asked to sign. Mrs Curtis asked why she should sign the document and was told Chemical Cleaning would not accept liability for certain risks, including damage to beads and sequins. In fact, the document purported to exempt Chemical Cleaning from liability for any damage at all. The dress was returned with a stain and Mrs Curtis claimed damages. The English Court of Appeal considered that the defendant was not able to rely on the exemption clause to exclude its liability for the damage. The defendant's assistant had misrepresented the breadth of the exemption clause in the document and, as a result, the clause did not become part of the contract.[38] Additionally, the labelling of the signed document as a 'receipt' may have been sufficient to displace the effect of signature because Curtis might reasonably have understood the document not to contain contractual terms.[39]

These examples of the application of the exceptions to the default rules of incorporating terms favour the interests of consumers in the face of exclusions clauses that would deny them compensation for harm arising from a breach of contract. There are also examples of outcomes that are less favourable to consumers. For example, in *Thompson v London, Midland and Scottish Railway Co* the plaintiff fell when her train drew up at a station but did not align her carriage with the platform.[40] The ticket had been bought for the plaintiff by her niece. Despite being illiterate and unable to read her ticket, the plaintiff was held to be bound by a term found on the train timetable, which stated that ticket holders had no claim against the company for 'injury (fatal or otherwise) loss,

[35] *Olley* [1949] 1 KB 532 (CA).
[36] *Chapelton* [1940] 1 KB 532.
[37] *Curtis* [1951] 1 KB 805 (CA).
[38] ibid 809–10.
[39] ibid 809.
[40] *Thompson* [1930] 1 KB 41 (CA).

damage or delay however caused'.[41] Lord Denning described this case as a 'bleak winter for our law of contract'.[42]

D. Consumer Contracts and the Rise of Mandatory Statutory Protections

Ultimately, concerns about the impact of overreaching exclusion clauses on consumers were addressed by legislation using mandatory rules to protect parties to standard form contracts from overreaching exclusion clause,[43] via the Unfair Contract Terms Act 1977,[44] and subsequently, the protections for consumers in the Unfair Contract Terms Regulations 1999 and 1994, and the CRA.[45] The CRA, sections 31, 47 and 57 provide that a term in a contract to supply goods, digital content or services is not binding on the consumer to the extent that it would exclude or restrict the trader's liability arising under the terms implied by that Act.[46] Section 65 provides that a trader 'cannot by a term of a consumer contract or by a consumer notice exclude or restrict liability for death or personal injury resulting from negligence'. Section 62 provides that an unfair term of a consumer contract or notice is not binding on the consumer.[47]

Mandatory rules limiting the scope of parties' contracting power are commonly seen as a response to the abuses of bargaining power in profoundly unequal relationships, particularly between consumers and traders.[48] Dagan and Heller suggest mandatory rules in contract are further informed by the object of ensuring that 'people do not use contract – one of law's main autonomy-enhancing devices – in ways that are predictably autonomy-reducing'.[49] Exclusion clauses that take away consumers' rights to redress for breaches of contractual obligations of due care in the provision of services or the acceptable quality of goods erode the very basis of the parties' contracts. They may be presumed not to represent the genuine informed choice of consumers, and in any event, because of their impact on future rights, should not be treated as autonomy enhancing.

In the context of contractual interpretation, courts have taken Parliament's decision to enact protective legislation responding to concerns about overreaching exclusion clauses to support a more straightforward approach in determining the meaning and

[41] ibid 43.

[42] *George Mitchell* [1983] QB 284 (CA) 297.

[43] H Collins, *Regulating Contracts* (Oxford, Oxford University Press, 1999) 47–48.

[44] Following Law Commission and Scottish Law Commission, *Exemption Clauses: Second Report* (Law Com No 69; Scot Law Com No 39, 1975).

[45] Previously the Unfair Terms in Consumer Contracts Regulations 1999, replacing the Unfair Terms in Consumer Contracts Regulations 1994 (UTCCR).

[46] See CRA: for goods ss 9–17, 28, 29; digital content ss 34–37 and 41; services ss 49–52.

[47] A similar development occurred in Australia in 1974, through the consumer protection provisions in the Trade Practices Act 1974 (Cth), now the Australian Consumer Law. This legislation prohibits attempts to exclude or limit liability for failures to comply with the statutory rights of quality, or 'consumer guarantees' in that legislation (s 64) as well as containing a regime rendering void unfair terms in standard form contracts (Pts 2–3).

[48] *George Mitchell* [1983] QB 284 (CA) 298–99; R Catterwell, 'Autonomy and Institutionalism in the Law of Contract' (2022) 42 *OJLS* 1067, 1073.

[49] H Dagan and M Heller, 'The Autonomy Default Paradigm in Contract Law' (2024), available at papers.ssrn.com/sol3/papers.cfm?abstract_id=4754123.

scope of contracts outside the regime.[50] Thus, Lord Wilberforce in *Photo Production Ltd v Securicor Transport Ltd* explained:[51]

> It is significant that Parliament refrained from legislating over the whole field of contract. After this Act, in commercial matters generally, when the parties are not of unequal bargaining power, and when risks are normally borne by insurance, not only is the case for judicial intervention undemonstrated, but there is everything to be said, and this seems to have been Parliament's intention, for leaving the parties free to apportion the risks as they think fit and for respecting their decisions.

These kinds of statements direct courts to respect the contractual allocation of risk of parties of equal bargaining power rather than to use contractual devices for balancing out responsibilities. They leave open the proper approach to contracts within the protective regimes and to the question arising prior to interpretation, of identifying the terms of the contract. An extension of the reasoning might be that in the face of protective legislation applying to some kinds of exclusion clauses and some aspects of consumer contracts, there is no need for anything but a standardised approach to the application of contract rules and principles regardless of the kind of contract in question. Another interpretation would be that where the parties are of unequal bargaining power, courts should be alive to that reality in applying those rules and principles. The distinction may be more notional than real.

As we have seen, rules of incorporation allow attention to the context through the exceptions to those rules. The context of a consumer transaction will therefore remain relevant. The same point applies in interpretation. This is because the interpretation of exclusion clauses, as with other contract terms, requires ascertaining the meaning that 'the document would convey to a reasonable person'.[52] That reasonable person is, however, placed in the position of the parties. Moreover, the context and purpose of the contract are relevant to its interpretation.[53] This would suggest that the context of a consumer contract cannot entirely be ignored, and indeed is likely to be relevant to understanding the meaning given to the words used and also the characterisation of particular provisions.[54] Equally the context and status of the consumer must be relevant in determining in situations of incorporation whether for the purposes of the signature rule the document signed would reasonably be understood as a contractual document[55] and, in unsigned contracts, the salience of notice.[56]

However, the question of how courts should apply the standard rules for determining the scope and meaning of consumer contracts now rarely comes before the courts.[57]

[50] See, eg, *George Mitchell* [1983] QB 284 (CA) 296–97; *Photo Production Ltd v Securicor Transport Ltd* [1980] AC 827 (HL) 843, 851 ('*Photo Production*'); *Bank of Credit and Commerce International SA v Ali and others* [2001] UKHL 8, [2001] 2 WLR 735 [60]; *Toll* [2004] HCA 52, (2004) 219 CLR 165, 182–83. See also *Granville Oil & Chemicals Ltd v Davis Turner & Co Ltd* [2003] EWCA Civ 570, [2003] 1 All ER Comm 819 [31]; *Esso Australia Resources Ltd v Federal Commissioner of Taxation* [1999] HCA 67, (1999) 201 CLR 49 [24].

[51] *Photo Production* [1980] AC 827 (HL) 843.

[52] *Investors Compensation Scheme Ltd v West Bromwich Building Society* [1998] 1 WLR 896 (HL) 912 ('*ICS*'). See also discussion in A Robertson, 'Purposive contractual interpretation' (2019) 39 *Legal Studies* 230, 231–12.

[53] *Mount Bruce Mining Pty Ltd v Wright Prospecting Pty Ltd* [2015] HCA 37, (2015) 256 CLR 104 [46].

[54] See section III below.

[55] See, eg, *Curtis* [1951] 1 KB 805 (CA).

[56] See, eg, *Parker-Grennan v Camelot UK Lotteries Ltd* [2024] EWCA Civ 185 ('*Parker-Grennan*').

[57] But see consideration of these kinds of question in *Australian Competition and Consumer Commission v Smart Corporation Pty Ltd* [2021] FCA 347 [71]; *Australian Securities and Investments Commission v Auto*

This is because there is little ongoing litigation on consumer contracts, particularly unpacking the kind of neat and knotty contractual problems that informed earlier cases.[58] Litigation is costly. Moreover, much of the effective enforcement of consumer protection statutory protections is done by regulators, often without going to court.[59] The lack of litigation on consumer contracts in more recent times has led to an absence of examples and analysis of the demands and challenges of consumer contracts in doctrinal terms.[60] In much of the case law, consumer contracts have moved out of sight of contract law, to become creatures of statute.

It is possible that much the same approach has been taken in scholarly literature. Contract texts often discuss consumer contracts separately from commercial contracts and commonly do not inquire into the way in which the status of the consumer may affect the courts approach to the application of contract doctrine. Taken further, the combined effect of an absence of case law, a deference to consumer protection legislation as resolving concerns about inequality of bargaining power or consumer welfare, and the imperative in 'other' kinds of contracts to give effect to party autonomy, may lead to an absence of consumer contracts from discussions about contract doctrine. There may, in other words, develop a practical and conceptual divide between consumer contracts as governed by legislation and commercial contracts as the central subject of judge-made contract law.

Admittedly, this is a useful distinction because it captures the kinds of tensions contract scholars have repeatedly observed within the law of contract, particularly over the interpretation and application of exclusion clauses. Thus, Brownsword has drawn attention to the tension between 'market individualism' and 'consumer welfarism' in contract.[61] Correlating consumer contracts with welfarist concerns and then allocating them conceptually to the field of mandatory statutory rules is a way of containing this tension. Yet consumer contracts are still contracts, and importantly, consumer protection legislation is premised on them being such. Consumer contracts also form a significant proportion of the contracts that are made.[62] We should take them seriously as contracts. They are also interesting doctrinally.

There remain interesting doctrinal questions to be addressed about consumer contracts subject to statutory regimes, including about the extent to which contract

& General Insurance Company Limited [2024] FCA 272 [66]: consumer protection legislation applying to the terms of a contract apply to 'the term on its proper construction; that is, the meaning-content of the term.'

[58] There are some exceptions. See, eg, *O'Brien* [2001] EWCA Civ 1279, [1] (Hale LJ): 'It would make an excellent question in an undergraduate contract law seminar or examination. Like all good questions, it is easy to ask and difficult to answer.'

[59] See S Bright, 'Unfairness and the Consumer Contract Regulations' in A Burrows and E Peel (eds), *Contract Terms* (Oxford, Oxford University Press, 2007) 176. See also Australian Competition and Consumer Commission, *Unfair Contract Terms: Industry Report* (March 2013).

[60] But for a good example of a consumer contract raising questions of both statute and common law see *Glasser v Atay* [2023] EWHC 2539 (KB) ('*Glasser*').

[61] R Brownsword, *Contract Law: Themes for the Twenty-First Century*, 2nd edn (Oxford, Oxford University Press, 2006) 137. See also Adams and Brownsword (n 2); R Brownsword, 'Regulating Transactions: Good Faith and Fair Dealing' in G Howells and R Schulze (eds), *Modernising and Harmonising Consumer Contract Law* (Munich, Sellier European Law Publishers, 2009) 89–113; R Brownsword, 'The Law of Contract: Doctrinal Impulses, External Pressures, Future Directions' (2014) 31 *Journal of Contract Law* 73; R Catterwell, 'Autonomy and Institutionalism in the Law of Contract' (2022) 42 *OJLS* 1067, 1073; MJ Trebilcock, *The Limits of Freedom of Contract* (Boston, Harvard University Press, 1993) 164.

[62] On the significance that should be given to 'ordinary' people's contracts, see also Dagan and Heller (n 49).

principles and rules should adapt to the inequality of bargaining power and information asymmetries characterising consumer contracts. These questions require attention for the proper application of the statute, and also in developing contract doctrine. Thus, for example, in the court considered the consequences of a lump sum payment term for barristers' services being void as unfair under the Consumer Rights Act. Justice Turner held that there was no scope to allow a *quantum meruit* clam for the work done under the contract. This result arose under common law principles and the policy of the statute. Turner J held that the parties had stipulated for a lump sum payment, not a divisible contract, which precluded a *quantum meruit* claim for any work that had been done.[63] Additionally, a *quantum meruit* approach at common law was precluded by the policy of the statutory regime,[64] which should not allow parties to recover in *quantum meruit* a comparable sum excluded by the relevant term being unfair. Turner J considered that:[65]

> [I]f a quantum meruit approach were permissible in this case, it would have the potential to disincentivise traders from ensuring that the terms under which they contracted were fair. Otherwise they could opt to incorporate unfair terms in the hope that they would not be challenged but confident that there would be a safety net providing for the payment of a reasonable sum in the event that they were.

This conclusion is disputed by Rory Gregson. Gregson disputes the contractual bar on a *quantum meruit*, claiming that 'once the unfair "no refunds" term was struck out' the barristers could have been treated as earning the contract price as they performed their obligations.[66] Gregson further argues that even the protective policy of the CRA should not allow consumers to receive services for free.[67] Regardless, the case demonstrates the relevance to both statutory interpretation and contract law of engaging fully with consumer contracts as contracts.

III. Applying Contract Rules to Consumer Contracts

The presence of mandatory statutory rules applying to clauses in consumer contracts raises the relationship between those rules and the contractual defaults, such as concerning incorporation of terms, and also the possibility of insights from contract defaults informing the application of the statute.

A. Incorporating Terms

As we have seen, courts have at times used the requirement of reasonable notice of terms in unsigned contracts as a means of exercising some control over unfair terms. They have done this by focusing on the time at which the notice was provided and by holding that greater notice, such as would be 'fair and reasonable', is required to

[63] *Glasser* [2023] EWHC 2539 (KB), [71]–[75], citing *Cutter v Powell* (1795) 6 TR 320, 101 ER 573 and *Barton v Jones* [2023] UKSC 3, [2023] AC 684.
[64] *Glasser* (ibid) [76].
[65] ibid [77].
[66] R Gregson, 'All or Nothing' (2024) 83 *CLJ* 27, 29.
[67] ibid.

incorporate unusual terms.[68] Thus, at common law, unusual terms, which may also be unfair terms under the CRA, will not be incorporated into an unsigned standard form consumer contract unless consumers are given reasonable notice of those terms before the contract is made in a form that is proportionate to the significance of the term.[69]

After the passing of consumer protection statutes controlling the overreaching use of unfair terms and exclusion clauses, it may be that some common law rules reduce the opportunity to apply consumer protection legislation. For example, if a term has not been incorporated into a standard form contract between a trader and consumers, the term will not be subject to review under the unfair terms law on the ground that it is not, in fact, a term of a contract.[70] The distinction between challenging a purported term on the ground that it is not incorporated into the contract, and on grounds of unfairness under the CRA, may be of little significance to an individual consumer who does not wish to be bound by the term.[71] If the term is not incorporated into the contract between the trader and the consumer, it will not be binding on the consumer, and a challenge to the term under the CRA will be unnecessary to achieve this result.

It might be argued that if the term is one that the trader holds out as being part of its standard form contracts with consumers, then the term should be treated as such for the purposes of review under the CRA, regardless of whether the term is actually incorporated into the contract.[72] This approach, by allowing a wide range of purported terms to be reviewed for unfairness, is consistent with the consumer protection purposes of the CRA.[73] It is also arguably not overly onerous to hold a trader to its own representation about the terms that form part of its standard form contracts with consumers for the purpose of review under the CRA.[74]

However, a finding that the term was not incorporated may provide a more secure and direct protection in many cases than subjecting the term to review for unfairness, or even characterisation as an exclusion clause void as limiting liability for a breach of statutory implied terms. There is therefore no reason for courts to take a narrower approach to the relevant contract rules on incorporation so as to allow greater scope for the review of unfair terms under the CRA. In this sense, the directive not to distort doctrine from *Photo Production Ltd v Securicor Transport Ltd* remains valid even in the domain of consumer contracts.[75] That said, the context of consumer contracting should

[68] See *Interfoto* [1989] QB 433 (CA) 443; E Macdonald, 'The Duty to Give Notice of Unusual Contract Terms' (1988) *Journal of Business Law* 375.

[69] *Oceanic* (1988) 165 CLR 197 (HCA) 228.

[70] *Goodlife Foods Ltd v Hall Fire Protection Ltd* [2018] EWCA Civ 1371, (2018) 178 Con LR 1 [5] ('*Goodlife*'); *Bates v Post Office Ltd (No 3: Common Issues)* [2019] EWHC 606 (QB) [1055(1)] ('*Bates*').

[71] E Macdonald, 'The Emperor's Old Clauses: Unincorporated Clauses, Misleading Terms and the Unfair Terms in Consumer Contracts Regulations' (1999) 58 *CLJ* 413, 419.

[72] For a case where the representation of the trader was relevant in determining when the contract was made, see *Baltic Shipping Co v Dillon 'Mikhail Lermontov'* (1991) 22 NSWLR 1 (CA) 24.

[73] For recognition of the relevance of consumer protection objectives in interpreting legislation, see *Henville v Walker* [2001] HCA 52, (2001) 206 CLR 459, 489.

[74] Macdonald advocated a similar 'purposive' approach to identifying the terms that may be subject to review under the UCTL. Macdonald argued that 'it should be sufficient for the purposes of [the UTCCR] if standard clauses were intended to be used as standard terms': Macdonald (n 71) 419. It is suggested that the test should be whether the terms were held out by the trader as forming part of the standard form contract with consumers; it should not be necessary to prove intention on the part of the trader.

[75] See *Photo Production* [1980] AC 827 (HL) 843.

be a relevant factor when considering the fact of incorporation, whether by notice or signature.

One important issue arising when considering a contract made online will be to identify which of the many hyperlinked terms form the terms of that contract.[76] In the UK, it has been suggested that while a signed contractual document may incorporate standard terms contained in another document or online,[77] that will only be the case where the incorporated/online terms are clearly identified.[78] Notice may be required of onerous terms contained in those other documents or links but 'buried' in the small print.[79] But most contracts made online are not 'signed' in the traditional sense. They are either 'clickwrap' contracts, where the purchaser will have been required to click on a dialogue box that states that the purchaser agrees to the terms of the contract prepared by the seller before proceeding with the transaction, or 'browse wrap' contracts, where the purchaser is given notice of the seller's standard terms through a hypertext link displayed on the web page used to purchase the goods.[80]

In Australia, clickwrap contracts have been considered to be binding on the basis that a 'click' is akin to a signature.[81] This characterisation can be accepted where the status of 'clicking' as agreeing to terms is clearly explained and there is a direct link to the relevant terms. It is less convincing in scenarios where consumers are acting under pressures of time to secure a purchase (for example, purchasing high-demand concert tickets) or where they are faced with multiple sets of hyperlinked terms (for example, terms of service, terms of website use and privacy policies). The signature rule only applies in circumstances where the person signing should reasonably be aware they are signing a contract as opposed to something else.[82] Properly characterised, at least some click-to-consent scenarios may properly be treated as falling within this exception, on the ground that the click signals consent to the transaction – not the hyperlinks. Additionally, it may be unconvincing to treat a click as akin to a signature in cases where a consumer must click through multiple links to find the terms[83] or where it is unclear what terms are included in the click consent.[84]

[76] See also E MacDonald, 'Incorporation of Standard Terms in Website Contracting — Clicking "I Agree"' (2011) 27 *Journal of Contract Law* 198; JM Paterson, 'Consumer Contracting in the Age of the Digital Natives' (2011) 27 *Journal of Contract Law* 152.

[77] *Do-Buy 925 Ltd v National Westminster Bank plc* [2010] EWHC 2862 (QB) [92]; *Higgins & Co Lawyers v Evans* [2019] EWHC 2809 (QB), [2020] 1 WLR 141 [77].

[78] *Impala Warehousing and Logistics (Shanghai) Co Ltd v Wanxiang Resources (Singapore) Pte Ltd* [2015] EWHC 25 (Comm); *Bates* [2019] EWHC 606 (QB) [1055].

[79] *Bates* [2019] EWHC 606 (QB) [1055]; *Blu-Sky Solutions Ltd v Be Caring Ltd* [2021] EWHC 2619 (Comm), [2022] 2 All ER (Comm) 254, [99], referring to *Peekay* [2006] EWCA Civ 386, [2006] 2 Lloyd's Rep 511, [43]; *Goodlife* [2018] EWCA Civ 1371, (2018) 178 Con LR 1 [53].

[80] See generally MacDonald (n 76).

[81] See, eg, *eBay International AG v Creative Festival Entertainment Pty Ltd* [2006] FCA 1768, (2006) 170 FCR 450 (assuming a click is akin to a signature); *Surfstone Pty Ltd v Morgan Consulting Engineers Pty Ltd* [2016] QCA 213, [2017] 2 Qd R 66.

[82] *Toll* [2004] HCA 52, (2004) 219 CLR 165 [57].

[83] E Mik, 'Contracts Governing the Use of Websites' [2016] Sing JLS 70.

[84] See D Clifford and JM Paterson, 'Data Rights and Contract Law: Formation, Incorporation and Vitiating Factors' in D Clifford, KH Lau and JM Paterson (eds), *Data and Private Law* (Oxford, Hart Publishing, 2023) ch 8 discussing whether the terms of an online privacy notice should be treated as incorporated into an online consumer contract.

In the UK, *Parker-Grennan v Camelot UK Lotteries Ltd* was suggested by the Court of Appeal to be the first case considering what needs to be done to incorporate standard terms and conditions into a contract for goods or services made online where the consumer clicked agreement to terms available through a hypertext link.[85] Interestingly, the analysis proceeded on the basis that terms were incorporated not by signature but by notice.[86] This meant the trader needed to do 'what was reasonably sufficient to bring the various Terms and Conditions to the notice of [the consumer]'.[87] In the case in question, the consumer was held to have been given sufficient notice through hypertext in a context where the terms themselves were not unusual or onerous.[88] However, the court also suggested that a hypertext link to incorporate terms may not be sufficient in other scenarios, such as where a consumer was not given time to read the terms before the contract needed to be concluded or was required to click through multiple links.[89] Given many commercial contracts are now made online, this decision has wider implications beyond the 'residual' category of consumer contracts, and perhaps illustrates the commonality of issues across both categories in the digital world.

B. Scope of Liability and Notice

As already noted, statutes such as the CRA proscribe terms that purport to exclude or restrict liability arising under statutory implied terms in contracts for goods, digital content and services to consumers, as well as liability for negligence.[90] While parties cannot exclude or restrict liability, it remains possible for parties to limit the scope of the transaction undertaken. At a broad level of abstraction, there is no real distinction between excluding and defining the scope of contractual liability. Nonetheless, in practice courts recognise the distinction, and it informs drafting practices.[91] This should be a matter of substance, not form.[92] At one time, much was made of the distinction between excluding liability and settling the basis of the contract in cases under the Misrepresentation Act 1967, section 3. The distinction led to terms excluding or limiting liability for misrepresentation being subject to scrutiny for fairness while non-reliance clauses, which had much the same effect, were upheld,[93] provided they did not attempt to 'rewrite history'.[94] *First Tower Trustees Ltd v CDS (Superstores International)*

[85] *Parker-Grennan* [2024] EWCA Civ 185, [6]. Also noting that the summary of the rules for incorporation into a contract in the leading contract text, *Chitty*, predated the digital era: [3].

[86] ibid [26]–[31].

[87] ibid [31].

[88] ibid [34].

[89] ibid [47].

[90] CRA, ss 31 and 57; Australian Consumer Law, s 64.

[91] *Halsbury's Laws of England*, 5th edn (London, LexisNexis, 2019) vol 22, para 183.

[92] See JM Paterson and E Bant, 'Misrepresentation, Misleading Conduct and Statute through the Lens of Form and Substance' in A Robertson and J Goudcamp (eds), *Form and Substance in the Law of Obligations* (Oxford, Hart Publishing, 2019).

[93] *Thornbridge Ltd v Barclays Bank plc* [2015] EWHC 3430 (QB) [112]; *Barclays Bank plc v Svizera Holdings BV* [2014] EWHC 1020 (Comm), [2015] 1 All ER (Comm) 788 [61]; *Sears v Minco plc* [2016] EWHC 433 (Ch) [80]; *Marz Ltd v Bank of Scotland plc* [2017] EWHC 3618 (Ch) [260].

[94] *Raiffeisen Zentralbank Osterreich AG v The Royal Bank of Scotland Plc* [2010] EWHC 1392 (Comm), [2011] Bus LR D65 [314]. See also *JP Morgan Chase Bank v Springwell Navigation Corp* [2010] EWCA Civ 1221, [2010] 2 CLC 705 [181].

Ltd introduced a different approach, more consistent with the protective purpose of the legislation, which considered the substantive effect of the provision in question.[95] Nonetheless, the point remains that a contracting party is entitled to say 'I will do A but not B'. Exclusions of liability for reasonable care in doing A will be void under the Act. The decision not to do B cannot be so challenged in this way.

The point is also recognised by the unfair terms regime in the CRA. Section 64 provides that, provided it is 'transparent and prominent', a term of a consumer contract may not be assessed for fairness to the extent that 'it specifies the main subject matter of the contract'. By contrast, exclusion clauses are included in the grey list of terms that are likely to be unfair.[96] In *Director General of Fair Trading v First National Bank plc*,[97] Lord Bingham and Lord Steyn suggested that the categories of terms excluded from review for unfairness should be interpreted narrowly.[98] Lord Bingham explained that:[99]

> The object of the [CRA] is to protect consumers against the inclusion of unfair and prejudicial terms in standard-form contracts into which they enter, and that object would plainly be frustrated if [the exemption provisions] were so broadly interpreted as to cover any terms other than those falling squarely within it.

Lord Steyn stated that the CRA exemption of terms that relate to the main subject matter of the contract:[100]

> [M]ust be given a restrictive interpretation. Unless that is done [the exemptions] will enable the main purpose of the scheme to be frustrated by endless formalistic arguments as to whether a provision is a definitional or an exclusionary provision. Similarly, [the exemption] dealing with 'the adequacy of the price or remuneration' must be given a restrictive interpretation. After all, in a broad sense all terms of the contract are in some way related to the price or remuneration. That is not what is intended.

Additionally, terms falling within the categories identified in the grey list of the kinds of terms that may be unfair should not be treated as falling within the excluded categories.[101]

Even accepting this guidance, in some cases, difficult questions may arise as to how to distinguish between terms that define the subject matter of the contract and terms that may affect the subject matter without defining it. The category of terms that define the main subject matter of the contract and hence are exempted from review under the CRA might cover many of the terms of a standard form consumer contract. Consider, for example, a contract for the sale of furniture. Does the main subject matter only cover the specified furniture, or does it extend to the time of delivery, terms of delivery and the terms of payment (ie furniture to be delivered by the trader, on a specified date and paid

[95] *First Tower Trustees Ltd v CDS (Superstores International) Ltd* [2018] EWCA Civ 1396, [2019] 1 WLR 637 [67] and [98]. See also *Cremdean Properties v Nash* [1977] 241 EG 837 (CA) (non-reliance clauses subject to s 3 of the Misrepresentation Act 1967 as in substance they are limiting liability).

[96] CRA, Sch 2(1)–(2).

[97] *Director General of Fair Trading v First National Bank plc* [2001] UKHL 52, [2002] 1 AC 481 ('*Director General of Fair Trading*').

[98] ibid [12], [34]. See also *Office of Fair Trading v Abbey National plc* [2009] UKSC 6, [2010] 1 AC 696 [43] and [104] ('*OFT*').

[99] *Director General of Fair Trading* (n 97) [12].

[100] ibid [34].

[101] *Glaser* [2023] EWHC 2539 (KB) [36] (Turner J).

for in cash)? The issue becomes more complicated where a bundle of services are to be provided. Consider, for example, a contract for a package holiday. In such a case, is the main subject matter the holiday destination or also the transport to that destination and the tours and activities offered on arrival?

Difficult questions about the scope of the subject matter exemption may also arise in respect of exclusion or limitation clauses.[102] Such terms were clearly not intended to be exempted from review under the CRA, given that they are prominently included in the 'grey list' of terms that may be unfair.[103] However, the very purpose of exclusion clauses is to define the scope of a trader's legal obligations.[104] Moreover, many clauses that limit or exclude a trader's liability can alternatively be drafted as part of the term that sets out the subject matter of the contract.[105] Consider, for example, a contract for a holiday by train, which provides that, 'in the event of disruption to the train lines, alternative transport will be arranged'.[106] Phrased this way, the exclusion clause would not appear to form part of the main subject matter of the contract, which is a holiday by train. However, the contract might alternatively state that it is for a 'holiday by train, bus or such other forms of transport as are available'. Is the qualification on train travel now part of the term defining the main subject matter of the contract?[107] Paolissa Nebbia gives the example of a contract for a 'luxury holiday'.[108] Nebbia argues that if the contract creates an expectation that 'accommodation will be of first class standard', this expectation may be legitimate even if the contract provides that accommodation will be in a luxury hotel or 'if this is not available, in a lower class hotel'.[109]

Given the consumer protection purpose of the CRA, should the question of whether a term falls within the exemption for terms defining the main subject matter of the contract be determined by reference to the perceptions and expectations of consumers presented with the term? Certainly, the Law Commissions of England and Wales and of Scotland considered that 'it is implicit in the [unfair terms regime] that the consumer's expectations are an essential part of how "subject matter" is itself defined'.[110] The Law Commissions stated that whether a term 'relates to the definition of the subject matter depends (at least in part) on how the "deal" was presented to the consumer'.[111] Certainly in interpreting a contract the 'parties' personal characteristics and preferences' are not relevant,[112] and nor are their individual interests as compared to the overall purpose of the contract.[113] However, in seeking to ascertain the

[102] E Macdonald, *Exemption Clauses and Unfair Terms* (Haywards Heath, Tottel Publishing, 2006) 216.

[103] Australian Consumer Law, s 25; Australian Securities and Investments Commission Act 2001 (Cth), s 12BH.

[104] See generally B Coote, *Exception Clauses: Some Aspects of the Law Relating to Exception Clauses in Contracts for the Carriage, Bailment and Sale of Goods* (London, Sweet & Maxwell, 1964).

[105] See also Macdonald (n 102) 103.

[106] ibid 218.

[107] *cf* Law Commission and Scottish Law Commission, *Unfair Terms in Contracts: A Joint Consultation Paper* (Law Com CP No 166; Scot Law Com DP No 119, 2002) [3.23]; Law Commission and Scottish Law Commission, *Unfair Terms in Contracts* (Law Com No 292; Scot Law Com No 199, 2005) [3.58].

[108] P Nebbia, *Unfair Contract Terms in European Law* (Oxford, Hart Publishing, 2007) 131.

[109] ibid.

[110] Law Commission and Scottish Law Commission (2002) (n 107) [3.59].

[111] ibid [3.23] and [3.58]. See also Macdonald (n 102) 217–19.

[112] Robertson (n 52) 233.

[113] ibid 234.

meaning that would be conveyed to a reasonable person in the position of the parties,[114] the circumstances of the consumer must be relevant in determining what the contract conveys as its 'main subject matter'. The consumer, for example, may be likely to focus on the headline claims over the nuances of fine print and to take words at face value without attributing specialised or trade meanings to them.

The influence of the typical or average consumer was nonetheless doubted as relevant to the assessment of what amounts to the main subject matter of the contract under the unfair terms regime preceding the CRA in *Office of Fair Trading v Abbey National plc*.[115] However, the matter has been resolved by the statute in favour of considering the perceptions of the average consumer. The revised regime in the CRA at section 64(2) now provides that a term is only excluded from assessment for unfairness 'if it is transparent and prominent'. Under section 64(4), a term is 'prominent' if 'it is brought to the consumer's attention in such a way that an average consumer would be aware of the term'. This approach is resonant to the requirements of notice in incorporating terms, which goes to the proportionality of the efforts to bring the term to the notice of consumers to be bound, having regard to the unusual or onerous nature of the term.

The approach also affirms that there is force in the distinction between the main subject matter and an exclusion clause, which is by nature framed as an exception to the obligations rather than as defining the limits of them. In *Green v Petfre (Gibraltar) Ltd (t/a Betfred)* the court held that exclusion clauses in an online betting contract did not concern the main subject matter of the contract for the purposes of section 64 of the CRA.[116]

C. Imbalance in Unfair Terms and General Defaults

While contractual principles of construction and incorporation play a key role in determining the application of the mandatory protective provisions of the CRA, contract default rules are relevant in making the assessment as to whether a term is ineffective as unfair. The CRA section 62(4) sets out the test for an unfair term, providing:

> A term is unfair if, contrary to the requirement of good faith, it causes a significant imbalance in the parties' rights and obligations under the contract to the detriment of the consumer.

Whether the term causes an imbalance in the parties' rights and obligations under the contract may be the most straightforward aspect of the test of an unfair term. It involves a factual inquiry into whether the term is 'weighted' in favour of the trader.[117] As explained in *Director General of Fair Trading v First National Bank* by Lord Bingham, this imbalance may be found in 'the granting to the trader of a beneficial option or

[114] *ICS* [1998] 1 WLR 896, 912–13; *Pacific Carriers Ltd v BNP Paribas* [2004] HCA 35, (2004) 218 CLR 451, 461–62.

[115] *OFT* [2009] UKSC 6, [2010] 1 AC 696 [80] and [113]. Note the different approach taken in Case C-26/13 *Kásler v OTP Jelzálogbank Zrt* [2014] 2 All ER (Comm) 443 and Case C-143/13 *Matei v SC Volksbank România SA* ECLI:EU:C:2015:127 discussed in *Chitty on Contracts* (n 6) para 41-374.

[116] *Green v Petfre (Gibraltar) Ltd (t/a Betfred)* [2021] EWHC 842 (QB) [182] ('*Green*'). See also *R (ex p Donegan) v Financial Services Compensation Scheme Ltd* [2021] EWHC 760 (Admin) [143].

[117] *Director General of Fair Trading* [2001] UKHL 52, [2002] 1 AC 481 [17].

discretion or power, or by the imposing on the consumer of a disadvantageous burden or risk or duty'.[118]

The test of an unfair term under the CRA also requires an unfair term to cause a *significant* imbalance in the rights and obligations of the parties under the contract, Accordingly, having identified an imbalance in the rights and obligations of the parties arising under the contract, it must be considered whether that imbalance can be classed as 'significant'. In *Director General of Fair Trading v First National Bank*, Lord Bingham thought the requirement would be satisfied 'if a term is so weighted in favour of the trader as to tilt the parties' rights and obligations under the contract significantly in his favour'.[119]

In many cases, whether a term in a standard form contract causes a significant imbalance in the rights and obligations of the parties under the contract may be assessed by considering the extent to which the term detracts from the rights consumers would otherwise hold under the common law of contract.[120] Contract provides a range of 'default' rules governing the rights and obligations of the parties to a contract. This allocation of rights and obligations, having evolved over a long period of time under constant judicial scrutiny, may represent at least a presumptively fair balance between the rights and interests of contracting parties. The imbalance in the parties' rights and obligations caused by a term that attempts to realign the effect of common law rules may, accordingly, be significant.[121]

In *Director General of Fair Trading v First National Bank*, Lord Millett indicated some support for the relevance of the default position under the common law in determining whether a term is unfair. Lord Millett said that 'It is obviously useful to assess the impact of an impugned term on the parties' rights and obligations by comparing the effect of the contract with the term and the effect it would have without it'.[122] The Office of Fair Trading has also favoured using the common law as a reference point for what might constitute a significant imbalance in the parties' rights and obligations.[123] This approach has been confirmed by the European Court of Justice. In *Aziz*, it explained that:[124]

> [I]n order to ascertain whether a term causes a 'significant imbalance' in the parties' rights and obligations arising under the contract, to the detriment of the consumer, it must in particular be considered what rules of national law would apply in the absence of an agreement by the parties in that regard. Such a comparative analysis will enable the national court to evaluate whether and, as the case may be, to what extent, the contract places the consumer in a legal situation less favourable than that provided for by the national law in force. To that end, an assessment should also be carried out of the legal situation of that consumer having regard to the means at his disposal, under national legislation, to prevent continued use of unfair terms.

Consider, for example, a termination clause that gives the trader broad rights to terminate the contract, even in the event of a trivial breach by the consumer. In the absence

[118] ibid.

[119] ibid.

[120] C Willett, *Fairness in Consumer Contracts: The Case of Unfair Terms* (London, Routledge, 2007) 47.

[121] Office of Fair Trading, 'Unfair Contract Terms Guidance: Guidance for the Unfair Terms in Consumer Contracts Regulations 1999' (September 2008) 10.

[122] *Director General of Fair Trading* [2001] UKHL 52, [2002] 1 AC 481 [54].

[123] Office of Fair Trading (n 121) 10.

[124] Case C-415/11 *Aziz v Caixa d'Estalvis de Catalunya, Tarragona i Manresa* [2013] 3 CMLR 5 [68] ('*Aziz*').

of any countervailing factors elsewhere in the contract, this type of clause may be characterised as causing a significant imbalance in the rights and obligations of the parties under the contract. Only the trader, not the consumer, is given the right to terminate for trivial beaches of contract. The imbalance may also be characterised as 'significant'. Broad termination clauses go beyond the common law default position, under which a trader will typically only be entitled to terminate a contract in response to significant breach or a repudiation of the contract by the consumer.

The other aspect of the test of unfairness is whether a significantly imbalanced term is contrary to the requirements of 'good faith'.[125] The European Court of Justice has held that the good faith element goes to 'whether the seller or supplier, dealing fairly and equitably with the consumer, could reasonably assume that the consumer would have agreed to such a term in individual contract negotiations'.[126] This approach allows a court to consider whether the consumer should reasonably expect the term in question might be included, usually to protect the interests of the supplier,[127] or whether there was an aspect of 'unfair surprise'.[128] Consistently in *Director General of Fair Trading v First National Bank*, Lord Millett suggested that in assessing whether a term was unfair under the unfair terms regime now contained in the CRA, courts might consider:[129]

> [T]he effect of the inclusion of the term on the substance or core of the transaction; whether if it were drawn to his attention the consumer would be likely to be surprised by it; … and whether, in such cases, the party adversely affected by the inclusion of the term or his lawyer might reasonably be expected to object to its inclusion and press for its deletion.

Again, in *ParkingEye v Beavis*, the Supreme Court considered that combined factors of whether consumers might reasonably have expected the term, or conversely been surprised by it, were relevant to the test of unfairness.[130] Whittaker argues that this idea of some sort of hypothetical bargain between a reasonable consumer and the trader should not trump the clear mandate of the statutory regime to address significant imbalance in contracts that are not individually negotiated.[131] Consumers might reasonably expect that a contract for goods or services will contain some terms protecting the interests of the trader, but that does not necessarily make those terms fair. Conversely, however, highly unusual terms should be treated with greater suspicion, which is consistent with the inquiry in considering the incorporation of terms by notice.

IV. Consumer Protection and Contract Law

Contract law has an ongoing relevance to consumer contracts, and the challenges of consumer contracts have much to contribute to the general law of contract. Consumer contracts are strongly regulated by protective statutory regimes, including protections

[125] *Chitty on Contracts* (n 6) para 41-297.

[126] Case C-415/11 *Aziz* [69]. See also Joined Cases C-84/19 *Profi Credit Polska SA v QJ*, C-222/19 *BW v DR* and C-252/19 *WL v CG* [2020] OJ C378/7 [96].

[127] Willett (n 120) 49.

[128] Case C-415/11 *Aziz* [75] (Opinion of AG Kokott).

[129] *Director General of Fair Trading* [2001] UKHL 52, [2002] 1 AC 481 [54].

[130] *Parkingeye Ltd v Beavis* [2015] UKSC 67, [2016] AC 1172 [106].

[131] *Chitty on Contracts* (n 6) para 41-309.

from unfair terms and ameliorating the effect of overreaching exclusion clauses. The application of protective statutes is centrally dependent on the existence of a contract. In particular, what I have argued are the default rules of incorporation determine the scope of the contract to which the mandatory statutory provisions apply. There does not need to be any contortion of principle in this approach. The application of the rules, and even more so their exceptions, will properly be influenced by the context of the contract applying to consumers. Additionally, courts may draw on contract rules and principles in the characterisation of contract terms required by the statutory regime.

Nonetheless, one consequence of the overlay of statutory rules over consumer contracts has been a tendency in contract scholarship to treat consumer contracts as distinct from the main field of contract law. This trend is understandable, given that the thick overlay of statute requires some independent treatment of consumer contracts. It also reflects the overall paucity of new case law on consumer contracts. The application of contract law to consumer contracts is less visible than in earlier times, not because of a lack of relevance, but because the cost and time of litigation means consumer disputes are not often litigated in court. The trend may further be seen as consistent with the idea of a general law of contract applying to all contracts, rather than applying differently to different kinds of contracts.

Hugh Collins has observed that contract law is simply unable to respond to concerns about the ill effects of inequalities of bargaining power in specific kinds of contracts, because, by necessity, contract law operates at a higher level of abstraction to cover all contracts.[132] Collins argues that one of the strengths of the private law of contract developed in the nineteenth century was its level of abstraction, which permitted the regulation of a variety of contractual relationships.[133] This approach empowered parties themselves to define the terms of their contracts.[134] The commitment to this underlying philosophy also made it difficult for contract law to respond to different types of contracts without undermining its own internal logic of rules fitting to 'contract' rather than to particular types of contracts.[135] The outcome of this thinking, however, is often not to broaden the domain and purposes of contract to cover consumer protection. Instead, the fact of statutory intervention is used to hive consumer contracts off from mainstream, or commercial contracts, which become the paradigm of contract law.[136]

The difficulty with separating consumer transactions from contract law is that it narrows the domain of contract law significantly. It excludes the kind of transactions that most people are familiar with and privileges a specific kind of commercial contract where the parties are of relatively equal bargaining power or can be presumed to be so. This characterisation of contract has an impact on how the underlying purposes of contract are understood. It is easier to justify a strict view of contract premised on an objective theory of reasonable parties where ideas of 'welfarist' or 'fairness' concerns (or more accurately the relativities of the interpersonal relationship) are limited to

[132] Collins (n 43) 47–48.
[133] ibid 46.
[134] ibid 47.
[135] ibid 47–48.
[136] See S Hedley, 'Two Laws of Contract, or One?' in TT Arvind and J Steele (eds), *Contract Law and the Legislature: Autonomy, Expectations, and the Making of Legal Doctrine* (Oxford, Hart Publishing, 2020).

exceptional cases at the margins. In turn, this tendency to understand contracts as involving a particular paradigm of contractual equality may deflect attention from a more ongoing recognition that contextual considerations of information asymmetry or unequal bargaining power may necessitate a different set of assumptions in the application of contract doctrine, or even the framing of default rules and their exceptions.

Collins does provide a more nuanced view. He argues that the private law of contract continues to retain 'welfarist regulation within its normative discourse'.[137] Collins argues that 'the norms underlying the social and economic regulation', such as consumer protection statutes, have been 'fitted into vague private law doctrines that qualified freedom of contract, such as abuse of rights, unconscionability and good faith'.[138] However, these doctrines are treated as exceptional in modern contract law, narrowly confined and constrained to unusual cases. Focusing on these doctrines as the embodiment of contextual or even welfarist sentiment underestimates the inherent flexibility of core default rules, such as those surrounding the incorporation of terms. The very innovation of context, circumstances or reasonableness provides an inherent adaptivity and capacity to respond to the realities of the contractual relationship.

This then leads to the question of how to redress the balance and reaffirm the unity of contract law applying across different kinds of contracts, while being alive to the application differences in principles and rules applying to specific contracts, especially those subject to mandatory protective regimes. Of course, courts cannot develop law that is not before them, and scholars cannot comment purely on hypothetical challenges. Nonetheless, some consumer protection cases are litigated (usually when the subject matter in question is of high value).[139] Courts considering commercial contracts sometimes make reference to the different result that might apply under a consumer contract.[140] Class actions in consumer cases may also increasingly raise the profile of the unique considerations applying in these contexts.[141] Additionally, some cases involving consumers have made their way to the courts, typically where the stakes are high, such as for gambling contracts[142] or properly settlements.[143]

It is incumbent on courts and scholars in discussing general principles derived from case law to be alive to the status of the parties, and the influence that may hold on the application of those principles and rules. Conversely, it is important to take care in the application of statutory rules to interrogate the underlying contract doctrines on which those regimes commonly build. The lessons from this inquiry are important in providing an accurate reflection of the scope of the law of contract. They also may help illuminate the challenges and possible responses to the harsh effects of standard form contracts on small business parties, who may share many of the burdens of lack

[137] Collins (n 43) 49.
[138] ibid.
[139] *O'Brien* [2001] EWCA Civ 1279; *Green* [2021] EWHC 842 (QB).
[140] See, eg, *Amiri Flight Authority v BAE Systems Plc* [2003] EWCA Civ 1447; [2004] 1 All ER (Comm) 385, 392–393 [15]–[16]; *Cargill International Trading Pte Ltd v Uttam Galva Steels Ltd* [2019] EWHC 476 (Comm) [89].
[141] See, eg, *Karpik v Carnival plc* [2023] HCA 39, (2023) 280 CLR 640 (choice of law clauses); *Toyota Motor Corporation Australia Ltd v Williams* [2023] FCAFC 50 (damages).
[142] *Parker-Grennan* [2024] EWCA Civ 185.
[143] *Glaser* [2023] EWHC 2539 (KB).

of power and information seen in contracts with consumers.[144] Indeed, it may be some of the challenges of contracting online – including over incorporating terms through hypertext, hidden exclusions as well as automated and algorithmic contracts – will again raise issues common to all contracts, thus supporting the reunification of the commercial and 'residual' categories, at least for some kinds of analysis.

V. Conclusion

This chapter has considered the relationship between contract default rules and the mandatory rules introduced by consumer protection statutes in consumer contracts regulated by these statutes. It has suggested that the rules applying to incorporating terms can be considered contractual default rules. One of the attractions of default rules is that they are clear and unequivocal as well as applying across the body of contracts. This is true of incorporation rules, although courts have considerable flexibility to adapt the rules of particular contexts through the application of the exceptions to the rules. In consumer contracts, the work in readdressing inequalities of bargaining power and information that was previously done by these exceptions is now achieved through mandatory statutory regimes applying to attempts to exclude liability for breaches of statutory implied terms and limitations on unfair terms.

Contract default rules on incorporation and characterisation precede the application of the mandatory statutory regime, which underlines the point that consumer contracts remain very much part of the general law of contract, which is only impoverished by ignoring them. Mandatory statutory consumer protections applying to consumer contracts do not remove interesting questions of contract doctrine. They refocus them. They demand attention on the role of context, and the extent to which rules of incorporation and characterisation should be alive to inequalities of bargaining power and information asymmetries. Common issues in responding to the new modes of contracting in the digital age may go some way to addressing this neglect as the issues are common to both commercial contracts and the residual category that includes consumer contracts.

[144] See, eg, *Bates* [2019] EWHC 606 (QB).

9

Frustration Dissected: Mandatory and Default Rules

JONATHAN MORGAN[1]

I. Introduction

Considering contract doctrines as 'mandatory' or 'default' rules illuminates the law on frustration. This chapter contends that there is no single unified 'doctrine of frustration'.[2] It is an unhappy composite of rules with different rationales which would better be kept apart. When a contract's performance becomes *illegal* after a change in the law,[3] the obligations cease automatically as a matter of *mandatory public policy*. Contract law must necessarily contain a doctrine of 'frustration by supervening illegality'. It can hardly recognise obligations to break the law. But that rationale cannot extend to other interruptions. Consistency between different departments of the law (criminal and contract law) is immaterial to the problem of contracts that become more difficult, more expensive or uneconomic to perform. Contract law should therefore formalise a bifurcation between supervening illegality (a *mandatory* rule of public policy) and the *default* rules on 'frustration by change of circumstances' (whether impossibility, impracticability or failure of purpose – categories which remain disaggregated for the purposes of this chapter).

In those latter situations, it will be argued, contracting parties / drafters have primary responsibility to deal with interruptions, whereas the court's role is simply to enforce the agreed allocation of risk. (As with any question of interpretation, this often raises difficulties about construction and implication). It is questionable whether the courts should be any more ambitious than that. The chapter doubts their capacity to devise appropriate 'defaults' to govern changes of circumstances.[4] If the law's

[1] I would particularly like to thank Ewan McKendrick and David Foxton for their comments (and to Sir David also for lending me a copy of his PhD thesis, discussed below).

[2] W Day, 'Shades of Frustration' in E Peel and R Probart (eds), *Shaping the Law of Obligations: Essays in Honour of Professor Ewan McKendrick KC* (Oxford, Oxford University Press, 2023) 111 ('there is no such thing as "the" doctrine of frustration').

[3] Or, eg, outbreak of war triggering offences of 'trading with the enemy'.

[4] *cf* A Robertson, 'Default Rules, Interpretation and Risk Allocation', this volume, ch 3 (distinguishing default rules from 'interpretive devices' ('merely a mechanism for determining what was implicitly agreed'), and arguing that frustration is better understood as a default rule).

aim were improved economic efficiency, the necessary information is unavailable. It is equally doubtful whether excusing non-performance for reasons of fairness and justice is cogent. (Commercial law is otherwise ostentatiously uninterested in substantive fairness, just prices, etc.[5])

Nor does 'logic' necessitate an impossibility defence. On the contrary, freely excusing non-performance would be inconsistent with English contract law's fundamental premises; namely, the default strictness of contractual obligations and, in remedies, the primacy of compensation over specific relief. It is never legally impossible to pay damages, save through bankruptcy. (And, obviously, it would cut across the entire bankruptcy regime to suggest that, of itself, bankruptcy discharged all the debtor's obligations by 'frustration'.)

The common law is said[6] to have moved historically from the 'absolute contract' rule of *Paradine v Jane*,[7] through *Taylor v Caldwell's* implied term theory of excuse,[8] to frustration as judicially imposed relief for radical change of circumstances.[9] (In that leading case, Lord Radcliffe thought the implied term rationale suffered a 'logical difficulty', 'obscuring the true action of the court'.[10]) Despite the judges' longstanding and uncharacteristic preoccupation with frustration's jurisprudential basis,[11] it perhaps 'matters little which theory is avowed'.[12] Lord Wilberforce concluded that 'they shade into one another'.[13] There can be little if any practical difference between 'construction', 'implication' and Lord Radcliffe's preferred 'legal rule' when 'the crucial question must be answered … by reference to the particular contract which the parties made'.[14]

Even a professor hesitates to refight old battles so authoritatively dismissed as academic.[15] Yet this chapter argues that distinct advantages accrue from approaching 'interruption' questions through objective interpretation. They become a subset of the general and universal exercise of deciding the meaning, explicit and implicit, of contracts. It is, *pace* Lord Radcliffe, no more 'obscure' or 'illogical' than assigning objective meanings that might not have occurred to the parties, in any other context. That is a 'commonplace' matter: while doubtless 'artificial' to attribute 'an intention which [the parties] did not have (as a matter of fact)', it is nevertheless: 'an exercise which the courts have been willing to undertake for as long as commercial contracts have come before

[5] *cf mandatory consumer protection*, eg, NI Silber, 'Debts, Disasters, and Delinquencies: The case for placing a mandatory force majeure provision into consumer credit agreements' (2010) 34 *New York University Review of Law and Social Change* 760.

[6] Though this is a major over-simplification: C Jayathilaka, 'A Tale of Too Many Doctrines: Supervening Impossibility and the Sale of Goods' (2025) 88 *MLR* 433.

[7] (1646) Aleyn 26, 82 ER 897.

[8] (1863) 3 B&S 826, 122 ER 309.

[9] *Davis Contractors v Fareham UDC* [1956] AC 696.

[10] [1956] AC 696, 728.

[11] E Peel, *Frustration and Force Majeure*, 4th edn (London, Sweet & Maxwell, 2022) § 16-006 (unusual preoccupation suggests judicial anxiety about effect on sanctity of contracts).

[12] *Davis Contractors v Fareham UDC* [1956] AC 696,728 (Lord Radcliffe).

[13] *National Carriers Ltd v Panalpina (Northern) Ltd* [1981] AC 675, 693.

[14] ibid 717 (Lord Roskill).

[15] 'Academic (adj): Not leading to a decision; unpractical; strictly theoretical or formal' (OED). Even a learned civilian commentator describes debates about the juristic basis of frustration as 'theoretical ornaments': W Lorenz, 'Contract Modification as a Result of Change of Circumstances' in J Beatson and D Friedman (eds), *Good Faith and Fault in Contract Law* (Oxford, Oxford University Press, 1995) 376.

them for construction'.[16] The usual rules of construction apply, including a necessary liberality when implying terms into brief (eg, oral) agreements, and a converse reluctance to reinterpret or supplement detailed, professionally drafted written contracts.

Thus reverting to 'construction and implication' need not, and would not, license Denningesque intervention '[to] do therein what is just and reasonable'.[17] However, in one respect only, it could potentially exert a desirable liberalisation. If the rigorous test for implication of a term 'in fact' were satisfied, the court could properly find that an interruption was to *suspend* obligations, or to extinguish only *part* of the contract.[18] At the moment, the only permissible conclusion on holding a contract 'frustrated' is to order its immediate and automatic discharge. That strict rule makes obvious sense when supervening illegality prohibits performance. It is, just as obviously, quite nonsensical as a commercial response to many other interruptions. It is telling that in the only appellate English COVID-19 contract case to date, the tenants applied (unsuccessfully) for rent relief on the basis of express and implied terms in the lease (and on restitution for failure of basis) – but did *not* rely on frustration as such.[19]

For parties which desire flexibility and/or a wider category of excuses, the remedy is in their own hands. Contractual devices available include 'force majeure',[20] 'cancellation', 'frustration'[21] and 'material adverse change'[22] clauses; best-efforts standards; 'break', assignment, sub-letting and agreed-termination clauses;[23] and 'hardship', rent-review, price-adjustment, unilateral modification[24] and renegotiation clauses (or some combination of all these). Conversely, the parties may reaffirm contract law's usual strictness, and preclude any possibility of frustration applying, through an emphatic statement of the absolute nature of the relevant obligations.[25]

The chapter finishes by noting that the legislature can also intervene in a crisis. Wars and pandemics threaten systemic economic turmoil. *Mandatory*, emergency powers to modify, suspend and cancel contractual obligations may be thought expedient. Crucially, discretionary intervention under statutory powers is limited to the crisis at hand. Such legislation therefore does not affect the common law's narrow approach to 'frustration'. Indeed, the general law of contract is freed to maintain its default strictness.

[16] *Bromarin AB v IMD Investments Ltd* [1999] STC 301, 310 (Chadwick LJ).

[17] *British Movietonews v London and District Cinemas* [1951] 1 KB 190, 201.

[18] *cf* G McMeel, 'The juridical basis of frustration revisited' [2020] *Lloyd's Maritime and Commercial Law Quarterly* 297, 302 (noting 'distinctiveness of the implication technique, *especially for crafting solutions which eschew total discharge*') (emphasis added).

[19] *Bank of New York Mellon (International) Ltd v Cine-UK Ltd* [2022] EWCA Civ 1021, [2023] 2 P&CR 19 (rejecting implied term suspending rent during pandemic restrictions). *cf* E McKendrick, 'Covid, contracts and change of circumstances' [2024] *Lloyd's Maritime and Commercial Law Quarterly* 34, 41 (frustration not argued 'presumably' because tenants 'did not wish to lose the benefit of their lease for the future').

[20] eg E McKendrick, 'Force Majeure Clauses: The gap between doctrine and practice' in A Burrows and E Peel (eds), *Contract Terms* (Oxford, Oxford University Press, 2007).

[21] M Bridge, 'Force Majeure Clauses: Character, Scope and Protection' in PS Davies and Hans Tjio (eds), *Fraud and Risk in Commercial Law* (Oxford, Hart Publishing, 2024).

[22] eg AA Schwartz, 'A "standard clause analysis" of the frustration doctrine and the material adverse change clause' (2010) 57 *University of California Los Angeles Law Review* 789.

[23] *cf Canary Wharf v European Medicines Agency* [2019] EWHC 335 (Ch).

[24] SG Kahn, 'Unilateral modification clauses in long term contracts' (1986) *International Business Law Journal* 145.

[25] eg, *ACG Acquisition v Olympic Airlines SA* [2012] EWHC 1070 (Comm), [2012] 2 CLC 48; *Salam Air SAOC v Latam Airlines Group SA* [2020] EWHC 2414 (Comm), [2021] 1 CLC 795.

To reiterate: this chapter does not question the existence of frustration by supervening illegality. That mandatory rule does not depend on party intentions, express or implied.[26] Indeed, it may override them. Such illegality cases have nothing to do with other problems of changed circumstances. That these fundamentally distinct doctrines share the name 'frustration' is confusing.

II. The Mandatory Rule: Contracts Frustrated by Supervening Illegality

This is a doctrine of public policy. Its proper analogue is not the doctrine of common mistake,[27] but contracts that are illegal from the outset (such as a contract to commit a crime). As Treitel stresses, the law here is not solely concerned with justice for the contracting parties *inter se*.[28] Because the public interest can outweigh the parties' interests, 'special rules' govern this area (contrasted with all other 'frustration' cases).[29] Most strikingly, that supervening illegality may override even express risk-allocation. Also, as we discuss first, illegality explains one of the mysteries of frustration doctrine: its automatic and total effect.

The automatic, total discharge rule has been affirmed by the highest authority throughout frustration's modern history. Yet it has often been criticised. The justification for the rule is opaque. As McKendrick comments, automatic discharge was simply assumed in *Taylor v Caldwell* with 'little by way of reasoning in support of [the court's] conclusion that both parties were excused'.[30] The most emphatic statement, repeatedly approved, is Lord Sumner's: 'frustration brings the contract to an end forthwith, without more and automatically'.[31] Here too, McKendrick questions whether this 'immediate termination' is as fair or as 'necessary' as Lord Sumner claimed. We must dig beneath the leading cases' shallow reasoning to find the justification, 'if there is one', for the automatic discharge rule.[32] McKendrick argues that it suits the narrow scope of the English frustration doctrine, making sense in cases of outright impossibility (like *Taylor v Caldwell*) as well as illegality cases. But only in the latter is McKendrick's explanation, we suggest, persuasive.

When a contract is frustrated by supervening illegality, then certainly 'the automatic discharge of both parties is the simplest way to ensure that performance does not take

[26] cf *Codelfa Construction Pty Ltd v State Rail Authority (NSW)* (1982) 149 CLR 337, 380 (Aickin J) ('Normally the parties to a contract proceed upon the assumption, usually implicit rather than explicit, that the contract [performance] can be lawfully completed').

[27] *cf Great Peace Shipping Ltd v Tsavliris (International) Ltd (The Great Peace)* [2002] EWCA Civ 1407, [2003] QB 679 [61], [85].

[28] Peel (n 11) 8-003. *cf Patel v Mirza* [2016] UKSC 42, [2017] AC 467 [262 (i)] (Lord Sumption) ('Whatever rationale one adopts for the illegality principle, it is manifestly designed to vindicate the public interest as against the interests and legal rights of the parties').

[29] Peel (n 11) 8-003.

[30] E McKendrick, 'Frustration: Automatic Discharge of Both Parties?' in A Dyson, J Goudkamp and F Wilmot-Smith (eds) *Defences in Contract* (Oxford, Hart Publishing, 2017) 144.

[31] *Hirji Mulji v Cheong Yue Steamship Co* [1926] AC 497, 505.

[32] McKendrick (n 30) 152.

place and the policy of the law is upheld'.[33] Hence the rule that was already 'authoritatively laid down' by the mid-nineteenth century, that outbreak of war rendering trading with the enemy illegal 'at once [works] an absolute dissolution' of such a contract.[34] The rationale is clear: 'the presumed object of war being as much to cripple the enemy's commerce as to capture his property, a declaration of war imports a prohibition of commercial intercourse'.[35] For maximum efficacy the 'prohibition' must be immediate, total and automatic. (It also follows that substituting damages for the (illegal) primary obligation would stultify the policy: if the aim is 'to cripple the enemy's commerce' it would make no sense to compensate 'the enemy's' lost expectations).

But with other interruptions of performance, the case for automatic total discharge is typically much weaker. In *Taylor v Caldwell* perhaps, it 'recognised the practical reality of the events'.[36] The Surrey Music Hall had burned to the ground. But outright impossibility is not the only instance of 'non-illegality' frustration. Lord Wright said frustration was 'as numerous and diverse as are the possibilities of the performance of a contract being interrupted' (necessitating 'A certain elasticity').[37] The variability of interrupted performance sits ill with the stringent and undifferentiated *effect* of frustration. As Bridge observes:

> [T]he case for automatic frustration appears to hinge on the futility of further performance and to presuppose therefore the application of frustration only in extreme circumstances. There are, nevertheless, numerous cases of impossibility of performance that do not necessarily strike at the root of the contract … These cases, orphaned by the rule of automatic frustration … may be referred to as instances of excused non-performance and concern temporary or partial impossibility. A rule of automatic discharge … consigns these cases to a sort of no-man's land.[38]

Supervening illegality apart, it is unclear why English law seems so strongly committed to automatic discharge. It appears inconsistent with its judicial champions' other pronouncements. Frustration's *flexibility* was central to Lord Wright's decision in *Joseph Constantine v Imperial Smelting*.[39] Yet Lord Wright also influentially approved Lord Sumner's *inflexible* theory of frustration's effect.[40] The contradiction is hard to understand. Lord Wright even explained why automatic discharge is unlikely to reflect what the contracting parties expected to happen. It is equally incompatible with the 'justice' explanation of frustration – also advocated by both Lords Sumner and Wright. These points require further explanation.

Lord Wright explained that a court decides 'not what the parties actually intended, but what as reasonable men they should have intended', given the drastic change of

[33] ibid 154.

[34] *Esposito v Bowden* (1857) 7 Ellis & Blackburn 763, 792; 119 ER 1430, 1440 (Willes J). *cf* Manisty, *arguendo*, *Esposito v Bowden* (1857) LJ (QB) 17, 19: 'The mere declaration of war does not rescind the contract. It only suspends it.'

[35] *Esposito v Bowden* (1857) 7 Ellis & Blackburn 763, 779; 119 ER 1430, 1436 (Willes J).

[36] McKendrick (n 30) 153.

[37] *Denny Mott & Dickson v James B Fraser* [1944] AC 265, 274.

[38] MG Bridge, 'Frustration and excused non-performance' (2021) 137 *LQR* 580, 589.

[39] [1942] AC 154.

[40] *Joseph Constantine v Imperial Smelting* [1942] AC 154, 187 (also *Denny Mott & Dickson v James B Fraser* [1944] AC 265, 274).

circumstances.[41] Yet he also rejected the idea that all-or-nothing discharge reflects these notional 'intentions'. The court cannot assume that

> if they had thought of [the interrupting event, the contracting parties] would have said: 'Well, if that happens, all is over between us'. On the contrary, they would almost certainly on the one side or the other have sought to introduce reservations or qualifications or compensations. As to that the court cannot guess. What it can say is that the contract either binds or does not bind.[42]

Analysis of commonly agreed clauses supports this prediction. *Force majeure* clauses usually provide for *suspension or adjustment* of obligations (ie, Lord Wright's 'reservations, qualifications or compensations'). While sometimes contracts do include express 'cancellation' clauses (eg, the GAFTA provisions on export prohibitions), even these typically contain an initial 'grace period' of suspension before the contract is finally 'cancelled'.[43]

Extending automatic discharge beyond illegality also contradicts frustration's 'fairness' justification. Lord Sumner famously deemed it 'a device by which the rules as to absolute contracts are reconciled with a special exception which justice demands'.[44] While frequently followed, numerous criticisms can be made.[45] 'Justice' is not really an explanation and yields no workable test to identify frustrated contracts.[46] As Treitel continues: 'Still less does the "just solution" theory determine the type of relief which, in English law, can be given'– indeed, the law falls short of 'the comprehensive apportionment of loss which might be regarded as the "just solution"'.[47]

In short, automatic total discharge is necessarily entailed by the public policy basis of frustration *for supervening illegality*. Whereas generalised, as it has been, to *other* cases of interrupted performance, it renders frustration 'a blunt instrument, drastic in its effects but rarely employed'.[48]

Supervening illegality's most striking 'special rule' is its potential to override agreed contractual allocations of the risk. Again, this flows from the basis in public policy. Parties obviously cannot contract directly out of the mandatory rules on illegality ('We agree to disapply the rule *ex turpi causa*'). That axiom was extended to indirect circumvention in *Ertel Bieber & Co v Rio Tinto Co*.[49] The sale of sulphur ore between a British and a German company would obviously have been frustrated by illegality upon the

[41] *Joseph Constantine v Imperial Smelting* [1942] AC 154, 185.
[42] *Denny Mott & Dickson v James B Fraser* [1944] AC 265, 275.
[43] Bridge (n 21) 21–22, 25.
[44] *Hirji Mulji v Cheong Yue Steamship Co Ltd* [1926] AC 497, 510 (again approved by Lord Wright: *Joseph Constantine v Imperial Smelting* [1942] AC 154, 184).
[45] See text to nn 209–27 below.
[46] PS Atiyah, *Essays on Contract* (Oxford, Clarendon Press, 1986) 273 ('fairness' neither a 'theory' of frustration nor a 'technique' for application – rather it is 'the end purpose … of all legal techniques'); Peel (n 11) 16-009.
[47] Peel (n 11) 16-009. *cf* American Law Institute, *Restatement (Second) of Contracts* (1981) § 272(2) ('the court may grant relief on such terms as justice requires').
[48] Bridge (n 38) 580 (NB ibid fn 1: 'Supervening illegality raises issues of its own and is not dealt with in this article').
[49] [1918] AC 260.

outbreak of the war in 1914 (ie, criminalised as trading with the enemy). However, the 1910 and 1912 sale contracts stated (emphasis added):

> [S]hould war or any other cause, over which the buyers … have no control, prevent their receiving such ore, the obligation to receive under this contract shall be reduced in proportion, or *suspended during the continuance of such impediment…*

The House of Lords held this 'suspension' void for public policy; it could not prevent the contract of sale being frustrated. For Lord Atkinson, the contract still benefited the enemy (German) company: the clause 'does not deprive the [buyers] of the full enjoyment of all benefits of the contract, but merely postpones that enjoyment for an uncertain time leaving it ultimately certain and secure'.[50] That the clause prevented direct or immediate trading with the enemy was insufficient. Lord Sumner stated that the 'higher public obligation' of obeying the (criminal) law 'discharges any private obligation to the contrary'.[51]

Many leading cases on supervening illegality concern trading with the enemy. It affected innumerable contracts on the outbreaks of both major twentieth-century wars (providing much of the raw material from which frustration 'somewhat empirically evolved').[52] Prohibiting trading with the enemy is an especially potent head of public policy.[53] The *Rio Tinto* decision gave it broad scope in striking down the 'suspension' clause.[54] Indeed, contemporary commentators criticised *Rio Tinto* for seeming inconsistency with well-established rules against the expropriation of enemy aliens' property and contractual rights.[55] (Instead, the law *suspended* such rights' enjoyment: eg, the British tenant of a building owned by a German landlord paid rent to the official custodian, which would reimburse the enemy landlord only once the war ended.) The *Rio Tinto* clause would have had precisely this suspensory effect. Its invalidation was in McNair's opinion 'specious and dangerous', undermining the principle against expropriation.[56] Foxton suggests that *Rio Tinto's* date (1918) influenced its outcome. Following four years of total war, and the allied powers' hardening attitude to Germany's ultimate readmission to world commerce when the war was over, the House of Lords' decision was 'harsh, but wholly in keeping with the public mood'.[57]

Thus, sufficiently important public policy may drastically curtail contractual obligations. By contrast, lesser prohibitions will not always entail frustration. It is a perennially difficult question of statutory construction whether the sanction of contractual invalidation is intended, over and above the fines or penalties stipulated.[58] As with any illegality

[50] ibid 279–80 (*cf* Lord Dunedin at 275: suspended obligation 'represents a present value which may be realized by means of assignation [sic] to neutral countries').

[51] [1918] AC 260, 285.

[52] *Joseph Constantine v Imperial Smelting* [1942] AC 154, 193 (Lord Wright). See C MacMillan, 'English Contract Law and the Great War: The Development of a Doctrine of Frustration' (2014) 2 *Comparative Legal History* 278 (trading-with-enemy cases 'bolstered' frustration's 'extraordinary' development).

[53] Peel (n 11) § 8-006 ('of exceptional strength'). *cf Blackburn Bobbin v Allen* [1918] 1 KB 540, 549 (McCardie J) (trading with enemy a 'severe and far-reaching' prohibition).

[54] *cf* 'grace period' in GAFTA export-prohibition clause; Bridge (n 21).

[55] D Foxton, 'Property, Liberty and Obligation: Aspects of the Judicial Role in the Great War' (PhD Thesis, University of London, 2000) ch 2.

[56] AD McNair, *Essays and Lectures upon some Legal Effects of War* (Cambridge, Cambridge University Press, 1920) 67.

[57] Foxton (n 55) 205 (see further 508).

[58] See, eg, *Archbolds (Freightage) Ltd v Spanglett Ltd* [1961] 1 QB 374, 389.

plea, 'it is unacceptable that the court should, on the first indication of unlawfulness affecting any aspect of a transaction, draw up its skirt and refuse all assistance'.[59] Aside from contracts expressly forbidden by statute,[60] public policy is served better 'by refusing to nullify a bargain [for illegality] save on serious and sufficient grounds'.[61] It has long been recognised that nullification itself violates the policy favouring freedom of contract.[62] Reconciling these competing concerns involves a broad weighing of policy factors.[63] This jurisprudence is equally relevant to *supervening* illegality and contracts alleged to be illegal from the outset.

Even if one obligation becomes incapable of lawful performance, liability may remain for other obligations under the contract.[64] (Note Weir's criticism of the 'characteristically sloppy English ellipse' deeming *whole contracts* to 'evanish', rather than particular obligations only.[65]) Take a sale needing an export licence. If the government refuses to issue the licence, it clearly becomes impossible for the seller lawfully to export the goods. However, even if *that* obligation has been frustrated, the contract will usually place responsibility for obtaining necessary permissions on one of the parties. That party would be liable for failing to obtain the licence. Note this does not permit the parties to contract around the export control regime. It does not make contractually obligatory what the export regulations forbid. Rather, the collateral obligation to obtain permission allocates responsibility for failing to comply with the mandatory regulations.

Beatson J wisely noted how 'Lord McNair deplored the tendency to include impossibility arising from supervening illegality within the conception and terminology of frustration'.[66] Day has also recently argued that frustration here depends on public policy and has nothing to do with party intentions, being 'an entirely different doctrine'.[67] We strongly agree. It is time to take such calls seriously.[68] There should be a formal division between frustration by illegality, and all other situations of interrupted performance.

III. Changes of Circumstances: Party Agreement

Most 'frustration' cases have nothing to do with public policy. The problem posed is which party should bear the risk of things turning out differently from what was

[59] *Saunders v Edwards* [1987] 1 WLR 1116, 1134 (Bingham LJ).

[60] *Henderson v Dorset University NHS Trust* [2020] UKSC 43, [2021] AC 563 [74]–[75].

[61] *Vita Food Products Inc v Unus Shipping Co Ltd* [1939] AC 277, 293.

[62] *Printing and Numerical Registering Co v Sampson* (1875) LR 19 Eq 462, 465 (Jessel MR) (applied in *SR Projects Ltd v Rampersad* [2022] UKPC 24 [86] ('salutary words')).

[63] *Patel v Mirza* [2016] UKSC 42, [2017] AC 467.

[64] *cf Matthey v Curling* [1922] 2 AC 180 (Atkin LJ, dissenting in Court of Appeal, would have held tenant's *covenant to repair* frustrated by military occupation, but lease itself (and tenant's obligation to pay rent) *not* frustrated).

[65] T Weir, '*Nec Tamen Consumebatur* … Frustration and Limitation Clauses' [1970] *CLJ* 189 ('a simplicity of formulation which is bound to delude').

[66] *Islamic Republic of Iran Shipping Lines v Steamship Mutual Underwriting Association (Bermuda) Ltd* [2010] EWHC 2661 (Comm), [2011] 1 Lloyd's Rep 195 [100] (citing AD McNair, *Legal Effects of War* (3rd edn, Cambridge, Cambridge University Press, 1948) 134).

[67] Day (n 2) 121 (noting the relevant 'policy' in *domestic* illegality is consistency within the legal system, whereas in *foreign* illegality it is comity between different systems).

[68] *cf* G Williams, *The Law Reform (Frustrated Contracts) Act 1943* (London, Stevens, 1944) 25 ('unfortunate that the terminology of "frustration" has obscured the distinction' between impossibility and illegality).

expected. That is largely a matter for the parties themselves – arguably it should be *exclusively* their responsibility, and no 'doctrine of frustration' is needed.

That suggestion sounds radical and unorthodox. In fact, though, it would make little practical difference. The English doctrine of frustration is notoriously strict, a last-ditch plea.[69] Courts have been consistently unimpressed by a century's assorted international crises – world wars, closure of the Suez Canal (an artery of world trade), or the global COVID-19 pandemic. The doctrine's enduring narrow scope deliberately places responsibility for pricing and managing contingencies on parties drafting contracts.

A sophisticated drafter has such questions at the forefront of their mind: 'The language of commerce is the language of risk'.[70] This is epitomised by the traditional paradigm English commercial case: carriage of goods by sea. The obvious and insistent risks pertaining to marine shipment, and payment for cargoes afloat, make risk-allocation the central feature of such contracts. It is indeed true for *all* commercial contracts.

As noted, contractual devices to effect the allocation of risk are many – not exhausted by 'force majeure' clauses *eo nomine*. The basic structure of a transaction also allocates many of its fundamental risks. Judge Posner states:

> The normal risk of a fixed-price [sale] contract is that the market price will change. If it rises, the buyer gains at the expense of the seller (except insofar as escalator provisions give the seller some protection); if it falls, as here, the seller gains at the expense of the buyer. The whole purpose of a fixed-price contract is to allocate risk in this way.[71]

He accordingly held that a distressed buyer could not invoke a *force majeure* clause when the price of a commodity fell dramatically: the clause had not been 'intended to buffer [the buyer] against the normal risks' of a falling market, since that would 'nullify a central term of the contract'.

Frustration was similarly inconsistent with the overall transaction in *Canary Wharf v European Medicines Agency*.[72] The agency (a government body of the European Union (EU)) had executed a 25-year lease for office accommodation in London, but argued that the lease was frustrated by the United Kingdom's subsequent decision to leave the EU (which accordingly relocated the European Medicines Agency (EMA) to another (continuing) member state, after 'Brexit'). Marcus Smith J analysed the lease's structure closely. By entering a 25-year commitment, with the express right to sub-let or assign the lease but crucially *without* a break clause,[73] the lessee EMA (indeed, both parties) had assumed the risk of events affecting the suitability of the premises. Should such contingencies occur, however unforeseeably, the lessee had by agreement limited its recourse to assignment or sub-letting.[74] To suggest that Brexit had frustrated the lease

[69] *National Carriers Ltd v Panalpina (Northern) Ltd* [1981] AC 675,688 (Lord Hailsham LC) (leases frustrated 'not never but hardly ever').

[70] R Fentiman, 'Legal Risk in International Commercial Disputes' in M Dyson (ed), *Regulating Risk through Private Law* (Cambridge, Intersentia, 2018) 285.

[71] *Northern Indiana v Carbon County Coal Co*, 799 F 2d 265, 275 (1986).

[72] [2019] EWHC 335 (Ch).

[73] Lessee (EMA) had initially wanted a break clause but lessor (Canary Wharf) resisted this: [2019] EWHC 335 (Ch) [76], [218], [224].

[74] *cf* [2019] EWHC 335 (Ch) [249](1) 'the Lease is remarkably sophisticated … [and] *made provision in terms for the allocation of this risk*' (original emphasis of Marcus Smith J).

would effectively have reinserted the break clause that the lessee had unsuccessfully failed to insist upon in negotiations.[75]

Canary Wharf illustrates the role of unilateral powers (including termination) in planning against a long-term agreement's inevitable uncertainties: 'parties may agree to a discretionary power … to create an adequate response to future uncertainty … [as] a "governance mechanism" that enables adjustment of obligations'.[76] The corollary is that when drafters *omit* such powers of adjustment, *inflexible* commitments result (eg, the lessee's rent obligation in *Canary Wharf*). The suite of available risk-allocation options justifies a strong scepticism toward court-imposed 'frustration'. As in the old retort from *Paradine v Jane*: if the parties wanted an excuse, they should have included it in the contract.[77]

That presumption is strong but not absolute. The court might conclude that although unstated, the contract on its true construction has an implicit shared basis, making its obligations conditional on the continued existence of some state of affairs. There is, then, a residual place for the 'construction theory' of frustration (to use the familiar label). Indeed, it is hard to see how anyone could oppose this 'theory'. When obligations are implicitly or inherently conditional, the court is simply enforcing what was agreed. It would over-extend the good sense of *Paradine v Jane* to make it *compulsory*. *Paradine* is simply a non-interventionist starting point. The loss *presumptively* lies where it falls – but parties are free to reallocate it as they please.

This is, unashamedly, an 'internal' explanation.[78] All contractual obligation is voluntarily assumed,[79] and judges may need to decide by 'construction of the particular contract, whether the obligation is absolute or whether it is qualified'.[80] By contrast, on what authority could the courts wield 'a dispensing power'?[81] Contrary to recent criticism that it would 'obscure the distinctiveness' of cases about failed agreed basis,[82] it is a major advantage to classify these questions as 'mundane contractual interpretation'.[83]

'Mundane' or otherwise, questions of interpretation are frequently not straightforward. In particular, it may be difficult to identify the *implicit* limits of an unqualified obligation – ie, one prima facie absolute.[84] The general approach to construction and

[75] Though the EMA did negotiate a 'substantial inducement' of £40m rent reduction: [2019] EWHC 335 (Ch) [93].

[76] H Collins, 'Discretionary Powers in Contracts' in D Campbell, H Collins and J Wightman (eds), *Implicit Dimensions of Contract – Discrete, Relational, and Network Contracts* (Oxford, Hart Publishing, 2003) 226.

[77] *Dermott v Jones* 69 US 1, 8 (1864).

[78] *cf* AJ Morris, 'Practical reasoning and contract as promise: Extending contract-based criteria to decide excuse cases' [1997] *CLJ* 147 (frustration occupies difficult borderline between unambiguously 'internal' meaning and externally imposed solution, but applicably only in cases 'of most extreme egregiousness').

[79] *Transfield Shipping Inc v Mercator Shipping Inc (The Achilleas)* [2008] UKHL 48, [2009] 1 AC 61 [12] (Lord Hoffmann) ('logical to found liability for [consequential] damages upon the intention of the parties (objectively ascertained) because all contractual liability is voluntarily undertaken').

[80] *Joseph Constantine v Imperial Smelting* [1942] AC 154, 185 (Lord Wright).

[81] ibid.

[82] H Dagan and O Somech, 'When Contract's Basic Assumptions Fail' (2021) 34 *Canadian Journal of Law & Jurisprudence* 297, 301.

[83] *pace* Dagan and Somech (ibid) 308.

[84] *cf Blackburn Bobbin v Allen* [1918] 1 KB 540, 547 (McCardie J) ('the *ever-embarrassing duty* of deciding whether an implied term shall be read into a given contract [when] serious change of circumstances occurs') (emphasis added).

implication is directly relevant here.[85] With detailed, professionally drafted contracts, there is a strong presumption that the parties mean what they say and have exhaustively specified the agreement. There is little room for corrective reinterpretation, nor an entire new term.[86] As Lord Hoffmann observed: 'when [a contract] does not expressly provide for what is to happen when some event occurs [the] most usual inference … is that nothing is to happen … [The] loss lies where it falls.'[87] Given this 'usual inference', and the court's acceptance of losses lying undisturbed, to identify a 'gap' in the contract (or a 'windfall') begs the question.[88]

But the presumption is not absolute. Even in professionally drafted contracts, there may be obligations, or qualifications, which (although unsaid) are irresistibly entailed by what has been expressly agreed.[89] To juxtapose two further observations of Lord Hoffmann, the interpreter 'must take into account that legal documents are drawn up by people who can be expected to have chosen their words with care and not to have left things out'.[90] But even professionally drafted standard forms may – indeed notoriously they do – include 'superfluous words … [clumsy] draftsmanship … redundancies or loose ends'.[91] And there is still greater scope for courts to supplement brief agreements, through 'interpretation'. Even high-value contracts may be agreed without anything written down, their formation deduced from context and conduct alone ('arising from the briefest and most informal exchange').[92] Such oral contracts will probably have few express terms beyond the most fundamental (eg, percentage of estate agent's commission on a successful sale). The court may need to imply further terms to deal with less common contingencies (eg, at precisely what stage of the transaction is the agent's commission earned?).[93] That might include a term conditioning the parties' obligations on a continuing state of affairs (eg, the existence of the concert hall in *Taylor v Caldwell*).

Party agreement is central. However, the court must ascertain what it is that the parties have agreed. With a well-drafted, detailed contract (eg, the *Canary Wharf*

[85] *Chandris v Isbrandtsen-Moller Co* [1951] 1 KB 240, 244 (Devlin J) (contracting parties 'are apt to use words, phrases or clauses which, taken literally, are wider than they intend').

[86] *Marks and Spencer plc v BNP Paribas* [2015] UKSC 72, [2016] AC 742; *Bank of New York Mellon (International) Ltd v Cine-UK Ltd* [2022] EWCA Civ 1021, [2023] 2 P&CR 19 [140] (Flaux C) (with 'detailed documents prepared by lawyers, the scope for implication is limited').

[87] *Attorney General of Belize v Belize Telecom Ltd* [2009] UKPC 10, [2009] 1 WLR 1988 [17]. *cf* A Kull, 'Mistake, Frustration and the Windfall Principle of Contract Remedies' (1991) 43 *Hastings Law Journal* 1 (if risk unallocated, neither illogical nor arbitrary to leave it where it falls; whereas re-allocation without contractual authority imposes significant administrative costs without compelling social advantage).

[88] F Wilmot-Smith, 'Contract and unjust enrichment in the High Court of Australia' (2020) 136 *LQR* 196 (approved as 'sound criticism' in *Dargamo Holdings Ltd v Avonwick Holdings Ltd* [2021] EWCA Civ 1149, [2022] 1 All ER (Comm) 1244 [75] (Carr LJ)).

[89] eg, *Jones v Lydon* [2021] EWHC 2321 (Ch) (agreement that copyright-holders make licensing decisions by majority vote entailed further *implied* obligation that all copyright-holders (including dissenters) *execute* licences agreed by majority); *Glynn v Margetson* [1893] AC 351; *Tesco v USDAW* [2024] UKSC 28, [2025] ICR 107.

[90] Lord Hoffmann, 'Language and lawyers' (2018) 134 *LQR* 553, 573.

[91] *Beaufort Developments (NI) Ltd v Gilbert-Ash NI Ltd* [1999] 1 AC 266, 273–74 (Lord Hoffmann) (on JCT standard forms); *cf Burrell & Sons v Green & Co* [1914] 1 KB 293, 303 (Bailhache J) ('charterparties often contain many redundant words').

[92] *Devani v Wells* [2019] UKSC 4, [2020] AC 129 [59], [63] (Lord Briggs). See further *Realestate.com.au Pty Ltd v Hardingham* [2022] HCA 39, (2022) 277 CLR 115.

[93] *Devani v Wells* [2019] UKSC 4, [2020] AC 129 [29], [33] (Lord Kitchin).

lease) this presents few difficulties.[94] The court simply enforces the express agreement. It should not give undue emphasis to rules such as *contra proferentem*, ie, should not read down *force majeure* clauses as supposedly derogating from valuable contractual rights.[95] The 'presumption' is of dubious relevance since the rights never existed in an unqualified state, but always *subject to* the *force majeure* provisions.[96]

Professionally drafted written contracts have limited scope for unspoken limits on *ex facie* absolute obligations. (Especially not when even specifically unforeseeable risks are routinely 'priced and allocated [in contracts] as part of the package of a more broadly framed risk').[97] By contrast, with less sophisticated agreements characterised by 'informality, brevity or the absence of skilled professional assistance', the courts place 'greater emphasis on the factual matrix' rather than the text.[98] This allows greater scope for implicit limits. Yet all construction cases turn on their particular facts. As Lord Wright once cautioned, decisions about interpretation 'may help by way of analogy and illustration' but they can never be applied directly to differently worded contracts with different contexts 'as if they embodied rules of law'.[99] It has therefore been mistaken, we suggest, to synthesise decisions about the implicit limits of particular obligations into a general default rule of 'frustration'.[100]

IV. Changes of Circumstances: A Default Rule?

The orthodox understanding, however, is that in addition to the (mandatory) rule on supervening illegality, English law also contains a *default* rule which discharges contracts upon a sufficiently radical change of circumstances. This section argues there is *no necessity* to excuse promisors whose obligations become impossible to perform. Once it is appreciated that impossibility is neither necessary nor sufficient to 'frustrate' a contract, the doctrine's essential indefinability becomes clear. (Courts therefore strive to keep the doctrine narrow, to limit the uncertainty created.)

Judges appreciate that a wide frustration doctrine would 'tend to sap the foundations of contract law'.[101] Every contract (except an instantaneous exchange) binds the parties

[94] *cf Canary Wharf v European Medicines Agency* [2019] EWHC 335 (Ch) [26(4)] (Marcus Smith J) ('even a sophisticated contract which, on its face, *appears* to make provision for all subsequent vicissitudes may find itself defeated by the truly unforeseen') (emphasis in original).

[95] *cf* R Catterwell, 'Frustration and assumption of risk' (2022) *Journal of Business Law* 76; R Catterwell, 'Party Intention, Default Rules and Contract Theory', this volume, ch 4.

[96] *MUR Shipping v RTI Ltd* [2022] EWCA Civ 1406, [2023] 1 Lloyd's Rep 463 [54]; but *cf* [2024] UKSC 18, [2025] AC 675 [45].

[97] GG Triantis, 'Contractual allocations of unknown risks: A critique of the doctrine of commercial impracticability' (1992) 42 *University of Toronto Law Journal* 450, 452 (*cf* 483 rejecting 'the myth that unforeseen risks are not allocated').

[98] *Wood v Capita Insurance Services Ltd* [2017] UKSC 24, [2017] AC 1173 [13] (Lord Hodge).

[99] *Luxor (Eastbourne) Ltd v Cooper* [1941] AC 108, 130.

[100] *cf* AL Corbin, *Corbin on Contracts: Volume 6* (St Paul, Minn, West Publishing Co, 1962) 358 ('all generalizations [about frustration] should be regarded as tentative working rules, continually to be tested and re-examined in the light of … the customs, business practices, feelings and opinions of men – the prevailing *mores* of the time and place').

[101] *Blackburn Bobbin v Allen* [1918] 1 KB 540,552 (McCardie J) (criticising *Krell v Henry* [1903] 2 KB 740 as an exceptional, perilous rule).

to do things in the future. This is inherently risky. The future is known to be uncertain. In French, *contrater, c'est prévoir* ('to contract is to foresee').[102] Given these facts of life, no system of contract law could entertain a wide, general defence of 'changed circumstances'. Every party always runs the risk that their contract may prove less profitable – or even ruinous. Long-term binding obligations would become unachievable if every contingency affecting the contract's value *ipso facto* 'frustrated' the contract.[103]

The historical development of English law's single 'doctrine of frustration' was catalysed by the crisis of the First World War.[104] (It may be noted that in 1918, a committee appointed by the Board of Trade recommended against a wider statutory power of intervention: if all pre-1914 contracts were to be dissolved by the wartime economic dislocation, the 'general cancellation' would bring 'disaster' to the national economy and British international trade.[105]) As argued above, supervening illegality (which featured prominently, as trading with the enemy) should never have been woven into a general common law frustration doctrine,[106] but kept distinct. Other 'strands' included destruction of specific subject matter (*Taylor v Caldwell*).[107] But it would be mistaken to derive a general rule of discharge by *impossibility*. Blackburn J had reasoned from longstanding decisions discharging contracts for personal services upon death / incapacitation.[108] This specific rule seems unarguably correct.[109] Agency too is generally dissolved by death of the principal.[110] But must *all* events that make performance impossible discharge the obligation?

English law has no such general doctrine.[111] Many cases illustrate the contrary.[112] A leading modern American case raised a question strongly analogous to *Taylor v Caldwell*. An opera company claimed damages when it had to cancel its production in a theatre owned by the defendant, because power cuts made safe performance impossible.[113] The United States Court of Appeals held by a majority, in accordance with *Taylor v Caldwell*, that the unexpected interruption of the electricity supply excused the defendant. That this was not an inevitable conclusion is shown by the

[102] G Ripert, *La Règle Morale dans les Obligations Civiles*, 4th edn (Paris, Pichon & Durand-Auzias, 1949) 151.

[103] *cf Davis Contractors v Fareham UDC* [1956] AC 696, 731 (Lord Radcliffe) (were mere hardship an excuse, 'an untold range of contractual obligations [would become] unenforceable').

[104] C MacMillan, 'English Contract Law and the Great War: The Development of a Doctrine of Frustration' (2014) 2 *Comparative Legal History* 278; Foxton (n 55) ch 5.

[105] *Report of Board of Trade Committee in Respect of Pre-War Contracts* (Cd 8975, 1918).

[106] *cf* American Law Institute (n 47) § 264 ('Prevention by Government Regulation' as another 'specific instance' of generic 'impracticability': comment (a)).

[107] *cf* ibid § 263 ('Destruction, Deterioration … of Thing Necessary for Performance').

[108] *Hyde v Dean of Windsor* (1596) Cro Eliz 552, 78 ER 798. *cf* American Law Institute (n 47) § 262; *Robinson v Davison* (1871) LR 6 Ex 269.

[109] *Blackburn Bobbin v Allen* [1918] 1 KB 540, 547 McCardie J ('Death and illness are unceasing features of human society' and discharging performance in such cases 'seems just and reasonable').

[110] PG Watts and FMB Reynolds, *Bowstead & Reynolds on Agency*, 23rd edn (London, Sweet & Maxwell, 2023) 10-015–10-016.

[111] *Joseph Constantine v Imperial Smelting* [1942] AC 154, 163 (Viscount Simon LC) ('Discharge by supervening impossibility is not a common law rule of general application, like discharge by *supervening illegality*') (emphasis added).

[112] eg *CTI Group Inc v Transclear SA (The Mary Nour)* [2007] EWHC 2070 (Comm), [2007] 2 CLC 518 [38]; and [2008] EWCA Civ 856, [2008] 2 CLC 112 [14].

[113] *Opera Company of Boston v Wolf Trap Foundation for the Performing Arts*, 817 F 2d 1094 (1987).

dissenting judgment, reasoning that the readily foreseeable risk of electrical outages should have remained with the defendant venue, which could have addressed the risk (physically) by using portable generators or (contractually) by expressly shifting it to the plaintiffs.

In 1869 Hannen J stated: 'There can be no doubt that a man may by an absolute contract bind himself to perform things which subsequently become impossible, or to pay damages for the non-performance.'[114] Nevertheless, can it be *fair* to hold a party liable for failing to achieve the impossible? Is it even *cogent* to recognise legally binding obligations to do impossible things? Does not 'ought' imply 'can'?[115]

These objections are misplaced. Neither fairness, nor logic, requires an impossibility defence. To suggest otherwise runs contrary to two deep, structural features characterising contracts in the common law tradition. First, duties are usually strict, indeed absolute: not so much fault-insensitive as fault-blind. Secondly, the paramount remedy is payment of damages for breach, rather than enforcement of the primary obligations. (Comparison with civilian systems highlights these common law doctrines' mutually supportive quality: the civilian tradition's more stringent, performance-focused remedies require a more forgiving approach to breach and to the anterior definition of obligations, including the generous re-interpretation of 'harsh' terms.)[116] 'Frustration' contradicts strict liability while remaining irrelevant to liability in damages.

Contract law's (presumptive) strictness is ubiquitous: the question is *whether* the contract was performed, not *why* it wasn't. This is usually taken for granted and rarely explained, nor often even articulated.[117] 'It is *axiomatic* that … it is, in general, immaterial why the defendant failed to fulfil his [contractual] obligation, and certainly no defence to plead that he had done his best.'[118] In a system characterised by these absolute, fault-insensitive obligations, it would be oddly selective to object to strict liability *only* when breach has become unavoidable. On a fault-informed view, *Paradine v Jane*-style hostility to the excuse of changed circumstances does not seem *uniquely* 'problematic'. The pervasive default strictness of the entire law of contract would equally stand condemned.[119]

In practice, few seem to object to contract law's strict approach (with which the narrow frustration doctrine coheres). First, many contractual obligations are not duties on the promisor *to do* anything, but rather impose 'duties *that*' a certain state of affairs exists.[120] A seller is contractually bound to guarantee, eg, the condition or the existence of the goods, but it would be odd to suggest they were obliged to take action to

[114] *Baily v De Crespigny* (1869) LR 4 QB 180, 185.

[115] *cf* A Slavny, 'Should Tort Law Demand the Impossible?' in P Miller and J Oberdiek (eds), *Civil Wrongs and Justice in Private Law* (Oxford, Oxford University Press, 2020).

[116] M Pargendler, 'The Role of the State in Contract Law: The Common-Civil Law Divide' (2018) 43 *Yale Journal of International Law* 143.

[117] SA Smith, *Contract Theory* (Oxford, Oxford University Press, 2004) ch 10 ('The puzzle of strict liability'). Although *cf* B Nicholas, 'Fault and Breach of Contract' in J Beatson and D Friedman (eds), *Good Faith and Fault in Contract Law* (Oxford, Oxford University Press, 1994); O Ben-Shahar and A Porat (eds), *Fault in American Contract Law* (Cambridge, Cambridge University Press, 2010).

[118] *Raineri v Miles* [1981] AC 1050, 1086 (Lord Edmund-Davies) (emphasis added).

[119] *cf* Nicholas (n 117): fault ignored precisely because '*Paradine v Jane* is part of the basic furniture of [the common lawyer's] mind'.

[120] E Eldridge, 'Rights That' (2024) 44 *OJLS* 808.

bring about (say) the warranted mileage of a car or existence of a shipwreck.[121] Here then, the 'moral' objection to obligations to take impossible *actions* seems beside the point. Absolute obligations may also suit the parties. '[A] man might by apt words bind himself that it shall rain to-morrow or that he will pay damages.'[122] As Holmes pointed out,[123] this would not oblige the promisor actually to do that which they obviously cannot control (the weather). Such an impossible promise would (Holmes conceded) be problematic in 'the moral world'. But the promise's sole *legal* effect is to place non-occurrence at the promisor's *risk*.[124] The promisor is obliged to pay damages should it not happen.[125] Contract law does not compel performance of the problematic primary, fine-weather promise.[126] An obligation regarding a *state of affairs* is (unlike a duty *to do something*) simply not susceptible of an imperative to comply.[127]

Given this fundamental rule of contract remedies, an impossibility defence is not logically required. By contrast, such a defence *would* be required if literal enforcement were contract law's primary remedy. Accordingly then, impossibility is a recognised equitable defence in the exceptional situations where English courts would otherwise order specific performance (eg, sales of land). First, and obviously, courts do not make orders in vain.[128] Judges realise the likely 'lack of respect for the court in seeking to achieve the unachievable'.[129] Secondly and moreover: 'It is unthinkable that a court should put a man at risk of imprisonment [for contempt] by making an order which it knows, at the time of making the order, is impossible of performance.'[130] No such objections could be raised to liability in *damages*. Payment of compensation is *always legally possible*.[131] That is not to deny the universal truth that debtors frequently cannot pay. But as Judge Posner put it (with understatement, perhaps):

> [W]hile one can think of all sorts of reasons why, when the time came to pay, the buyer might not have the money, rarely would the seller have intended to assume the risk that the buyer might, whether through improvidence or bad luck, be unable to pay.[132]

[121] ibid (citing *Dick Bentley v Harold Smith (Motors)* [1965] 1 WLR 623 and *McRae v Commonwealth Disposals Commission* (1951) 84 CLR 377).

[122] *Baily v De Crespigny* (1869) LR 4 QB 180, 185 (Hannen J). *Jones v St John's College Oxford* (1870) LR 6 QB 115, 127 (Hannen J) ('Undoubtedly, it may be an unusual or an unwise contract to enter into, but there is no reason why a man should not … in direct terms enter into a contract to perform an impossibility').

[123] OW Holmes, *The Common Law* (Boston, Little Brown & Co, 1881) 288–300.

[124] *Northern Indiana v Carbon County Coal Co*, 799 F 2d 265, 276 (1986) (Posner J): 'a promisor might want his promise to be unconditional, not because he thought he had superhuman powers but because he could insure against the risk of nonperformance better than the promisee, or obtain a substitute performance more easily'.

[125] Holmes (n 123) 301 ('The only universal consequence of a legally binding promise').

[126] *cf Hall v Wright* (1859) E B & B 765, 790–791; 120 ER 695, 705 (Martin B) ('assuming that it could not reasonably be expected … that the [incapacitated] defendant should marry the plaintiff [as promised], I can see no reason why he should not compensate her for the breach of the contract').

[127] Eldridge (n 120) 825.

[128] *New Brunswick Co v Muggeridge* (1859) 4 Drewry 686, 698; 62 ER 263, 268 (specific performance would be 'idle and nugatory'). *cf* Eldridge (n 120) 826 ('duties *that*' are a discrete category of obligations that equity will not enforce).

[129] *Attorney-General v Guardian Newspapers Ltd (No 1)* [1987] 1 WLR 1248, 1269 Browne-Wilkinson V-C (citing also King Canute and danger of law appearing an ass) (refusing injunction to restrain publication of 'confidential' information that had been widely distributed).

[130] *Udall v Capri Lighting Ltd* [1988] QB 907, 915 (Balcombe LJ).

[131] Smith (n 117) 385 ('fault is automatic … because, in principle, the only valid excuse for failure to satisfy a monetary obligation is insolvency. Unless one is bankrupt, payment is always possible').

[132] *Northern Indiana v Carbon County Coal Co*, 799 F 2d 265, 276–77 (1986).

It would be bizarre indeed if a debtor's impecuniosity thereby discharged their debts, as a matter of contract law.

Thus, against the pervasive background regime of strict liability and the damages remedy, there is no logical necessity for a general 'impossibility' defence. *A fortiori* for broader excuses of 'impracticability' (performance becoming more onerous or expensive)[133] or 'frustration of purpose' (performance, while possible, now worthless or pointless for the recipient).[134] These categories overlap: 'in matters of business, a thing is said to be impossible when it is not practicable; and a thing is impracticable when it can only be done at an excessive or unreasonable cost'.[135] While this has expanded into an 'impracticability' doctrine in US law (albeit still rarely applied),[136] English law has resisted the extension. Courts are understandably sceptical about a doctrine (impracticability) that

> ultimately represents the ever-shifting line, drawn by courts hopefully responsive to commercial practices and *mores*, at which the community's interest in having contracts enforced according to their terms is outweighed by the commercial senselessness of requiring performance.[137]

It may be noted that courts seem more receptive to frustration when there has been state intervention.[138] Surveying frustration's formative development in the First World War, MacMillan finds an important, albeit implicit, legal distinction. Despite the unprecedented scale of the economic disruption, English courts still 'sought to uphold existing contracts wherever possible and discharged contracts only infrequently'. In Macnair's contemporary view, the judges had been determined to debunk the erroneous 'layman's' impression that the war had simply dissolved all contracts.[139] Yet courts proved more sympathetic when an interruption stemmed from *government* action (such as requisition), rather than more general wartime hardships (eg, shortages and rising prices). In MacMillan's view, 'although judges did not state this', in practice they discharged contracts only 'where the disruption had been caused by direct governmental intervention'.[140] For example, holding that an express contractual power to extend time for performance did not prevent frustration by indefinite, compulsory government redirection of the building contractor's workforce and materials, the House of Lords

[133] American Law Institute (n 47) § 261.

[134] ibid § 265; *Krell v Henry* [1903] 2 KB 740. (*cf Maritime National Fish v Ocean Trawlers* [1935] AC 524, 528–29 (Lord Wright) ('The correctness of [*Krell v Henry*] has been questioned … The authority is certainly not one to be extended').

[135] *Moss v Smith* (1850) 9 CB 94, 103; 137 ER 827, 831 (Maule J): *cf Horlock v Beale* [1916] 1 AC 486, 499 (Lord Atkinson).

[136] *Transatlantic Financing Corpn v US* 363 F 2d 312 (1966) ('While it may be an overstatement to say that increased cost and difficulty of performance never constitute impracticability, to justify relief there must be more of a variation [in cost] … than is present in this case').

[137] *Transatlantic Financing* ibid.

[138] *cf The Mary Nour* [2008] EWCA Civ 856, [2008] 2 Lloyd's Rep 526 [23] (a 'prohibition of export rendering the shipment of the goods unlawful' would (unlike failure of supply) 'usually' frustrate, being 'a supervening event not contemplated by the contract').

[139] AD McNair, *Essays and Lectures Upon Some Legal Effects of War* (Cambridge, Cambridge University Press, 1920) 74.

[140] MacMillan (n 104) 300.

reasoned that those 'most unprecedented and arbitrary powers' could not have been contemplated by the contracting parties.[141]

Again, *Baily v De Crespigny* has been influential.[142] The court in *Baily* endorsed the general rule that where statutory compulsion prevents compliance with a contractual obligation, 'the statute repeals the covenant'.[143] The rule was not absolute.[144] Yet parties are 'presumed to be contracting on the supposition that the law will remain such as it is' and 'words, shewing a contrary intention, ought to be pretty clear to rebut that presumption'.[145] Even here though, frustration ultimately depends on the circumstances. Government control of the national economy was doubtless, in 1914–18, 'most unprecedented'. It would now be rather less surprising, given modern expansion of the state's role, cemented after the 1939–45 war. Even in the US, 'government's manifold interventions in the economy' are now 'a pervasive factor'.[146] The risks of modern property investment include reductions in value by government restrictions on use, as much as damage by 'fire and tempest'.[147] With changes in law, equally, *res perit domino* (ie, the owner bears the risk). A century after the Great War, commercial parties are taken to assume the risk of many sorts of state regulation which may obstruct contractual performance or adversely affect its value.[148]

Orthodoxy then recognisees a flexible 'doctrine of frustration' in English contract law. But it is intractable. Any attempt to derive clear rules, even prima facie rules, seems doomed. We could attempt to isolate at least a handful of hard-edged rules, such as discharge for *res extincta*.[149] This would purchase certainty at the high cost of arbitrariness. As Bridge comments, delineating frustration by 'different events of impossibility' (such as physical destruction) 'presents a visible line but does not command acceptance for its intrinsic rationality'.[150] Alas for 'intrinsic rationality', Sir Mackenzie Chalmers codified this doctrine in sections 6 and 7 of the Sale of Goods Act (SGA) 1893.[151] The High Court of Australia exposed the absurdity of the statute compelling courts to hold the contract 'void' in all *res extincta* cases.[152] It may be (as in *McRae*) that the only

[141] *Metropolitan Water Board v Dick Kerr & Co* [1918] AC 119, 134 (Lord Atkinson).

[142] (1869) LR 4 QB 180. *cf Dick Kerr* [1918] AC 119,140–41.

[143] *Brewster v Kitchell* (1697) 1 Salk 198, 91 ER 177.

[144] *cf Matthey v Curling* [1922] 2 AC 180; *Codelfa Construction Pty Ltd v State Rail Authority (NSW)* (1982) 149 CLR 337 (compare majority and Brennan J, dissenting (whether breach excused when nuisance injunction prevented timely performance)); *Eyre v Johnson* [1946] KB 481, 484 (Denning J) ('illegality as to the performance of one clause which does not amount to frustration in any sense of the word, does not carry with it the necessary consequence that the party is absolved from paying damages').

[145] *Mayor of Berwick v Oswald* (1854) 3 El & Bl 653, 665; 118 ER 1286, 1291 (Maule J dissenting).

[146] *Northern Indiana v Carbon County Coal Co*, 799 F 2d 265, 278 (1986).

[147] *Amalgamated Investment & Property Co v John Walker & Sons* [1977] 1 WLR 164, 175 (Lawton LJ) (instancing the 'hazards' of planning permission, fiscal and legislative changes, 'Listed' buildings, and compulsory purchase).

[148] *cf Bank of New York Mellon (International) Ltd v Cine-UK Ltd* [2022] EWCA Civ 1021, [2023] 2 P&CR 19 [143] (Flaux C) (thinking it 'debateable' whether the restrictions of the 2020–21 COVID legislation were 'unprecedented', given that 'some restrictions have been imposed historically during previous pandemics, including the Great Plague').

[149] *Taylor v Caldwell* (1863) 3 B & S 826, 122 ER 309; *Couturier v Hastie* (1856) 5 HLC 673, 10 ER 1065.

[150] M Bridge, 'Frustration and excused non-performance' (2021) 137 *LQR* 580, 585.

[151] *cf* criticising the resulting 'confusion' and 'inconsistent and contradictory results' (overlapping rules in SGA s 7, s 20 (passage of risk) and the 'doctrine of frustration'): Jayathilaka (n 6).

[152] *McRae v Commonwealth Disposals Commission* (1951) 84 CLR 377.

sensible interpretation of a given contract makes the seller *responsible* – and liable – for the goods' non-existence. As Atiyah argued, the SGA should therefore be seen as enacting 'merely a prima facie rule of construction' rather than a rigid rule of law.[153] But this is not the natural reading of the statute. Lord Goff blamed Chalmers specifically for English law's uncharacteristically doctrinaire ('Romanistic') rule.[154] Outside this misguided codification, however, courts can tailor 'frustration' to the circumstances.

Assuming the law therefore rejects clear-albeit-arbitrary categories, frustration doctrine suffers the opposite vice. The concept of obligations made 'radically different' is easy to state but troublesome to apply.[155] The Latin tag, *Non haec in foedera veni*,[156] merely disguises the difficulties with 'the decent obscurity of a learned language'. To put such a 'test' into effect, we must

> pinpoint the instance when the difference in degree becomes the difference in kind … [That] is too burdensome for any court … [The] judge is essentially unaided in [performing] … this uncalibrated balance.[157]

Rix LJ, in a leading modern restatement, reasoned that an overall test was needed 'if [frustration] is not to descend into a morass of quasi-discretionary decisions'.[158] However, his Lordship immediately accepted that the 'circumstances [of frustration] can be so various as to defy rule-making' and his so-called 'test' was in fact a 'multi-factorial' weighing of numerous relevant factors.[159]

While such 'uncalibrated balancing' is challenging,[160] the actual outcomes in 'frustration' cases largely seem sensible. The undifferentiated *effect* of frustration in English law may well reinforce the judicial caution. Automatic total discharge is (obviously) a drastic and inflexible remedy. As argued above, it is appropriate for supervening *illegality* but typically inappropriate for other changed circumstances. Courts understandably approach frustration reluctantly, unless automatic total discharge would be a suitable outcome. As noted, this inflexible remedy requires cases of partial failure of supply (etc) to be resolved, somehow, outside the envelope of 'frustration'.[161]

V. A Broader Default? Commercial Expectations

So far, this chapter has argued that lumping together different types of 'frustration' into one doctrine has been regrettable. Supervening illegality should be sharply distinguished. In all other cases where contracts are discharged for change of circumstances,

[153] PS Atiyah, '*Courturier v Hastie* and the sale of non-existent goods' (1957) 73 *LQR* 340.

[154] R Goff, 'The Search for Principle' (1983) 69 *Proceedings of the British Academy* 169, 173.

[155] LE Trakman, 'Frustrated contracts and legal fictions' (1983) 46 *MLR* 39, 48 (invites 'judicial speculation … surmise … after-the fact conjecture').

[156] *Davis Contractors v Fareham UDC* [1956] AC 696, 729 (Lord Radcliffe). *cf Edwinton Commercial Corporation v Tsavliris Russ (Worldwide Salvage & Towage) Ltd (The Sea Angel)* [2007] EWCA Civ 547, [2007] 2 Lloyd's Rep 517 [84] Rix LJ ('It is ironic that Aeneas's shabby excuse to Dido has become the watchword of the modern doctrine of frustration').

[157] JH Schlegel, 'Of Nuts, and Ships, and Sealing Wax, Suez, and Frustrating Things: The Doctrine of Impossibility of Performance' (1969) 23 *Rutgers Law Review* 419, 439.

[158] *The Sea Angel* [2007] EWCA Civ 547, [2007] 2 Lloyd's Rep 517 [110].

[159] ibid [111].

[160] *cf* Day (n 2) 124 on Rix LJ's 'one-size-fits-all' formula ('wretched').

[161] Bridge (n 38).

this is properly explained by the court deciding that there are implicit, unstated limits on apparently absolute obligations: 'asking whether the obligation is implicitly conditional from an objective point of view … emerges from an objective interpretation of their agreement, not from an effort to discover the parties' subconscious thoughts'.[162] (Given this *objective* approach, identifying implicit terms should not be dismissed as a 'pious … legal fiction'.)[163] As observed already, it is perilous to infer *general* rules of law from the construction of *particular* contracts. The synthesis labelled 'frustration' is doubtful, accordingly. Courts *only* need ask whether the obligations should be understood as, objectively, qualified in the circumstances that have arisen. The further stage of turning from construction of the agreement to apply a separate 'doctrine of frustration' is arguably redundant.[164] Ockham's Razor prunes out the additional step.

The suggestion that there is no 'doctrine of frustration' save for supervening illegality is undoubtedly radical. Lawyers of a gradualist temperament might wonder whether the orthodox doctrine could be retained, justified and explained. We doubt this. But the present section and the next examine the possibility of rehabilitating frustration as a useful 'default'. One strong reason to make the attempt is Andrew Robertson's chapter in the present volume.[165] Robertson criticises exclusive reliance on construction. As he argues, courts face a difficult task in trying to infer unspoken allocations of risk.[166] This involves an ad hoc 'open-ended inquiry' which is 'elusive … [producing] inconsistent or unpredictable results'.[167] Robertson therefore defends the use of default rules (including frustration). These offer identifiable and distinctive substantive content, embodying an underlying principle of justice 'which will govern in the absence of a contractual allocation'.[168]

This is consistent with Lord Leggatt's comment that there would be 'very little to the law of contract' if it were restricted to enforcing what the parties have *expressly* agreed.[169] Significantly, the law supplements agreements with *default rules* that are (Lord Leggatt claims) 'generally optimal when they reflect prevailing social norms and expectations and therefore create rights and obligations which reasonable parties would be likely

[162] J Nadler, 'Impossibility and Frustration' in M Chen-Wishart and P Saprai (eds), *Research Handbook on The Philosophy of Contract Law* (Cheltenham, Edward Elgar, 2025 forthcoming). *cf Realestate.com.au Pty Ltd v Hardingham* [2022] HCA 39, (2022) 277 CLR 115 [17] (Kiefel CJ and Gaegler J) ('intention' in contract law must be understood *objectively*, ie, 'not a search for the uncommunicated subjective motives or intentions of the parties').

[163] *Scott v Del Sel* 1920 2 SLT 373, 376–77 (Lord Sands) ('to do homage to a very sacred legal principle – the sanctity of contract').

[164] *cf* CJ Slade, 'The myth of mistake in the English law of contract' (1954) 70 *LQR* 385; JC Smith, 'Contracts – Mistake, frustration and implied terms' (1994) 110 *LQR* 400; J Morgan, 'Common mistake in contract: Rare success and common misapprehensions' [2018] *CLJ* 559; Day (n 2).

[165] Robertson (n 4).

[166] Robertson (ibid) section III dismisses the 'obviousness' test (for implication) as 'not a legal standard but a "*deus ex machina*"'. However, 'obviousness' plays a significant constraining role since it must be obvious not simply that *some* term might have been agreed, but which *particular* term: eg, *Bank of New York Mellon (International) Ltd v Cine-UK Ltd* [2022] EWCA Civ 1021, [2023] 2 P&CR 19 [139]; *Yoo Design Services Ltd v Iliv Realty PTE Ltd* [2021] EWCA Civ 560 [51(vii)] (Carr LJ) (must show 'either that there was only one contractual solution or that one of several possible solutions would without doubt have been preferred'). *cf* A Robertson, 'Purposive Contractual Interpretation' (2019) 39 *Legal Studies* 230, 243 (test of 'singular apt solution' superior to 'vague' obviousness).

[167] Robertson (n 4) section IV.

[168] ibid.

[169] *Barton v Morris* [2023] UKSC 3, [2023] AC 684 [125].

to agree between themselves'.[170] Defaults can also help 'avoid unfair outcomes in cases where parties, whether through inertia, lack of opportunity or foresight, or deliberate choice, have not negotiated express terms to cover certain significant contingencies'.[171] As Lord Leggatt suggests, such gaps are unavoidable given constraints on drafting. Exhaustive contracts would be expensive to draft,[172] and *absolute* exhaustiveness is simply impossible: 'Even the most comprehensive and carefully drafted written contract cannot anticipate and provide expressly in advance for every possible contingency'.[173]

This is a clear and authoritative judicial endorsement of 'majoritarian' defaults. A gap-filling rule should supply, by implication of law, what that the majority of contracting parties desire. Such rules reduce drafting costs (as Lord Leggatt notes). They are also attractive theoretically. We can reconcile contract law's doctrines with *voluntary* agreement by emphasising contractors' tacit assent to the background law. As Barnett's seminal analysis maintained, that assent is more plausible the closer are the legal defaults to contractors' 'commonly-held … commonsense expectations'.[174] The task of ascertaining their expectations accurately is important given default rules' 'stickiness' – the various reasons why contractors might fail to contract away from them, even when they are not optimal for the transaction in question.[175] The likelier 'default' rules are not to be displaced, the more important it is to set them accurately.[176]

From this perspective, frustration would be a good 'default rule' if it reflects what the majority of contracting parties expect: Lord Leggatt's 'prevailing social norms and expectations'. Unfortunately, it is extremely difficult to identify what those 'prevailing expectations' might be. The premise assumes there *are* stable and homogeneous expectations to be 'identified'. Yet that foundational assumption has been queried as a general matter, using such empirical evidence as exists.[177] On 'frustration' specifically, Dagan and Somech question the cogency of resorting to custom. Common standards evolve as 'public solutions to *recurring* problems'.[178] Yet 'frustration' involves unusual, even extraordinary situations – which thus 'defy the conditions in which such [customary] solutions emerge'.

Terms may (even today) be implied into contracts by trade usage, but that must be proven through evidence.[179] More commonly, however, terms implied by law (ie,

[170] ibid [128].

[171] ibid.

[172] ibid [127] ('commerce would be stultified if time and cost was routinely incurred in discussing and making provision for [unlikely] situations').

[173] ibid.

[174] RE Barnett, 'The sound of silence: Default rules and contractual consent' (1992) 78 *Virginia Law Review* 821.

[175] L Bernstein, 'Social norms and default rules analysis' (1993) 3 *Southern California Interdisciplinary Law Journal* 59; R Korobkin, 'The Status Quo Bias and Contract Default Rules' (1998) 83 *Cornell Law Review* 608.

[176] O Ben-Shahar and JAE Pottow, 'On the stickiness of default rules' (2006) 33 *Florida State University Law Review* 651.

[177] L Bernstein, 'The Questionable Empirical Basis of Article 2's Incorporation Strategy: A Preliminary Study' (1999) 66 *University of Chicago Law Review* 710; L Bernstein, 'The Myth of Trade Usages: A Talk' (2018) 23 *Barry Law Review* 119.

[178] H Dagan and O Somech, 'When Contract's Basic Assumptions Fail' (2021) 34 *Canadian Journal of Law & Jurisprudence* 297, 306.

[179] *Exxonmobil v Texaco* [2003] EWHC 1964 (Comm), [2003] 2 Lloyd's Rep 686 [21]; *Gibson v Small* (1853) 4 HLC 353, 397; 10 ER 499, 516 (Parke B) ('The custom of trade, *which is a matter of evidence*, may … annex incidents to all written contracts …') (emphasis added).

standardised default rules) emerge from a judge's trained intuitions of what 'the nature of the contract itself implicitly requires, no more, no less'.[180] As Lord Denning once explained, the courts are here 'imposing' rules upon contractual 'relationships … of common occurrence', with the terms 'not founded on the intention of the parties, actual or presumed, but on more general considerations [of] what would be reasonable in the general run of such cases'.[181] As the critic must allow, judges have a keen appreciation of the realities of commercial life. Courts digest what is commercially reasonable from a diet of concrete litigation.

Nevertheless, the court invariably has no *direct* evidence of such expectations (again, by contrast with the proof required for 'trade custom' implied terms). The evidence may indeed be inadmissible. Lord Reed states: 'The behaviour of the reasonable man is not established by the evidence of witnesses, but by the application of a legal standard by the court'; to lead such evidence would be 'beside the point' and 'misconceived'.[182] To claim that judicially formulated default rules track 'prevailing social norms' (to quote Lord Leggatt) – ie, reflecting typical contracting parties' *actual* expectations – involves heroic assumptions. The proposition is that in the absence of hard evidence, courts can identify the terms 'which reasonable parties would be likely to agree between themselves' by intuition alone. It is a convenient fiction.

It is a potentially harmful one, too, being obfuscatory. Burton, noting the absence and likely impossibility of reliable empirical evidence about contracting parties' actual expectations, argues correctly that 'empirical majoritarian' default rules 'collapse into a *hypothetical* majoritarianism'.[183] But that label, Burton argues, is entirely misleading: 'It adds nothing but rhetoric to attribute [the proposed default] to a [hypothetical] majority'.[184] It would be more transparent to accept that *normative* choices have to be made: ie, identifying what defaults rational parties *ought to* want. This has no real basis in (actual) expectations. Using the 'façade' or 'illusion' of 'hypothetical consent' seeks to 'spread a cloak of objectivity and contractual liberty over an analyst's independent conclusions'.[185] (Or, we might add, a court's.)

If this critique is accepted, and it is impossible to justify frustration by reference to contracting parties' actual (typical) expectations, we must examine the more 'openly normative' justifications put forward for the doctrine. First, that frustration enables the court to allocate risks in an economically efficient way. Secondly, that frustration allows absolute obligations to be reconciled with justice. Neither normative justification succeeds.

[180] *Liverpool City Council v Irwin* [1977] AC 239, 254 (Lord Wilberforce).

[181] *Shell (UK) Ltd v Lostock Garage Ltd* [1976] 1 WLR 1187, 1196.

[182] *Healthcare at Home Ltd v The Common Services Agency* [2014] UKSC 49, [2014] 4 All ER 210 [3] (approving [2013] CSIH 22, 2013 SC 411 [60] (Lord Carloway): 'other juridical creations, such as the man on the Clapham omnibus (delict) *or the officious bystander (contract)*' (emphasis added)).

[183] SJ Burton, "Collapsing Illusions: Standards for Setting Efficient Contract and Other Defaults" (2016) 91 *Indiana Law Journal* 1063, 1067.

[184] *cf Healthcare at Home Ltd v The Common Services Agency* [2014] UKSC 49, [2014] 4 All ER 210 [2] (Lord Reed) (the 'intellectual tradition of defining a legal standard by reference to a hypothetical person' involves 'legal fictions').

[185] Burton (n 183) 1072.

VI. A Broader Default? Of 'Efficiency' and 'Justice'

Stephen Smith's influential metric for the success of private law theories scrutinises their 'fit' with the legal rules, including making 'transparent' sense of the understandings and attitudes of judges and others. Smith's metric also assesses the (moral) attractiveness, or 'justification', of the theory.[186] At first sight, both 'economic efficiency' and 'justice' appear *attractive* justifications for frustration. In a world of scarce resources, should the law (including contract law) not aim to minimise waste and maximise the allocation of resources to their most productive use? And should not *all* law (including contract law) aspire to just outcomes? Yet while both candidate justifications sound well, they are highly abstract, and translating them into concrete doctrine will be controversial (ie, less universally attractive). But even accepting them as abstract 'justifications', both *fit* poorly with contract doctrine.

'Economic analysis of law' has manifestly little 'fit' with English law. Even Posner accepts that many US judges fail to reason explicitly from economic premises.[187] Posner instead suggests that common law doctrines are economically efficient notwithstanding, as if evolving by some unconscious process of natural selection.[188] Leaving aside the question of whether contract law really is 'efficient', Posner's defence encounters serious objections. It utterly fails to give a 'transparent' account of the law, as conceived and explained by its participants. As Smith notes, this style of argument either means that judges must be suffering from false consciousness (unable to recognise that their decisions really derive from the logic of economic efficiency) or engaged in mass deception (consciously using economic analysis, yet disguising it in their judgments).[189] Neither seems remotely plausible.

On frustration specifically, Posner and Rosenfield recommend that courts allocate risks of interruptions to the party better placed to bear it at least cost – for example, by investing in precautions to prevent it or insuring against its occurrence.[190] Usually the promisor is best placed to make the necessary decisions. But where the *promisee* can bear the risk at lower cost, the court should discharge the promisor's liability by holding the contract frustrated (thus transferring the risk to the promisee).

Judge Posner claims this 'fits' frustration doctrine.[191] For example, the rule that a farmer is excused from an obligation to sell crops growing in a particular field if the crop fails through no fault of the farmer's.[192] Posner argues that this risk is better born by the *buyer*, being likely a wholesaler / merchant 'which buys from a variety of growers not all of whom will be hit by blight in the same growing season, [and therefore] in a better

[186] Smith (n 117) ch 1.

[187] eg *McCarty v Pheasant Run Inc* 826 F 2d 1554 (1987) (Illinois courts do not refer in terms to 'Learned Hand' efficiency test of reasonable care – but in substance courts apply 'the same factors, and in the same relation, as in the Hand Formula').

[188] RA Posner, *Economic Analysis of Law* (Boston, Little, Brown & Co, 1972) 320–21. See further, eg, G Priest, 'The Common Law Process and the Selection of Efficient Rules' (1977) 6 *Journal of Legal Studies* 65.

[189] Smith (n 117) 24–32.

[190] RA Posner and AM Rosenfield, 'Impossibility and related doctrines in contract law: An economic analysis' (1977) 6 *Journal of Legal Studies* 83.

[191] *Northern Indiana v Carbon County Coal Co*, 799 F 2d 265 (1986).

[192] *Howell v Coupland* (1876) 1 QBD 258.

position to buffer the risk of blight than the grower is'. There is no need to leave the risk where it lies initially (on the farmer / seller) to produce efficient incentives: 'The grower has every incentive to avoid the blight; so if it occurs, it probably could not have been prevented.'[193] Judge Posner explains *Krell v Henry* similarly.[194] Henry, the hirer, would not have intended to insure Krell, the owner, against the risk of the coronation procession being postponed 'since Krell could always relet the room, at the premium rental, for the coronation's new date'.[195] Since Krell was better placed to absorb the loss (ie, by reletting the room later), the contract was correctly held frustrated.

Yet such reasoning is completely absent from the leading English cases. Secondly, as Treitel points out, Posner's explanation of *Krell v Henry* involves historical hindsight.[196] We know today that there was a rearranged coronation in October (rather than June) 1902, and that the postponed procession, despite a curtailed route, still traversed Pall Mall in London. But what if the procession had taken a different route, or what if King Edward VII's appendicitis had proved fatal, or what if Britain had become a republic? Omniscience is not available to courts deciding cases 'in real time', still less to parties contracting for performance in the unknowable future.

Perhaps we could defend Posnerian risk-allocation on the basis that rational parties, knowing that they cannot know the future, should be taken to delegate the question of excuse to a future court. Precisely because the court can intervene ex post facto, using hindsight, to allocate the risk most efficiently.[197] (This claim about what rational contractors *should* prefer is contested. Kraus and Scott argue that it is rational for parties to reject courts' hindsight advantage (given the costs of ex post judicial reformulation); indeed, while it would be simple *expressly* to delegate decisions using vague formulae such as 'unfair change of circumstances' that the court can apply using hindsight, this is rare in the practice of contract drafting.[198] Gillette similarly finds a 'wide variety' of techniques to allocate (or re-allocate) risks; none appears sufficiently widespread to ground a singular 'majoritarian' default; both detailed ex ante and delegated ex post mechanisms have their differing costs; and the court should therefore simply enforce the parties' choice between the available techniques, without seeking to second-guess it.[199] Notably, empirical evidence suggests that even sophisticated contractors do not attempt to draft force majeure clauses that reflect Posner and Rosenfield's complex 'cheapest risk bearer' approach.)[200]

[193] Criticised: AO Sykes, 'The doctrine of commercial impracticability in a second-best world' (1990) 19 *Journal of Legal Studies* 43, 90–91.
[194] [1903] 2 KB 740.
[195] *Northern Indiana v Carbon County Coal Co*, 799 F 2d 265, 277 (1986).
[196] Peel (n 11) §7-016 (noting that Posner also ignores the wasted expenditure by parties like Krell, and their 'considerably reduced' profits at the October procession).
[197] *cf* A Bagchi, 'Retrospective risk allocation' (2022) 85 *Law & Contemporary Problems* 1 (ex post intervention to promote 'fairness').
[198] JS Kraus and RE Scott, 'Contract Design and the Structure of Contractual Intent' (2009) 84 *New York University Law Review* 1023.
[199] CP Gillette, 'Commercial Rationality and the Duty to Adjust Long-Term Contracts' (1985) 69 *Minnesota Law Review* 521.
[200] U Benoliel, 'The Impossibility Doctrine in Commercial Contracts: An Empirical Analysis' (2020) 85 *Brooklyn Law Review* 393 (contracts filed with US Securities and Exchange Commission).

Even were hindsight permissible,[201] it is doubtful that courts could intervene 'efficiently'. The optimal assignment of commercial risks is difficult even for experienced businesspeople. Speaking generally, Judge Frank Easterbrook observes:

> Allocating risks by contract is no easy matter, and only a long process of experimentation in the marketplace reveals the best terms … All of the provisions for creating incentives and allocating risks have their advantages and disadvantages; … no one combination of these terms is right for all people at all times.[202]

Wise courts appreciate their limited capacity to make 'optimal' risk-allocations: 'Judges are not always the most commercially-minded, let alone the most commercially experienced, of people, and should, I think, avoid arrogating to themselves overconfidently the role of arbiter of commercial reasonableness.'[203]

These general concerns are sharpened in the context of economic analysis. Declaring its 'failure' to transform legal doctrine, even in the US, Eric Posner blames the 'normative weaknesses' of economic models: if simple, such models 'exclude relevant variables', but when more complex and realistic, 'the optimal rule depends on empirical conditions that cannot be observed'.[204] On the Posner/Rosenfield model of frustration specifically, Posner (Eric) accepts that it is challenging for contract drafters to assign (and insure against) all conceivable risks, ex ante. But he doubts whether 'courts have the information necessary to repair the insurance market' by intervening ex post, through frustration.[205] Similarly, Sykes concludes that the difficulty of obtaining necessary evidence (about, eg, risk-bearing capacity, loss aversion, moral hazard) makes it 'exceptionally difficult to formulate [an efficient] default rule' of frustration. Sykes finds the US doctrine comprises 'highly unpredictable rules that are devoid of any apparent economic foundation'.[206] Triantis agrees that the unworkability of Posner and Rosenfield's recommendations doom them to failure.[207] Answers to 'subtle' questions about the cheapest bearer of risk are necessarily unpredictable. Yet only *clear* rules can guide party behaviour. The best judicial policy may be restraint, simply enforcing the contract as it stands, since it is preferable that one party clearly *knows* (ex ante) they will be liable and can plan accordingly, even if not necessarily the 'most efficient' risk-avoider.

Economics' supposed 'inevitability' notwithstanding,[208] it has had notoriously little impact on English law. By contrast, support abounds for justifying frustration as the implementation of *fairness and justice*. The doctrine has been authoritatively labelled 'a

[201] Contrary to much English authority, eg, *Court Line Ltd v Dant & Russell Inc* [1939] 3 All ER 314, 318 (Branson J) (must decide using probabilities as they appeared at the time of the frustrating event 'and not the certainty arrived at after the event'); *Bank Line v Arthur Capel* [1919] AC 435, 454 (Lord Sumner) ('Rights ought not to be left in suspense or to hang on the chances of subsequent events. The contract binds or it does not bind, and the law ought to be that the parties can gather their fate then and there').

[202] *Industrial Representatives Inc v CP Clare Corporation*, 74 F 3d 128 (1996).

[203] *Skanska Rashleigh Weatherfoil Ltd v Somerfield Stores Ltd* [2006] EWCA Civ 1732 [22] (Neuberger LJ).

[204] EA Posner, 'Economic Analysis of Contract Law after Three Decades: Success or Failure?' (2003) 112 *Yale Law Journal* 829, 854 (and *passim*).

[205] ibid 849.

[206] Sykes (n 193) 93–94.

[207] Triantis (n 97).

[208] FH Easterbrook, 'The Inevitability of Law and Economics' (1989) 1 *Legal Education Review* 3, 3 ('If there were an abundance of every good thing, there would be no need for law … If there is scarcity, law cannot be understood apart from economic thought').

special exception which justice demands'.[209] Orthodoxy maintains that 'justice' underlies frustration,[210] at least to a significant degree.[211] However, this orthodoxy is problematic. First, as noted already, the inflexible and drastic *effect* of upholding a frustration plea is inconsistent with the doctrine's supposed concern with justice and fairness. A jurisdiction to adjust or suspend obligations, and to apportion losses between the parties, would cohere much better with a basis in 'justice'.[212] English law, however, insists on automatic total discharge.[213] That may be just as unfair as letting the contract stand (with the misfortune transferred). Rejecting the frustration plea in *Panalpina*, Lord Russell reasoned:

> If a principle of achieving justice be anywhere at the root of the principle of frustration, I ask myself why should justice require that a useless site be returned to the lessor rather than remain the property of the lessee? (It is not suggested that a just solution can be achieved by somehow sharing the bad luck between lessor and lessee by, for example, a reduction of rent.)[214]

The court will simply leave the loss where it falls, if such crude intervention would not produce an obviously fairer result.

The Law Reform (Frustrated Contracts) Act 1943 is, arguably, only a limited correction of the common law, effectively a statutory change-of-position defence. Robert Goff J influentially took this view, holding that the statute was 'designed to prevent unjust enrichment' but *not* 'designed to apportion the loss between the parties'.[215] Admittedly this remains controversial (given the dearth of authority on the Act). There is support for loss-sharing,[216] or simply a broad judicial discretion over calculating the statutory 'just sum'.[217] Nevertheless, there is a telling contrast between the 1943 Act and other jurisdictions' frustration statutes which clearly mandate taking *all* losses and gains into account.[218]

Moreover, frustration's supposed concern with 'justice' (half-hearted at best, in its remedies) fits poorly with commercial law's wider approach. Courts do not otherwise intervene to rebalance agreements that prove unwise. According to a recent leading case: 'it is not the function of a court when interpreting an agreement to relieve a party

[209] *Hirji Mulji v Cheong Yue Steamship Co Ltd* [1926] AC 497, 510 (Lord Sumner).

[210] *The Super Servant Two* [1990] 1 Lloyd's Rep 1, 8 (Bingham LJ) (the fairness basis 'established by the highest authority, [and] not open to question').

[211] *Canary Wharf v European Medicines Agency* [2019] EWHC 335 (Ch) [25] (Marcus Smith J) ('Whilst … the object of the doctrine is to do justice … what is "just" and what is "unjust" is coloured by the nature of the doctrine and the juridical basis upon which it operates'); *The Sea Angel* [2007] EWCA Civ 547, [2007] 2 Lloyd's Rep 517 [112]–[113] (Rix LJ) ('underlying role' of justice; it does not supersede the detailed rules on frustration, albeit their 'application cannot be divorced from considerations of justice').

[212] JL Harrison, 'A Case for Loss Sharing' (1983) 56 *Southern California Law Review* 573. *cf* Kull (n 87).

[213] Consistent with a strong general tendency of the common law, albeit one that is now fading: T Weir, 'All or Nothing' (2004) 78 *Tulane Law Review* 511.

[214] *National Carriers Ltd v Panalpina (Northern) Ltd* [1981] AC 675, 709.

[215] *BP v Hunt* [1979] 1 WLR 783, 799.

[216] Williams (n 68) 35–39.

[217] *BP v Hunt* [1981] 1 WLR 232, 243 (Lawton LJ); *Gamerco SA v ICM Fair Warning (Agency) Ltd* [1995] 1 WLR 1226.

[218] E McKendrick, 'Frustration, Restitution, and Loss Apportionment' in A Burrows (ed), *Essays on Restitution* (Oxford, Oxford University Press, 1991); American Law Institute (n 47) § 272(2); *cf National Carriers Ltd v Panalpina (Northern) Ltd* [1981] AC 675, 707 (Lord Simon of Glaisdale) ('The Act of 1943 seems unlikely to vouchsafe justice in all cases').

from the consequences of his imprudence or poor advice';[219] it would be 'illegitimate' to rewrite contracts 'in the name of commercial good sense'.[220] Lords Sumption and Neuberger sum up: 'Leaving aside challenges going to the reality of consent, … the courts do not review the fairness of men's bargains either at law or in equity'.[221] Indeed even vitiating factors (affecting 'the reality of consent') are cautiously limited in English law, because of judicial concerns about 'unacceptable uncertainty in the sphere of commercial transactions'.[222] Lord Diplock once commented on 'justice' in commercial law (rebuking Lord Denning):[223]

> [T]he fact that the [judge] may think that one of the parties was unwise in agreeing to assume a particular misfortune risk or unlucky in its proving more expensive to him than he expected, has nothing to do with the merits of the case or with enabling justice to be done. The only merits of the case are that parties who have bargained on equal terms in a free market should stick to their agreements. Justice is done by seeing that they do so …

Or, to quote Judge Easterbrook again:[224]

> [A] court cannot improve matters by intervention after the fact. It can only destabilize the institution of contract, increase risk, and make parties worse off … Parties to contracts are entitled to seek, and retain, personal advantage; striving for that advantage is the source of much economic progress. Contract law does not require parties to be fair, or kind, or reasonable, or to share gains or losses equitably.

These citations could be multiplied. They exemplify contract law's deeply non-interventionist character. To hail frustration as an 'exception that justice demands' is therefore a startling anomaly. Why such peculiar solicitude about contracts that become impracticable or impossible to perform, amid the widespread unconcern with other harsh contracts? Given its incongruity,[225] not to mention its intractability, the 'fairness' explanation of frustration should also be rejected. Instead, courts should treat interruptions as a question of construction (and implication).[226] Objective interpretation of the contract in its context, mindful always that the judicial role is to interpret what the parties agreed and not to improve upon it. No court has 'carte blanche … to make up a solution of its own' to '[mend] the parties' bargain'.[227]

[219] *Arnold v Britton* [2015] UKSC 36, [2015] AC 1619 [20] (Lord Neuberger).

[220] ibid [77] (Lord Hodge).

[221] *Cavendish Square Holding BV v El Makdessi* [2015] UKSC 67, [2016] AC 1172 [13].

[222] *Pakistan International Airline Corporation v Times Travel (UK) Ltd* [2021] UKSC 40, [2023] AC 101 [50] (Lord Hodge) (economic duress) (*cf* R Bigwood and J Dietrich, 'Uncertainty in Private Law: Rhetorical Device or Substantive Legal Argument?' (2021) 45 *Melbourne University Law Review* 60).

[223] *The Maratha Envoy* [1978] AC 1, 8. *cf* Lord Sumption, 'A question of taste: The Supreme Court and the interpretation of contracts' (2017) 17 *Oxford University Commonwealth Law Journal* 301, 310 ('fairness has nothing to do with commercial contracts').

[224] *Industrial Representatives Inc v CP Clare Corporation*, 74 F 3d 128 (1996).

[225] *cf* G Jones and W Goodhart, *Specific Performance*, 2nd edn (London, Butterworths, 1996) 15 (change of circumstances insufficient to frustrate contract could nevertheless make it 'too harsh and oppressive to grant specific performance').

[226] Note *Iris Helicopter Leasing Ltd v Elitaliana Srl* [2021] EWHC 2459 (Comm) [25] (Jacobs J) (rejecting frustration plea which would have upset a clear contractual allocation of risk: 'the very reverse of the proper approach to frustration … [producing] the unjust result which, as Rix LJ says [in *The Sea Angel* [2007] EWCA Civ 547], is a result which the doctrine of frustration should not produce').

[227] *Sara & Hossein Asset Holdings Ltd v Blacks Outdoor Retail Ltd* [2023] UKSC 2, [2023] 1 WLR 575 [61] (Lord Briggs, dissenting).

VII. Mandatory Legislation Interventions: Emergency Relief for Systemic Shocks

This chapter advocates frustration's bifurcation, and a narrow treatment of the branch dealing with change of circumstances. The recommendation relates to ordinary, common law principles. Given a sufficiently widespread crisis, the *legislature* can – and does – intervene to modify contractual obligations. The government's main priority is the crisis itself: fighting the war or (in a pandemic) protecting public health. However, politicians must also address the consequent economic turmoil – some caused by the very measures used by the government to address the crisis. The enemy must be defeated, whether Nazi Germany or COVID-19. But not by destroying the national economy.

Contract lawyers should note a number of distinctive features about such legislation. First, its breadth. Courts can be empowered to intervene on the basis of broad 'hardship', inconceivable under strict, narrow common law frustration. Secondly, and relatedly, legislation may confer wide remedial discretion to adjust contracts. Thirdly, and obviously, Parliament has the constitutional authority to impose such drastic changes, and government the capacity to weigh up the costs and benefits of departing from contract law's normal strict approach. Fourthly, the dramatic departure is clearly signalled to contracting parties by the legislation (*cf* the gradual evolution of judicial doctrine). When it is desirable to influence behaviour (eg, discourage contract performance that might spread contagious disease),[228] legislation provides superior 'education' in a 'public policy crisis where coordination and swift action are important'.[229]

Fifthly, the legislature has the crucial power to alleviate financial pressures by the distribution of *public funds* (ie, not limited, as the court is, to allocating losses between the contracting parties). Finally, and significantly, such legislation is conceived as *exceptional* – limited in scope and duration to the immediate crisis. It is *not* a permanent or universal rejection of contract law's longstanding narrow approach to frustration.

Space precludes an exhaustive chronicle of such interventions. Some examples will illustrate. In the COVID-19 pandemic of 2020–21, the United Kingdom Parliament legislated for limits on enforcement of landlords' obligations (eg, repossession for non-payment of rent), followed by a six-month moratorium on commercial rental obligations.[230] These interventions were of limited scope. For wider 'relief', HM Government relied on 'exhortation' rather than formal legislation.[231] Most businesses acted with the cooperative forbearance encouraged by this Cabinet Office 'Guidance' (likely through commercial good-sense than any spirit of obedience).[232] Scant litigation has followed the pandemic, despite the colossal commercial disruption caused by government restriction on everyday activities. The few English cases to go to court were

[228] DA Hoffman and C Hwang, 'The Social Cost of Contract' (2021) 121 *Columbia Law Review* 979.

[229] AJ Casey and A Niblett, 'The Limits of Public Contract Law' (2022) 85 *Law & Contemporary Problems* 51, 58.

[230] Coronavirus Act 2020, ss 81–82; Commercial Rent (Coronavirus) Act 2022. *cf* K Barnett and M Harding, 'Contract in the Time of COVID-19' in B Bennett and I Freckelton (eds), *Pandemics, Public Health Emergencies and Government Powers* (Annandale, Federation Press, 2021) (surveying the Australian legislation).

[231] E McKendrick, 'Covid, contracts and change of circumstances' (2024) *Lloyd's Maritime and Commercial Law Quarterly* 34.

[232] Cabinet Office (HM Government), *Guidance on responsible contractual behaviour in the performance and enforcement of contracts impacted by the Covid-19 emergency* (London, 7 May 2020).

dispatched with the usual, strict approach.[233] (These highly predictable results confound US scholars' claims that (American) frustration doctrine's *vagueness* encouraged the 'Great Renegotiation' of contracts during the pandemic.)[234]

Why did COVID-19 apparently cause less havoc for contracting parties than would have been expected (given the limited scope of the statutory relief and the common law's customary narrowness)? First, commercial contracts usually now contain hardship, *force majeure*, or similar clauses. The ubiquity of such mechanisms makes recourse to 'frustration' less likely.[235] However, one might predict simply a different style of dispute, about the meaning of those exculpatory clauses.[236] A second factor easing the economic impact of COVID lockdowns was business interruption insurance. As McKendrick notes, a significant case about such policies' pandemic coverage was fast-tracked to the Supreme Court to give 'quick and clear guidance to the market'.[237] Thirdly, and perhaps crucially, the British Government itself paid workers whose services were unusable during the lockdowns (eg, employment in 'non-essential' shops). This state 'furlough' scheme was instituted to prevent mass redundancies. It also cushioned the losses of the legally shuttered (employing) businesses. Its total cost to UK taxpayers was *£97 billion*.[238]

The allocation of public funds is not an available solution for courts hearing a frustration case. Even a wide remedial discretion presupposes that losses are born by one or other party, or shared between them. Such a discretion to apportion was conferred by the Liabilities (War-Time Adjustment) Act 1941. It enabled the court to impose an 'equitable and reasonable' adjustment of obligations of persons 'in serious financial difficulties owing to war circumstances': section 1(1). Contemporary commentators gave this power a qualified welcome.[239] Adjustment of debts (without the stigma of bankruptcy proceedings) was a 'palliative' which would 'do more good than harm'. Yet, complained Finer, it was a 'delusion' to believe that modifying contracts could accomplish 'so grandiose an object as the national preservation of small-scale business' (and 'judges who have this duty set on them may well be perplexed'). Only much wider government action to spread the burden of wartime economic restrictions could achieve that. (Viscount Simon LC had acknowledged the limits of contract adjustment, when introducing the Liabilities (War-Time Adjustment) Bill).[240]

When the 1941 legislation was modestly extended in 1944, the Attorney-General faced MPs complaining that although the legislation was sometimes useful, many

[233] *Bank of New York Mellon (International) Ltd v Cine-UK Ltd* [2022] EWCA Civ 1021, [2023] 2 P&CR 19. J Morgan, 'Frustration and the pandemic' (2021) 137 *LQR* 563 (earlier cases).

[234] *cf* Y Givati, Y Kaplan and Y Listokin, 'Excuse 2.0' (2024) 109 *Cornell Law Review* 629.

[235] McMeel (n 18) 309–10 ('the prolixity of modern contractual documentation routinely ousts recourse to … doctrinal tools').

[236] *cf MUR Shipping BV v RTI Ltd* [2024] UKSC 18, [2025] AC 675 (not a COVID dispute).

[237] McKendrick (n 231) 42–43; *FCA v Arch Insurance* [2021] UKSC 1, [2021] AC 649.

[238] Public Accounts Committee, *40th Report of 2022-23 Parliamentary Session (COVID Employment Support Schemes)* (London, House of Commons, 2023).

[239] M Finer, 'The Liabilities (War-Time Adjustment) Act, 1941' (1941) 5 *MLR* 120.

[240] HL Deb, col 871 (25 March 1941) ('no ingenuity on the part of any Lord Chancellor will ever restore the position of individual citizens who have suffered … immense loss. It is a loss which we must endure and put up with for essential purposes').

creditors were also persons of small means (eg, owners of holiday boarding houses), no less economically precarious than the debtors who had been seeking relief under the Act.[241] The only satisfactory solution (in these MPs' opinion) was government compensation. But Sir Donald Somervell AG declared it was 'quite impossible for the Government to attempt to pay … losses which result from the war over the whole community', adding, 'At any rate it is outside this Bill'.[242]

Compensation from public funds is, naturally, a popular solution.[243] But there are competing claims, not least in wartime or other public emergencies. It is certainly not the *court's* role to allocate losses to the taxpayer without express statutory mandate: 'it is for those who fill and empty the public purse to decide when, by whom, on what conditions and within what limitations such compensation is to be made available'.[244]

When statutory compensation *is* available, it can influence frustration decisions. In *Baily v de Crespigny*, statutory compulsion to permit a railway station to be built on his land excused the defendant, when sued for breach of a restrictive covenant owed to the plaintiff.[245] The court suggested the result would have differed had the legislation made the railway company liable to compensate the defendant: 'this would have indicated that the legislature did not intend that the defendant should be freed from liability on his covenant, although he was disabled from performing it'.[246] But that was not the way the legislation had been structured. The plaintiff therefore had to put up with the loss of the covenant, being 'one of a numerous class of persons injured by the construction of a railway, for whom the legislature has not provided compensation'.[247]

Cases about frustration of charterparties in World War I might also have been influenced by a judicial desire to divide Admiralty compensation for requisitioned shipping. This point was not as openly acknowledged as it (characteristically) was in contemporary US cases.[248] However, MacMillan argues that the House of Lords' 1916 decision that the charterparty in *Tamplin v Anglo-Mexican* had *not* been frustrated by the ship's requisition was a pragmatic way to give something to both sides.[249] The owners were still paid hire by the charterers at the (pre-war) agreed rate; the charterers, although unable to use the ship, themselves received the Crown compensation, conceived as hire paid (now at significantly higher wartime rates) under a sub-charter to the Admiralty. The strategy is perhaps confirmed by Lord Atkinson's objection, in dissent, that the Crown's payment of 'sub-hire' to the charterers was 'irrelevant' and had 'obscured' the true legal position.[250]

[241] HC Deb, cols 1779–812 (11 October 1944).
[242] ibid col 1783. NB the Liabilities (War-Time Adjustment) Act 1944, s 11 abolished the Revenue's automatic priority over debtors' assets in insolvency (the 'really fresh attitude' to government sacrifice advocated by Finer (n 239) 123).
[243] *Report of Board of Trade Committee* (n 105) 7 (compensation was 'raised [by consultees] in many different forms').
[244] *Burmah Oil v Lord Advocate* [1965] AC 75, 134 (Viscount Radcliffe, dissenting).
[245] (1869) LR 4 QB 180.
[246] ibid 188.
[247] ibid 189.
[248] cf *The Isle of Mull* 257 F 798 (1919) and 278 F 131 (1921).
[249] *Tamplin v Anglo-Mexican* [1916] 2 AC 397; MacMillan (n 104) 290–92.
[250] [1916] 2 AC 397,422.

Lord Parker even suggested that the Admiralty payment should itself somehow be divided between owners and charterers.[251] While some courts struggled to put this into effect,[252] the dictum came to be seen as incorrect.[253] War compensation was due only to those physically dispossessed from their property (like the shipowners), not those with merely *contractual* interests in property (like charterers, or merchants who had agreed to buy goods subsequently requisitioned for military use).[254] Equally, only outright takings of property attracted compensation from the Defence of the Realm (Losses) Commission, while mere restrictions on its use did not.[255] The line drawn might have been unsophisticated,[256] but it defined the limits of public compensation *clearly*. In short, the question of state support may be influential *upon* frustration, but is certainly not determined *by* the contractual position.

As emphasised above, legislative interventions have been conceived as emergency measures. They are time-limited. The brief lifespan of the Commercial Rent (Coronavirus) Act 2022 permitted it little impact in practice. McKendrick suggests the Act was therefore an 'experiment that has failed'.[257] However, the limited nature of such legislation is vital. Judges may view broad discretion with distaste. Scrutton LJ extrajudicially criticised the broad powers to modify wartime contracts in the Courts (Emergency Powers) Act 1917. The judges had to do justice in imitation of 'Solomon, or the legendary Cadi under a palm tree', having been 'given a free hand, with no guidance' by Parliament.[258] Nor was Scrutton the only critical judge.[259] Yet because such jurisdictions confer extraordinary statutory powers, they cannot be generalised across 'ordinary' contract law.[260]

Waddilove emphasises this point.[261] He accepts that most of the time, contract law should contain predictable rules. A general, vague excusatory doctrine 'risks the dissolution of contract altogether if not properly confined'. But faced with a cataclysm beyond the scope of contracting parties to predict, or for the tools of contract law to resolve, Waddilove advocates a different paradigm. His historical model is the special court constituted by the Fire of London Disputes Act 1666. By allocating losses in 'just' and 'proportionate shares' (when tenants were otherwise 'not relievable [from the burden of repairs] in any ordinary course of Law')[262] the 'Fire Court' facilitated London's rapid reconstruction after that year's Great Fire. Waddilove notes the emergency process's

[251] ibid 428.
[252] *Chinese Mining Co v Sale & Co* [1917] 2 KB 599.
[253] Foxton (n 55) 497 ('sloppy thinking').
[254] ibid chs 2–3.
[255] ibid.
[256] ibid 340 ('a crude and essentially physical test'), 360 (enduring strength of 'traditional concepts of property').
[257] McKendrick (n 221) 49.
[258] TE Scrutton, 'The War and the Law' (1918) 34 *LQR* 116.
[259] *Wauters v Association Internationale* (1918) 34 TLR 577 (Rowlatt J) (the legislation made judges 'dictators'); *North Metropolitan Electric v Stoke Newington Corp* [1921] 1 Ch 455, 468 Lawrence J ('much embarrassed by … a power so arbitrary in its nature').
[260] *North Metropolitan Electric v Stoke Newington Corp* [1921] 1 Ch 455, 468 ('It must however be remembered that this … emergency power [is] conferred upon the Court only because of the great dislocation of almost all commercial transactions caused by the greatest war in which England has ever been engaged').
[261] DP Waddilove, 'Anticontract' (2024) 61 *American Business Law Journal* 135.
[262] 1666 Act, Preamble.

distinctive design features compared to ordinary contract law; a reactive, ex post response to particular facts. Excuse as 'a complete release of obligation' cutting across the contractual allocation of risks, prioritising *fair* resolution as a matter of public good. Such particularistic discretion is 'inherently irregular', the antithesis of the law's settled clarity – an approach 'fundamentally without rules … [lacking] any internal consistency'. While this might sound disruptive at best, dystopian at worst, Waddilove insists that such discretion can be safely circumscribed by emergency legislation. Through tight legislative parameters, a Fire Court is securely 'cabined from the system of regular contract law'. Indeed, its insulation reinforces the 'regular' law's desirably settled nature.[263]

Legislation can thus impose an exceptional mandatory jurisdiction to rebalance contracts in times of public crisis. There are dangers in such a course. A 1918 government committee believed that the then-current First World War legislation had relaxed contractual obligations sufficiently, advising against a further extension of discretionary relief.[264] It was particularly undesirable to undermine the sanctity of cross-border contracts, undermining British companies' reliability in international trade. Indeed, to cancel any contract ('but one mesh in the great web of contractual obligations') could ultimately bring economic 'disaster'.[265] While critical commentary on contract law in the COVID pandemic envisages a wider excuse for non-performance,[266] this too could exacerbate economic harm. Bloomfield and Gordon note how failure of individual contracts within strategic supply chains 'can cascade into macro-level shocks' (as commonly experienced during the global pandemic).[267] Imposing *greater* liability for such breaches of contract (to make failing suppliers internalise the economic disruption to the wider public) would, they argue, help incentivise optimal levels of economic 'resilience'. One reason for recurrent drugs shortages in America, it appears, is the readiness of the US law to excuse manufacturers from contractual liability (when, eg, federal regulators take action against unsafe factories).[268] Even if the 'impracticability' excuse makes sense between manufacturers and their immediate customers, the drug manufacturers' excused failures impose harm and suffering on the ultimate downstream consumers (eg, cancer patients) – a clear and grave form of externality. In other words, excusing too readily in a crisis itself risks macro-economic damage and other societal disruption.[269]

[263] Waddilove (n 261) 155 ('Fire courts, in short, keep law good by filtering out hard cases to relieve pressure that could potentially distort the regular system of contract law').

[264] *Report of Board of Trade Committee* (n 105).

[265] Prefiguring the 'exhortation' strategy in the COVID-19 crisis a century later, the Committee (ibid) thought legislation unnecessary since, throughout the war, most businesses had acted in a spirit of 'give and take' – so adjustments could be left to the 'good sense and good feeling' and indeed the 'patriotic spirit' of contracting parties.

[266] eg McKendrick (n 221), C Mitchell, 'What does Covid-19 teach us about English contract law?' (2024) 44 *Legal Studies* 313.

[267] D Bloomfield and J Gordon, 'The law and economics of resilience' (2026) 103 *Washington University Law Review* (forthcoming).

[268] K Reinmuth, 'Default Difficulties: The Case for Regulatory Intervention in Merchants' Reliance on Default Rules That Harm Consumers' (2025) 77 *Stanford Law Review* 779.

[269] Givati, Kaplan and Listokin (n 234) 673 (contracting parties should *share* losses, not allocate according to a zero-sum game, 'from a broad macroeconomic perspective … [when] mass bankruptcies and a downward economic spiral are imminent').

Decisions of national economic policy are obviously for the political, not judicial, branches of government. Yet when they adjudge such drastic intervention to be necessary, the policy may be implemented without the drawbacks of common law. The departure from ordinary contract principle is announced clearly through legislation, and by the same means cleared decisively away when the crisis has passed.[270]

VIII. Conclusions and Summary

To summarise this long chapter, and its unorthodox propositions about the supposedly unified 'doctrine of frustration':

(1) There is no *single* 'doctrine of frustration'.

(2) There is a *mandatory* rule imposing 'frustration by supervening illegality'. It is a doctrine of public policy, necessary to ensure consistency between contractual obligation and the criminal law. Supervening illegality 'kills the contract itself and discharges both parties automatically'.[271] Parties cannot agree to disapply or relax this rule.[272] Its proper analogue is in textbook chapters on contracts unenforceable because of (initial) illegality.

(3) All other changes of circumstances raise quite different questions. Namely, the allocation of risks (and losses) for events affecting performance.

(4) Such risk-allocation is primarily a matter for the parties. There is no room for mandatory rules;[273] even the usefulness of gap-filling *defaults* is open to serious doubt. Much of the point of contracts is to undertake, and allocate, risks in a future world / marketplace *known to be uncertain*. Contractors structure and price contracts around such risks, using, eg, *force majeure*, cancellation, best-efforts or other clauses. '[The] acceptance of risk is a natural and inevitable consequence of contracting … [Contractual] risk cannot validly be assumed to be transferred away from its natural location unless the contrary is explicitly stated.'[274]

(5) English contract law typically imposes absolute *obligations de résultat*.[275] It would be inconsistent to allow a general impossibility or impracticability defence (which would substantially reconfigure the strict obligations into 'best endeavours'). However, an *ex facie* unqualified obligation may contain implicit limits – ie, being conditional on certain matters. This is a question of objective construction.

(6) This explanation is 'internal'. By contrast, the leading modern English explanation of the frustration doctrine declares it must be imposed by the court.[276] Yet it was

[270] But *cf* MacMillan (n 104) (frustration's common law development during the 1914–18 war was 'no doubt bolstered by … the radical provisions of the emergency legislation').

[271] *Joseph Constantine v Imperial Smelting* [1942] AC 154, 163.

[272] *Ertel Bieber & Co v Rio Tinto Co* [1918] AC 260.

[273] *cf* Dagan and Somech (n 178) 316 ('the prescription that the parties are not bound by an agreement whose basic assumption failed … is immutable … If contract is to serve people's self-determination, contract law *must* comply with this' (emphasis in original)).

[274] T Roberts, 'Commercial Impossibility and Frustration of Purpose: A Critical Analysis' (2003) 16 *Canadian Journal of Law & Jurisprudence* 129, 132, 145.

[275] Nicholas (n 117).

[276] *Davis Contractors v Fareham UDC* [1956] AC 696, 728 Lord Radcliffe ('the parties themselves have become so far disembodied spirits that their actual persons should be allowed to rest in peace. In their place there rises … the court itself').

fallacious to reason that a contract's objective meaning cannot extend to matters that the parties did not, in fact, subjectively contemplate.[277]

(7) This interpretive exercise need not be confined to effecting automatic complete discharge (an 'implied contingent condition subsequent'). A contract might provide (either expressly or *implicitly*) for (say) the suspension of obligations during a non-permanent interruption of performance.

(8) Courts are properly cautious about implying terms to govern interrupted performance,[278] especially in detailed professionally drafted agreements.[279] Bingham MR's warning about the 'intrusive … extraordinary' power to imply terms[280] remains apposite here. As Flaux C recently declared, even assuming the COVID-19 crisis (and government response) were truly 'unprecedented', that was 'no reason to disregard or disapply fundamental principles of the law of contract'.[281]

(9) The residual 'doctrine of frustration' (ie, outside supervening illegality), as conceived by orthodox understandings (although not by this chapter), is a *default* rule. Contracting parties are free to allocate risks of interruption differently, and frequently do.[282] Indeed, the 'narrow forgiveness' offered by the frustration doctrine positively 'amounts to an invitation to contracting parties to depart from the common law'.[283]

(10) Orthodoxy holds that once the process of construction (interpretation and implication) is exhausted, the court must turn to the 'doctrine of frustration'.[284] We argue this is regrettable for a number of reasons.[285]

   (a) First, some of the supposed doctrine's rules are appropriate *only* for supervening illegality. Automatic complete discharge is necessary as a matter of public policy. But its drastic effect is often unsuitable for commercial interruptions.

   (b) Secondly, while prima facie rules govern certain standard situations (death in employment; destruction of specific subject-matter), these are misleading if extrapolated into a general doctrine (eg, 'physical impossibility'). Outside the standard situations, however, frustration 'doctrine' is indefinable.[286] Corbin exaggerated little in commenting that 'the court must exercise its equity powers and pray for the wisdom of Solomon'.[287]

[277] *Bromarin AB v IMD Investments Ltd* [1999] STC 301, 310. *cf Realestate.com.au Pty Ltd v Hardingham* [2022] HCA 39, (2022) 277 CLR 115 [50] (Gordon J) ('Older cases decided before the ascendancy of the objective theory of contract should be approached with caution').

[278] *Bank of New York Mellon (International) Ltd v Cine-UK Ltd* [2022] EWCA Civ 1021, [2023] 2 P&CR 19 [140] (Flaux C) ('the test for implication is a stringent one and … nowhere near satisfied in these cases').

[279] ibid [140].

[280] *Philips Electronique SA v British Sky Broadcasting Ltd* [1995] EMLR 472, 481.

[281] *Bank of New York Mellon (International) Ltd v Cine-UK Ltd* [2022] EWCA Civ 1021, [2023] 2 P&CR 19 [143] (rejecting counsel's invitation to 'apply the law in a fresh light').

[282] *Canary Wharf v European Medicines Agency* [2019] EWHC 335 (Ch) [38] ('Contracts, these days, seek to anticipate everything').

[283] Bridge (n 21) 13.

[284] *Canary Wharf v European Medicines Agency* [2019] EWHC 335 (Ch) [26(4)] ('even a sophisticated contract … may find itself defeated by the truly unforeseen').

[285] *cf* Robertson (n 4).

[286] A familiar legal problem (eg, *Buckland v The King* [1933] 1 KB 767, 772 (Scrutton LJ)).

[287] Corbin (n 100) 371–72 ('When neither custom not agreement determines the allocation of a risk').

(c) Thirdly, there is no evidence of any consistent expectation about what courts should do to resolve such difficulties, across the diverse universe of possible contracts, parties and interruptions.[288] Frustration conceived as a 'doctrine' (rather than merely decisions about individual contracts) must therefore be an 'external' judicial imposition (and not a 'majoritarian' default).

(d) Fourthly, however, the basis justifying such an 'external' rule is uncertain. The two leading candidates ('economic efficiency' and 'justice') both fail.

(11) Economic analysts recommend that frustration allocates risks 'efficiently' to the party able to bear them at least costs.[289] While economic efficiency is an appealing goal in the abstract, implementing it exceeds real-world judicial capacity, given limited available information about contracting parties' risk-absorbing abilities. This explanation also has absolutely no support from reasoning in English frustration cases.

(12) While courts have frequently explained frustration doctrine as a device to reconcile absolute obligations with the needs of justice and fairness,[290] this explanation is also dubious (despite its comparative popularity). Why should this kind of 'unfairness' alone attract anomalous judicial solicitude? English law is otherwise notoriously reluctant to reopen hard bargains. Furthermore, if the doctrine were truly rooted in fairness the court should adjust the contract, not impose automatic total discharge for frustration.

(13) Legislation may ordain a different approach in the face of widespread economic disruption. Such a regime is *mandatory*. Courts have been empowered by statute to suspend, modify or cancel unexpectedly burdensome contracts in wars, pandemics and other systemic crises, not purely as a matter of fairness to hard-pressed individuals, but to preserve national economic stability. The advantages of emergency legislation are three-fold. First, the displacement of ordinary contract doctrine, in the public interest, is clearly signalled. Secondly, Parliament can also allocate public funds to mitigate losses that would otherwise lie with individual contractors. Thirdly, legislative intervention is limited in scope and time to the crisis that requires it. Such exceptional statutory intervention proves the narrow (common law) rule.

[288] More plausibly, parties have different expectations: *The Eugenia* [1964] 2 QB 226, 238 (Lord Denning MR) ('Each [party] would have sought to insert reservations or qualifications of one kind or another').

[289] Posner and Rosenfield (n 190).

[290] *Hirji Mulji v Cheong Yue Steamship Co Ltd* [1926] AC 497, 510 (Lord Sumner).

10

Date of Breach as a Sticky Default Rule and the Role of the Court in Assessing Reasonable Mitigatory Measures

KATY BARNETT*

I. Introduction

As Jonathan Morgan has noted, it is possible to identify whether a contractual rule is default or mandatory by looking at whether the rules can be changed by the parties or not.[1] If a rule cannot be changed, it is mandatory; if it can be contracted around, it is a default rule. Therefore, to assess the nature of a given rule it is necessary to consider whether parties can negotiate around it in their contracts. The exemplars of default rules are those which apply to implication of terms and termination, but parties can also, of course, stipulate the quantum of damages, or exclude certain heads of damages. Morgan argues that contractual remedies, including those rules which govern the assessment expectation damages, can be seen as 'default rules' in some instances.[2]

It can be more difficult, however, to assess the status of a particular rule, if it is a rule from which the parties do not generally depart, although it is possible that they *could* negotiate around it if they wanted to. In this collection, Robertson has argued that default rules allocate risk in the absence of express agreement.[3] Given that the date from which damages are measured will affect the quantum of damages, any changes will affect the allocation of risk. The dearth of case law on this issue suggests that parties do

* Thank you to the participants in Melbourne Law School–Cambridge Law Faculty Research Partnership Workshop on Default and Mandatory Rules in Contract and Commercial Law, 15 April to 13 May 2024, and to those who commented on drafts of this chapter, including Ryan Catterwell, Adam Kramer, Harold Luntz (may his memory be a blessing), Jonathan Morgan, Peter Radan and David Winterton. Any errors remain my own.

[1] J Morgan, 'Contract remedies as default rules' in R Halson and D Campbell, *Research Handbook on Remedies in Private Law* (Cheltenham, Edward Elgar, 2019) 472, 472. See R Catterwell, 'Party Intention, Default Rules and Contract Theory', this volume, ch 4, who identifies a spectrum of what counts as a 'default rule' from narrow to extremely broad.

[2] Morgan (n 1) 485–87, where Morgan argues that expectation damages are not necessarily the optimal default rule.

[3] A Robertson, 'Default Rules, Interpretation and Risk Allocation', this volume, ch 3.

not generally contract around the rule that damages are assessed as at date of breach. The 2002 ISDA Master Agreement may be an exception to this general trend.[4]

Catterwell has argued in this collection that there is a default presumption in favour of common law remedies applying.[5] The question is the extent to which this presumption applies to the granular rules of the remedies themselves. Morgan has argued that the rules of mitigation give effect to the bargain the parties are presumed to have intended, and thus could operate as default rules.[6] It is accepted in this chapter that the date of breach rule is intrinsically intertwined with the principles of mitigation, and that, as Dyson and Kramer have asserted, courts are prepared to depart from it.[7] It is also accepted, for the purposes of this chapter, that Summers is correct to assert that if a party makes a choice to respond to a breach in an unusual way, the court tends to assume that the party has responded in the usual way (for better or for worse) and in this way, principles of mitigation are built into the assessment of loss itself.[8] In this chapter, it will be argued that 'legal causation' does not provide an adequate justification for mitigation or remoteness principles either, and that a more fine-grained approach is needed.

As Korobkin notes, some default rules have a '*status quo* bias': once a particular rule becomes the norm, parties are more reluctant to depart from it than they otherwise would be.[9] These rules are 'stickier' than others. The date of breach rule could perhaps best be described being on the 'very sticky' end of the default spectrum.[10] The reason for this is that there is generally no need for parties to stipulate in the contract for a different date – although they *could* if they wanted to – because the principles of mitigation allow courts to depart from the rule of thumb when the circumstances require it.[11]

The decision to depart from the date of breach rule is generally that of the court, when assessing the quantum of loss, and depends broadly upon whether a substitute performance is available on the market. Courts assess damages on the presumption that the non-breaching party *immediately* goes onto the market as at the date of breach, to find a substitute performance, in order to mitigate. But this is only where there is a liquid market in which substitute performances are readily available.

This chapter will be structured as follows. In section II, I will consider the function of default rules, and the history and function of the date of breach rule. In section III, I consider the general exceptions to the date of breach rule, which explains why

[4] Thank you to Louise Gullifer and Jonathan Morgan for pointing me in the direction of this possible exception. The contract is created by the International Securities and Derivatives Association, Inc: www.isda.org/book/2002-isda-master-agreement-mylibrary. It allows for amended dates of assessment of 'in the event of early termination.

[5] Catterwell (n 1).

[6] J Morgan, 'Smuggling Mitigation into White & Carter v McGregor: Time to Come Clean?' (2015) *Lloyd's Maritime and Commercial Law Quarterly* 575. See criticisms of this view in A Summers, *Mitigation in the Law of Damages* (Oxford, Oxford University Press, 2024) 70–71.

[7] A Dyson and A Kramer, 'There is no "Breach Date Rule": Mitigation, Difference in Value and Date of Assessment' (2014) 130 *LQR* 259.

[8] Summers (n 6) ch 2. See also K Barnett, 'Substitutive Damages and Mitigation in Contract Law' (2016) 23 *Singapore Academy of Law Journal* 795.

[9] R Korobkin, 'Status Quo Bias and Contract Default Rules' (1998) 83 *Cornell Law Review* 608.

[10] The concept of a 'sticky' default rule is discussed in H Dagan and M Heller, 'Autonomy Defaults' (1 February 2025), available at ssrn.com/abstract=4754123 or dx.doi.org/10.2139/ssrn.4754123.

[11] Dyson and Kramer (n 7); Summers (n 6).

parties are generally not incentivised to stipulate any change in their contracts. There is adequate flexibility in the response of the court. The court simply treats the date of breach rule as a rule of thumb, readily departed from if the circumstances require it, and hence there is no need for the parties to change anything in their contracting practices. In section IV I consider the difficult case of *The Golden Victory*, where the minority considered that courts could not depart from the date of breach rule for reasons of certainty. This must be wrong, for the reasons considered in sections II and III. Contracting parties do not need to stipulate a different date in their contracts because the courts have the ability to depart from it in a way that is likely to meet the needs of contracting parties (as a matter of efficiency, autonomy and individual justice).

II. The Function of Default Rules and the History and Function of the Date of Breach Rule

A. The Function of Default Rules More Generally

The function of default rules more generally is contested. In their landmark article, Ayres and Gertner argue that default rules 'fill in the gaps in incomplete contracts' in order to generate economically efficient outcomes, reflecting the rules that the majority prefers.[12] Dagan and Heller have queried this and argued that some defaults exist, not to promote efficiency, but to enhance societal autonomy.[13] As Gullifer has argued, in the commercial sphere, default rules also have the benefit of providing legal certainty, coordination and harmonisation.[14]

It is argued that all of these functions are present in the date of breach rule. In different ways, the date of breach rule promotes efficiency and cooperation, but also seeks to allow maximal autonomy for the non-breaching party, in the way that they respond to breach. The rule also provides legal certainty. In what follows, I discuss first the history of the rule (how parties and the courts came to this rule) and then what the policy concerns behind the date of breach rule are.

B. The History of the Date of Breach Rule

The institution of contract *qua* contract is a relatively late development; it was not until the nineteenth century that lawyers consistently treated contract as such, and not as species of debt or tortious obligation.[15] Although Summers has situated the beginnings

[12] I Ayres and R Gertner, 'Filling Gaps in Incomplete Contracts: An Economic Theory of Default Rules' (1989–1990) 99 *Yale Law Journal* 87, 87. But see Korobkin (n 9) 610, criticising the focus on efficiency.
[13] Dagan and Heller (n 10).
[14] L Gullifer, 'The Nature and Function of Default Rules in Commercial Law' in B Häcker and J Ungerer (eds), *Default Rules in Private Law* (Hart Publishing, forthcoming).
[15] J Baker, *An Introduction to English Legal History*, 5th edn (Oxford, Oxford University Press, 2019) 375.

of principles of mitigation as arising rather earlier,[16] the legal principles establishing the expectation measure for damages for breach of contract only coalesced even later, in the mid-nineteenth century. While courts from the sixteenth century onwards made awards which arguably reflect a consciousness of expectation damages,[17] the constraints of pleadings and the division of courts into Common law and Chancery meant that theses principles were not clearly developed. Moreover, damages were a question for the jury, and thus the principles upon which damages were calculated were opaque.[18]

The development of principles of contract damages when a thriving global market for goods had arisen explains why courts start from a presumption that damages are calculated from the date of breach.

An important contributor to the development of rules governing the calculation of contract damages was the development of liquid markets, where fungible replacements for the subject matter of contracts could readily be purchased. The rise of contracts for the sale of shares and stock were an important part of the shift towards an explicit awards of expectation damages in England, because shares and stock were intrinsically fungible.[19] A series of English cases between 1799 and 1810 applied the rule of expectation damages to contracts for sale of stock in a rising market.[20] Consequently, by 1805, Lord Redesdale made the following statement regarding the choice between expectation damages and specific performance in the context of a sale of stock:

> Unquestionably the original foundation of these decrees [for specific performance] was simply this: that damages at law would not give the party the compensation to which he was entitled, that is, would not put him in a situation as beneficial to him as if the agreement were specifically performed. On this ground the court, in a variety of cases, has refused to interfere where, from the nature of the case, the damages must necessarily be commensurate to the injury sustained … *For instance, in agreements for the purchase of stock, it is the same thing to the party where or from whom the stock is purchased, provided he receives the money that will purchase it.*[21]

In other words, damages were adequate, because they allowed the plaintiff to purchase a substitute performance, in part because the shares were entirely fungible.

However, this alone was not enough. It was also necessary to have a market where goods were sufficiently fungible to enable damages to be adequate. Once liquid markets arose, it was possible for judges to apply a date of breach rule as a rule of thumb in the early twentieth century. It was therefore not necessary for parties to stipulate anything

[16] Summers (n 6) 13 cites *Vertue v Bird* (1676) 3 Keb 766, 84 ER 1000, followed by a series of 19th-century cases.

[17] D Ibbetson, 'The assessment of contractual damages at common law in the late sixteenth century' in M Dyson and D Ibbetson (eds), *Law and Legal Process: Substantive Law and Procedure in English Legal History* (Cambridge, Cambridge University Press 2013) 126.

[18] W Swain, *The Law of Contract 1670–1870* (Cambridge, Cambridge University Press, 2015) 10, 23–29, 101–06.

[19] MJ Horwitz, 'The Historical Foundations of Modern Contract Law' (1974) 87 *Harvard Law Review* 917, 937. Note that some of Horwitz's conclusions have been questioned: AWB Simpson, 'The Horwitz Thesis and the History of Contracts' (1979) 46 *University of Chicago Law Review* 533.

[20] *Shepherd v Johnson* (1802) 2 East 211, 102 ER 349; *M'Arthur v Seaforth* (1810) 2 Taunt 257, 127 ER 1076; *Payne v Burke* (1799) discussed at 2 East 212, note (a); 102 ER 350, note (a). As Horwitz notes, it is apparent that the US shifted to an expectation measure 10 years earlier than the UK.

[21] *Harnett v Yielding* (1805) 2 Sch & Lef 549, 553–54; [1803–1813] All ER Rep 704, 705 (emphasis added).

different, because the case law indicated that courts were prepared to depart from the rule where necessary.

Slater v Hoyle & Smith,[22] a case from the early twentieth century, is illustrative of the way in which the law developed. The buyers purchased 3,000 pieces of bleached cotton cloth from the sellers for six pounds, nine shillings per piece, but they were unhappy with the quality of the pieces provided and refused to accept the remaining pieces due under the contract. The sellers (plaintiffs) sued the buyers for their refusal to accept delivery. The buyers (defendants) counterclaimed for breach of warranty in relation to the cloth that had been delivered and failure to deliver cloth of the requisite quality in relation to the remaining pieces due under the contract.

In fact, the buyers had a follow-on contract to sell some of the pieces to a third party and had delivered the pieces to the third party for the contracted-for price, with no reduction in price (as if the goods had not been defective). The sellers had not known of the follow-on contract but argued that it should be considered in assessing the buyers' loss. The court held that circumstances peculiar to the buyer were irrelevant in calculating damages, and the fact that the buyers had sold some of the pieces for full price did not reduce the damages payable for breach of warranty.[23]

However, courts do not invariably apply the rule in *Slater v Hoyle & Smith*.[24] Subsequent sales have been considered, including where a sub-sale involved a latent defect, as in *Bence Graphics International Ltd v Fasson UK Ltd*,[25] and where there was a delay in delivery, as in *Wertheim v Chicoutemi Pulp Co*.[26] In section III, I will discuss these exceptions in more detail and explain how they lead date of breach to become a sticky default rule insofar as the parties to the contract are concerned.

However, before moving to this topic, I will tie the historical and evolutionary development of the law into the broader policy concerns reflected in the rules governing mitigation and the date of breach rule.

C. The Policies Behind Mitigation and the Date of Breach Rule

I have argued elsewhere that principles of mitigation (including the date of breach rule) reflect a variety of policy aims,[27] using Andrew Robertson's division between interpersonal justice considerations and community welfare considerations.[28] The rule for

[22] *Slater v Hoyle & Smith* [1920] 2 KB 11.

[23] ibid 14–15 (Bankes LJ); 17–18 (Warrington LJ); 21–25 (Scrutton LJ). See also *Clark v Macourt* [2013] HCA 56, (2013) 253 CLR 1 [111], [130]–[133] (Keane J).

[24] See eg, *Euro-Asian Oil SA v Credit-Suisse AG* [2018] EWCA Civ 1720 [68]–[74] (Simon LJ) (a case involving contracts akin to string contracts) which rejected *Slater v Hoyle & Smith* [1920] 2 KB 11.

[25] *Bence Graphics International Ltd v Fasson UK Ltd* [1998] QB 87.

[26] *Wertheim v Chicoutemi Pulp Co* [1911] AC 301.

[27] K Barnett, 'The Policy Behind Remoteness in Contract Damages: Beyond Voluntary Assumption of a Risk or Gap Filling' in A Goymour and J O'Sullivan, *Politics, Policy and Private Law Volume 2* (Oxford, Hart Publishing, 2025, *in press*) 49, 64–67. *cf* Summers (n 6) who asserts that the only clear explanation for these rules is 'factual causation'.

[28] A Robertson, 'Rights, Pluralism and the Duty of Care' in D Nolan and A Robertson (eds), *Rights and Private Law* (Oxford, Hart Publishing, 2012); A Robertson, 'On the Function of the Law of Negligence' (2012) 33 *OJLS* 31; A Robertson, 'Policy-based reasoning in duty of care cases' (2013) 33 *Legal Studies* 119.

assessment of damages as at date of breach is simply a 'rule of thumb', which may not accurately reflect what actually occurred, but allows a court and the parties to make a rough and ready guess as to what the damages will likely be.

While Summers and Kramer argue that 'legal causation' can explain many of the problems in mitigation, 'legal causation' is simply a cover for a variety of policy decisions.[29] The label 'causation' occludes the policy considerations behind the courts' decisions, notwithstanding Summers' elegant analysis of 'common sense causation' which identifies autonomy and predictability as keys.[30] This simply underlines further that these questions are policy decisions, not decisions about causation at all.

As Wayne Courtney has argued, in contract law questions of factual causation are not relevant to mitigation, and nor are new intervening acts, but the court does consider the reasonableness of the plaintiff's reliance on the defendant's promise to perform.[31] When it becomes unreasonable for the plaintiff to expect that the defendant will perform their obligations, the defendant will no longer be liable for any losses sustained by the plaintiff. The predictability of the plaintiff's loss is taken into consideration, as well as the ease with which the plaintiff may stem that loss. Courts do not require plaintiffs to perform impossibilities, and they respect party autonomy and award damages even if the mitigating act causes more loss.[32]

Summers and Kramer have argued, too, that party choice and autonomy are pivotal to the court's willingness to look into subsequent events.[33] Summers has expanded on this in his recent book, and argues that this approach reflects the fact that, in assessing damages and mitigation, courts simply assume that the plaintiff took the usual 'no breach' position.[34] In a case like *Slater v Hoyle & Smith* this means that the cross-claimant was presumed to have had to sell the defective cotton and buy replacement cotton in the calculation of damages. However, a plaintiff can choose not to take the usual mitigatory action, and must wear the consequences of this, either for good or for ill. In *Slater v Hoyle & Smith*, the decision not to take the usual action turned out to be positive for the non-breaching party, but it could equally well have been negative, as Summers notes.[35] Either way, the non-breaching party would have to wear the consequences.

The real benefit of Summers' analysis is his discussion of the *res inter alios acta* rule, and his careful consideration of the reasons courts make an assessment as to whether a subsequent contract is related to the breach or not. Summers argues that this decision comes down to whether the subsequent contract is predictable or not, and the extent to which the plaintiff's decision is an autonomous choice.[36] While Summers' argument is compelling, rather than seeing this as 'factual causation' or 'common sense causation' the rule is better understood as reflecting certain policy concerns which seek to ensure interpersonal justice between the parties in a given dispute, including the predictability

[29] Barnett (n 27).
[30] Summers (n 6) ch 5.
[31] W Courtney, 'Contract Damages and the Promisee's Role in its Own Loss' (2018) 42 *Melbourne University Law Review* 406, 427–31.
[32] J Edelman, *McGregor on Damages*, 22nd edn (London, Sweet & Maxwell, 2024) [10-005].
[33] Dyson and Kramer (n 11) 265; Summers (n 6) ch 6.
[34] Summers (n 6) 185–86.
[35] ibid 185–86, 196–97.
[36] Summers (n 6) ch 9.

of a particular response to a breach, and the extent of control a non-breaching party has over the choices they make in response to a breach.

The emphasis upon autonomy reflects in part the nineteenth-century ideal of contract as a vehicle for the free will of the parties. This links to the community welfare concern noted by Dagan and Heller, to ensure that contract is autonomy maximising. I have argued elsewhere that mitigation rules reflect a well-recognised and overriding general policy of the law in favour of encouraging self-help by plaintiffs.[37] However, there are also aspects of interpersonal justice concerns in the assessment. In assessing whether the plaintiff's subsequent actions will be taken into account or not, it is necessary to consider (as a matter of interpersonal justice) whether the plaintiff's mitigatory actions are predictable. The more predictable a consequence, the more likely a court is to find that the defendant should have had that consequence in mind.

However, there are also other policy considerations underlying the date of breach rule. Because it is a default rule which parties do not generally depart from, parties are incentivised to mitigate efficiently,[38] and this also makes court processes and proceedings more efficient. The rule is efficient because the plaintiff is the person who is best situated to ameliorate the loss,[39] or in economic terms, the 'least cost avoider'.[40] Hence, the date of breach rule reflects both interpersonal justice considerations (namely, that it is unfair for the defendant to be liable if the plaintiff could have reasonably acted to stop the loss from occurring) and community welfare considerations (namely, that it is in the interests of society at large if the party who is best situated to heal the contractual breach does so).

Efficiency is not the only policy concern which contains both interpersonal justice considerations and community welfare considerations. Jonathan Morgan has argued that the mitigation rules not only foster efficiency, but also cooperation between the parties, reflecting a second community welfare consideration.[41] The incentive for a plaintiff to seek a replacement performance means that a dysfunctional relationship can be discontinued, reflecting a concern to allow for a 'clean break', both as a matter of interpersonal justice in a dysfunctional relationship, but also as a matter of community welfare.[42] Similarly, David Campbell argues that there is a relational aspect to the rules governing breach and mitigation.[43] Commercial contracts are often made in the context

[37] Barnett (n 8).

[38] *cf* Summers (n 6) 68–71 who eschews efficiency, self-help and cooperation as explanations, and prefers a wholly causal explanation (in the expanded sense of legal causation, not factual causation).

[39] MG Bridge, 'Mitigation of damages in contract and the meaning of avoidable loss' (1989) 105 *LQR* 398, 409–10; Barnett (n 8) 806–08.

[40] G Calabresi and D Melamed, 'Property Rules, Liability Rules, and Inalienability: One View of the Cathedral' (1972) 85 *Harvard Law Review* 1089, 1094.

[41] Morgan (n 6).

[42] This policy operates in other areas of private law. See E Bant and M Bryan, 'Defences, Bars and Discretionary Factors' in E Bant and M Bryan (eds), *Principles of Proprietary Remedies* (Sydney, Thomson Reuters, 2013) [11.120].

[43] See, eg, D Campbell, 'The Relational Constitution of Remedy: Co-operation as the Implicit Second Principle of Remedies for Breach of Contract' (2005) 11 *Canadian Bankruptcy Reports (5th)* 455; D Campbell, 'A Relational Critique of the Third Restatement of Restitution § 39' (2011) 68 *Washington & Lee Law Review* 1063, 1093–09; D Campbell, 'What Do We Mean by the Non-Use of Contract?' in J Braucher, J Kidwell and W Whitford (eds), *Revisiting the Contracts Scholarship of Stewart Macaulay: On the empirical and the lyrical* (Oxford, Hart Publishing, 2013) 159, 179–81.

of an ongoing relationship, and the parties continue to deal with each other after the particular contract in question has been terminated. The rules governing mitigation incentivise both parties to minimise their losses, move on and make a new contract later. This can be seen to reflect a community welfare desire to uphold the institution of contracting and cooperation.

Relatedly, there is also the consideration of certainty, a utilitarian community welfare concern. Michael Bridge argues that it is preferable to have a clear and commercially certain date of breach rule which does not require the court to consider subsequent transactions.[44] Where a market is liquid, any distribution of benefit and burdens between plaintiff and defendant as a result of mitigatory principles will be limited to ensuring that the courts do not have to untangle too much. Similarly, Stephen Waddams argues that the rule is founded on convenience, and crystallisation of the buyer's entitlement at an early stage.[45] While the policy considerations of commercial certainty and limiting the forensic inquiry required by the court can be seen to underlie the rule, these rules are only efficient in a liquid market, where forensic inquiries into subsequent events would be too costly and inefficient. Outside a liquid market, where it is not easy to obtain a substitute performance, courts are ready to look into subsequent events. Moreover, the potential for efficiency to explain mitigation should not be overstated, because a claimant will still be deemed to have mitigated in a rising market, although there is no inefficient waste of resources in this situation.[46]

Consequently, while Summers and Kramer's description of the law is adopted in section III below, the policy concerns of the date of breach rule are better understood through a legal pluralist lens. The law does not march to a single beat.

III. Exceptions to the Date of Breach Rule

As noted above, contracting parties do not usually depart from the date of breach rule in their contracting, even though they could if they wished. In Australia at least, the courts acknowledge that the reasons why the court may decide to use a different date to measure damages have to do with coherence and fairness. While compensation of loss, certainty and efficiency are one goal of contract damages, it is important that contractual principles be coherent. Mitigation is in tension with the principle of full compensation. I have argued elsewhere that mitigation rules reflect a well-recognised and overriding general policy of the law in favour of encouraging self-help by plaintiffs, and that this rule is concerned with issues of distributive justice.[47] However, in so doing, the law does not expect impossibilities of the plaintiff.

As discussed under heading B below, one of the most important exceptions to the breach date rule arises where immediate mitigation is unreasonable or impossible to

[44] Bridge (n 38) 408–09; MG Bridge, 'Defective goods and sub-sales' [1998] *Journal of Business Law* 259, 259; MG Bridge, 'Markets and damages in sale of goods cases' (2016) 132 *LQR* 405.

[45] SM Waddams, *The Law of Damages*, 5th edn (Toronto, Canada Law Book Co, 2012) [1.1480]–[1.1540], [15.100].

[46] '*The Asia Star*' [2010] 2 SLR 1154 [26]–[29]; Waddams (n 45) [15.70].

[47] Barnett (n 8).

achieve for some reason. This is particularly the case where the plaintiff has acquired an asset which they would not otherwise have acquired and the asset is not readily marketable at the time of acquisition, or if the plaintiff does not discover a defect in the subject matter of the contract until some time has elapsed after acquisition, or if the plaintiff is 'locked in' to holding the asset for some other reason.[48] The presence of a liquid market is pivotal to the decision the court makes, as is the possibility of mitigation.

A. Subsequent Events: Consequential Losses

It is necessary to take into account subsequent events when calculating consequential losses flowing from the breach of contract. Nothing more need be said about this exception, other than the obvious point that consequences only become evident when events unfold, and therefore it is essential to look at subsequent events. Consequential losses are, of course, subject to limitations upon liability, including causation, remoteness and mitigation.

B. Subsequent Events: When the Court Overrides the 'Date of Breach' Rule for Reasons of 'Justice'

While the date of breach rule is a default rule, the court may override it for reasons of 'justice' in relevant circumstances. The use of the word 'justice' can be criticised on the basis that it is uncertain, so the meaning is explained here. The date of breach rule of thumb presumes that a plaintiff can readily obtain a substitute on the market. However, if a plaintiff cannot actually obtain a substitute on the market, and it would be unfair to presume that they could do so. Instead, the date of assessment of damages is moved to a date when the plaintiff *could* reasonably resort to the market, to ensure that the plaintiff is not treated unfairly. This tends to happen where the market is not liquid.

If the plaintiff is for some reason unable to mitigate, the date when it becomes reasonable or possible to mitigate may be used instead to calculate the value of the substitute performance. As Kramer and Dyson have argued, these situations may arise in the following circumstances:[49]

(1) when a plaintiff is legally 'locked out' of the market ('string contracts') because the plaintiff has a subsequent sub-contract to on-sell the subject matter of the contract and the defendant knows of this;
(2) where a plaintiff is practically 'locked out' of the market: in other words, the subject matter of the contract is not readily able to be resold because of subsequent circumstances, despite efforts by the plaintiff to resell;
(3) where a plaintiff is 'locked in' for reasons other than financial reasons: this may be because they cannot purchase an alternative on the market or resell for practical limitations relating to the subject matter of the contract;

[48] *Smith New Court Securities Ltd v Scrimgeour Vickers (Asset Management) Ltd* [1997] AC 254, 265–66.
[49] Dyson and Kramer (n 11).

(4) where a plaintiff is 'locked in' for financial reasons: ie, if they are unable to purchase a substitute performance because they are impecunious, the court may take this into account in deciding whether a failure to mitigation is reasonable, if the impecuniosity flows from the breach (or is 'intrinsic' to it); and
(5) where the subject matter of the contract has a latent defect which only becomes evident at a later date, the court may use a later date (either when the defect was discovered, or when it became possible for the plaintiff to mitigate the effect of the defects).

Each of these instances will be discussed in turn.

i. When a Plaintiff is Legally 'Locked Out' of the Market ('String Contracts')

This occurs when the non-breaching party has a sub-contract which provides that they *must* transfer those specific widgets to a third party for a specified price, and that the breaching party knows of this. In those circumstances, the court does not generally expect the non-breaching to mitigate because they will be unable either to sell the goods on the open market or purchase non-defective substitute goods on the market. This is sometimes called a 'string contract'.[50] In these circumstances, if the defendant knows or ought to know of the sub-contract, the correct measure of damages is the loss of profit on resale.[51]

However, in *Kwei Tek Chao v British Traders and Shippers Ltd*, the plaintiff's argument that it was entitled to the loss of profit on a sub-sale did not succeed, as there was no evidence that the parties contemplated resale or knew of a string contract at the time when the contract was made.[52] Thus, *Hadley v Baxendale* remoteness and the contemplation of the parties may operate to preclude recovery of a loss of profit even if the plaintiff is 'locked out' of the market. Remoteness and mitigation are not entirely intertwined.

ii. Where a Plaintiff is Practically 'Locked Out' of the Market (Subject Matter of the Contract not Readily Marketable)

If the subject matter of the contract is rare and there are no other sellers of that subject matter on the market at the time when breach occurs, the court does not generally expect the non-breaching party to mitigate immediately upon breach. They will only be expected to mitigate once this becomes possible (if it becomes possible at all).

In *Kwei Tek Chao v British Traders and Shippers Ltd* the market for a particular good was not liquid, and this was taken into account in calculating damages.[53] London exporters (the sellers) contracted under a cif contract to sell 20 tons of a chemical known as

[50] See eg, in GA Mulligan, 'Damages for Breach: Quantum, Remoteness and Causality' (1955) 72 *South African Law Journal* 152.
[51] *Kwei Tek Chao v British Traders and Shippers Ltd* [1954] 2 QB 459, 490 (Devlin J); *Johnson v Perez* (1988) 166 CLR 351, 356–57 (Mason CJ).
[52] *Kwei Tek Chao v British Traders and Shippers Ltd* [1954] 2 QB 459, 489 (Devlin J).
[53] [1954] 2 QB 459.

Rongalite C to buyers in Hong Kong. The seller's forwarding agents forged bills of lading purporting to show that the shipment had been made on 31 October 1951, and the bank paid the purchase price accordingly. In fact, the goods had not been shipped at that time, and were not shipped until 17 December 1951. The sellers were not involved in the forwarding agents' fraud. When the goods eventually arrived in Hong Kong, the goods were unable to be sold because an embargo had been placed upon the importation of goods of this type by Chinese authorities. The goods were 'virtually unsaleable' on the market. Accordingly, the difference in value was between the contract price (£590 per ton) and the salvage value as at the date of delivery, when the chemical was unsaleable (£70 per ton). In obiter dicta in *Johnson v Perez*, Mason CJ indicated that the situation would be similar where there was no market for a particular kind of shares, and the shares had been loaned to the defendant, but the defendant had breached its contract by failing to return the shares at the stipulated time when the market was fluctuating.[54]

In English law, it is clear that the inability to sell real property as a result of a falling market is a reason to use a later date of assessment of damages,[55] particularly if reasonable mitigating actions are taken, such as immediate re-advertisement of the property. The situation is less clear in Australian law. While some cases have adopted the English approach,[56] in another line of cases, courts have been unsympathetic to inelasticity in the market for real property and have measured damages as the difference in value between the contract price and the property's market value as at the date of the breach,[57] even if the property was difficult to sell, and the plaintiff was only able to sell to a third party over a year later.[58] In these cases, the plaintiff's exposure to fluctuating property prices has been regarded as arising from the plaintiff's own free decision. In one case, it was said that the vendor failed to mitigate by terminating the contract and should have obtained protection against the consequences of a falling market by seeking specific performance instead.[59] It is worth wondering whether this line of Australian cases reflects sound principle, given the discussion above.

iii. Where a Plaintiff is 'Locked In' (for Reasons Other than Financial Reasons)

In *Smith New Court Securities Ltd v Scrimgeour Vickers (Asset Management) Ltd*,[60] a case of deceit, the plaintiff had purchased shares with an intention that it would sell the shares gradually at a later stage. It later did this and suffered a substantial loss. The

[54] *Johnson v Perez* (1988) 166 CLR 351, 356–57, citing *Asamera Oil Corp v Sea Oil & General Corp* (1978) 89 DLR (3d) 1.

[55] *Hooper v Oates* [2013] EWCA Civ 91, [2014] Ch 287. See J Morgan, 'Mitigation and the date of assessment of damages in sales of land' (2013) 29 *Journal of Professional Negligence* 125.

[56] Most notably in *Lords v Von Thomann (No 2)* [2014] WASC 320.

[57] It is unsettled in Australian law whether the relevant 'date of breach' is the date of completion or the date of the acceptance of the repudiation. The issue was left open in *C & P Syndicate Pty Ltd v Reddy* [2013] NSWSC 643 [197] and *Ng v Filmlock Pty Ltd* [2014] NSWCA 389, (2014) 88 NSWLR 146 [45]. In *Lords v Von Thomann (No 2)* [2014] WASC 320 [159], it was concluded that the relevant date was the acceptance of the repudiation.

[58] *Ng v Filmlock Pty Ltd* [2014] NSWCA 389, (2014) 88 NSWLR 146; *C & P Syndicate Pty Ltd v Reddy* [2013] NSWSC 643.

[59] *C & P Syndicate Pty Ltd v Reddy* [2013] NSWSC 643 [192]–[194].

[60] *Smith New Court Securities Ltd v Scrimgeour Vickers (Asset Management) Ltd* [1997] AC 254.

House of Lords found that the plaintiff had been 'locked in' to holding certain shares, and it could not have sold the shares at the date of acquisition.[61] The plaintiff's mitigating acts (selling the shares at a later date) were appropriate in the circumstances. While this shows a willingness to consider situations where a claimant is 'locked' in, it might be objected that the case is not applicable to contract, because courts are more prepared to award generous damages in tort where the wrong is deliberate and contumelious.[62]

However, generally, a court might consider changing the date of assessment of damages situations where a plaintiff is 'locked in' for reasons other than financial reasons in contract. An example of this is *Vieira v O'Shea*.[63] The plaintiff bought an interest in a racehorse in reliance on the defendant veterinarian's advice that the horse was free of health problems. In fact, the horse had a pre-cystic lucency in its left hind leg at the time of purchase, and later required surgery which prevented it from racing and reduced its value. Damages for breach of contract were assessed according to the difference between the price the plaintiff had paid for his interest in the horse and the actual value of the interest at the earliest date at which the plaintiff could reasonably have been expected to sell the interest (more than two years after the acquisition of the interest in the horse). The plaintiff did not discover the horse's unhealthy condition until six months after purchase and was therefore effectively 'locked in' and unable to sell the interest until the horse's condition was improved.[64] Accordingly, it was reasonable to delay sale until that time.[65]

Sometimes a plaintiff may be effectively 'locked in' to a contract because they are reasonably seeking performance of the contract, and damages may be measured from the date where they decide not to press for performance.[66]

iv. *Where a Plaintiff is 'Locked In' (for Financial Reasons)*

Where a plaintiff is 'locked in' to a contract for financial reasons (because they cannot afford to purchase a substitute) the difficulty faced in such cases is not simply the presence or absence of a liquid market, or a contractual or practical inability to access that market, unlike the other categories of case mentioned. There *is* a liquid market by which the plaintiff could mitigate their losses, and there is no reason why the plaintiff cannot access that market, other than their own lack of money. Nonetheless, depending upon the circumstances, impecuniosity can be a relevant reason for a failure to mitigate.[67]

Burns v MAN Automotive (Aust) Pty Ltd illustrates how these issues may play out in contract, although the decision of the majority is unsatisfactory for its lack of focus on mitigation.[68] In July 1977, Mr Burns, the plaintiff, entered into a hire purchase

[61] ibid 267–68 (Lord Browne-Wilkinson), 285 (Lord Steyn) (Lords Keith, Mustill and Slynn agreed with Lords Browne-Wilkinson and Steyn).
[62] Barnett (n 27).
[63] *Vieira v O'Shea* [2012] NSWCA 21.
[64] ibid [46].
[65] ibid [45].
[66] See eg, *Laird v Pim* (1841) 151 ER 852; 7 M & W 474, 478.
[67] *Dodd Properties (Kent) Ltd v Canterbury City Council* [1980] 1 WLR 433.
[68] *Burns v MAN Automotive (Aust) Pty Ltd* (1986) 161 CLR 658 ('*Burns v MAN Automotive*'). See K Barnett, 'Mitigation and Remoteness in Contract: Policy and Principle' (2019) 36 *Journal of Contract Law* 5.

agreement for a diesel prime mover, from MAN Automotive (Aust) Pty Ltd (MAN), the defendant. MAN warranted that the engine was fully reconditioned and was aware that Mr Burns was an interstate haulier who intended to use the prime mover for his business. In fact, the engine had never been reconditioned and constantly broke down. In July 1978 Mr Burns discovered that the engine was severely defective and asked MAN to repair the engine. They refused. He could not afford to repair the engine himself and instead, continued to use the prime mover for less profitable short-haul cartage within Queensland. In November 1979 the prime mover broke down entirely and was repossessed by the hire purchase company. The trial judge found that if the prime mover had complied with the warranty, Mr Burns could have expected it to operate for four years and awarded Mr Burns's loss of earnings for that full four-year period. Mr Burns had also made actual losses as he had been forced to undertake less lucrative intrastate haulage. The trial judge awarded damages for this loss too. The Queensland Court of Appeal held that Burns could not recover either his loss of potential earnings or his actual losses once he discovered the true state of the engine in 1978. Mr Burns appealed to the High Court of Australia.

The joint majority judgment of Wilson, Deane and Dawson JJ held that mitigation was not relevant, and that remoteness principles determined the measure of damages.[69] The losses suffered after the breakdown of the truck were said to be too remote and not within the contemplation of the parties, and the plaintiff was not 'locked in' to the contract.[70] With respect, this analysis is unconvincing.[71] The analysis of the joint majority surely involves a consideration of mitigatory principles, because the plaintiff's losses were limited to those suffered before July 1978, seemingly precisely because the joint majority considered this was when he could reasonably have been expected to mitigate his loss.

Gibbs CJ considered that the plaintiff's losses were not too remote, and his impecuniosity was largely caused by the breach, so that the four years of lost profit should be recoverable.[72] Nonetheless, he found that it was unreasonable for the plaintiff to have carried on the business and would not have allowed recovery of the losses arising from the short-haul intrastate cartage.[73]

Brennan J, in dissent, held that a defendant should be liable for all foreseeable losses *until* the time that it is reasonable to expect the injured party to mitigate his losses. He upheld the trial judge's decision on the basis that it was unreasonable to expect the plaintiff to mitigate because his impecuniosity was directly caused by the breach. According to Brennan J, there was no justification for treating the plaintiff's impecuniosity as an extrinsic cause of the lost profits or as rendering the profits too remote.[74] The reasoning in *The Liesbosch* to that effect that impecuniosity was an extrinsic cause should not be applied.[75] The cause of loss of profits was at all times the unfitness of the prime mover.

[69] *Burns v MAN Automotive* (1986) 161 CLR 658, 662.
[70] ibid 667–68.
[71] Barnett (n 68).
[72] *Burns v MAN Automotive* (1986) 161 CLR 658, 659–60.
[73] ibid 660.
[74] ibid.
[75] *Owners of Dredger Liesbosch v Owners of Steamship Edison (The Liesbosch)* [1933] AC 449. In fact, *The Liesbosch* has later been overruled in English law: see *Lagden v O'Connor* [2004] 1 AC 1067 [8] (Lord Nicholls), [12] (Lord Slynn), [61] (Lord Hope), [81] (Lord Scott) and [90] (Lord Walker).

The plaintiff's decision to conduct short-haul cartage was also directly related to the unfitness of the prime mover. This case, and the shift away from *The Liesbosch*, illustrate the point that decisions as to whether something is a regarded as 'cause' or not is a policy decision.[76]

v. Where the Subject Matter of the Contract has a Latent Defect which Only becomes Evident at a Later Date

Again, the choice of a later date of assessment is at least partially intertwined with questions of mitigation: the plaintiff cannot be expected to mitigate until the defect with the subject matter of the contract has been discovered.

The date of breach rule can be overridden by a court if the subject matter of the contract has a latent defect which only becomes evident upon a later date. The date of assessment may be the date upon which the flaw has become fully evident, or even a later date, if the consequences of the breach are not fully known. However, the flaw must be 'intrinsic' (ie, present at the time of making the contract, and related to the breach of contract) rather than 'extrinsic'. In *Twycross v Grant*, Cockburn CJ gave the example of the sale of a racehorse that subsequently sickened and considered two possibilities: where the horse had a latent disease at the time of sale (in which case the flaw was 'intrinsic'); and where the horse contracted a disease after the sale (in which case the flaw was 'extrinsic').[77] Although these observations were made in the context of the tort of deceit, a similar principle would apply to breach of contract, although the measure to be applied would prima facie be the expectation measure. Thus, if the horse was been warranted to be sound, and it in fact had a latent (but intrinsic) disease which later led to its death, the fair time to assess the difference in value would be the value of the horse at the time of contracting, and the value of the horse at its death,[78] because it was only at the time that the intrinsic problem with the horse became evident. This would be subject to any actions which should reasonably have been taken to mitigate the loss. Alternatively, if the horse died from an entirely unrelated disease which it contracted after purchase, this would be an 'extrinsic' event, and the correct date for assessment of damages would be the date of breach.

In fact, this approach has been taken in cases, including *Van den Hurk v Martens & Co Ltd*.[79] In that case the plaintiffs bought drums of sodium sulphide from the defendants, who knew that the plaintiffs intended to export them. The drums were delivered to the plaintiffs in Manchester, but were not opened, because it was impracticable to open and reseal them before use. The plaintiffs then delivered the drums to customers in Genoa and Lyons, but because of congestion on French railways, this took longer than expected. When the customers opened the drums some months later, they discovered that the chemical within was not in fact sodium sulphide, but sodium hydroxide (caustic soda), and rejected them. The plaintiffs sought to have the difference in value measured not from the date of the contract, but the later date, when the defect was

[76] Barnett (n 68).
[77] *Twycross v Grant* (1877) 2 CPD 469, 544–45 (Cockburn CJ).
[78] Presumably the value of the horse upon its death would be very low.
[79] *Van den Hurk v Martens & Co Ltd* [1920] 1 KB 850.

discovered. Bailhache J found that the appropriate date in the circumstances was the later date.[80] There is an overlap with the 'string contract' cases discussed earlier, because it was relevant that the defendants knew that the chemical was for resale.

Burns v MAN Automotive can also be viewed in this way. Effectively, the majority decided that Burns's impecuniosity was an 'extrinsic' event, and the correct date to measure damages was the date at which the flaw in the engine was found. Conversely, Brennan J in dissent held that Burns's impecuniosity was 'intrinsic', that it flowed at all times from the breach of warranty and was within the contemplation of the parties given their knowledge of Burns's reliance on the engine of the prime mover and his business. Perhaps, in Summers' terms, it depends upon whether one believes Burns had a real choice to mitigate, in determining whether the impecuniosity was 'extrinsic' or 'intrinsic'.[81] Autonomy and choice are important interpersonal justice policy considerations which affect a way in which a court considers these matters.

As *Vieira v O'Shea* indicates, even if the plaintiff knows of the defect, if they are prevented from taking immediate steps to mitigate the loss because of circumstances beyond their control (in that case, the horse had to be treated before mitigation could occur) the date of assessment of damages may be deferred until that time. Thus, this may have some overlap with the category of a plaintiff being 'locked in' for other reasons.

C. Subsequent Events: Where a Repudiation is Accepted and Subsequent Events Affect the Plaintiff's Loss

Where a contract is repudiated before the date for full performance was due, difficult questions arise as to measurement of damages, particularly when subsequent events occur which would have actually made the loss greater or lesser. If the subsequent event is inevitable, then the situation is simple: it should be taken into account.[82] But if the subsequent event was not inevitable, the courts face the question of whether to take it into account. In *Bwllfa and Merthyr Dare Steam Collieries Ltd v Pontypridd Waterworks Co* Lord Macnaughten said (in the context of an arbitrator's assessment of compensation under statute):

> In order to enable him to come to a just and true conclusion, it is his duty … to avail himself of all information at hand at the time of making his award which may be laid before him. Why should he listen to conjecture on a matter which has become an accomplished fact? Why should he guess when he can calculate? With the light before him, why should he shut his eyes and grope in the dark?[83]

The situation which arose in *Golden Strait Corporation v Nippon Yusen Kubishika Kaisha*[84] was precisely such a situation. A contract was repudiated before the full performance was due, and subsequent events which did actually occur would have

[80] ibid 853.
[81] Summers (n 6) 112–13.
[82] *The Mihalis Angelos* [1971] 1 QB 164 (failure of ship to reach handover port inevitable).
[83] [1903] AC 426, 431 (Lord Macnaughten).
[84] *Golden Strait Corporation v Nippon Yusen Kubishika Kaisha (The Golden Victory)* [2007] UKHL 12, [2007] 2 AC 353.

(at least arguably) lessened the loss suffered by the plaintiff. It is to this case that we now turn.

IV. The Problem of *The Golden Victory*

In *The Golden Victory* the House of Lords decided by a narrow majority that, where one party had repudiated a contract before the date of performance, subsequent events occurring after breach could be taken into account in calculating loss. Golden Strait Corporation chartered *The Golden Victory*, a tanker, to Nippon Yusen Kubashika Kaisha in July 1998, for seven years (one month more or less at the charterers' option). Among other things, the charterparty provided that both Golden Strait and Nippon Yusen each had a right to cancel the charterparty if war or hostilities were to break out between any two or more of named countries, including the United States, the United Kingdom (UK) and Iraq. In December 2001, when the charter still had four years to run, Nippon Yusen repudiated the contract. Golden Strait accepted the repudiation and claimed damages for breach of contract, and the matter went to arbitration in 2002. Importantly, Golden Strait could not easily obtain a substitute charter with someone else on the same terms, because the charter market had since collapsed. In an interim decision, the arbitrator decided, among other things, that there had been repudiation, and the earliest date for redelivery of the tanker was 6 December 2005. While the interim arbitral award was being appealed, the Second Gulf War broke out on 21 March 2003. Nippon Yusen would have validly terminated the charter upon the outbreak of war, because they were fundamentally disenchanted with it.

Golden Strait argued that it should be entitled to damages from the date of breach to 6 December 2005. Nippon Yusen argued that it should only be liable to damages from the date of breach to 21 March 2003 because it would have terminated the charter validly on that date anyway. The essential question for the court was whether damages should be measured as if at the date of breach (without the knowledge of the war) or as at the date of assessment, in light of the outbreak of war.

The arbitrator held that damages should take into account the outbreak of war, a decision which was upheld by trial judge and then by the English Court of Appeal. Mance LJ (with whom Auld and Tuckey LLJ agreed) said that the considerations of certainty, finality and ease of settlement that underlie the normal measure of contract damages had to

> yield to the greater importance of achieving an assessment of damages and compensation which more accurately reflects the actual loss which the owners can, at whatever is the date of assessment, now be seen to have suffered as a result of the charterers' repudiation.[85]

Golden Strait appealed to the House of Lords. As noted at the outset of this chapter, the House of Lords took two different approaches.

[85] *Golden Strait Corporation v Nippon Yusen Kubishika Kaisha* [2005] EWCA Civ 1190, [2006] 1 WLR 533 [26] (Mance LJ).

In the majority, Lord Scott, Lord Carswell and Lord Brown decided that Golden Strait was entitled to damages only until 21 March 2003 (when war broke out). It was said that it was necessary to depart from the 'date of breach' rule in exceptional circumstances, such as these.[86] Lord Scott argued that Golden Strait had been deprived of 'the contractual benefit of the charterparty' which included a right to terminate the charterparty in the event of outbreak of war. By seeking compensation to 6 December 2005, Golden Strait was 'seeking compensation exceeding the value of the contractual benefits of which they were deprived', which would offend the contractual principle that a plaintiff should not be put in a better position than they would have been in but for the breach.

In the minority, Lord Bingham and Lord Walker delivered separate judgments.[87] Lord Bingham said that the date of breach rule should have been retained, and events occurring after breach should be irrelevant. The decision of the Court of Appeal below was said to undermine 'the quality of certainty which is a traditional strength and major selling point of English commercial law and involves an unfortunate departure from principle'.[88] He also said that certainty in commercial affairs, finality, consistency and coherence were essential principles undergirding English contract damages.[89]

The decision has been criticised. For example, Francis Reynolds argues that both the majority (with the emphasis on fairness and preventing over-compensation) and the minority (with the emphasis on commercial certainty) miss the point, and that the breach should give rise to damages because of the plaintiff's interest in performance.[90] Morgan has criticised the decision on a policy basis, arguing that to assess damages using hindsight encourages parties to use delay tactics in litigation where this would be advantageous.[91] On the other hand, Andrew Burrows has praised the majority judgment for applying 'a true compensatory approach'.[92]

Harvey McGregor has suggested that *The Golden Victory* has no direct connection with mitigation but has ramifications for the inherent relationship between the rules of mitigation and the rules as to time of assessment of damages. He argued that, by their decision to take into account matters occurring after breach, the majority may have opened the way to revisiting some cases where a transaction entered into by aggrieved party after breach has been left out of account.[93] Mitigation can, however, be seen to provide a solution to the problem of this case, as will be argued below.

Victor Goldberg has suggested that the prima facie calculation of the loss should be the remaining value of the charter as at the date of breach, discounted by the possibility (as at the date of acceptance of the repudiation) that the war clause would have been

[86] *The Golden Victory* [2007] UKHL 12, [2007] 2 AC 353 [30]–[38] (Lord Scott), [80]–[81] (Lord Brown).

[87] Lord Walker substantially agreed with Lord Bingham, however: see *The Golden Victory* [2007] UKHL 12, [2007] 2 AC 353 [42].

[88] ibid [1] (Lord Bingham).

[89] ibid [23] (Lord Bingham).

[90] F Reynolds, 'The *Golden Victory* – A Misguided Decision' (2008) 38 *Hong Kong Law Journal* 333.

[91] J Morgan, 'A Victory for "Justice" over Commercial Certainty' (2007) *CLJ* 263.

[92] A Burrows, *Remedies for Torts, Breach of Contract and Equitable Wrongs*, 4th edn (Oxford, Oxford University Press, 2019) 174. For another approving view of the case, see Q Zhou, 'Damages for repudiation: an *ex ante* perspective on the Golden Victory' (2010) 32 *Sydney Law Review* 579.

[93] H McGregor, 'The Role of Mitigation in the Assessment of Damages', in D Saidov and R Cunnington (eds), *Contract Damages: Domestic and International Perspectives* (Oxford, Hart Publishing, 2008) 332, 345–46.

exercised.[94] It is suggested that this is a suitable starting point. In fact, Lord Bingham made the point in dissent that, if the war had been probable as at the date of repudiation, the damages would have been discounted by that probability as at the date of termination.[95]

David McLauchlan and Nick Hegan have argued that the difference in value should have been between the value of the remainder of the charter and the value of any substitute charter to mitigate the loss.[96] While it was impossible to obtain a substitute charter on equivalent terms, it might have been possible obtain a substitute charter on less advantageous terms and calculate the difference in value thereby. And, as McLauchlan and Hegan point out, it cannot be assumed that the substitute charterer would have terminated when war broke out (despite Lord Brown's assumption to this effect in *The Golden Victory*).[97] Hence they say:

> It is usually accepted that, where there is a ready market for the subject-matter of the contract, the so-called 'duty' to mitigate means that a plaintiff cannot claim damages in respect of subsequent adverse market moves which could have been avoided. In other words, the plaintiff's damages are calculated as if the mitigating transaction had occurred. We would argue that the same approach should apply here, given that it was accepted that a substitute term charter was available; in other words, the owners' damages should be calculated assuming a substitute charter had been obtained. Of course, charter rates having fallen, the owners would have to have paid an upfront sum to obtain the substitute charter on exactly the same terms, which sum would clearly have been calculated by reference not only to the difference between the contract and market rates but also to the low likelihood of cancellation at the time of acceptance of the repudiation. Damages should therefore be equal to that sum, and the fact that the owners chose not to seek the replacement charter was their own risk or advantage (depending on future rises and falls in the charter market).[98]

Although *The Golden Victory* is controversial, the majority's view in *The Golden Victory* was upheld in *Bunge SA v Nidera BV*.[99] Nidera BV contracted to buy 25,000 metric tonnes of Russian milling wheat from Bunge SA. The contract contained a clause allowing either party to cancel the contract in the event of a 'prohibition of export, blockade or hostilities or in case of any executive or legislative act done by or on behalf of the government of the country of origin of the goods [Russia]'. On 5 August 2010, the Russian Government announced an embargo on sales of wheat, running from 15 August 2010 to 31 December 2010. On 9 August 2010, Nidera informed Bunge of the embargo (which had not yet come into force) and purported to cancel the contract. Bunge did not accept the cancellation, but on 11 August 2010, it treated it as a repudiation and sued for damages. In the event, the Russian Government's embargo came into force on 15 August 2010, as promised. Bunge sued for damages for the difference between the contract price and the market price as at 11 August 2010, namely US$3,062,500. Nidera

[94] V Goldberg, *Rethinking the Law of Contract Damages* (Cheltenham, Edward Elgar, 2019) 44–45.

[95] *The Golden Victory* [2007] UKHL 12, [2007] 2 AC 353 [21] (Lord Bingham).

[96] D McLauchlan and N Hegan, 'Contract Damages: Fundamental Principle, Fundamental Disagreement' (2008) 46 *Canadian Business Law Journal* 89, 92–93.

[97] ibid 91. See *The Golden Victory* [2007] UKHL 12, [2007] 2 AC 353 [82] (Lord Brown).

[98] McLauchlan and Hegan (n 96) 92–93.

[99] *Bunge SA v Nidera BV* [2015] UKSC 43, [2015] 2 Lloyd's Rep 469. See also *Ageas (UK) Ltd v Kwok-Fit (GB) Ltd* [2014] EWHC 2178.

argued that, while the termination had been premature, given that the embargo had in fact come into force when the time for shipment would have arisen, the sale would not have gone ahead in any case.

The unanimous UK Supreme Court applied *The Golden Victory* and found that Bunge was only entitled to nominal damages, because the sale would never have gone ahead. Bunge (unsuccessfully) tried to distinguish the *The Golden Victory* on the basis that it involved the supply of a service over an extended time, while this was just a one-off sales contract. The Supreme Court held that Nidera was only entitled to nominal damages of US$5. Lord Sumption (speaking for the court) said:

> Commercial certainty is undoubtedly important, although its significance will inevitably vary from one contract to another. But it can rarely be thought to justify an award of substantial damages to someone who has not suffered any.[100]

Kramer argues that *Bunge SA v Nidera BV* was a simple case of 'but for' causation, and not a case where subsequent events were taken into account.[101] In other words, even if Nidera had not breached, Bunge would still have suffered an identical loss because Nidera would have validly terminated some six days later once the embargo came into force. The Supreme Court clearly contemplated in *Bunge SA v Nidera BV* that mitigation and date of breach were two ways of asking the same question in many instances.[102]

How then, with this in mind, is the problem faced in *The Golden Victory* best approached? First, as suggested by Goldberg and McLauchlan and Hegan, the court could calculate the value of the remainder of the charter as at the date of the acceptance of the repudiation and discount that value according to the possibility as at that date Nippon Yusen might have validly terminated in the future (on the basis that a war with the named parties was clearly contemplated and seen as a possibility).[103]

The court does not seem to have looked at the question of mitigation carefully, and simply assumed that it was possible, without looking at it closely. It would be necessary to ascertain whether substitute charterers were available (even on less advantageous terms). This leads to three possibilities:

(1) If substitute charterers were available immediately, damages would be the difference in value between the value of the remainder of the charter as above, and the substitute charter as at the date of acceptance of the repudiation (as per the majority).
(2) If substitute charterers were not available (eg, Golden Strait was practically 'locked out' of the market) then a later date of assessment should be taken for the difference in value, calculated at the point when it was reasonable or possible for Golden Strait to mitigate.[104]

[100] *Bunge SA v Nidera BV* [2015] UKSC 43, [2015] 2 Lloyd's Rep 469 [23] (Lord Sumption).

[101] A Kramer, 'Contract Damages' in W Day and S Worthington (eds), *Challenging Private Law: Lord Sumption on the Supreme Court* (Oxford, Hart Publishing, 2020) 74, 78.

[102] See particularly, *Bunge SA v Nidera AV* [2015] UKSC 43, [2015] 2 Lloyd's Rep 469 [16], [21] (Lord Sumption).

[103] As per the suggestion in Goldberg (n 95) 44–45. See also *The Elena D'Amico* [1980] 1 Lloyd's Rep 75, 87 (Robert Goff J).

[104] There is some suggestion in the argument of the respondents that there was no 'available market' for rehire for a certain period of time: see *The Golden Victory* [2007] UKHL 12, [2007] 2 AC 353, 364 (submissions of the

(3) If it was not possible for Golden Strait to mitigate at all (even on less advantageous terms), the proper date would be the date of the earliest date of redelivery (as per the minority).

As McLauchlan and Hegan say:

> [I]n these 'market' cases it can certainly be argued that it is beside the point whether the plaintiffs 'ended up' being better off because there is an earlier question to be answered. That question is whether termination for repudiation or breach has the effect of reallocating market risk to the plaintiffs. If there is such a reallocation, it follows from the principles applied in mitigation cases that subsequent market changes are for the plaintiffs', not the defendants', account. Of course, this does not mean that the plaintiffs were under an 'obligation' to deal with the risk, only that they must be treated as if they had. Such a principle not only promotes certainty and efficiency of settlement, it makes good economic sense by placing responsibility for dealing with market risk in the hands of those best able to do so.[105]

The reference to the party most able to deal with market risk links back to the question of 'least-cost avoider' earlier in this chapter. Part of the policy of the law is to place the risk on that party.

Several points can be made in the wake of this discussion. First, the date of breach rule exists for reasons of certainty and efficiency. It does not seek to measure exact losses but provides an efficient 'rule of thumb' by which parties and judges can readily calculate what losses might occur. It incentivises mitigation and self-help. It is a sticky default rule because it is not in the interests of parties to contract around it. Courts are better situated to assess when a fair date of assessment would be, having regard to the policy considerations behind mitigation and the market-based history of the development of contract damages rules. Even in a complex case such as *The Golden Victory*, considerations of the principles of mitigation can provide guidance as to the correct calculation of damages.

V. Conclusion

It has been suggested in this chapter that the date of breach rule of assessment is subject to a *status quo* bias, and therefore the parties do not often depart from it. It has been suggested that there are numerous policy reasons behind the operative policy governing mitigation and the date of breach rule, including promotion of autonomy, efficiency, promotion of cooperation, and interpersonal justice concerns about what response is predictable and what a reasonable plaintiff should do. It seems likely from the paucity of cases raising the issue that parties do not depart from the rule (by and large) because the court itself is better situated to depart from the rule when it is necessary to do so.

respondents). It seems that the arbitrator did not allow consideration of the actual facts regarding the market and the availability of a substitute charter. In my view, this led to the problems faced in the case right up to the House of Lords.

[105] McLauchlan and Hegan (n 96) 93.

The date of breach rule is both intrinsically intertwined with principles of mitigation and a rule of thumb for judges. It is important to understand the relationship between mitigation and the date of breach rule to ascertain when judges will calculate damages as from a different date. This also helps ascertain the rational response to difficult cases like *The Golden Victory*. Courts should not treat the date of breach rule as immutable, precisely because the parties rely on the courts to make the necessary adjustments, in positions where there is not a liquid market.

11

The Express Modification of Contract Law's Default Remedial Rules

DAVID WINTERTON*

I. Introduction

Contract law contains various default rules. In the remedial context, perhaps the most fundamental such rule stipulates that, following breach, the innocent party is entitled to an award of ('expectation') damages, which aims to put this party into 'the same situation … as if the contract had been performed' (hereinafter, 'the *Robinson v Harman* principle').[1] Although an order for specific performance or an injunction mandating performance of a contractual promise is occasionally available, a damages award aiming to approximate the plaintiff's 'non-breach position'[2] is the standard response to the breach of any enforceable (positive)[3] contractual obligation.[4] Contracting parties are, of course, permitted a certain degree of latitude to depart from this default position, but there are limits upon the extent to which this is permitted.[5]

The *Robinson v Harman* principle is also subject to various restrictions that impact the extent to which the claimant's counterfactual, non-breach position is precisely

* I thank members of the Faculty of Law at the Sydney University and the University of Hong Kong respectively, for valuable feedback on earlier versions of this chapter. I also thank the following people for helpful written comments on earlier drafts: Professor Andrew Robertson, Professor Katy Barnett, Professor John Murphy, Professor Wojciech Sadurski, Jane Chan, Dani Christelis, Maya Eswaran, Jack Pembroke-Birss, Tim Pilkington, Scott Ralston and Jess Pens.

[1] *Robinson v Harman* (1848) 1 Ex 850, 855; 154 ER 363, 365 (Parke B).

[2] See Adam Kramer, *The Law of Contract Damages*, 3rd edn (Oxford, Hart Publishing, 2022) 14–15. It is generally accepted that a plaintiff may alternatively seek to recoup its 'wasted expenditure'.

[3] It is acknowledged that coercive relief is more readily available to enforce a promise to refrain from performing a certain act. See *Doherty v Allman* (1878) 3 App Cas 709 (HL), where Lord Cairns LC stated that: 'If parties, for valuable consideration, with their eyes open, contract that a particular thing shall not be done, all that a Court of Equity has to do is to say, by way of injunction, that which the parties have already said by way of covenant, that the thing shall not be done; and in such case the injunction does nothing more than give the sanction of the process of the Court to that which already is the contract between the parties.'

[4] That specific performance is presumptively available in certain cases obviously does not contradict this claim since the plaintiff always has the choice to claim damages instead.

[5] See section II.

replicated.[6] The most theoretically significant of these restrictions is probably the rule that precludes the recovery of losses that are too remote. Whether this doctrine is itself best understood as a default rule or as upholding the parties' agreed allocation of the risks associated with non-performance remains a matter of ongoing debate.[7] But the recovery of damages for 'consequential loss'[8] is also subject to restriction on various other grounds, such as by reference to the avoidable loss rule of mitigation, the intervening cause doctrine, or on account of the claimant's contributory negligence.[9] It is beyond the scope of this chapter to consider whether any of these further restrictions on recovery are properly characterised as default rules.[10]

The central ambition of the present chapter is instead to examine the effect, under Anglo-Australian law, of attempts by contracting parties to modify, via express stipulation, certain default rules that would otherwise apply when responding to an actual, or anticipated, breach of contract.[11] It should immediately be noted that, in addition to the possibility of statutory modification, there are two other potential means by which contract law's default remedial rules might be modified. The first is through the drawing of a necessary implication from the parties' agreement.[12] The second, and more contestable, possible mode of modification is via the derivation of an implicit risk allocation from an objective construction of the parties' agreement. Both additional methods of modification also merit further consideration. But this too is a task that cannot be undertaken here.

The remainder of this chapter consists of three substantive sections. Section II considers attempts to modify the default rules that govern the assessment of damages for breach of contract by express stipulation. After briefly outlining the central features of the law governing the enforceability of liquidated damages clauses, it is argued that the wholesale exclusion of a breaching party's liability to pay damages does not prevent the creation of a valid contractual obligation to perform and that the default interpretation

[6] Note that while most of the rules that qualify the *Robinson v Harman* principle *reduce* the damages payable, rules concerned with identifying when certain consequential benefits that were derived from the breach of contract are properly disregarded have the opposite effect.

[7] For contrasting views, see A Kramer, 'An Agreement-Centred Approach to Remoteness and Contract Damages' in N Cohen and E McKendrick (eds), *Comparative Remedies for Breach of Contract* (Oxford, Hart Publishing, 2005) 249; and A Robertson, 'The Basis of the Remoteness Rule in Contract' (2008) 28 *Legal Studies* 172. For judicial support for an 'agreement-oriented' view, see *Transfield Shipping Inc v Mercator Shipping Inc* [2009] AC 61 ('*The Achilleas*') [22]–[26] (Lord Hoffmann) and [31]–[37] (Lord Hope).

[8] This is a legal term of art, the meaning of which is considered in section II.B.ii.

[9] Other notable restrictions on the recovery of recovery are the 'reasonableness' restriction on 'cost of cure' claims and the exclusion, in certain contexts, of compensation for non-pecuniary loss.

[10] For some consideration, see J Morgan, 'Contract Damages as Default Rules' in D Campbell and R Halson (eds), *Research Handbook on Remedies in Private Law* (Cheltenham, Edward Elgar, 2019) 476–93 and J Morgan, 'On the Nature and Function of Remedies for Breach of Contract' in S Worthington and G Virgo (eds), *Commercial Remedies: Resolving Controversies* (Cambridge, Cambridge University Press, 2017) 23–45.

[11] I hereafter use the term 'default remedial rule' to describe those default rules that determine the court's response to a breach, or anticipated breach, of a legal obligation. For detailed examination of the ambiguities that arise in relation to the meaning of the word 'remedy', see P Birks, 'Rights, Wrongs and Remedies' (2000) 20 *OJLS* 1 and S Smith, *Rights, Wrongs and Injustices: The Structure of Remedial Law* (Oxford, Oxford University Press, 2019).

[12] Consider, for example, the question that arose in *Soteria Insurance Ltd v IBM United Kingdom Ltd* [2022] EWCA Civ 440, [2022] 2 All ER (Comm) 1082 as regards whether the parties' express exclusion of recovery of 'indirect or consequential Losses … loss of profit, revenue [or] savings (including anticipated savings), data … goodwill [or] reputation' also excluded, by necessary implication, the recovery of 'wasted expenditure'.

of express exclusions of liability for 'consequential loss' should be to preclude recovery for any adverse consequences of a breach that do not consist merely in failing to receive the promised performance. Section III considers the legal effect of an express term specifying a preference for a particular response to breach, arguing that although courts should be reluctant to enforce clauses expressly stating a preference for coercive relief, they should generally give effect to clauses directing them only to award damages. Finally, section IV considers the impact of contractually incorporating an express term purporting to modify the law's default damages rules on the availability of coercive relief. Here it is argued that including a liquidated damages provision generally cannot render damages 'adequate' for the purposes of determining the availability of specific performance or an injunction, and that the incorporation of an express term excluding or limiting a breaching party's damages liability is generally relevant in determining whether ordering coercive relief is justified.

II. The Effect of the Express Modification of Contract Law's Default Damages Rules on Damages Recovery

This section considers attempts to modify the default rules that govern the assessment of damages for breach of contract by express stipulation. Part A outlines the central features of the Anglo-Australian law governing the enforceability of liquidated damages provisions. The purpose of doing so is not merely to describe the rules that limit the extent to which the parties can expressly agree on compensation exceeding the sum that would otherwise be awarded, but also to provide the necessary background for an argument advanced in section IV concerning whether coercive relief is available where the parties' have agreed to liquidate the damages payable upon breach. Part B considers a distinct way that contracting parties may modify the operation of the default rules that otherwise apply following contractual breach; namely by incorporating a clause that excludes liability to pay damages for non-performance, or via the inclusion of a clause that limits such liability to a lesser amount than otherwise would be recoverable. The use of such clauses raises several important practical and theoretical issues,[13] but the discussion here is limited to considering just two. The first is whether it is permissible to exclude *any* liability to pay damages following the failure to perform a contractual promise. The second is the effect of incorporating an express exclusion (or limitation) of liability for 'consequential loss'.

A. The Enforceability of 'Agreed Damages' Clauses

One obvious way in which contracting parties may expressly modify contract law's default remedial rules is by stipulating what damages are payable upon breach. It

[13] For more detailed consideration of the default (and mandatory) rules applicable to such clauses, see J Paterson, 'Mandatory Statutory Rules, Consumer Contracts and Contractual Interpretation', this volume, ch 8.

is trite to observe that such 'liquidated damages' clauses will be enforceable to the extent that they are not properly characterised as 'penal'.[14] Under the old law of penalties, now significantly modified in both the United Kingdom (UK) and Australia,[15] enforceability required simply that the agreed amount payable upon breach had to constitute a genuine pre-estimate of the likely loss that the innocent party was predicted to suffer in consequence of the relevant breach. One important, and surprisingly unsettled, question that had arisen in that context was 'whether a liquidated clause can only represent legally recoverable loss, or all loss', notably including those that would be irrecoverable because 'too remote'.[16] While it has been observed that 'There is authority favouring the "legally recoverable loss" test',[17] the decision of the English Court of Appeal in *Robophone Facilities Ltd v Blank*[18] stands as authority for the opposing view.

In *Cavendish Square Holding BV v Talal El Makdessi; ParkingEye Ltd v Beavis*,[19] the UK Supreme Court reformulated the test governing when such a clause is 'penalty', and therefore unenforceable, in addition to confirming that the jurisdiction to relieve against penalty clauses only arises in relation to provisions triggered by breach. In relation to the former, it was held that a liquidated damages provision is 'penal' when the relevant secondary obligation imposes a detriment on the breaching party that is either 'out of all proportion to any legitimate interest of the innocent party in the enforcement of the primary obligation',[20] or 'exorbitant or unconscionable when regard is had to the innocent party's interest in … performance'.[21]

The law that regulates contractual penalty clauses in Australia is both similar and importantly distinct from that which governs in England. In Australia, the approach to determining whether a liquidated damages clause is a 'penalty' occurs in two stages. At the first stage of analysis, the court asks whether the penalty rule is engaged by asking whether, on its proper construction, the agreed remedy is in the nature of a security right to ensure the promisor's fulfilment of a condition (ie, the relevant provision need not be triggered by a breach of contract).[22] At the second stage of analysis, as all members of the High Court of Australia held in *Paciocco*, the court asks whether the amount payable constitutes a 'penalty' in the relevant sense. Although there was some

[14] See, for example, *Andrews v Australian & New Zealand Banking Group Ltd* [2012] HCA 30, (2012) 247 CLR 205 ('*Andrews*').

[15] *Cavendish Square Holding BV (Appellant) v Talal El Makdessi* [2015] UKSC 67, [2016] AC 1172; *Paciocco v Australia and New Zealand Banking Group Ltd* [2016] HCA 28, (2016) 258 CLR 525 ('*Paciocco*').

[16] See JD Heydon, *Heydon on Contract* (Sydney, Lawbook Co, 2019) 965.

[17] ibid, citing *Lansat Shipping Co Ltd v Glencore Grain BV* [2009] 1 Lloyd's Rep 658 [22]. See also *Ringrow Pty Ltd v BP Australia Pty Ltd* [2005] HCA 71, (2005) 224 CLR 656 [21] (the Court): 'In typical penalty cases, the court compares what would be recoverable as unliquidated damages with the sum of money stipulated as payable on breach'.

[18] *Robophone Facilities Ltd v Blank* [1966] 1 WLR 1428 (CA) 1448–1449 (Diplock LJ).

[19] *Cavendish Square Holding BV v Talal El Makdessi; ParkingEye Ltd v Beavis* [2015] UKSC 67, [2016] AC 1172 ('*Cavendish*').

[20] ibid [32] (Lord Neuberger PSC and Lord Sumption JSC, with whom Lord Carnwath JSC agreed and Lord Clarke JSC delivered a concurring judgment).

[21] ibid [255] (Lord Hodge JSC).

[22] See *Andrews* [2012] HCA 30, (2012) 247 CLR 205 [11] (the Court); *Paciocco* [2016] HCA 28, (2016) 258 CLR 525 [23]–[26] (Kiefel J). For more detailed analysis, see N Tiverios, *Contractual Penalties in Australia and the United Kingdom: History, Theory and Practice* (Sydney, Federation Press, 2019) 104–20.

divergence in the precise formulation adopted by the various judgments delivered in *Paciocco*, the essential focus of the inquiry is on whether, on its proper construction, the collateral stipulation proportionately protects a 'legitimate interest',[23] or is not (primarily) concerned to punish non-performance.[24]

According to the dominant approach in *Paciocco* and *Cavendish*, the relevant question in determining whether a clause is 'penal' is 'whether a provision for the payment of a sum of money on default is out of all proportion to the interests of the party which it is the purpose of the provision to protect'.[25] As this formulation makes clear, it is unnecessary that the agreed amount constitute a genuine pre-estimate of the plaintiff's probable loss, albeit that this is one uncontroversial way that this test can be satisfied. Nevertheless, as the *Paciocco* decision itself clearly establishes, the sum stipulated by a valid liquidated damages clause may exceed, even greatly exceed, the projected loss provided that this amount is not 'out of all proportion' to the plaintiff's 'legitimate interests'. Thus, under the new approach, it is no longer necessary that the sum agreed upon as damages constitutes an (even rough) approximation of the amount that the plaintiff would otherwise have been entitled to recover in a claim for breach of contract.

Perhaps the most important question that arises in relation to the penalty doctrine concerns its most plausible justification. Although it is beyond the scope of this chapter to consider this difficult and longstanding puzzle,[26] the rule's recent reconfiguration in both Australia and the UK has present salience for at least two reasons. One is that this reconfiguration raises important questions regarding the express modification of contract law's default remedial rules that previously did not arise, including: (1) when an interest is properly regarded as 'legitimate';[27] and (2) how difficulties concerning the incommensurability (or 'incomparability')[28] of money and certain (legitimate) non-financial interests should be navigated.[29] The other reason is that the law's recent reformulation may have important implications for other questions that arise concerning the extent to which the parties' contract may modify contract law's default rules. One such question, examined in section IV, is whether incorporating an 'agreed damages' clause into a contract can render damages 'adequate' for the purpose of assessing the appropriateness of coercive relief.

[23] *Paciocco* [2016] HCA 28, (2016) 258 CLR 525 [29] (Kiefel J, French CJ agreeing), [279] (Keane J).

[24] ibid [159] (Gageler J).

[25] See, eg, *Paciocco* [2016] HCA 28, (2016) 258 CLR 525 [29] (Kiefel J, French CJ agreeing) and *Cavendish* [2015] UKSC 67, [2016] AC 1172 [32] (Lord Neuberger PSC and Lord Sumption JSC, with whom Lord Carnwath JSC agreed and Lord Clarke JSC delivered a concurring judgment).

[26] For consideration of some possibilities, see N Tiverios, 'Doctrinal approaches to the law of penalties: A post-*Andrews* intention-based defence of relief against fixed contractual penalties' in S Degeling, J Edelman and J Goudkamp (eds), *Contract in Commercial Law* (Sydney, Thomson Reuters, 2016) 457–92. *cf* R Stevens, 'Rights Restricting Remedies' in A Robertson and M Tilbury (eds), *Divergences in Private Law* (Oxford, Hart Publishing, 2016) 159, 171–76.

[27] See, eg, E Peden, 'The Enigma of Legitimate Interest after *Paciocco*' (2019) 35 *Journal of Contract Law* 263.

[28] For explanation of the difference between incommensurability and incomparability, see R Chang, 'Introduction' in R Chang (ed), *Incommensurability, Incomparability, and Practical Reason* (Cambridge, MA, Harvard University Press, 1998).

[29] For consideration of the claim that 'incommensurability' is an ever-present concern in judicial decision-making, as well as its implications, see P Sales and F Wilmot-Smith, 'Justice for Foxes' (2022) 138 *LQR* 583.

B. The Enforceability of Exclusion (or Limitation) of Liability Clauses

This section considers the effect of incorporating clauses that wholly or partially exclude the liability to pay damages following breach. Two central claims are made. The first is that the wholesale exclusion of a breaching party's liability to pay damages does not prevent the creation of a valid contractual obligation to perform as promised. The second is that the default interpretation of express exclusions of liability for 'consequential loss', which may be modified by the parties' agreement, should be that such clauses preclude recovery for any adverse consequences of a breach that do not consist merely in a failure to receive the promised performance.

i. Is it Possible to Wholly Exclude the Liability to Pay Damages?

The most fundamental question regarding the use of exclusion clauses is whether the liability to pay damages in substitution for providing the promised performance following breach can be wholly excluded. According to Devlin J in *Firestone Tyre Co v Vokins*, the effect of such an exclusion is to render the relevant promise 'illusory' so that 'there is not in law a contract at all'.[30] This is essentially the same view as that advanced by Professor Coote in his landmark study of 'Exception Clauses'.[31] Coote there proposed that such clauses

> are substantive rather than procedural in their effect … [so that a] clause which made purported contractual rights wholly unenforceable would not have effect merely as a shield to claims for damages. It would, in fact, prevent those rights from accruing in the first place.[32]

This view has been persuasively challenged by Professor Stevens on the basis that it ignores the critical distinction between the concepts of obligation and liability.[33] An alternative, and preferable, view is accordingly that exclusions of liability, even purported wholesale exclusions, constitute a *defence* to liability rather than having any effect on the existence of the underlying (primary) right (or correlative obligation) created by the parties' agreement. That this is the better view is perhaps most clearly demonstrated by the fact that, following the performance of an obligation that is wholly unenforceable, no action for restitution of its value will lie,[34] which confirms that the obligation is not in fact a legal nullity.

The possibility that the relevant obligation may be coercively enforced via an injunction or an order for specific performance also demonstrates that the view favoured

[30] *Firestone Tyre Co v Vokins* [1951] 1 Lloyd's Rep 32, 39 (Devlin J): 'It is illusory to say: "We promise to do a thing, but we are not liable if we do not do it."'.

[31] See B Coote, *Exception Clauses: Some Aspects of the Law Relating to Exception Clauses in Contracts for the Carriage, Bailment and Sale of Goods* (London, Sweet & Maxwell, 1964); B Coote, *Contract as Assumption: Essays on a Theme* (Oxford, Hart Publishing, 2010) ch 6.

[32] See Coote (ibid) 7.

[33] See R Stevens, 'Binding our Future Selves' in P Davies and M Raczynska (eds), *Contents of Commercial Contracts: Terms Affecting Freedoms* (Oxford, Hart Publishing, 2020) 13, 22–24.

[34] See, eg, *Moses v Macferlan* (1760) 2 Burr 1005, 1012; 97 ER 676; *Thomas v Brown* (1876) 1 QBD 714 and R Stevens, *The Laws of Restitution* (Oxford, Oxford University Press, 2023) 73–74 and 123.

by Devlin J and Coote is unsustainable. Where, however, the relevant contractual obligation is incapable[35] of being coercively enforced, one can at least see the intuitive appeal of this view since arguably here the wholesale exclusion of damages liability does, in substance, if not in form, effectively provide the promisor with an unfettered discretion whether to perform. But as already explained, the fact that an obligation is unenforceable does not mean it is devoid of legal effect. Thus, even where coercive relief is wholly unavailable, a total exclusion of damages liability does not prevent creation of the underlying right, even if this right is incapable of being enforced.

ii. The Effect of Excluding Liability for 'Consequential Loss'

A less fundamental – but probably more practically important – question that arises in this context concerns the impact of contractually incorporating an express exclusion (or limitation) of liability for 'consequential loss'.[36] The relevant authorities here disclose two main views regarding the effect of such clauses. The historically dominant view in the English authorities, hereafter labelled 'the *Croudace* view' after one of the leading authorities instantiating it,[37] is that 'consequential loss' means only those adverse consequences of a contractual breach that (but for the exclusion) might be recovered under the second limb of the rule in *Hadley v Baxendale*.[38] One difficulty this view confronts is that it is not clear precisely which results of a breach of contract are properly regarded as falling within the second – as opposed to the first – limb of the *Hadley* formulation,[39] particularly since it has been held that the two limbs in *Hadley* are not analytically distinct but are in fact based on the same underlying principle.[40] Arguably, another difficulty with this approach is that it attributes to commercial parties an understanding of a legally complex distinction of which they may be unaware.[41]

[35] Certain difficulties arise here. For some obligations, while specific enforcement is *theoretically* possible, in practice it is never ordered. For other obligations, while coercive relief is generally not available, it may exceptionally be ordered. Moreover, a wholesale – or even partial – exclusion of damages liability for the breach of a particular obligation may well strengthen the case for the making of an order for coercive relief, as explained below in section IV.

[36] For detailed discussion, see J Carter, 'Exclusion of liability for Consequential Loss' (2009) 25 *Journal of Contract Law* 118.

[37] As Carter (ibid) 118 explains, the 'modern root' of this view is *Croudace Construction Ltd v Cawoods Concrete Products Ltd* [1978] 2 Lloyd's Rep 55.

[38] (1854) 9 Ex 341, 156 ER 145 ('*Hadley*'). The second limb is generally associated with the following statement: 'Now, if the special circumstances under which the contract was actually made were communicated by the plaintiffs to the defendants, and thus known to both parties, the damages resulting from the breach of such a contract, which they would reasonably contemplate, would be the amount of injury which would ordinarily follow from a breach of contract under these special circumstances so known and communicated.'

[39] The first limb covers 'damages … such as may fairly and reasonably be considered either arising naturally, *ie*, according to the usual course of things, from such breach of contract itself, or such as may reasonably be supposed to have been in the contemplation of both parties, at the time they made the contract, as the probable result of the breach of it' (ibid).

[40] See, eg, *Jackson v Royal Bank of Scotland* [2005] UKHL 3, [2005] 1 WLR 377 [47]–[48] (Lord Walker, with whom Lord Nicholls and Lord Brown agreed).

[41] See Carter (n 36) 126. The claim is only arguable because on one highly plausible view of what constitutes an 'agreement' the parties need not be aware of the content of the legal obligations that it creates. See further R Stevens, 'What is an Agreement' (2020) 136 *LQR* 599.

But there may be an even more fundamental problem with the *Croudace* view. As many prominent commentators have observed, it is strongly arguable that the *Hadley* rule does not in fact constitute an accurate description of the truly justified limit (or limits) on recovery that the remoteness rule seeks to capture.[42] At the very least, it has long been appreciated that it is unlikely that the various instances in which the recovery of certain adverse consequences of a contractual breach have been denied on the grounds that such consequences are too remote can be reduced to a single principle or test.[43] If either of these propositions is correct, it is not surprising that any attempt to define contractual stipulations that purport to limit liability for 'consequential loss' solely by reference to the two limbs in *Hadley* will tend to be more productive of confusion than clarity.

An alternative view, historically less popular in England,[44] is that references to 'consequential loss' in exclusion (or limitation) of liability clauses describe 'everything beyond the normal measure of damages'.[45] This, for example, was the view taken by Nettle JA in the Victorian Court of Appeal decision in *Environmental Systems Pty Ltd v Peerless Holdings Pty Ltd*,[46] notably invoking the view expressed in *McGregor on Damages*.[47] Significantly, *McGregor* there defines the normal measure of loss as 'that which every claimant in a like situation will suffer in the need to rectify the wrongful act',[48] with the effect that 'consequential loss' denotes 'losses which are particular to … [the] claimant's individual circumstances'.[49] Put differently, 'consequential loss' denotes any way in which the plaintiff has been made materially worse off compared to its projected non-breach position that does not consist merely in a failure to receive the promised performance. Notably, this may even include those adverse consequences of the breach that it was the objective purpose of the relevant obligation breached to prevent if that purpose included obtaining some *consequential* benefit that was contingent upon obtaining the promised performance.[50]

[42] See, eg, A Tettenborn, '*Hadley v Baxendale* Foreseeability: A Principle beyond Its Sell-by Date?' (2007) 23 *Journal of Contract Law* 120; Kramer (n 7); Robertson (n 7); Stevens (n 26) 159, 163–70 and V Niranjan, 'The Contract Remoteness Rule: Exclusion, Not Assumption of Responsibility' in A Dyson, J Goudkamp and F Wilmot-Smith (eds), *Defences in Contract* (Oxford, Hart Publishing, 2017) 187.

[43] See, eg, L Fuller and W Perdue, 'The Reliance Interest in Contract Damages: 1' (1936) 46 *Yale Law Journal* 52, 85, observing that 'it is clear that the test of foreseeability is less a definite test itself than a cover for a developing set of tests'. See also, L Hoffmann, '*The Achilleas*: Custom and Practice or Foreseeability?' (2010) 14 *Edinburgh Law Review* 47, 53, observing, in relation to the indeterminacy of the *Hadley* rule, that this 'degree of indeterminacy … is usually a symptom of other unexpressed factors operating beneath the surface'.

[44] But see *Caledonian North Sea Ltd v British Telecommunications Plc* [2002] 1 Lloyd's Rep 553 (Lord Hoffmann); *Hotel Services Ltd v Hilton International Hotels (UK) Ltd* [2000] 1 All ER (Comm) 750; *Star Polaris LLC v HHIC-PHIL Inc* [2016] EWHC 2941 (Comm) and *Transocean Drilling (UK) Ltd v Providence Resources Plc* [2016] EWCA Civ 372 [11]–[35].

[45] See *Environmental Systems Pty Ltd v Peerless Holdings Pty Ltd* [2008] VSCA 26, approved in *Waterbrook at Yowie Bay Pty Ltd v Allianz Insurance Pty Ltd* [2008] NSWSC 1451 [77].

[46] *Environmental Systems Pty Ltd v Peerless Holdings Pty Ltd* [2008] VSCA 26 [85]–[93].

[47] See J Edelman, *McGregor on Damages*, 22nd edn (London, Sweet & Maxwell, 2024) [3-014]–[3-020], where the same essential view continues to be endorsed today. It may therefore fairly be labelled the 'McGregor view': see, eg, Carter (n 36) 119.

[48] See Edelman (ibid) [3-008], using the term 'normalised loss'.

[49] ibid [3-016].

[50] As now explained, that such 'loss' may not be recoverable where 'consequential loss' is excluded constitutes the main distinction between the McGregor view and the *Croudace* view.

The impetus for the development of the *McGregor* view is that the *Croudace* view adopts a meaning of consequential loss that conflicts with its ordinary linguistic usage by commercial parties.[51] If the first limb of the *Hadley* rule is sometimes understood to include adverse effects of the breach that extend beyond merely failing to receive the promised performance, this is probably correct.[52] Of course, the two views could be made to converge if a more restrictive view of the first limb of *Hadley* is taken, according to which it is synonymous with the deprivation of performance entailed by the breach itself. But the first limb of *Hadley* has historically not been so circumscribed. The truth of this proposition is demonstrated by the House of Lords' leading decision in *The Heron II*,[53] which was arguably wrongly decided.[54] The profits that the claimants failed to obtain as a result of the fall in the Basrah sugar market following the defendant carrier's delayed delivery were held to be recoverable as damages under *Hadley's* first limb on the basis that, at contract formation, such profits 'may reasonably be supposed to have been in the contemplation of both parties … as the probable result of the breach'.[55]

As between the *Croudace* and *McGregor* views, it is suggested that the latter is preferable for the reasons outlined above. However, as Carter has noted, 'When stated as an abstract proposition', neither of these two alternative views can be correct. Apart from the cases supporting them, 'consequential loss' 'could not be regarded as some sort of legal term of art attracting a presumption in favour of a particular (legal) meaning'[56] since the objective meaning of the language used within its relevant context always determines the meaning of *any* contractual utterance.[57] But this fact is expressly acknowledged in the most recent version of *McGregor*,[58] and its recognition is consistent with identifying the term's most conceptually coherent default interpretation from which justifiable departure in a particular case must be demonstrated via a process of construction.

As to what constitutes the conceptually preferable interpretation of 'consequential loss' in the context of a clause excluding liability in damages to compensate for certain kinds of loss, the most obvious answer, as foreshadowed above, is that the term denotes any deterioration in the innocent party's projected non-breach position that does not consist merely in a failure to receive the promised performance. An alternative, and narrower, definition of 'consequential loss' would limit the category to include only those consequential benefits of performance that it was not part of the objective purpose of the relevant promise to deliver, an approach that probably roughly

[51] See Carter (n 36) 125 and Edelman (n 47).

[52] However, one source of the difficulties in this area may be the existence of disagreement regarding what is the best interpretation of the word 'consequential' itself.

[53] *C Czarnikow Ltd v Koufos* [1969] 1 AC 350 ('*The Heron II*').

[54] See, eg, R Epstein, 'Beyond Foreseeability: Consequential Damages in the Law of Contract' (1989) 18 *Journal of Legal Studies* 105, 125.

[55] It is noteworthy in this context that *The Heron II* is arguably inconsistent with *The Achilleas*, though much more than can be said here would be needed to substantiate this claim.

[56] Carter (n 36) 119.

[57] See, eg, G Leggatt, 'Making Sense of Contracts: The Rational Choice Theory' (2015) 131 *LQR* 454; L Hoffmann, 'Language and Lawyers' (2018) 134 *LQR* 553.

[58] See Edelman (n 47) [3-016].

corresponds with the *Croudace* view.[59] In any event, the first interpretation of 'consequential loss' appears to be consistent with the way the term is typically understood when used in the formulation of other abstract legal principles. A prominent recent example of this is the way that the term was used by the majority judgment of the High Court of Australia in *Cessnock City Council v 123 259 932 Pty Ltd* when restating the legal rules that facilitate the recovery of 'wasted expenditure' as damages for breach of contract.[60]

Despite this, if the proposed default interpretation of 'consequential loss' in the context of express attempts to exclude liability for such loss is adopted, one potential complication that arises is the absence of any widespread agreement regarding what it means for a monetary award to compensate (or 'substitute') for a failure to receive the promised performance.[61] While Professors Smith and Webb have each claimed that a 'cost of cure' award is the primary 'substitutionary' measure of damages on the basis that such an award provides the innocent party with that sum of money necessary to obtain the promised performance from elsewhere,[62] Professor Stevens has argued that a 'difference in value' award,[63] which attempts to quantify the market value of what was promised but not provided,[64] is the true 'substitutionary' measure. Although these two measures often coincide, occasionally they diverge, most obviously when a 'cost of rectification' award is possible.

One important practical implication of this difference in opinion is that, in contrast to Smith and Webb, an award of the cost of curing a defectively performed contractual obligation is, for Stevens, one for 'consequential loss'. On the view advocated here, such an award would thus appear to be irrecoverable if the parties' contract incorporated a clause purporting to exclude liability for such loss. One way to avoid this

[59] Notably, it may be observed that 'damages … such as may fairly and reasonably be considered either arising naturally, i.e., according to the usual course of things, from such breach of contract itself' might be viewed as another way of describing the deprivation that consists merely in a failure to deliver the promised performance, while 'such as may reasonably be supposed to have been in the contemplation of both parties, at the time they made the contract, as the probable result of the breach of it' might be viewed as another way of describing those *consequences* of performance that it was the objective purpose of the relevant contractual obligation to provide. For a similar analysis, see Stevens (n 26) 171–76.

[60] See *Cessnock City Council v 123 259 932 Pty Ltd* [2024] HCA 17 [120] (Edelman, Steward, Gleeson and Beech-Jones JJ): 'The calculation of a plaintiff's consequential loss will permit the plaintiff to recover expenditure reasonably incurred in anticipation of, or reliance on, the performance of the contractual obligation that was breached but only to the extent that the expenditure would have been recovered but cannot now be recovered.'

[61] Some commentators deny the possibility of awards of substitutionary damages at all, but this view is difficult to maintain in the face of authorities such as *Clark v Macourt* [2013] HCA 56, (2013) 253 CLR 1 and *MDW Holdings Limited v James Norvill* [2022] EWCA Civ 883, [2023] 1 All ER 929.

[62] See S Smith, 'Substitutionary Damages' in C Rickett (ed), *Justifying Private Law Remedies* (Oxford, Hart Publishing, 2008) 93; and C Webb, 'Performance and Compensation: An Analysis of Contract Damages and Contractual Obligation' (2006) 26 *OJLS* 41. For similar accounts, see B Coote, Contract Damages, *Ruxley*, and the Performance Interest' (1997) *CLJ* 537 and J Edelman 'Money Awards of the Cost of Performance' (2010) 4 *Journal of Equity* 122.

[63] See, eg, R Stevens 'Damages and the Right to Performance: A Golden Victory or Not?' in J Neyers, R Bronaugh and S Pitel (eds), *Exploring Contract Law* (Oxford, Hart Publishing, 2009) 171.

[64] For detailed discussion, see D Winterton, 'Two Conceptions of the "Performance Interest" in Contract Damages' in R Halson and D Campbell (eds), *Research Handbook on Remedies in Private Law* (n 10) 132; and D Winterton, 'Claims for the Value of the Lost Contractual Performance' (2019) 45 *University of Western Australia Law Review* 75.

conclusion would be to recognise that 'difference in value' awards, on the one hand, and (at least some)[65] 'cost of cure' awards, on the other hand, constitute two distinct ways of compensating for the claimant's failure to receive the promised performance. An alternative approach would be to invoke the narrower interpretation of 'consequential loss' canvassed above, whilst also recognising that 'cost of cure' awards are made precisely when they can be said to give effect to the objective purpose of the contractual obligation that was breached. Either analysis would lead to the conclusion that the recovery of (at least some) 'cost of cure' awards is not excluded by the existence of an enforceable contractual exclusion of liability for 'consequential loss'.

III. The Impact of Express Party Agreement as to the Appropriate Response to Breach

Contracting parties may expressly stipulate a preference for a particular kind of response to breach. This section considers what impact, if any, the expression of such a preference should have upon judicial rulings. Since damages constitute the law's default response to contractual breach, the most important instance of this phenomenon is where the parties incorporate a clause that expressly stipulates a preference for the availability of specific performance (hereafter, a 'specific relief' clause).[66] It is argued that the incorporation of such a clause does no more than provide some relevant evidence regarding whether the making of such an order is justifiable. Alternatively, contracting parties might expressly agree that one or the other party should be confined only to recovering damages upon the occurrence of a breach. Here it is argued, conversely, that such clauses should normally be given effect, albeit that departure from this position may occasionally be justified. Finally, it should be noted that the parties also may expressly stipulate that a particular *measure* of damages is recoverable, but it is beyond the scope of the present chapter to consider the enforceability of such clauses.[67]

A. Express Agreement that Coercive Relief should be Ordered

It is generally accepted that coercive relief in the form of an order for specific performance (or the granting of a mandatory injunction)[68] is only available when damages are 'inadequate'.[69] Alternatively, it has been said that such an order is available

[65] It may be that the cost of cure' is sometimes awarded as a monetary substitute for the promised performance and sometimes is awarded to make good the adverse consequences of the breach.

[66] See S Rowan, 'For the Recognition of Remedial Terms Inter Partes' (2010) 126 *LQR* 448, 449.

[67] For some consideration of the enforceability of 'cost of cure damages clauses', 'restitution clauses' and 'penalty [or punitive damages] clauses', see the discussion in Rowan (n 66) 455.

[68] As noted above (n 3), injunctions to enforce promises not to perform an act are more readily available.

[69] See *Harnett v Yielding* (1805) 2 Sch & Lef 549; *Adderley v Dixon* (1824) 1 Sim & St 607, 610; 57 ER 239, 240–41 (Leach VC); and *Sudbrook Trading Estate Ltd v Eggleton* [1983] 1 AC 444.

when, by such relief, 'the court … [can] do more perfect and complete justice',[70] or 'it would not be just in all the circumstances to be confined to damages',[71] though it is debatable whether or not these rival formulations constitute distinct tests of availability or are simply different ways of articulating the same principle. Against that background, contracting parties might expressly stipulate that, in relation to particular obligations or breaches, specific performance should be ordered or that common law damages are to be regarded as 'inadequate'. The question thus arises as to whether the incorporation of such a term constitutes anything more than the mere 'wishful thinking' that some have claimed it amounts to.[72]

The assertion that the inclusion of such an express term makes no difference whatsoever derives from the elementary proposition that 'the parties cannot dictate to a court how its discretion should be exercised'.[73] Although this leads naturally to the conclusion that it is 'doubtful whether, at least for the time being, clauses which provide for such relief are enforceable',[74] it has nevertheless been claimed that 'the exercise of the [court's] discretion may at least take into account the inclusion of an express intention to the effect that these remedies are preferred by the parties', so that it 'can do no harm to state this [remedial preference]'.[75] Judicial support for such a view was also expressed in one of the few reported cases to consider the issue directly, *Warner Brothers Pictures Inc v Nelson*.[76] Justice Branson there observed that:

> Of course, the parties cannot contract themselves out of the law; but it assists, at all events, on the question of evidence as to the applicability of an injunction in the present case, to find the parties formally recognising that in cases of this kind injunction is a more appropriate remedy than damages.[77]

That the jurisdiction of the court cannot be ousted by the parties' express agreement was emphatically reiterated in the more recent English Court of Appeal decision in *Quadrant Visual Communications Ltd v Hutchinson Telephone UK Ltd*.[78] There, Stocker LJ observed that 'Once the court is asked for the equitable remedy of specific performance, its discretion cannot be fettered'.[79] Notably, specific performance was refused in *Quadrant* on the discretionary basis that the plaintiff did not come to equity with 'clean hands', which arguably limits the decision's more general significance. Although more optimistic than some other commentators as regards the potential impact of

[70] See, eg, *Wilson v Northampton and Banbury Junction Rly Co* (1874) 9 Ch App 279, 284 (Lord Selborne LC); *Rainbow Estates Ltd v Tokenhold Ltd* [1999] Ch 64, 72 (Lawrence Collins QC).

[71] See *Paolucci v Makedyn Pty Ltd* [2021] NSWCA 215 ('*Paolucci*') [96] (Leeming JA, White and McCallum JJA agreeing) [96].

[72] See, eg, J Carter and M Tilbury, 'Remedial Choice and Contract Drafting' (1998) 13 *Journal of Contract Law* 5, 34, fn 112.

[73] See *Seddon on Deeds*, 2nd edn (Sydney, Federation Press, 2022) [6.25].

[74] See Rowan (n 66) 451.

[75] See *Seddon on Deeds* (n 73) [6.25], also suggesting that the inclusion of such a clause may be particularly appropriate for certain kinds of obligations contained in deeds (giving the examples of promises concerning confidentiality and restraint of trade).

[76] *Warner Brothers Pictures Inc v Nelson* [1937] 1 KB 209.

[77] ibid 221.

[78] *Quadrant Visual Communications Ltd v Hutchinson Telephone UK Ltd* [1993] BCLC 442 ('*Quadrant*').

[79] ibid 451 (Stocker LJ). To similar effect, see ibid 452 (Butler-Sloss LJ).

these kind of clauses, Rowan offers effectively the same conclusion regarding these authorities, concluding that:

> Until there is judicial authority to the contrary, it would … be unsafe to regard specific relief clauses as being anything other than evidential in value, probative to the question of whether damages are adequate.[80]

A similar, albeit more expansive, view was expressed by Professor Carroll in one of the few sustained academic analyses of the effect of incorporating a specific relief clause.[81] According to Carroll,

> Affording a clause of this nature an evidentiary role as to the parties' intentions at the time of contracting on the adequacy of damages and what is regarded as the appropriate remedy for breach would appear to be uncontroversial … [but] ultimately may be the most that will be achieved by including one in a contract.[82]

Alongside the evidential role suggested by Branson J in *Warner Bros*,[83] Carroll also advances the more controversial proposition that express agreement as to the appropriateness of 'specific relief … [could] play a more general role as a factor … to be weighed against other discretionary considerations' in deciding whether coercive relief should be ordered.[84] Additionally, she suggests that some support for this proposal can be derived from Spry's suggestion that 'the fact that specific performance has been stipulated tends to diminish the weight of [but not render completely irrelevant] other considerations such as hardship to the defendant', which may count against the making of such an order.[85]

The plausibility of Carroll's contention that express agreement as to the appropriateness of specific relief could play a more substantive, rather than merely evidential, role in determining whether specific performance should be ordered is doubtful. One difficulty with this proposal is that it is unclear precisely how any such a weighing process should be carried out, though this evaluative challenge arguably confronts judges *whenever* coercive relief is requested in preference for an award of damages, at least if the availability of coercive relief is to be determined by whether 'it would not be just in all the circumstances to be confined to damages'.[86]

A more fundamental problem with Carroll's proposal is that, aside from its potential evidential value, it is unclear why, given the nature of the task that confronts the judge in this context, the parties' expression of a preference for coercive relief should have *any* bearing upon the court's assessment of whether coercive relief should be ordered.[87]

[80] See Rowan (n 66) 453.

[81] R Carroll, 'Agreements to Specifically Perform Contractual Obligations' (2012) 29 *Journal of Contract Law* 155.

[82] ibid 180.

[83] Additionally, she proposes that the existence of such a clause may make a costs order in favour of the plaintiff more likely if 'specific relief' is ultimately refused ibid 179, citing the decision in *Longwood Station Ltd v Coast Capital Savings Credit Union* 2007 BCSC 1564 in support.

[84] Carroll (n 81) 179.

[85] ibid 180, discussing ICF Spry, *The Principles of Equitable Remedies*, 9th edn (Sydney, Lawbook Co, 2014) 79–80.

[86] See *Paolucci* [2021] NSWCA 215 [96].

[87] See further Smith (n 11) chs 4–5.

To elaborate further, it may be accepted that the defendant's promise to perform a sufficiently certain act – when accompanied by consideration and an intention to create legal relations – provides sufficient reason for that promise to be enforced by the state. But when determining what constitutes the appropriate mode of enforcement, additional considerations become relevant, potentially including 'public interest' considerations,[88] and it is not obvious why the parties' express stipulation as to their preferred mode of enforcement has any normative salience. Reduced to its essence, the central point is that, while it is generally accepted that the fact that the parties have made a sufficiently certain agreement justifies the recognition (and enforcement) of certain legal rights (and their correlative duties), this does not entail acceptance of the further proposition that party agreement regarding the appropriate mode of enforcing such rights is normatively relevant in determining how the state should enforce those rights.

It is arguable that Carroll's proposal depends upon one's view as to the best understanding of the test for determining whether specific performance should be ordered. If specific performance is only available when damages are 'inadequate', Carroll's proposal is only supportable if the existence of express agreement as to the appropriateness of specific relief is relevant to the court's determination of whether damages are indeed 'inadequate'. This must in turn depend upon whether the parties themselves can determine (or at least influence) the meaning of 'adequacy' in this context, a proposition that is highly doubtful for the reasons outlined above. If, on the other hand, specific performance is available whenever such an order is 'just in all the circumstances', this might more easily allow for the parties' prior agreement as to the appropriateness of such an order to be regarded as a material factor to be added to the scales when assessing whether such relief should be ordered. But even if this view is preferred, one still confronts the difficulty adverted to above that, in determining how a claimant's successfully asserted legal right should be enforced, considerations additional to those that determine whether that right exists become relevant,[89] and indeed those other considerations are often decisive.[90] Consequentially, apart from the possibility of providing some useful evidence of what the objective purpose of the relevant contractual obligation is (and, therefore, whether damages are 'adequate' in the relevant sense), it is far from clear that the parties' prior agreement that coercive relief should be ordered ought to have any bearing upon the judicial determination of whether such an order is appropriate.

Finally, the precise basis for Spry's contention that the existence of a specific relief clause 'tends to diminish the weight of … other considerations such as hardship to the defendant' is not obvious.[91] Accepting for present purposes that retention of the 'hardship' defence in its current form is justified, the rationale for this 'bar' to relief must be the desirability of recognising the possibility that the defendant's circumstances have so changed since the parties' agreement was made that it is not appropriate, all relevant

[88] See, for example, *Fearn v Board of Trustees of the Tate Gallery* [2023] UKSC 4, [2024] AC 1 (Lord Leggatt JSC) [130]–[133].

[89] See further, ibid.

[90] See, eg, *Co-operative Insurance Society v Argyll Stores* [1998] AC 1.

[91] Spry (n 85) 79–80.

matters considered, to coerce the affected party to perform their obligation(s). If so, it is far from obvious why the hardship defence should not equally apply in relation to any attempt to invoke a specific relief clause.

To recapitulate, it is clear that the court's discretion cannot be fettered by the contract and that the inclusion of a clause stipulating that coercive relief should be the default response to the breach of a particular contractual obligation may (at best) constitute relevant evidence in relation to what the purpose of the relevant contractual obligation is – and therefore, whether damages are indeed 'adequate' in the relevant circumstances. But, as noted, the better view may be that this is merely a threshold requirement that must be satisfied before an order for coercive relief becomes possible, with the overriding test being whether 'it would not be just in all the circumstances to be confined to damages'.[92] Even so, the preferable view is that it is ultimately for the court to determine whether ordering such relief is justified by reference to an assessment of all relevant considerations. Notably, such considerations do not include any agreement made by the parties as to their preferred method of enforcement because, while it is for the parties to create legal rights via their agreement, it is for the courts to determine both whether: (1) they have successfully done so; and (2) the precise mechanism by which such rights should be enforced.

B. Express Agreement that 'Damages Only' should be Awarded

In contrast to the position just considered, contracting parties may incorporate an express term stipulating that 'damages only' are recoverable upon the occurrence of a particular breach, thereby expressing a preference that coercive relief be wholly excluded.[93] Given the dearth of relevant authority in Australia and England and Wales regarding whether such clauses should be enforced, their effectiveness in these jurisdictions is unclear. By contrast, the enforceability of a 'damages only' clause is a question that has received more attention in other jurisdictions. For example, in the context of advancing a broader argument in favour of adopting specific performance as the default response to contractual breach, Jukier has observed that there is judicial support for the enforcement of such clauses in the United States and that the Convention on Contracts for the International Sale of Goods 1980 (CISG) expressly provides that parties may contract out of specific performance.[94] But the significance of this latter fact for non-US common law jurisdictions is unclear because, in contrast to the CISG, specific performance is not the presumptive response to contractual breach. It might accordingly be claimed that the reason to enforce a 'damages only' clause in a non-US common law jurisdiction differs in kind from the reason to enforce such clauses in jurisdictions where damages are not the law's default response to a breach of contract.

[92] See *Paolucci* [2021] NSWCA 215 [96].

[93] Such a clause has been referred to as a 'damages only' provision: see Carroll (n 81) 167.

[94] See R Jukier, 'Taking Specific Performance Seriously: Trumping Damages as the Presumptive Remedy for Breach of Contract' in R Sharpe and K Roach (eds), *Taking Rights Seriously* (Ottawa, Canadian Institute for the Administration of Justice, 2009) 85, 115.

So, what *should* be the effect of the parties' incorporation of a clause expressly stipulating that 'damages only' are recoverable upon the happening of a particular breach? In contrast to a clause expressly stating a preference for coercive relief, such a clause merely purports to direct the court *not* to order the more coercive mode of enforcing a contractual promise. While this does purport to constrain the range of remedial options open to the court, it does so only by removing the most coercive option. Such a clause accordingly constitutes a far less significant interference with the state's role in enforcing contractual rights, and in fact makes it easier to justify *any* kind of state enforcement of contractual promises.[95] It is suggested that such a clause is best interpreted as altering the content of the relevant primary obligation so that the relevant promise is now most accurately characterised as a disjunctive undertaking either to perform *or* to pay damages. It is accordingly suggested that enforcing such a clause is significantly easier to justify than enforcing a specific relief clause,[96] and that normally such clauses should be given effect, albeit that certain specific exceptions to this general principle may be justified.[97]

Regardless of whether this analysis is wholly accepted, the effect of a purported 'damages only' clause must, as Spry explains, ultimately be determined by reference to a proper construction of the relevant contract.[98] It seems safe to assume that an intention to exclude the availability of coercive relief will not be lightly drawn. As Lord Goff observed in *Stocznia Gdanska SA v Latvian Shipping Co*, albeit in the very different context of considering whether a seller's right to recover accrued instalments prior to the contract's 'rescission' had been abandoned, 'clear words are needed to rebut the presumption that a contracting party does not intend to abandon any remedies for breach of the contract arising by operation of law'.[99] A similar sentiment was also expressed more recently by Lord Leggatt in *Triple Point Technology Inc v PTT Public Co Ltd*.[100] Additionally, the High Court of Australia has affirmed the existence of the same principle in Australian law,[101] though again not in the specific context of considering the enforceability of a 'damages only' provision.

[95] The point here is that the state's enforcement of contractual promises, either via coercive orders or via an award of damages, requires justification. Arguably, such justification becomes easier if the most coercive means of enforcement is impermissible. To put the point another way, if an order requiring the performance of a contractual right was *never* available, the very existence of a *law* of contract would be easier to justify. Importantly, however, it would be harder to characterise this body of law as the law of *agreements*, since it might be said that, under such a legal regime, agreements were never *fully* enforceable.

[96] For an argument that may run counter to this proposal but is strongly supportive of the claims made earlier in relation to 'specific relief' clauses, see S Shiffrin, 'Remedial Clauses: The Overprivatization of Private Law' (2012) 67 *Hastings Law Journal* 407.

[97] Two possible exceptions may be: (1) where damages are 'inadequate' in a sense that could not have reasonably have been envisaged by the parties when their contract was made; and (2) where, due to the existence of an extensive exclusion of liability clause, the promise can only be effectively enforced via coercive relief. For further consideration of this second possibility, see section IV.B.

[98] See Spry (n 85).

[99] *Stocznia Gdanska SA v Latvian Shipping Co* [1998] 1 WLR 574, 585.

[100] *Triple Point Technology Inc v PTT Public Co Ltd* [2021] UKSC 29, [2021] AC 1148 [108].

[101] See *Concut Pty Ltd v Worrell* (2000) 176 ALR 693 [23] (Gleeson CJ and Gaudron and Gummow JJ), cited in Carroll (n 81) 167.

IV. The Impact of Express Modification of Contract Law's Default Damages Rules on the Availability of Coercive Relief

Section II of this chapter examined what impact the parties' express modification of default damages rules may have on the damages recoverable following a breach of contract. Section III considered whether incorporating an express term specifying a particular remedial preference should affect the relief ordered. The present section asks whether the modification of default damages rules can have any effect on the availability of coercive relief. One important question arising in this context, examined in Part A, is whether the presence of an enforceable liquidated damages clause affects the availability of such relief. It is argued that, although the parties' agreement to liquidate the damages payable upon breach may provide relevant evidence as regards whether damages are 'adequate' for the purposes of ordering coercive relief,[102] the presence of such a clause cannot generally be regarded as decisive evidence of the parties' agreement that coercive relief is inappropriate. A related question, considered in Part B, concerns the impact of including a clause limiting a breaching party's liability in damages upon the availability of coercive relief. The central claim advanced here is that including an exclusion clause in the parties' contract is necessarily relevant in deciding whether the available common law remedies are adequate.

A. The Impact of an 'Agreed Damages' Clause upon the Availability of Coercive Relief

An important question that arises in considering the extent to which contracting parties may alter the law's default remedial rules is whether the incorporation of a liquidated damages clause has the effect of precluding coercive relief, in the form of an order for specific performance or an injunction. At its most compelling, the argument in favour of this proposition is (roughly) as follows:

(1) At least according to the newly established law in both Australia and the UK, a liquidated damages provision can be included in a contract for at least two reasons:[103] (i) to render more certain and predictable potentially recoverable – but perhaps difficult to prove or predict – financial losses that may be suffered following breach; and (ii) to allow for the possibility of compensation for damage to other legitimate (financial and non-financial) interests for which damages may be either irrecoverable or difficult to prove.

[102] Relevantly, where damages cannot be quantified with the requisite degree of certainty to mandate recovery.

[103] A possible further reason not considered is that the inclusion of such a clause may deter breach. Under the old law of penalties, this objective was apparently illegitimate. But arguably, this is no longer the case under the contemporary approach provided that the relevant test is nevertheless satisfied.

(2) At least in some circumstances (ie, where damages are relevantly unquantifiable[104]), a liquidated damages provision may be construed as reflecting the parties' agreement as to what constitutes an accurate pre-estimate of the loss likely to result from the relevant breach.
(3) Therefore, at least in such cases, the sum of money recoverable by reference to the liquidated damages provision is 'adequate' (in the relevant sense) and, assuming that coercive relief is only available when damages are 'inadequate',[105] such relief therefore should not be ordered.[106]

But this argument is ultimately unpersuasive as a matter of principle, in addition to lacking support in the relevant authorities.[107] Reduced to its essence, this is because such an argument fails properly to account for the incommensurability (or incomparability) of money and non-pecuniary damage that is conventionally understood to provide the principal justification for conditioning the availability of coercive relief upon the inadequacy of damages.[108]

To elaborate further, one controversial question that arises regarding the availability of specific performance is whether mere difficulty in the quantification of damages is, by itself, sufficient grounds for the making of such an order. While it has been said that difficulty in quantifying damages is indeed a sufficient reason for ordering specific performance,[109] it may be that there is a critical distinction between mere 'evidential' (or 'forensic') difficulties in quantification and difficulties of proof that do not have 'a forensic root'.[110] On this view, only difficulties of the latter kind are sufficient to justify ordering specific performance.[111] But whatever the correct position in principle, courts have generally accepted that the unquantifiability of damages does sometimes provide a proper basis for ordering specific performance.[112]

[104] See R Austen-Baker, 'Difficulties with Damages as a Ground for Specific Performance' (1999) 10 *King's College Law Journal* 1, distinguishing between mere 'evidential' (or 'forensic') difficulties in quantification and 'intrinsic' difficulties.

[105] As noted earlier, the test is sometimes expressed in alternative terms: see cases cited at n 75.

[106] Of course, the parties could include a clause in their contract stipulating that the liquidated sum is without prejudice to any other relief that may be sought or that it should be taken as estimating the recoverable loss. Nevertheless, while of potential evidential relevance to the court's assessment as to whether coercive relief should be ordered, the existence of the latter kind of clause should still not be decisive of the issue.

[107] But see *BearingPoint Australia Pty Ltd v Hilliard* [2008] VSC 115 and *Idamenco (No 123) v Butterworth* [2013] NSWSC 357, which notably both involved application for *interlocutory*, rather than final, injunctive relief. In *Butterworth*, McDougall J held (at [20]) that the existence of an enforceable 'liquidated damages' clause was 'the governing consideration' in determining whether an injunction should be ordered on the basis that: 'here the parties agreed on the consequences of breach, the Court should be slow to substitute its own judgment that some further and more onerous restraint is necessary. It should instead act on the basis that the contract itself indicates the adequacy of damages as a remedy for breach.'

[108] For discussion of the extent to which this is an ever-present concern in judicial decision-making, see Sales and Wilmot-Smith (n 29).

[109] See, for example, HG Beale (ed), *Chitty on Contracts*, 35th edn (London, Sweet & Maxwell, 2021) ch 31, citing *AB v University of XYZ* [2020] EWHC 2978 (QB) [102] and *Bath and North East Somerset District Council v Mowlem Plc* [2004] EWCA Civ 115 [16] (Mance LJ, Park and Brooke LJJ agreeing): 'difficulty of quantification is an acknowledged basis for treating damages as an inadequate remedy'.

[110] See Austen-Baker (n 104) 2.

[111] See Austen-Baker (ibid) distinguishing between 'extrinsic' and 'intrinsic' difficulties in quantification.

[112] See, eg, *AB v University of XYZ* [2020] EWHC 2978 (QB) [102].

Accordingly, if what generally renders damages inadequate in the relevant sense is that non-pecuniary loss will likely result from the breach, there is a flaw in the argument that was outlined above for the proposition that the parties' inclusion of a liquidated damages clause may sometimes render damages adequate for the purposes of determining the availability of coercive relief. The flaw is that, just because a liquidated damages clause can be used to protect legitimate non-financial interests, it does not follow that the parties' inclusion of such a clause reflects their agreement that the stipulated sum constitutes an accurate pre-estimate of the recoverable compensation for any damage to these interests. As noted, it is also doubtful that the parties can themselves stipulate what is meant by the 'adequacy' standard in this context.

The more natural interpretation of a liquidated damages clause is accordingly that it constitutes recognition by the parties of the possibility of damage to the interests of the non-breaching party that are 'insusceptible of evaluation and assessment in money terms'.[113] Put differently, while incorporating a liquidated damages clause may be preferable to simply relying on the applicable default rules of damages assessment because it provides for additional, or more easily proven, financial compensation, this does not remove the problem of incommensurability (or incomparability) noted above that, at least in part, provides the foundation for the equitable jurisdiction to order coercive relief. The fact that the parties have liquidated the damages payable upon breach cannot therefore be invoked as proof of the adequacy of damages where, in the absence of the liquidated damages clause, damages would be inadequate.

Additional support for the view just outlined derives from the point made above in section III that the 'court's discretion [to order equitable relief] cannot be fettered by the contract'.[114] Since the better view is that the parties cannot dictate to a court that damages are inadequate, it also must be true that the parties cannot indirectly fetter the court's discretion as to the adequacy of damages by the inclusion of a liquidated damages clause. At best, such a clause may provide some evidence as to the interests that the parties' bargain sought to protect.

This analysis also derives authoritative support from the English Court of Appeal decision in *Bath and North East Somerset District Council v Mowlem Plc*,[115] which Brereton JA cited with approval in the New South Wales Court of Appeal's decision in *Tullet Prebon (Australia) Pty Ltd v Purcell*.[116] In *Mowlem*, the Council sought an interim injunction requiring Mowlem to grant access to another contractor to the project site following a delay in performing its promise to restore a historic spa in Bath. The existence of a clause liquidating damages for breach by delay in the amount of £12,000 per week did not prevent the requested injunction from being granted. According to Mance LJ, the existence of the relevant liquidated damages clause did not preclude a finding that damages were inadequate – and ultimately the granting of the requested injunction – on the basis that the agreed amount did not represent the Council's actual projected loses, which included loss of tourists, loss of trade in relation

[113] See *Andrews* [2012] HCA 30, (2012) 247 CLR 205 [11].
[114] See *Meagher, Gummow and Lehane* (n 79) [20-005].
[115] *Bath and North East Somerset District Council v Mowlem Plc* [2004] EWCA Civ 115 ('*Mowlem*').
[116] *Tullet Prebon (Australia) Pty Ltd v Purcell* [2010] NSWCA 150 [100].

to hotels and restaurants, and loss of parking income, in circumstances where at least some of those losses may have been irrecoverable on the grounds of remoteness.[117]

B. The Impact of Contractually Incorporating an Exclusion (or Limitation) of Liability Clause upon the Availability of Coercive Relief

As we have just seen, the decision to include a liquidated damages clause, even if occasionally decisive, cannot generally be regarded as precluding the availability of coercive relief. But what is the impact upon the availability of injunctive relief of incorporating an express contractual term that excludes or limits the liability to pay damages of one of the parties in relation to certain breaches of contract?

This question arose directly for consideration in the English Court of Appeal decision in *AB v CD*,[118] which concerned a licence agreement under which AB obtained the right to market CD's internet-based platform. The contract contained an express term purporting to exclude liability for loss of profits following a breach, or of any cause of action, and capping the damages recoverable under any head of claim at £17,000. After CD purported to terminate the parties' agreement, AB sought an interim injunction (until their dispute had been determined by arbitration) requiring CD not to terminate. In holding that the injunction should be granted, the Court of Appeal focused on the finding of Mance LJ in *Bath* that 'the primary obligation of a party is to perform the contract' and that the existence of a liquidated damages provision does not 'constitute an agreed price to permit Mowlem to breach the contract'.[119] Significantly, the Court further held that the existence of the exclusion clause in the parties' contract must be taken into consideration when deciding whether the available common law remedies were adequate to reflect 'the substantial justice of the situation'.[120]

If it is permissible for a contract to wholly exclude one party's liability to pay damages following breach – a proposition that was earlier defended[121] – there would be no reason to doubt that the existence of such a clause must be considered in determining whether the available common law remedies were adequate. But even if this view is rejected, it is less obvious that the damages may be regarded as inadequate when the parties have incorporated a clause excluding liability to pay damages

[117] *Mowlem* [2004] EWCA Civ 115 [20]: 'I consider that it is open to the Council, despite the liquidated and ascertained damages clause, to rely on the probable higher level of the actual loss that it would suffer without an injunction, in order to show that it would not be adequately compensated if it were left to a claim in damages. Even if one assumes that remoteness can be relevant in this context (as to which I need express no view), no question of remoteness arises in respect of such higher loss which relates to heads which would ordinarily be recoverable at law.'

[118] *AB v CD* [2014] EWCA Civ 229.

[119] ibid [25], [27]: 'an agreement to restrict the recoverability of damages in the event of a breach cannot be treated as an agreement to excuse performance of that primary obligation'.

[120] ibid [27]. See further P Davies, 'Injunctions in Torts and Contract' in S Worthington and G Virgo (eds), *Commercial Remedies: Resolving Controversies* (Cambridge, Cambridge University Press, 2017) 127 and P Turner, 'Inadequacy in Equity of Common Law Relief: the Relevance of Contractual Terms' (2014) *CLJ* 493.

[121] See section II.B.i.

compensating for some or all of the plaintiff's consequential loss. This is because, although the overriding remedial aim is to place the innocent party into as near a position as if the contract had been performed, it is generally accepted that the parties can expressly (or impliedly) limit the breaching party's obligation to do so. Accordingly, it might plausibly be claimed that, since the parties have bargained to restrict the scope of the breaching party's *secondary* duty to make good certain adverse consequence of the breach, this should inform the court's assessment of whether coercive relief is justified. But for the reasons advanced earlier in this chapter, and consistently with the logic of the Court of Appeal's decision in *AB v CD*, it is contended that the parties' agreement to restrict the scope of a party's secondary duty to make good certain adverse consequences of the breach cannot legitimately impact whether coercive relief is justified to give effect to the innocent party's *primary* right to performance of the relevant contractual promise.

V. Conclusion

The central ambition of this chapter has been to investigate the extent to which contracting parties can modify, via express stipulation, the default remedial rules that apply following an actual, or anticipated, breach of contract. Section II advanced two main claims. One was that the wholesale exclusion of the liability to pay damages upon breach does not prevent the valid creation of a contractual right to performance. The other was that, subject to party modification, the default interpretation of express exclusions of liability for 'consequential loss' should be to preclude damages being recovered to make good any adverse consequences of a breach that do not consist merely of failing to receive the promised performance. The central arguments advanced in section III were that incorporating an express term stipulating a remedial preference for coercive relief can do no more than provide (potentially relevant) evidence as to the justifiability of such an order and, conversely, that the expression of a preference for 'damages only' as a response to breach should normally be given effect. Finally, section IV also advanced two main claims. The first was that including an 'agreed damages' clause does not generally render damages 'adequate' for the purposes of adjudicating upon the availability of such relief. The second was that the contractual incorporation of an exclusion clause limiting a breaching party's damages liability is necessarily relevant in determining whether an order for coercive relief is justified.

12

Three Forms of Default Rules (in the Law of Unjust Enrichment)

RORY GREGSON*

I. Introduction

This chapter has two aims. The first is to show that lawyers use the label 'default rule' to describe three different concepts. It is important to untangle these three different senses of a 'default rule'. They operate differently, have different purposes, and have a complex relationship with each other.

The second aim is to examine the role of default rules in the law of unjust enrichment. The language of default rules is sometimes invoked in the law of unjust enrichment, and indeed this area provides potential examples of all three forms of default rules. But despite this, the role of default rules in unjust enrichment is underexamined. This chapter argues that, on closer inspection, default rules – in all three forms – have a smaller role in the law of unjust enrichment than is commonly supposed.

II. Three Forms of Default Rules

A. Distinguishing the Three Forms

The *Oxford English Dictionary* gives no fewer than nine definitions of the word 'default', one of which is 'designating an option, state, course of action, etc., which is adopted or reverted to in the absence of conscious choice or viable alternatives; (hence) usual, standard'. Thus, 'in default of' means 'in the absence of, for lack of'. When lawyers use the language of 'default rules', it is this sense of the word that they invoke.

However, close inspection reveals that lawyers use the phrase 'default rules' in three different ways, describing rules with three different formal features. All three categories of rules are defaults in the sense that they apply absent (in default of) some event occurring. But the relevant event is different in each of the three categories. Most often, lawyers

* I thank William Day, Katie Johnston and Jonathan Morgan for their comments.

use the phrase to describe rules which apply unless the parties agree that a different rule should apply. Second, and closely related, lawyers use the phrase to describe rules which apply unless one party communicates information to the other. Finally, lawyers sometimes use the phrase to describe rules which have exceptions: these are rules which apply unless a judge decides to apply an exception. For ease of exposition, I will label these 'classic defaults', 'information defaults', and 'rules with exceptions' respectively, and say something about each in turn.

Importantly, these three categories are not mutually exclusive. A single rule may have any combination of these three formal features.

B. Classic Default Rules

A default rule is classically defined as a rule which applies unless the parties agree otherwise.[1] To take some examples from the law of contract, the rules on quantification of damages are default rules, since the parties can enter an enforceable agreement that a different quantum is payable (subject to the rule against penalties and statutory controls).[2] The doctrine of frustration discharges the parties' obligations if performance becomes impossible or radically different.[3] This is a default rule,[4] since the parties can agree to a different allocation of risk, under which their obligations continue even if a supervening event renders performance impossible or radically different.[5] Much of the Sale of Goods Act 1979 consists of default rules. For instance, section 19 sets out rules on when title passes to the buyer, and these rules apply 'Unless a different intention appears'.

Classic default rules, then, are defined by their form: they are rules which apply unless the parties agree the content of a rule to apply instead. A classic default is therefore the opposite of a mandatory rule, which is usually understood to be a rule

[1] *Barton v Morris* [2023] UKSC 3, [2023] AC 684 [126]–[132] (Lord Leggatt); I Ayres and R Gertner, 'Filling Gaps in Incomplete Contracts: An Economic Theory of Default Rules' (1989) 99 *Yale Law Journal* 87, 87; R Craswell, 'Contract Law, Default Rules, and the Philosophy of Promising' (1989) 88 *Michigan Law Review* 489, 490; JS Johnston, 'Strategic Bargaining and the Economic Theory of Contract Default Rules' (1990) 100 *Yale Law Journal* 615, 615–16; RE Barnett, 'The Sound of Silence: Default Rules and Contractual Consent' (1992) 78 *Virginia Law Review* 821, 825; A Schwartz, 'The Default Rule Paradigm and the Limits of Contract Law' (1993) 3 *South California Interdisciplinary Law Journal* 389, 390; J Morgan, *Contract Law Minimalism: A Formalist Restatement of Commercial Contract Law* (Cambridge, Cambridge University Press, 2013) 91.

[2] Unfair Contract Terms Act 1977; Consumer Rights Act 2015, Pt 2. For discussion, see D Airey, 'When it's Mandatory to be "Reasonable": the Nature and Application of Reasonableness Under The Unfair Contract Terms Act 1977', this volume, ch 7 and JM Paterson, 'Mandatory Statutory Rules, Consumer Contracts and Contractual Interpretation', this volume, ch 8.

[3] *Taylor v Caldwell* (1863) 3 B & S 826, 834; 122 ER 309, 312 (Blackburn J); *Davis Contractors Ltd v Fareham UDC* [1956] AC 696 (HL) 729 (Lord Radcliffe).

[4] Except in the case of supervening illegality, where the doctrines operate as a mandatory rule: see J Morgan, 'Frustration Dissected: Mandatory and Default Rules', this volume, ch 9.

[5] *Ocean Tramp Tankers Corp v v/o Sovfracht (the Eugenia)* [1964] 2 QB 226 (CA) 238–39 (Lord Denning MR); *Associated Japanese Bank (International) Ltd v Credit Du Nord SA* [1989] 1 WLR 255 (QB) 268 (Steyn J); *Great Peace Shipping Ltd v Tsavliris Salvage (International) Ltd (the Great Peace)* [2002] EWCA Civ 1407, [2003] QB 679 [76] (Lord Phillips MR). For discussion, see J Morgan, 'Frustration Dissected: Mandatory and Default Rules', this volume, ch 9 and A Robertson, 'Default Rules, Interpretation and Risk Allocation', this volume, ch 3.

which the parties cannot opt out of. The title of this collection – 'Mandatory and Default Rules in Contract and Commercial Law' – refers to this dichotomy between mandatory rules and classic defaults.

C. Information Defaults

The label 'default rule' is also used to describe rules which apply unless one party communicates information to the other.[6] A good example is provided by the contractual remoteness test in *Hadley v Baxendale:* the default rule is that a claimant may not recover losses arising from 'special circumstances', unless they had communicated those special circumstances to the defendant before the contract was made.[7]

This default does not have the same form as the classic default rules discussed in the previous section. Classic defaults are rules which apply unless the parties agree otherwise. But the 'default' rule in *Hadley v Baxendale* is not displaced by the parties *bilaterally agreeing*, but rather by one party *unilaterally communicating* information to the other. Both classic defaults and information defaults, then, apply unless the parties do something, but that 'something' differs in each category. Classic defaults apply unless the parties agree the content of a rule which they wish to apply instead, whereas information defaults apply unless one party communicates certain information to the other.

An information default is therefore closely related to, though subtly distinct from, Ayres and Gertner's concept of a 'penalty default', which they explain as follows:

> Penalty defaults are designed to give at least one party to the contract an incentive to contract around the default rule and therefore to choose affirmatively the contract provision they prefer. In contrast to the received wisdom, penalty defaults are purposefully set at what the parties would not want – in order to encourage the parties to reveal information to each other or to third parties (especially the courts).[8]

A penalty default is therefore a category defined by a rule's rationale. It cuts across my threefold categorisation according to a rule's form. In principle, any rule could be designed to encourage one party to reveal information and so a default rule of any of the three forms could be a penalty default. Nevertheless, the form of an information default makes it an obvious choice to achieve this aim.

D. Rules with Exceptions

Finally, the phrase 'default rule' can be used to describe the idea that a rule has exceptions. For example, in chapter fourteen of this collection, Ying Khai Liew argues that the rule requiring certainty of intention for the creation of a trust does not apply

[6] For further examples, see S Hedley, 'Quality of Goods, Information, and the Death of Contract' (2001) *Journal of Business Law* 114.

[7] *Hadley v Baxendale* (1854) 9 Ex 341, 156 ER 145.

[8] Ayres and Gertner (n 1) 91.

in the usual way to *Quistclose* trusts,[9] and so 'the traditionally mandatory requirement of certainty of intention transforms into a default rule in the *Quistclose* context'. This is not a default rule in the classic sense. A classic default rule applies unless *the parties* agree that a different rule should apply. By contrast, here the language of 'default rule' describes the idea that a rule applies unless *the court* (not the parties) decides to make an exception.

Another example can be found in Lord Sales' essay entitled 'Default Rules in the Common Law: Substantive Rules and Precedent'.[10] Lord Sales discusses classic defaults such as the rules on quantification of damages for breach of contract. But he also describes precedent as a default rule. Again, this is not a classic default rule but a rule with exceptions: a precedent applies unless a judge (not the parties) chooses to depart from it.

The category of 'rules with exceptions' swallows the other two categories of default rules. A classic default is a rule subject to the exception that the parties can agree the content of a different rule to apply instead. An information default is a rule subject to the exception that it does not apply if one party communicates certain information to the other. However, the category of 'rules with exceptions' is much broader than classic defaults and information defaults, since the exception can be anything. Since many legal rules have exceptions, this third category captures large swathes of the law.

Describing a rule with exceptions as a 'default' rule is a perfectly natural use of language. The rule applies 'in default of' the judge applying an exception. However, in legal discourse, describing a rule with exceptions as a 'default rule' is best avoided. Classic defaults and (other examples of) rules with exceptions take radically different forms. Default rules in the classic sense, along with information defaults, are rules which apply unless the *parties* do something (either agree a different rule or communicate information). By contrast, (other examples of) rules with exceptions are rules which apply unless a *judge* applies an exception. Furthermore, these different forms of rules reflect different justifications, as explained below. The connotations associated with the language of 'default rules' are therefore unhelpful when discussing rules with exceptions.

To take another example, causing the death of another, with the intention to kill or cause grievous bodily harm, is murder. To my knowledge, nobody describes this as a 'default rule' just because it is a rule with exceptions such as acting in self-defence. Default rules and rules with exceptions are different concepts, best kept separate and described using different language.

E. Relationship

Classic defaults, information defaults, and rules with exceptions therefore describe three different formal features of rules. These are not mutually exclusive categories. A single rule may have any combination of these three formal features.

[9] *Quistclose Investments Ltd v Barclays Bank Ltd* [1970] AC 567 (HL).

[10] Philip Sales, 'Default Rules in the Common Law: Substantive Rules and Precedent' in B Häcker and J Ungerer (eds), *Default Rules in Private Law* (Oxford, Hart Publishing, 2025) 87.

For example, the rule in *Hadley v Baxendale*,[11] which is perhaps the most cited example of a default rule,[12] is an example of both a classic default and an information default. *Hadley* established the remoteness test for compensatory damages for breach of contract: a claimant may only recover losses

> either arising naturally, i.e., according to the usual course of things, from such breach of contract itself, or such as may reasonably be supposed to have been in the contemplation of both parties, at the time they made the contract, as the probable result of the breach of it.[13]

Thus, if 'special circumstances' increase the claimant's loss, the default rule limits the recoverable loss to that 'which would arise generally, and in the great multitude of cases not affected by any special circumstances'.[14] However, where the claimant had communicated the special circumstances to the defendant, then the increased loss will fall within the reasonable contemplation of the parties. The default rule (limiting recovery) is displaced and the claimant may recover the loss 'which would ordinarily follow from a breach of contract under these special circumstances'.[15]

The rule in *Hadley v Baxendale* is therefore an information default: the default is that abnormal loss arising from special circumstances is unrecoverable, *unless* the claimant communicated the special circumstances to the defendant. When *Hadley* is cited as an example of a default rule, it is often because of this: its operation as an information default.[16] But in addition, the rule in *Hadley* is also a classic default, since the parties can agree to opt out of the rule altogether by agreeing a liquidated damages clause.[17]

Similarly, a rule with exceptions may be either a classic default or a mandatory rule, depending on whether the parties can enter an enforceable agreement that a different rule should apply.

F. Purpose

Writing extra-judicially, Lord Sales argued that default rules serve four purposes. First, they save transaction costs by saving 'the parties the time and expense of expressly agreeing and recording any and all terms of their agreement'.[18] Second, they allow values to be injected into the law. Third, they serve the rule of law. Fourth, they alleviate information asymmetries.

[11] *Hadley v Baxendale* (1854) 9 Ex 341, 156 ER 145.

[12] Ayres and Gertner (n 1) 101–04; Johnston (n 1); Barnett (n 1) 867–88; R Korobkin, 'Status Quo Bias and Contract Default Rules' (1997–1998) 83 *Cornell Law Review* 608, 615–16; I Ayres and R Gertner, 'Strategic Contractual Inefficiency and the Optimal Choice of Legal Rules' (1992) 101 *Yale Law Journal* 729, 734; Sales (n 10) 92.

[13] *Hadley v Baxendale* (1854) 9 Ex 341, 354; 156 ER 145, 151 (Alderson B).

[14] ibid.

[15] ibid.

[16] Ayres and Gertner (n 1) 101–04; Johnston (n 1); Barnett (n 1) 867; Sales (n 10) 92–93.

[17] Korobkin (n 12) 615–16; Barnett (n 1) 868. Subject to the rule against penalties and the statutory controls in fn 2. And see also *Transfield Shipping Inc v Mercator Shipping Inc, The Achilleas* [2008] UKHL 48, [2009] 1 AC 61.

[18] Sales (n 10) 85.

It is important to distinguish the three different forms of default rules, since they serve different purposes. Taking each of Lord Sales' four purposes in turn, it is classic default rules which reduce transaction costs. Classic default rules, which apply unless the parties contract out of them, allow parties to enter legally binding agreements even if they have not made express provision about every contingency.[19] By contrast, rules with exceptions may *increase* transaction costs. The parties cannot be sure whether the judge will apply the default or depart from it, and so parties that want certainty must specify what they want to happen. Rules *without* exceptions would offer greater certainty, and so the parties would only need to contract out of them if they wanted a different result.

Second, all three forms of default rules inject values into the law through the choice of the content of the default rule. But this unremarkable since it is true of all legal rules. More precisely, Lord Sales' point is that 'the creation of default rules' through precedent gives effect to 'certain special values'.[20] While these values may be outweighed, 'a judge must grapple directly with why that is and justify the non-application of the presumptive rule by reference to compelling competing values which are themselves worthy of respect'.[21] Here, then, Lord Sales is primarily concerned with the behaviour of judges, and is giving a justification for rules with exceptions and not for classic defaults[22] or information defaults.

Third, and closely connected, it is rules with exceptions which serve the rule of law. Lord Sales argues that the law is shaped by many different incommensurable values, leading to 'a rule design spectrum'.[23] At one extreme, an indefeasible rule (applied by judges) gives certainty, but is inflexible and insensitive to countervailing values. At the other extreme, if a judge were to balance these incommensurable values in every case, 'the law does not govern; the judge does', leading to unpredictability and arbitrary decisions.[24] Lord Sales' concern here, then, is with the behaviour of judges, and this concern is addressed by using rules with exceptions. These occupy a middle ground between the two extremes, by giving a defeasible 'priority to one particular value (or set of values)'.[25] Lord Sales' concern here is not with the *parties* acting in an unpredictable or arbitrary way, and so information defaults (which apply unless one party reveals information to the other) and classic defaults (which apply unless the parties agree otherwise) do not address the concern.

Finally, information asymmetries are typically redressed by information defaults, which apply unless one party reveals information to the other. Accordingly, if the default rule is less advantageous to the party in question than the alternative, the party has an incentive to reveal information to the other. Ayres and Gertner,[26] as well as Lord Sales,[27] justify the rule in *Hadley v Baxendale* on this basis. If a promisee knows

[19] *Barton v Morris* [2023] UKSC 3, [2023] AC 684 [128]–[132] (Lord Leggatt).
[20] Sales (n 10) 86.
[21] Sales (n 10) 86.
[22] *cf* Korobkin (n 12).
[23] Sales (n 10) 83.
[24] Sales (n 10) 84.
[25] Sales (n 10) 84.
[26] Ayres and Gertner (n 1) 101–04.
[27] Sales (n 10) 92–93.

it has special circumstances which may increase its loss but which the promisor does not know, the information default in *Hadley v Baxendale* creates an incentive for the better-informed promisee to share that information with the promisor, so that they can recover the full extent of their loss. (However, there are good reasons to doubt that this incentive is effective in practice.)[28]

In summary, the three different forms of default rules generally serve different purposes. Although there is some overlap, it is typically classic defaults which reduce transaction costs, rules with exceptions which inject values into the law and serve the rule of law, and information defaults which redress information asymmetries.

III. 'Rules with Exceptions' in the Law of Unjust Enrichment

Having distinguished these three forms of default rule, this chapter now considers the role of each in the law of unjust enrichment. It first clears the ground by briefly considering rules with exceptions and information defaults, before focusing on classic defaults.

Many rules have exceptions, and this is true of many in the law of unjust enrichment. This chapter cannot address all rules with exceptions in unjust enrichment: this would require an entire book. Instead, this section examines an idea that has ramifications for the law of unjust enrichment as a whole: namely, the suggestion that there are some rules which apply to all unjust enrichment claims, unless there is a reason not to apply the rule. Mitchell, Mitchell and Watterson write:

> [M]any of the rules which collectively form the law of unjust enrichment can appropriately and fairly be applied in a variety of different situations, and the courts should not waste time and effort reinventing them from first principles in every unjust enrichment case, just as they should not reinvent, e.g. the rules governing causation and remoteness in every tort case. There may be good reasons for applying different rules in some tort cases, e.g. because fraudulent and negligent defendants merit different treatment, but it is still an appropriate and effective strategy for the courts to start with one set of rules and then ask when it is appropriate to depart from these. In the same way, the courts should be open to the idea that some unjust enrichment cases may be insufficiently alike to justify carrying rules over from one type of case to another. Nevertheless, this will frequently be a fair and reasonable course for them to take.[29]

Mitchell, Mitchell, and Watterson do not expressly use the language of rules with exceptions. Nevertheless, one might think of their suggestion in those terms: there are some general rules which apply to all unjust enrichment claims, subject to exceptions.

To take some examples, the general rule is that 'the defence of change of position is a general defence to all restitution claims (for money or other property) based on unjust

[28] Johnston (n 1); MA Eisenberg, 'The Principle of *Hadley v Baxendale*' (1992) 80 *California Law Review* 563, 587–98.

[29] C Mitchell, P Mitchell and S Watterson, *Goff and Jones: The Law of Unjust Enrichment*, 10th edn (London, Sweet & Maxwell, 2022) paras 1-12–1-13.

enrichment'.[30] However, a judge can depart from this default rule where the defence would 'stultify', 'subvert' or 'be inconsistent with' the unjust factor.[31] For instance, if the state unlawfully levies a charge, then the payor can use the *Woolwich* unjust factor to obtain restitution of the charge.[32] The rationale for this unjust factor is that the state should not be able to abuse its power and levy unlawful charges, and this would be undermined if the state were able to retain the charges by raising a change of position defence.[33]

Similarly, in *Investment Trust Companies v Revenue and Customs Commissioners*, the Supreme Court said that a claimant 'will not normally be [entitled to restitution] where the provision of the benefit was merely an incidental or collateral result of his expenditure'.[34] However, this rule does not apply to all unjust enrichment claims. For instance, cases of 'legal compulsion' or 'secondary liability' are said to be 'justified exceptions' to the rule against incidental benefits.[35]

On reflection, however, describing these rules as 'rules with exceptions' should be avoided. There is a voluminous literature on the definition of an 'exception' and indeed whether there is a stable concept of an 'exception' at all.[36] Just like the phrase 'default rule', the word 'exception' is used in different ways, to describe multiple different concepts. However, one important conceptual distinction is between an 'exception' to a rule and a rule not applying in the first place.[37] The word 'exception' implies that a case is prima facie caught by the rule, but that there is some countervailing reason why the rule should not apply.[38] Different *pro tanto* reasons point towards different results. In any particular case there is a *pro tanto* reason for applying the general rule, though this may be outweighed by *pro tanto* reasons for applying an exception. To take Lord Sales' example of precedent, 'the benefits flowing from predictability and certainty in the law' support the default rule of following precedent.[39] However, in some cases, the competing value of keeping the law 'in line with social expectations' may point towards making an exception and departing from the precedent.[40]

[30] *Haugesund Kommune v Depfa ACS Bank* [2010] EWCA Civ 579, [2012] QB 549 [122] (Aikens LJ). *cf Test Claimants in the FII Group Litigation v Revenue and Customs Commissioners* [2014] EWHC 4302 (Ch), [2015] STC 1471 [315] (Henderson J).

[31] *Test Claimants in the FII Group Litigation* (ibid) [315] (Henderson J).

[32] *Woolwich Equitable Building Society v Inland Revenue Commissioners* [1993] AC 70 (HL).

[33] *Test Claimants in the FII Group Litigation v Revenue and Customs Commissioners* [2014] EWHC 4302 (Ch), [2015] STC 1471 [309]–[315] (Henderson J).

[34] [2017] UKSC 29, [2018] AC 275 [52] (Lord Reed).

[35] A Burrows, '"At the Expense of the Claimant": A Fresh Look' [2017] *Restitution Law Review* 167, 177. See also C Mitchell, *The Law of Contribution and Reimbursement* (Oxford, Oxford University Press, 2003) para 3.31; A Burrows, 'In Defence of Unjust Enrichment' (2019) 78 *CLJ* 521, 542; S Watterson, 'At the Claimant's Expense' in E Bant, K Barker and S Degeling (eds), *Research Handbook on Unjust Enrichment and Restitution* (Cheltenham, Edward Elgar, 2020) 285. *cf Croxen v Gas and Electricity Markets Authority* [2022] EWHC 2826 (Ch) [208]–[209] (Zacaroli J).

[36] eg G Williams, 'The Logic of "Exceptions"' (1988) 47 *CLJ* 261; L Duarte d'Almeida, *Allowing for Exceptions: A Theory of Defences and Defeasibility in Law* (Oxford, Oxford University Press, 2015); L Bartels and F Paddeu (eds), *Exceptions in International Law* (Oxford, Oxford University Press, 2020).

[37] CO Finkelstein 'When the Rule Swallows the Exception' in L Meyer (ed), *Rules and Reasoning* (Oxford, Hart Publishing, 1999).

[38] ibid.

[39] Sales (n 10) 97.

[40] ibid, 97.

Different are the examples given above of 'rules with exceptions' in unjust enrichment. In cases where the general rule is disapplied, there is not even a *pro tanto* reason for applying that general rule. For instance, the defence of change of position tends to be justified on the basis that the defendant has an interest in the security of its receipt[41] or on the basis that innocent defendants should not be left worse off.[42] However, in a *Woolwich* claim, the defendant is the state which has unlawfully levied a charge. Here, the state has no legitimate interest in security of this receipt, and the state is not innocent. Consequently, there is not even a *pro tanto* reason in favour of applying the change of position defence. There is no reason to consider that the availability of the defence is the general rule, to which *Woolwich* claims form an exception. It is simply that the change of position defence never applies to *Woolwich* claims. Similarly, the value served by the incidental benefits rule is unclear,[43] and so the reason for applying it as a general rule is unclear.

It is therefore dangerous to think of these as rules with exceptions. It suggests that the rules are prima facie applicable to a wide range of cases, even where there is no reason to do so. This leads to well-documented problem of 'overgeneralisation',[44] with rules being applied beyond their justification and so claims succeeding where they should not.[45] Courts should never assume that a particular rule applies to all unjust enrichment claims subject to exceptions. Instead, courts should consider whether it is justified to apply to the rule to each claim.

In short, the change of position defence and incidental benefits rule are not general rules applying to all unjust enrichment claims, subject to some exceptions. Instead, they are rules that apply to some unjust enrichment claims but not others. To draw an analogy, contributory negligence is a defence to some torts and not others,[46] but it would be inaccurate and misleading to state a general rule that contributory negligence is a defence to all torts subject to some exceptions.

IV. 'Information Defaults' in the Law of Unjust Enrichment

Examples of information defaults in the law of unjust enrichment are hard to come by, but one possible example may be found in the change of position defence. This defence

[41] P Birks, *An Introduction to the Law of Restitution* (Oxford, Clarendon Press, 1989) 414–15; P Birks, *Unjust Enrichment* (Oxford, Oxford University Press, 2005) 219. Criticised E Bant, *The Change of Position Defence* (Oxford, Hart Publishing, 2009) 215.

[42] Bant (ibid) ch 8; R Stevens, 'The Unjust Enrichment Disaster' (2018) 134 *LQR* 574, 587; R Stevens, *The Laws of Restitution* (Oxford, Oxford University Press, 2023) 356.

[43] Stevens (2018) (ibid) 579; Stevens (2023) (ibid) 34–35.

[44] L Smith, 'Restitution: A New Start?' in P Devonshire and R Havelock (eds), *The Impact of Equity and Restitution in Commerce* (Oxford, Hart Publishing, 2019) 96. See also W Swadling, 'Ignorance and Unjust Enrichment: The Problem of Title' (2008) 28 *OJLS* 627; Stevens (2018) (n 42).

[45] eg, *TFL Management Ltd v Lloyds TSB Bank Plc* [2013] EWCA Civ 1415, [2014] 1 WLR 2006: disapproved in *Investment Trust Companies v Revenue and Customs Commissioners* [2017] UKSC 29, [2018] AC 275 [57] (Lord Reed).

[46] *Standard Chartered Bank v Pakistan National Shipping Corp (Nos 2 and 4)* [2002] UKHL 43, [2003] 1 AC 959; *Pritchard v Co-Operative Group Ltd* [2011] EWCA Civ 329, [2012] QB 320.

applies 'where an innocent defendant's position is so changed that … the injustice of requiring him … to repay outweighs the injustice of denying the plaintiff restitution'.[47] The requirement that the defendant is 'innocent' means that 'the defence is not open to one who has changed his position in bad faith, as where the defendant has paid away the money with knowledge of the facts entitling the plaintiff to restitution'.[48] One way that the defendant might acquire this knowledge is if the claimant tells the defendant of the facts which found their right to restitution.[49] In this particular fact pattern, the rule operates as an information default. The default rule is that the defendant may raise a change of position defence, but this default is displaced if the claimant tells the defendant of the facts which found their right to restitution and it is reasonable for the defendant to believe them. Like other information defaults, this rule redresses an information asymmetry. A mistaken claimant will often be in a better position to realise their mistake than the defendant, and so this rule creates an incentive for the claimant to speak up when something has gone wrong.

However, it may be unwise to think about this rule as an information default. The claimant informing the defendant of the facts that found their right to restitution is just one of many ways that the defendant could come to be in bad faith: the defendant might discover these facts itself, or may be informed by a third party. The scope of the rule is therefore broader than just an information default, and as such its rationale must go beyond redressing an information asymmetry. A more promising justification for the rule is that it ensures that undeserving defendants cannot benefit from the defence, rather than encouraging claimants to speak up. In other words, this is an accidental information default, rather than a rule deliberately crafted as such. Consequently, thinking of the rule as an information default is unlikely to be profitable.

V. 'Classic Defaults' in the Law of Unjust Enrichment

At first glance, the law of unjust enrichment seems to be one giant collection of classic default rules. The leading treatises say that claimant cannot bring an unjust enrichment claim if the defendant is contractually entitled to the relevant enrichment.[50] So, by entering a contract which says that the defendant is entitled to their enrichment, the parties can forestall an unjust enrichment claim. In this way, the parties can opt out of the law of unjust enrichment, making it a set of default, not mandatory, rules. Mitchell, Mitchell and Watterson say that a 'claim in unjust enrichment may be entirely excluded, displaced or limited by the existence of a contract'.[51] Similarly, for Virgo, 'the law of restitution should be considered to be subsidiary to the law of contract'.[52]

[47] *Lipkin Gorman v Karpnale Ltd* [1991] 2 AC 548 (HL) 579F (Lord Goff of Chieveley).
[48] ibid 580C (Lord Goff of Chieveley).
[49] *Jones v Churcher* [2009] EWHC 722 (QB), [2009] 2 Lloyd's Rep 94 [89] (Judge Havelock-Allen QC).
[50] A Burrows, *The Law of Restitution* (Oxford, Oxford University Press, 2011) 88–89; G Virgo, *The Principles of the Law of Restitution* (Oxford, Oxford University Press, 2015) 133–34; Mitchell, Mitchell and Watterson (n 29) para 1-17.
[51] Mitchell, Mitchell and Watterson (n 29) para 3-01.
[52] Virgo (n 50) 134.

The idea that the law of unjust enrichment consists of classic defaults also finds support in the cases. A good example is *Barton v Morris*.[53] There, a company called Foxpace wanted to sell its property, Nash House. Barton made two abortive attempts to purchase Nash House, losing £1.2m in forfeited deposits and costs. Foxpace and Barton then entered a new oral contract, in which Foxpace agreed to pay Barton £1.2m, if Barton introduced a purchaser who paid £6.5m for Nash House. Barton introduced a purchaser, who bought Nash House for just £6m.

Barton had therefore not earned the £1.2m, but the Supreme Court was divided three to two over whether Barton was entitled to be paid some lesser amount. The majority held that Barton was entitled to nothing. They interpreted the parties' agreement as an agreement that Barton would be paid 'if and only if' he introduced a purchaser who paid £6.5m, and so the agreement implicitly excluded an obligation to pay Barton if the property sold for less.[54] In the minority, Lord Leggatt and Lord Burrows interpreted the agreement as being 'silent' about what should happen if Barton introduced a purchaser who paid less than £6.5m.[55] This 'gap'[56] was filled by a default term implied by law, which said that Foxpace had to pay Barton the reasonable value of his service, which was assessed at £435,000.

Both the majority and the minority therefore resolved the case using the law of contract: the majority said that the contract implicitly excluded payment, while the minority said that a term implied by law provided for payment. The majority and minority agreed that because the terms of the contract determined whether or not Barton should be paid, there was no room for an unjust enrichment claim.[57] Lady Rose said:

> When parties stipulate in their contract the circumstances that must occur in order to impose a legal obligation on one party to pay, they necessarily exclude any obligation to pay in the absence of those circumstances … This excludes not only an implied contractual term but a claim in unjust enrichment.[58]

One might therefore say that the parties had contracted out of the default law of unjust enrichment.

This is supported by Lord Burrows' obiter dicta. Lord Burrows would have resolved the case using a term implied by law. But in the alternative, he suggested that if there was no term implied by law and the contract was silent about what should happen if the property sold for less than £6.5m, then Barton would be able to bring an unjust enrichment claim for restitution of the reasonable value of his service, with the unjust factor being failure of basis. Lord Burrows said: 'the silence in the contract meant that any default law should apply; and here there is the default law of unjust enrichment'.[59]

Similarly, if the parties contract expressly for a right to restitution, they may be contracting out of the default right to restitution offered by the law of unjust enrichment. This is shown by *Pan Ocean Shipping Co Ltd v Creditcorp Ltd (The Trident Beauty)*,

[53] *Barton v Morris* [2023] UKSC 3, [2023] AC 684.
[54] ibid [26] (Lady Rose).
[55] ibid [136] (Lord Leggatt).
[56] ibid [143], [160] (Lord Leggatt), [212] (Lord Burrows).
[57] ibid [96] (Lady Rose), [189]–[193] (Lord Leggatt), [226] (Lord Burrows).
[58] ibid [96] (Lady Rose).
[59] ibid [239] (Lord Burrows).

a case concerning the charter of a ship.[60] The shipowner assigned their rights under the contract to a third party called Creditcorp. The charterers therefore paid the hire to Creditcorp. The ship was damaged and could not be used, so the charterer sought restitution from Creditcorp.

The House of Lords denied the claim. The contract provided that the shipowner undertook to return 'any overpaid hire'. The shipowner had assigned its rights under the contract to Creditcorp, but not its obligations, and so the charterer's contractual right to restitution remained against the shipowner and not Creditcorp. In light of this, the charterer could not bring an unjust enrichment claim against Creditcorp. Lord Goff said: 'serious difficulties arise if the law seeks to expand the law of restitution to redistribute risks for which provision has been made under an applicable contract'.[61]

At first glance, then, the law of unjust enrichment seems to consist of classic default rules, which the parties can contract out of. However, this would be an overgeneralisation. The law of unjust enrichment is like the law of torts, in that it consists of many different causes of action, each founded on different reasons.[62] Some of these causes of action consist of default rules, others of mandatory rules, and yet others rules which are neither mandatory nor default. Some examples follow.

A. Non-Fraudulent Mistake

The rules on non-fraudulent mistake are accurately characterised as default rules, which the parties can contract out of. This can be illustrated by a variation on the facts of the *Trident Beauty*.[63] Suppose that there is a charter of a ship under which the shipowner undertakes to return 'any overpaid hire', and again the shipowner assigns their rights (but not their obligations) to Creditcorp, a third party. The charterer pays Creditcorp the hire. Forgetting that they have already paid, the charterer pays Creditcorp the hire for a second time.

Were it not for the contractual provision for restitution, this would be a classic case of a mistaken overpayment, and the charterer would have a claim for restitution of their second payment on the ground of mistake.[64] This is the default rule. However, just as in the real case, the contract provides that it is the shipowner who must refund 'any overpaid hire', and this implicitly excludes Creditcorp's obligation to make restitution. The parties can therefore opt out of the default rules on non-fraudulent mistakes.

B. Fraud, Duress, and Undue Influence

However, the rules applicable to *fraudulent* mistakes, along with duress and undue influence, are different. These are better understood as mandatory, rather than default, rules.

[60] [1994] 1 WLR 161 (HL).
[61] ibid, 166E–F.
[62] *Barnes v Eastenders Cash & Carry Plc* [2014] UKSC 26, [2015] AC 1 [102] (Lord Toulson); Burrows (2019) (n 35) 530; Smith (n 44); Mitchell, Mitchell and Watterson (n 29) paras 1-09–1-13; Stevens (2023) (n 42) ch 20.
[63] [1994] 1 WLR 161.
[64] *Kelly v Solari* (1841) 9 M & W 54, 152 ER 24.

This is clearest for fraud, since House of Lords authority establishes that it is impossible to exclude liability for one's own fraud.[65]

Matters are less clear when it comes to mistakes induced by fraudulent misrepresentations made by an agent. In *HIH Casualty and General Insurance Ltd v Chase Manhattan Bank*, an insurer sought to rescind an insurance policy on the ground that they had been induced to enter the policy by a fraudulent misrepresentation by the insured's agent.[66] The insured argued that the terms of the policy precluded rescission, pointing to a number of terms including one that said that the insured 'shall have no liability of any nature to the insurers for any information provided by any other parties'. The House of Lords rejected that argument, holding that the terms did not exclude the insurer's power to rescind. Three different arguments can be detected in the House's reasoning.

First, the ratio of the case was that it was unlikely that parties would agree to exclude claims for the agent's fraud, and so parties must use unambiguous language in order to do so.[67] The parties had not expressly excluded liability for fraud specifically so, as a matter of construction, the terms of the contract only excluded the power to rescind for *non-fraudulent* misrepresentations. On its own, this first argument suggests that the rules on fraudulent misrepresentations made by agents are default rules, which the parties can contract out of by using clear words.

A second argument was that if the policy was vitiated by fraud, then all the terms of the policy were vitiated by fraud, including any term excluding the power to rescind. As the insurer's consent to this term was vitiated, the insured could not rely on it. Lord Hobhouse said:

> Where a contract has been procured by the material fraud of one party … the party deceived has not given a true consent to be bound by the contract. He is entitled at common law to avoid the contract when he discovers the deceit.[68]

Similarly, Lord Bingham referred to the maxim that 'fraud unravels all'.[69]

The problem with this argument is that it suggests that the policy (including the exclusion clause) was *void* or unenforceable. However, fraud is usually understood to render a contract voidable.[70] A *voidable* contract is valid unless and until it is rescinded. This suggests that the insured should have been able to rely on the terms of the policy unless and until the policy was rescinded, including the exclusion clause which prevented the policy being rescinded. This is why, at common law, it is possible to exclude liability for non-fraudulent misrepresentations (though in England and Wales this is now qualified by statute).[71] On its own, this second argument does not explain

[65] *Pearson & Son Ltd v Dublin Corporation* [1907] AC 351 (HL); *HIH Casualty and General Insurance Ltd v Chase Manhattan Bank* [2003] UKHL 6, [2003] 1 All ER (Comm) 349 [16] (Lord Bingham), [98] (Lord Hobhouse), [121]–[122] (Lord Scott).

[66] *HIH Casualty and General Insurance Ltd v Chase Manhattan Bank* [2003] UKHL 6, [2003] 1 All ER (Comm) 349.

[67] ibid [16] (Lord Bingham), [24] (Lord Steyn), [68]–[69] (Lord Hoffmann), [97] (Lord Hobhouse), *cf* [123]–[127] (Lord Scott, dissenting).

[68] ibid [98].

[69] ibid [15]. See also *Pearson & Son Ltd v Dublin Corporation* [1907] AC 351, 362 (Lord James).

[70] *Derry v Peek* (1889) 14 App Cas 337 (HL).

[71] Misrepresentation Act 1967, s 3; Consumer Rights Act 2015, s 62.

why fraudulent misrepresentations are different and render the exclusion unenforceable and not merely voidable.

Finally, the House of Lords suggested that 'public policy' considerations prevented a party excluding liability for their own fraud. The House did not spell out what the policy was. The idea seemed to be that the courts will not use their public power to assist fraudsters 'to take advantage' of their fraud,[72] and conversely the courts will use their public power to protect victims of fraud. The House was divided on whether these public policy considerations also prevented a party excluding liability for their agent's fraud. Lord Hobhouse took the view that they did, since a principal should not be allowed to take advantage of their agent's fraud.[73] Lord Scott disagreed, suggesting that 'Public policy would, in my view, come into play only where the agent's principal knew of or was otherwise complicit in the fraud or where the agent was the alter ego of the principal, as an executive director may be of his company.'[74] But a majority of the court (Lord Bingham, Lord Steyn, and Lord Hoffmann) left open the question of whether public policy considerations prevented a party excluding liability for their agent's fraud,[75] thus leaving open the question of whether the rules on an agent's fraud are mandatory or default rules.

The same three arguments are in play if parties attempt to opt out of the law on duress. This is illustrated by *Borrelli v Ting*.[76] Ting was the chairman and CEO of Akai Holdings Ltd. Akai was wound up and the liquidators, under economic duress from Ting, entered into a settlement agreement in which Akai and the liquidators undertook 'not to sue or otherwise pursue any claims against Mr Ting' and to 'immediately cease all further investigations with a view to or in connection with issuing legal proceedings and/or making claims against Mr Ting'.

The liquidators sought to rescind the settlement and investigate Ting. Ting resisted this, arguing that the settlement itself excluded the liquidators' power to rescind the settlement. The Privy Council rejected that argument. Giving the board's advice, Lord Saville said that it would be an 'unacceptable proposition' to say 'that it is possible, by the use of illegitimate means, to obtain a binding agreement from which the party subject to the duress cannot withdraw'.[77] Lord Saville did not elaborate on why this was 'unacceptable', but the three arguments from *HIH* are potentially applicable. The three arguments are also potentially applicable to attempts to exclude liability for undue influence.

The following hypothetical example brings out the difference between these three arguments:

> A parent and their grown-up child agree that the latter will move in to help with the former's care. Aware of the law of undue influence and desiring to preserve the parent's ability to make gifts to the child, they enter a contract in which the child pays the parent £1,000 in

[72] *HIH Casualty and General Insurance Ltd v Chase Manhattan Bank* [2003] UKHL 6, [2003] 1 All ER (Comm) 349 [98] (Lord Hobhouse). See also *Pearson & Son Ltd v Dublin Corporation* [1907] AC 351, 362 (Lord James).

[73] ibid [98].

[74] ibid [122].

[75] ibid [16] (Lord Bingham), [24] (Lord Steyn), [76], [82] (Lord Hoffmann).

[76] *Borrelli v Ting* [2010] UKPC 21, [2010] Bus LR 1718.

[77] ibid [40] (Lord Saville).

> consideration for the parent agreeing not to pursue any undue influence claims against the child, whether arising in the past or future.
>
> Years pass and the parties indeed end up in a relationship in which the parent reposes trust and confidence in their child. The parent wants to thank the child for their care and so, without obtaining legal advice, the parent transfers title to his home to the child. The parent later seeks to rescind the transfer on the ground of presumed undue influence.

Applying the first argument, the parties have expressly excluded the power to rescind for duress or undue influence. If the rules on duress and undue influence are merely default rules, the parties have opted out of them and so the parent should not be able to rescind.

Applying the second argument, when the parties agreed to exclude the power to rescind, they did so voluntarily, free from any undue influence. The undue influence came later. Thus, the term excluding the power to rescind is not vitiated by undue influence, and so the child can rely on the term, preventing the parent rescinding.

However, the third argument still applies. Still present is the public policy of preventing the courts using their state power to aid those who practise undue influence, and instead using state power to protect the victims of undue influence. This suggests that the victim should still be able to rescind, and so the parties are prevented from excluding the power to rescind.

The child paid the £1,000 on condition that the parent would not pursue any undue influence claims against the child. If the parent then seeks to rescind the transfer of title, that condition has failed, and so the child may be able to seek restitution of the £1,000 on the ground of failure of basis or failure of condition.[78]

Thus, the first and second arguments do not apply so would not prevent the parties excluding the law on undue influence. However, the third argument still applies and prevents the parties excluding the law on undue influence. This suggests that the rules on duress and undue influence are, just like the rules on one's own fraud, mandatory rules.

C. Failure of Basis

Failure of basis claims are different again. The rules here are neither default rules, which the parties can opt out of,[79] nor mandatory rules, which apply regardless of what the parties agree. Instead, the rules on failure of basis give effect to what the parties have agreed. This is because the rationale for a failure of basis claim is that the parties agreed that C's enrichment of D is conditional.[80] The parties therefore agreed that, if the condition fails, D should not be entitled to the enrichment and so should return it to C. Thus, the claim for restitution gives effect to what the parties have agreed.[81]

[78] *Rowland v Divall* [1923] 2 KB 500 (CA).

[79] M Campbell, 'Doubting the Subsidiarity of Unjust Enrichment' [2021] LMCLQ 535, 539–42.

[80] *Fibrosa Spolka Akcyjna v Fairbairn Lawson Combe Barbour Ltd* [1943] AC 32 (HL) 65 (Lord Wright); Mitchell, Mitchell and Watterson (n 29) para 12-01; Stevens (2023) (n 42) ch 7.

[81] Stevens (2018) (n 42) 584–86; E Peel, 'Implied Terms and Restitution' in E Peel and R Probert, *Shaping the Law of Obligations: Essays in Honour of Professor Ewan McKendrick KC* (Oxford, Oxford University

This is illustrated by *Rowland v Divall*.[82] Rowland bought a car from Divall. It then transpired that the car was stolen, and the superior title holder recovered the car from Rowland. The Court of Appeal held that Rowland was entitled to restitution of the purchase price from Divall. Atkin LJ explained:

> It seems to me that in this case there has been a total failure of consideration, that is to say that the buyer has not got any part of that for which he paid the purchase money. He paid the money in order that he might get the property, and he has not got it.[83]

In a contract of sale, parties agree that payment of the price is conditional on receiving good title, and so they agree if the buyer does not get good title, then the seller has not earned the price and must return it. Thus, the failure of basis claim gave effect to the parties' agreement, rather than operating in default of the parties reaching an agreement.

The same point is shown by failure of basis claims which fail. Take *Dargamo Holdings Ltd v Avonwick Holdings Ltd*, which concerned the sale and purchase of shares in a company called Castlerose.[84] The purchaser paid the price, and the seller transferred the shares. Subsequently, the purchaser sought restitution of some of the purchase price, arguing that the parties had an understanding that the price was also intended to cover payment for the transfer of further assets, which the seller had never transferred.

The Court of Appeal rejected the claim. The parties' contract said that the only consideration for the payment was the transfer of shares in Castlerose, deliberately omitting mention of any other assets.[85] In light of this, Carr LJ explained:

> [W]here the basis of the consideration is expressly and unconditionally spelt out on the face of a valid and subsisting contract, as here, there is no proper scope for inquiring into an alternative basis that is plainly contrary to the express basis freely agreed between the parties. … [The] parties are simply being held to the express terms of the contract into which they chose to enter and with which terms they have fully complied on all sides.[86]

The parties had agreed that the seller's entitlement to the price was conditional on the buyer receiving only the shares in Castlerose. The purchaser had received the shares in Castlerose, so the agreed condition for the seller keeping the price was satisfied. Thus, the purchaser's claim for restitution failed because this gave effect to what the parties had agreed. There was not some default rule giving the purchaser a claim, which the parties had opted out of. Instead, the only rule was to give effect to what the parties had agreed.

Barton v Morris can be explained in the same way.[87] According to the majority, the parties had agreed that Barton would be paid if and only if the property sold for £6.5m, and they had agreed Barton would be paid nothing if the property sold for less. When the property sold for £6m, Barton's claim for restitution of the value of his service

Press, 2023); T Pilkington, 'Restitution for a Failure of Condition' (DPhil thesis, University of Oxford, 2023), available at ora.ox.ac.uk/objects/uuid:ece8d3aa-ddd4-4260-93bc-9bde77966b47; Stevens (2023) (n 42) 109.

[82] [1923] 2 KB 500 (CA).

[83] *Rowland v Divall* [1923] 2 KB 500, 506.

[84] [2021] EWCA Civ 1149, [2022] 1 All ER (Comm) 1244.

[85] *Dargamo Holdings Ltd v Avonwick Holdings Ltd* [2021] EWCA Civ 1149, [2022] 1 All ER (Comm) 1244 [112] (Carr LJ).

[86] ibid [133], [137].

[87] [2023] UKSC 3, [2023] AC 684.

failed because the parties had agreed that Barton should not be paid. Again, the legal rule was simply to give effect to what the parties had agreed. There was not some default rule giving restitution which the parties had opted out of.

Similarly, in *The Trident Beauty*,[88] the charterer's claim for restitution from Creditcorp failed because the parties had agreed that the shipowner, and not Creditcorp, would return any overpaid hire. They had therefore agreed that Creditcorp's entitlement to the hire was not conditional on the charterer's use of the ship. Again, the rules on failure of basis simply gave effect to the parties' agreement.

However, not everyone agrees that failure of basis claims should be understood as giving effect to the parties' agreement. Writing extra-judicially, Edelman J criticises this view on two grounds. First, he says that it rests on 'a contrived implied term; an agreement that restitution must follow a failure of the condition'.[89] Far from being 'contrived', this is necessarily implicit. When parties agree that one person's entitlement is conditional, they agree that they lose their entitlement if the condition fails, and so they agree to make restitution if the condition fails. Thus, agreeing that an entitlement is conditional is *the same as* agreeing a right to restitution if the condition fails, just expressed using different words.

Secondly, Edelman J writes that 'if such an implied term really existed, then … It would be an instance where restitution is expressly or impliedly agreed'.[90] Giving effect to this agreement through a failure of basis claim seems to contradict the law of contract, in cases where the parties' contract is void or unenforceable.[91] This is illustrated by the 'swaps' cases, such as *Westdeutsche Landesbank Girozentrale v Islington LBC*.[92] A council entered into an interest rate swap agreement with a bank, under which the bank was to pay a lump sum to the council and the council was to make payments, calculated by a formula tracking interest rates, to the bank every six months for the next 10 years. The bank paid the lump sum and the council made its first four payments. The House of Lords in *Hazell v Hammersmith and Fulham LBC* then held that interest rate swaps were ultra vires for councils and therefore the parties' contract was void.[93] The council stopped making its payments.

The House of Lords held that the bank was entitled to restitution of the lump sum it had paid to the council, less the payments that the council had already made, on the ground of 'failure of consideration'. On the account given in this chapter, this would mean that the bank and council agreed that the bank was paying on condition that the council make its payments, so the parties had agreed that if the council failed to make its payments then it was not entitled to the bank's payment and should return it, and the restitution claim gave effect to that agreement.

In a recent DPhil thesis, Pilkington argues that this cannot be right where a contract is void. He writes that 'the preferable view is that what it means for a contract to be void

[88] *Pan Ocean Shipping Co Ltd v Creditcorp Ltd* [1994] 1 WLR 161 (HL).

[89] J Edelman, Book Review (2024) 140 LQR 321, 325.

[90] ibid. See also P Jaffey, *The Nature and Scope of Restitution* (Oxford, Hart Publishing, 2000) 117.

[91] J Edelman, 'Liability in Unjust Enrichment when a Contract Fails to Materialise' in A Burrows and E Peel (eds), *Contract Formation and Parties* (Oxford, Oxford University Press, 2010) 178–79.

[92] [1996] AC 669 (HL). See also *Guinness Mahon & Co Ltd v Kensington and Chelsea Royal LBC* [1999] QB 215 (CA); *Cobbe v Yeoman's Row Management Ltd* [2008] UKHL 55, [2008] 1 WLR 1752; *School Facility Management Ltd v Christ the King College* [2021] EWCA Civ 1053, [2021] 1 WLR 6129.

[93] [1992] 2 AC 1 (HL).

is that the parties' agreement is a legal nullity' and so cannot affect legal relations.[94] A failure of basis claim, which gives effect to the parties' agreed right to restitution, is therefore not possible, as this would mean the parties' agreement affected their legal relations. Instead, in cases of void contracts, restitution is justified not by failure of basis but by 'absence of a juristic reason for a payment when it was made'.[95]

However, even if the parties' *contract* was void, their *agreement* need not be. A less radical approach would be to say that, even if the parties' agreement is void (or unenforceable) as a contract, it still may be given effect by a failure of basis claim. The two are distinct in both their effects and requirements. As for effect, a failure of basis claim only reverses a transfer of value from one party to another. It does not (in any other respect) put the parties into the position as if the contract were performed.[96] Thus, the backward-looking effect of a failure of basis claim does not contradict the voidness (or unenforceability) of the forward-looking effects of the contract. As for requirements, a failure of basis claim only requires the parties to have agreed a condition (by offer and acceptance). It does not require the other ingredients for a valid contract, such as consideration or – crucially – the capacity to contract.[97] Consequently, there is no contradiction to say that a contract is void (or unenforceable), but that a failure of basis claim gives effect to the parties' agreed right to restitution.

In short, a failure of basis claim is neither a mandatory nor a default rule. Instead, it gives effect to an agreed condition (and implicitly agreed right to restitution), though this agreement need not be valid and enforceable as a contract.

D. Recoupment and Contribution

The same is true of some, but not all, recoupment and contribution claims. These claims arise where C and D are both obliged to pay the same debt to X. If C pays X, then the debt of both C and D is discharged. D is then obliged to pay C to the extent that D ought to have borne the burden of paying the debt to X. If D ought to have borne the burden of paying the whole debt, then C has a right to 'reimbursement' or 'recoupment' against D.[98] If D ought to have borne the burden of paying only some of the debt, then C has a right to 'contribution' against D.[99] The claims are therefore justified by ensuring the burden of the debt falls where it should. This is sometimes (unfortunately)[100] described as the unjust factor of 'legal compulsion'[101] or 'secondary liability'.[102]

[94] Pilkington (n 81) 83.
[95] ibid 82–90.
[96] F Wilmot-Smith, 'Replacing Risk-taking Reasoning' (2011) 127 LQR 610, 622.
[97] Stevens (2018) (n 42), 585–86; Stevens (2023) (n 42) 111–15.
[98] eg *Brook's Wharf & Bull Wharf Ltd v Goodman Bros* [1937] 1 KB 534 (CA).
[99] Civil Liability (Contribution) Act 1978, s 1(1); *cf* s 2(2).
[100] R Gregson, 'Subrogation, Marshalling, and Property' in N Mrockova, A Nair and L Rostill (eds), *Modern Studies in Property Law: Volume 12* (Oxford, Hart Publishing, 2023) 275–76.
[101] Burrows (n 50) 436–37; A Burrows, *A Restatement of the English Law of Unjust Enrichment* (Oxford, Oxford University Press, 2012) 99.
[102] *Niru Battery Manufacturing Co v Milestone Trading Ltd (No 2)* [2003] EWHC 1032 (Comm), [2003] 2 All ER (Comm) 365 [31] (Moore-Bick J); Mitchell, Mitchell and Watterson (n 29) para 19-01.

The reason why, and extent to which, D ought to bear the burden of C and D's common debt varies from case to case.[103] In some cases, there is an agreement about where the burden should fall. In these cases, a recoupment or contribution claim, like a failure of basis claim, gives effect to what the parties have agreed, and is therefore neither a default nor mandatory rule. For instance, if a guarantor pays a principal debtor's debt, then the guarantor has a right to recoup their payment from the debtor.[104] This is because a guarantor agrees to pay if the principal debtor cannot and so, as between the debtor and the guarantor, the debtor agreed to bear the burden of paying the debt. Thus, in a case like this where the parties have agreed where the burden of the debt should fall, the recoupment claim gives effect to what the parties have agreed.

However, in other cases, there is no agreement about where its burden should fall. As a result, a recoupment or contribution claim cannot be giving effect to the parties' agreement. Instead, a recoupment or contribution claim operates as a default rule.

For example, in *Brook's Wharf and Bull Wharf Ltd v Goodman Bros*, the defendant imported squirrel skins, which they stored in the plaintiff's bonded warehouse.[105] This put both parties under a duty to pay customs duty on the import, which the plaintiff paid. The Court of Appeal held that the plaintiff was entitled to recover this amount from the defendant. Lord Wright MR explained:

> The plaintiffs were no doubt liable to pay the Customs, but, as between themselves and the defendants, the primary liability rested on the defendants. The liability of the plaintiffs as warehousemen was analogous to that of a surety. It was imposed in order to facilitate the collection of duties … The defendants as actual importers have obtained the benefit of the payment made by the plaintiffs …[106]

Here, then, the claim gave effect to a legal rule which said that the importer ought to bear the burden of paying the customs duties, since they obtained the benefit of the import. Nevertheless, this is best understood as just a default rule. If the parties had agreed that, as between the two of them, the warehouse should bear the burden of paying the customs duties, then there should be no recoupment claim.

VI. Conclusion

Lawyers use the phrase 'default rules' to describe three different forms of rules, which I have labelled 'classic defaults', 'information defaults' and 'rules with exceptions'. It is important to clearly separate these out, since they operate in different ways and serve different purposes. There are potential examples of all three in the law of unjust enrichment.

[103] Mitchell (n 35) ch 10; Mitchell, Mitchell and Watterson (n 29) paras 20-82–20-104; Smith (n 44) 107; C Mitchell, 'Other Reasons for Restitution' in E Bant, K Barker and S Degeling (eds), *Research Handbook on Unjust Enrichment and Restitution* (Cheltenham, Edward Elgar Publishing, 2020) 391.

[104] *Copis v Middleton* (1823) Turn & R 224, 37 ER 1083; *Hodgson v Shaw* (1834) 3 My & K 183, 40 ER 70.

[105] [1937] 1 KB 534 (CA).

[106] *Brook's Wharf & Bull Wharf Ltd v Goodman Bros* [1937] 1 KB 534, 546.

Rules with exceptions are rules which apply unless a judge decides that an exception applies. Although the change of position defence and incidental benefits rule are sometimes presented as rules with exceptions, the better view is that they should not be understood in this way. They are better understood as rules which apply to some unjust enrichment claims but not others.

Information defaults are rules which apply unless one party communicates information to the other, in order to redress information asymmetries between the parties. In the law of unjust enrichment, the rule that the change of position defence is only available to an innocent defendant could be understood in these terms, although other examples are difficult to come by.

Finally, classic defaults are rules which apply unless the parties agree otherwise. The law of unjust enrichment is sometimes presented as one giant collection of classic defaults. However, this is an overgeneralisation. It is true that some rules, such as those on non-fraudulent mistakes, constitute classic defaults. But other rules, such as those on fraud, duress and undue influence, constitute mandatory rules. And yet others, such as those on failure of basis, are neither classic defaults nor mandatory, but instead give effect to what the parties have agreed.

Overall, then, default rules in all their guises have a smaller role in the law of unjust enrichment than is commonly assumed.

13

Equity in Commerce: Why Do We Need Default Rules?

MAN YIP*

I. Introduction

There are two senses in which the term 'default rules' has been used. First, according to Lord Sales, default rules constitute an initial presumptive resolution of a legal dispute which can be overcome at the point of application. These are designed to accommodate both certainty and flexibility.[1] Because legal disputes are often underlined by 'competing incommensurable values', default rules support legal certainty by presumptively prioritising one of the values, thereby enabling rules to be formulated in a generalised and simple manner.[2] To ensure that the default position does not occasion injustice, any default rule may be disapplied where the requisite conditions are satisfied. Second, in contract law, the term 'default rules' refers by contrast to rules that would apply unless the contracting *parties* agree to the contrary.[3] The disapplication of the default position in contract law, subject to any statutory restrictions,[4] is determined by the contracting parties themselves. These rules are significant starting point for contract negotiation and in the absence of parties' agreement to the contrary, they will govern the contractual relationship.[5] Lord Sales' understanding of 'default rules', derived from surveying the general law terrain, is broader. On his account, a 'default' rule (or a prima facie rule) can be disapplied by other conditions: the conditions (and the alternative rule)

* I would like to thank Jonathan Morgan for his helpful comments. All errors and views remain my own.

[1] Lord Sales, 'Default Rules in the Common Law: Substantive Rules and Precedent' (Presentation at International Workshop on Default Rules in Private Law, Oxford, 24 March 2023).

[2] ibid.

[3] Jonathan Morgan, *Great Debates in Contract Law*, 3rd edn (Oxford, Hart Publishing, 2020) 135. Terms implied 'by law' are an example of default rules in contract law.

[4] *cf* D Airey, 'When it's Mandatory to be "Reasonable": The Nature and Application of Reasonableness under the Unfair Contract Terms Act 1977', this volume, ch 7; JM Paterson, 'Mandatory Statutory Rules, Consumer Contracts and Contractual Interpretation', this volume, ch 8.

[5] Morgan (n 3) ibid.

are determined by the court or statutes. After all, outside contract, relationships are not constituted by a bargain which affords an opportunity for parties to agree *ex ante* what the position should be in a particular situation. The two senses of the term are thus not inconsistent. It is suggested that the contractual sense may be conceived as a subset of the Lord Sales' understanding of the term. Simply put, the requisite conditions for replacing the 'default rule' with a different rule includes but is not limited to parties' agreement to the contrary.[6] In this chapter, I adopt the wider understanding of 'default' rules[7] but the discussion also deals with the narrower, contract-like type of default rules. In fact, a key line of inquiry in my chapter is understanding why in some cases party autonomy may be the condition for disapplying the default position but not in others.

Unlike default rules in contract law,[8] the topic of equitable default rules in the commercial context[9] has yet to receive in-depth treatment. And unlike default rules in contract law, which address how gaps in contracts should be filled, it is less clear what functions equitable default rules are meant to serve. The study is challenging but necessary. Equitable doctrines do not conform to the mould of common law rules and it may be seriously inquired as to the need for default rules in equity. Yet, equity has infiltrated commerce and supports its many activities. Would equity, in its *commercial* application, benefit from the well-known upsides of default rule design – such as saving in transaction costs and addressing informational asymmetries? Or does equity have different motivations for using default rules in different contexts and, if so, how would equitable default rules differ in design? The discussion unfolds as follows. Section II addresses the crucial preliminary issues that enhance our understanding of the role of default rules in the interface between equity and commerce, such as the functions of default rules; the nature and role of equity; and the different contexts in the commercial world. With the understanding set out in section II, we turn to examine the default rules that are found in three areas of fiduciary law in section III and discuss their specific functions in these areas. Fiduciary law, which regulates the conduct of a variety of actors in various contexts in the commercial world, is a rich terrain to examine the topic of equitable default rules in commerce. My analysis covers the principles applicable to relationship establishment, fiduciary duties and the equitable remedy of account of profits.

[6] *cf* YK Liew, 'From Mandatory to Default Rules: Trusts in the "Commercial" Context', this volume, ch 14 (adopting a broader understanding of 'default rules' which does not correspond fully with the meaning of default rules in contract law).

[7] Some may adopt the position that 'default rules' that are disapplied by conditions other than parties' agreement should be conceived as mandatory rules with exceptions. As Liew points out (ibid), this label is 'a contradiction of terms'.

[8] See, eg, I Ayres and R Gertner, 'Filling Gaps in Incomplete Contracts: An Economic Theory of Default Rules' (1989) 99 *Yale Law Journal* 87; I Ayres, 'Valuing Modern Contract Scholarship' (2003) 112 *Yale Law Journal* 881, 885–86; J Morgan, Contract Damages as Default Rules' in D Campbell and R Halson (eds), *Research Handbook on Remedies in Private Law* (Cheltenham, Edward Elgar, 2019) 476.

[9] This chapter will not consider *trusts*, as discussed brilliantly by Liew's chapter (n 6).

II. Preliminary Issues

A. Functions of Default Rules

Default rules are used in different areas of law and they may be used for different functions. For instance, they may be rules that fill a gap;[10] rules that are applied in the absence of alternatives;[11] or rules that incentivise contracting around the unattractive default position by encouraging the disclosure of material information (commonly known as 'penalty default' rules).[12] Not all default rules perform the same function, but they must perform *some* function through the prioritisation of a value represented by the preselected legal position. In the case of gap-filling, the preselected position may represent what is ordinarily considered fair and just: for instance, the default rule of prescribing equal-sharing of the beneficial ownership of family property between spouses may be said to endorse the value of equal partnership between a married couple.[13] In the case of penalty default rules, a position unfavourable to the parties – or at least the more informed party – is deliberately selected as the default to induce the informed party to contract out of the default by disclosing information to the counterparty with the aim of reaching a different and more favourable outcome.

B. Nature and Function of Equity

There may be two objections to the use of default rules in equity. First, if a default rule is a preselected position in law which can be disapplied and may be expressed in a generalised and simple form, the concept appears to be inconsistent with how equity operates. Equity is known to operate in a fact-sensitive manner, thereby allowing a plethora of values to be considered by the court in deciding what is a fair and just outcome. Many equitable principles by design do not prioritise one particular value, nor are they

[10] The private international law rule of presuming that the applicable foreign law is similar to the *lex fori* in cases where parties advanced a case that the issues involved were governed by a foreign law, but failed to plead the content of the foreign law, is also a rule that fills a gap (in this context, a gap in the evidence as to the content of the foreign law): see *FS Cairo (Nile Plaza) LLC v Brownlie* [2021] UKSC 45, [2022] AC 995 [118]–[112].

[11] In private international law, where a case involves international elements and may attract the application of foreign law, the law of the forum would be applied by default if neither party to the dispute advanced a case based on the application of foreign law (see *Brownlie* [2021] UKSC 45, [2022] AC 995 [113]–[118]).

[12] Ayres and Gertner (n 8) 97. The authors characterised (ibid 101) the *Hadley v Baxendale* principles of remoteness as a 'default of denying unforeseeable damages' as an example of a penalty default rule to induce the more informed party to disclose material information concerning his potential losses arising out of breach to the less informed party.

[13] Pre-*Stack v Dowden* [2007] UKHL 17, [2007] 2 AC 432: *Gissing v Gissing* [1970] 2 All ER 780 (HL) 792–93; *Midland Bank plc v Cooke* [1995] 4 All ER 562, 576. The common intention constructive trust is nowadays commonly applied to determine the beneficial ownership of property between unmarried cohabitees. In *Stack v Dowden* [2007] 2 AC 432 (HL) 459, Lady Hale observed that 'In the cohabitation context, mercenary considerations may be more to the fore than they would be in a marriage, but it should not be assumed that they always take pride of place over natural love and affection.'

formulated in a simple or certain manner as common rules often are. They address the need for flexibility in a different way from the 'default rule' kind of rule design.[14] Indeed, the inherent malleability of equitable doctrines, whether through the recourse to the label of 'unconscionability', a multi-factorial approach or the imposition of standards (instead of rules), has been abhorred for generating uncertainty and arbitrariness.[15]

By way of example, the test for setting aside a voluntary disposition in equity on the ground of mistake requires a causative mistake of sufficient gravity to render it unconscionable to leave the mistake uncorrected.[16] The court adopts a multi-factorial approach, including facts relating to 'the circumstances of the mistake and its consequences for the person who made the vitiated disposition', any relevant change of position and other relevant facts.[17] This formulation allows the court to take into account, amongst others, the competing values of protection of autonomy, security of receipt and avoiding undue prejudice to the recipient. Other examples include the second stage of the doctrine of proprietary estoppel, the residual jurisdiction to award equitable allowance to an errant fiduciary who is found liable to give an account of his profits, and the quantification of parties' respective interests in the property under the *Stack v Dowden* doctrine of common intention constructive trust where there is no express agreement on sharing.[18]

The reason why many equitable doctrines are open-textured is because, as Henry Smith has argued, 'a major theme of equity … is to solve complex and uncertain problems'[19] that are frequently unforeseen or unforeseeable.[20] On Smith's account, equity is 'meta-law': it is 'contextual and targeted' to enable common law (ie, first-order law) to be 'more formal and general'.[21] Much of equity, historically developed as exceptional interventions to 'remedy the deficiencies in the common law' ex post,[22] therefore do not function as default rules. Rather, these equitable doctrines represent the alternative legal positions that the courts apply to ensure that the 'default' common law position, in providing inadequate or no redress, does not occasion injustice. There are, of course, equitable doctrines/principles which are cast in relatively simple and certain terms and are not ex post corrective mechanisms[23] – for example, the requirements

[14] As Lord Sales has noted, the equitable open-textured standards type of rule design raises rule of law concerns. Lord Sales (n 1). *cf* D Klimchuk, 'Equity and the Rule of Law' in LM Austin (ed), *Private Law and the Rule of Law* (Oxford, Oxford University Press, 2014); M Harding, 'Equity and the Rule of Law' (2016) 132 *LQR* 278.

[15] See, eg, PBH Birks, 'Equity in the Modern Law: An Exercise in Taxonomy' (1996) 26 *University of Western Australia Law Review* 1; I Samet, *Equity: Conscience Goes to Market* (Oxford, Oxford University Press, 2018) 9–16.

[16] *Pitt v Holt* [2013] UKSC 26, [2013] 2 AC 108 [126].

[17] ibid [124]–[125].

[18] *Stack v Dowden* [2007] UKHL 17, [2007] 2 AC 432 [69].

[19] HE Smith, Equity as Meta-Law' (2021) 130 *Yale Law Journal* 1050, 1054. Although Smith confines his analysis to US law, they are applicable to the equitable jurisprudence of traditional common law jurisdictions such as England and Wales, Australia, Hong Kong and Singapore.

[20] ibid 1112.

[21] ibid 1100.

[22] Lord Briggs of Westbourne, 'Loose Ends in Accounting for Profits' in B Mcfarlane and S Elliott (eds), *Equity Today: 150 Years After the Judicature Reforms* (Oxford, Hart Publishing, 2023) 109. See also *Vauxhall Motors Ltd (formerly General Motors UK Ltd) v Manchester Ship Canal Co Ltd* [2019] UKSC 46, [2020] AC 1161 [63] (Lady Arden).

[23] The trust and the fiduciary doctrine are found in equity's exclusive jurisdiction.

for the creation of an express trust, as well as the no-conflict and no-profit rules that are applicable to fiduciaries. But if we look beneath the beguilingly simple formulation, fiduciary duties are a tool to enable 'after-the-fact compliance review' of fiduciary's conduct by the courts, having regard of the relevant facts and circumstances.[24] We will look at these duties more closely in section III.

The second objection is that even in respect of doctrines found in equity's exclusive jurisdiction, a major theme of equity is concerned with setting high standards for actors in valuable relationships or institutions in the society so as to protect them from opportunism.[25] At first blush, it appears perverse to that objective for equitable rules to be characterised as default rules, and not *mandatory* rules. To accord parties the freedom to decide which rules may be displaced may draw criticism that it blurs the distinction between equitable doctrines and contract, an institution that is surely founded on 'freely agreed obligations'.[26] To accord the discretion to the courts to disapply the rules may appear less objectionable but creates uncertainty for commercial parties, especially if the conditions for switching to an alternative are not clear. One may instinctively think that the alteration of equitable principles would result in the lowering of the standards that are expected of these actors and consequently the level of protection that the law accords to the relationship or institution. But this instinct is not necessarily correct. We need to first identify the equitable default rules and analyse the functions they serve and the conditions for their disapplication. The default rule may be disapplied by parties, the court or statute in circumstances where the high standards of equity are not required to apply in full rigour or at all. The investigation requires serious consideration of the proper role of party autonomy and that of the court/statute in setting the conditions for disapplying the equitable default rules in the commercial context. To do so, it is crucial that we unpack the phrase 'commercial context'.

C. The Commercial Contexts

That a different set of equitable principles may apply in the commercial context is often traced to the famous speech of Lord Browne-Wilkinson in *Target Holdings Ltd v Redferns*.[27] Whilst the commercial setting raises somewhat different considerations to those that arise in the traditional family context, it cannot be denied that equitable intervention is needed in a range of business relationships,[28] including transactions between

[24] RH Sitkoff, 'The Economic Structure of Fiduciary Law' (2011) *Boston University Law Review* 1039, 1044.

[25] See, eg, Lord Millett, 'Equity's Place in the Law of Commerce' (1998) 114 *LQR* 214, 216. Samet (n 15) ch 2 argues that equity's vocation is to promote the legal virtue of aligning liability imposed by legal rules with the moral accountability of the defendant's actions:.

[26] Morgan (n 8) 477. To be clear, I am not suggesting that there are no mandatory rules in contract law (*cf* duress, fraud) or there are no default rules in equity. It comes down to the degree of party autonomy that is allowed in each field.

[27] [1996] AC 421, 435. In *Pitt v Holt* [2013] UKSC 26, [2013] 2 AC 108 [92], Lord Walker proposed that different criteria might apply in respect of the application of the *Hastings-Bass* rule depending on whether the transaction was voluntary or contractual in nature.

[28] *F&C Alternative Investments (Holding) Ltd v Barthelemy* [2011] EWHC 1731 (Ch), [2012] Ch 613 [223].

sophisticated parties.[29] However, fierce disagreement persists in two main areas: first, whether the commercial context warrants the application of a different set of a principles from those that are applied in the domestic setting; and, secondly, the role of contract or contractarian thinking in shaping equitable principles in the commercial setting.[30] The first question may sometimes be conflated with the second question because contract is often (though not always) a dominant feature of the commercial context.[31]

Crucially, the label 'commercial context' is not a monolithic concept.[32] There are many different contexts in the commercial world,[33] and there is grave danger in relying on broad, sweeping generalisations, whether in relation to the commercial world or equity, to settle the debate. Not every transaction in the commercial context is a straightforward, arm's-length bargain. For instance, a transaction entered into between a commercial party and a consumer should be treated differently from a transaction entered into between two sophisticated parties.[34] The element of voluntariness in contract-making in the former scenario differs from that in the latter scenario, thereby giving rise to a need to differentiate the level of protection which the law should afford to the consumer as compared with a sophisticated business party. The broad generalisation that contracts are founded on 'freely agreed obligations' applies with far less force in the consumer context. Even in respect of non-consumer contracts, it has been noted that some contracting parties – such as professionals or small businesses – 'may share many of the characteristics of consumers which are thought to make the latter worthy of protection'.[35] For equity, the challenge is converse to that of contract law: about how much protection should be forgone in favour of other values.

Moreover, not all commercial transactions and enterprises have the same features, objectives and societal functions. Some business enterprises/transactions (most notably, the company) have strong social impact.[36] In deciding on how the law can facilitate and regulate their activities, especially under the prevailing Environmental, Social and Governance, and Corporate Social Responsibility movements, the law should not simply focus on private or economic interests. Even in respect of commercial activities that affect primarily private parties, the value of upholding standards needs to be balanced against

[29] Lord Briggs of Westbourne, 'Equity in Business' (2019) 135 *LQR* 567. See also *Hospital Products Ltd v United States Surgical Corp* (1984) 55 ALR 417, 456–57 (Mason J dissenting).

[30] Liew (n 6) has similarly considered these two explanations in the context of trusts arising in a 'commercial' context but ultimately dismissed them, on similar grounds, for being unhelpful in explaining the trend of moving from mandatory rules to default rules.

[31] *AIB Group (UK) Plc v Mark Redler & Co Solicitors* [2014] UKSC 58, [2015] AC 1503.

[32] Liew (n 6) similarly points out that 'The central difficulty with relying on "commercial" context as an explanation is that the term "commercial" does not yield a stable definition.' This results in the law not being able to define what counts as a 'commercial' context with sufficient precision so as to enable the courts to apply this.

[33] I have made this point in relation to trusts arising in the commercial context: see M Yip, 'The Commercial Context in Trust Law' (2016) *Conveyancer* 347.

[34] *Kew Green Group Ltd v Lamb* [2023] EWHC 1289 (KB) [151]. Beyond consumer protection legislation (Airey (n 4) and Paterson (n 4)), common law contract principles also take into account whether the contract was a freely negotiated one or not, in deciding the appropriate balance between freedom of contract and protection of vulnerable parties: see discussion in *Cavendish Square Holdings BV v Makdessi* [2015] UKSC 67, [2016] AC 1172 [35].

[35] *Cavendish v Makdessi* (ibid) [38].

[36] B Choudhury, *Corporate Duties to the Public* (Cambridge, Cambridge University Press, 2019) 8.

other values such as the pursuit of mutual interests or fostering cooperation.[37] Further, the circumstances might have changed, necessitating adjustment to how the law regulates the commercial activity. In contracts for professional services, on the other hand, upholding professional service standards and ethics is usually an important consideration.[38]

This is not to suggest that courts should adopt a very broad discretion in the application of equitable principles. Instead, in line with how equity operates, equitable doctrines ought to be context-sensitive. As we look at fiduciary law principles in the discussion to follow, it becomes clear that equity is already deploying context sensitivity, but the technique needs to be clearly articulated and openly assessed.

III. Fiduciary Law

Fiduciary regulation is a common feature of commercial activities. Many professionals and key commercial actors, such as directors, investment managers and agents, owe fiduciary duties to their principals in addition to their contractual and/or statutory duties. These various actors – many of whom perform very different functions to the trustee (the paradigmatic fiduciary) – play critical roles in the relevant commercial ventures. Fiduciary law is also an area of equity in which default rules are discussed, although attention is often directed to the duties that are owed and their breach.[39] In this section of the chapter, I examine the default rules that exist in three areas: the establishment of a fiduciary relationship; fiduciary duties; and account of profits. These three areas are interlinked because, as Finn has pointed out, a person 'is not subject to fiduciary obligations because he is a fiduciary; it is because he is subject to them that he is a fiduciary'.[40] As for account of profits, it is linked to the no-profit rule.

A. Commercial Fiduciary Accountability: A Jagged Frontier

At first blush, the default and mandatory rules debate relating to fiduciary law does not arise in respect of the criteria for establishing that fiduciary duties arise.[41] There are no concerns of regulation of behaviour or deterrence which require standards to be upheld. The central concern, at the stage of relationship establishment, is certainty in legal criteria,[42] so as to enable commercial people to plan their activities and mitigate risks accordingly. Even so, it is argued that a default rule inclination might be

[37] Morgan (n 8) 484, writing on contractual remedies as default rules, argues that the value of keeping promises must be balanced against other competing moral norms, 'including co-operation, forgiveness, and flexibility when circumstances change'.

[38] The irreducible core trustee duty to act honestly is assessed on an *objective* standard where professional trustees are concerned: see *Walker v Stones* [2001] QB 902, 938 (solicitor-trustees); *Fattal v Walbrook Trustees (Jersey) Ltd* [2010] EWHC 2767 (Ch) [81] (professional trustees).

[39] T Frankel, 'Fiduciary Duties as Default Rules (1995) 74 *Oregon Law Review*; S Worthington, 'Corporate governance: remedying and ratifying directors' breaches' (2000) 116 *LQR* 638, 662–65.

[40] P Finn, *Fiduciary Obligations* (Sydney, Law Book Co, 1977) 2. This reminds us that we should not adopt a status-based approach to determine who owes fiduciary duties.

[41] Frankel (n 39) 1233.

[42] S Worthington, 'Fiduciaries then and now' (2021) *CLJ* 154.

crystallising behind the 'jagged frontier'[43] of commercial fiduciary accountability. The frontier is 'jagged' because it is becoming harder to predict with certainty as to which commercial actor might owe fiduciary duties and what kind of fiduciary duties.

The classical approach towards determining who are fiduciaries may be stated simply: a fiduciary is someone who owes fiduciary duties by reason of her status (ie, falling within recognised categories of relationships), eg, trustee–beneficiary, director–company, solicitor–client and agent–principal.[44] But a fixed list, whilst certain, is not quite sufficient to deal with the myriad situations in which commercial actors may exercise discretion or manage property for another. Fiduciary duties may also arise on an ad hoc basis when certain characteristics are present, notwithstanding the lack of consensus on what these characteristics are and how many of these must be present for fiduciary duties to arise.[45] The attempts to unify the two approaches and come up with a proper account to explain when someone owes fiduciary duties are various. Reference is often made to Millett LJ's pronouncement in *Bristol & West Building Society v Mothew*:[46]

> A fiduciary is someone who has undertaken to act for or on behalf of another in a particular matter in circumstances which give rise to a relationship of trust and confidence. The distinguishing obligation of a fiduciary is the obligation of loyalty …

The idea of an 'undertaking' by the fiduciary[47] has inspired various explanatory accounts as to why and when fiduciary duties arise. One popular account is that fiduciary duties arise as a consequence of a *voluntary undertaking* by the fiduciary to act for the interests of another in abnegation of self-interest.[48] A person could be said to have voluntarily undertaken to act for another's interests by willingly occupying a certain office (as, eg, trustee, director) or through a mutual understanding derived from contractual arrangements. Modern case law nevertheless continues to stress that 'fiduciary responsibility, ultimately is an imposed not an accepted one', and the requirement of voluntariness is thus to be tested objectively.[49] As Sales J remarked in *F&C Alternative Investments (Holdings) Ltd v Barthelemy (No 2)*:[50]

> Fiduciary duties are obligations imposed by law as a reaction to particular circumstances of responsibility assumed by one person in respect of the conduct of the affairs of another.

[43] This label is borrowed from Fabrizio Dell'Acqua et al, 'Navigating the Jagged Technological Frontier: Field Experimental Evidence of the Effects of AI on Knowledge Worker Productivity and Quality' (September 2023) Harvard Business School Technology & Operation Management Unit Working Paper No 24-013. I use the phrase 'jagged frontier' to mean irregularity in imposing fiduciary accountability.

[44] J Edelman, 'When do fiduciary duties arise' (2010) 126 *LQR* 302.

[45] *Hospital Products Ltd v United States Surgical Corp* (1984) 55 ALR 417, 456–57 (Mason J).

[46] [1998] Ch 1 (CA) 18.

[47] A Scott, 'The Fiduciary Principle' (1949) 37 *California Law Review* 539, 540; Finn (n 40) 201.

[48] For academic literature, eg, AJ Duggan, 'Is equity efficient' (1997) 113 *LQR* 601, 622; Edelman (n 44); L Smith, 'Fiduciary Relationships – Arising in Commercial Contexts – Investment Advisor: *Hodgkinson v Simms*' (1995) 74 *Canadian Bar Review* 714; Worthington (n 42) (Worthington, relying on Sealy's work, would also include having control over another's property as a legally significant fact for finding that fiduciary duties arise). For case law, eg, *Hodgkinson v Simms* [1994] 3 SCR 377; *F&C Alternative Investment (Holdings) Ltd v Barthelemy (No 2)* [2011] EWHC 1731 (Ch), [2012] Ch 613 [225]; *Tan Yok Koon v Tan Choo Suan* [2017] 1 SLR 654 [194]. *cf* L Smith, *The Law of Loyalty* (Oxford, Oxford University Press, 2023) 69 (Smith does not think that fiduciary duties *only* arise by reason of the fiduciary's voluntary undertaking to act for another).

[49] *Vivendi SSA v Richards* [2013] EWHC 3006 (Ch) [139].

[50] [2011] EWHC 1731 (Ch), [2010] Ch 613 [225]. See also *Al Nehayan v Kent* [2018] EWHC 333 (Comm), [2018] 1 CLC 216 [159] (Leggatt J).

The limitation of the concept of 'voluntariness' in fully explaining when fiduciary duties arise is patent. Outside established categories of fiduciary relationships, it seems somewhat strained to say that commercial parties *voluntarily* assume fiduciary duties by reason of them consenting to undertake certain kinds of contractual obligations. They may not have *subjectively* consented to taking on the fiduciary obligations. In fact, they may not have even thought about fiduciary obligations at the time of contracting. If we were to adopt an objective assessment of voluntariness, the line between imposing fiduciary obligations and voluntarily assuming fiduciary duties becomes blurry. The voluntary assumption of fiduciary duties is, on one view, *inferred* from the parties' agreement, objectively interpreted, that one party should undertake certain contractual obligations. On another view, they are simply imposed on one party to ensure their proper performance of the contractual obligations.[51]

There is therefore renewed interest in the formulae of 'reasonable expectation'[52] or 'legitimate expectation'[53] of abnegation of self-interest as an alternative test, because the terminology makes plain the test's objectivity and de-emphasises the need for subjective consent. Importantly, a legitimate expectation of abnegation of self-interest could arise from one's undertaking to act for the interests of another.[54] In *Lehtimäki v Cooper*, Lady Arden regarded this as an 'additional' test and one that 'may not be appropriate in every case',[55] potentially suggesting that there is a default test that could be displaced in the right set of circumstances in favour of applying the 'reasonable expectation' test.[56] It is debatable as to what the default test is; one could also say there are several default tests that the court may apply in combination,[57] including the voluntary undertaking test, the test based on reposing trust and confidence,[58] vulnerability,[59] entrustment of property or discretion, etc. The precise conditions for

[51] Parties may, by contract, limit the scope of fiduciary duties. However, it remains contentious as to whether parties should be allowed to exclude a fiduciary relationship from arising altogether by contract. This type of 'contracting-out' was permitted in *Australian Securities & Investment Commission v Citigroup Global Markets Australia Pty Ltd (No 4)* [2007] 160 FCR 35 but was criticised by Finn for prioritising a 'contract-related view' of fiduciary relationship instead of regarding fiduciary law as 'an instrument of public policy maintaining and protecting the integrity of public and social institutions and practices': P Finn, 'Fiduciary Reflections' (2014) 88 *Australian Law Journal* 127, 142. *cf* AE Wood and L Hastings, 'A Response to Professor Finn's "Fiduciary Reflections"' (2014) 88 *Australian Law Journal* 314.

[52] In *Grimaldi v Chameleon Mining NL (No 2)* (2012) 287 ALR 22 [177], Finn J famously said that 'a person will be in a fiduciary relationship with another when and in so far as that person has undertaken to perform such a function for, or has assumed such a responsibility to, another as would thereby reasonably entitle that other to expect that he or she will act in that other's interest to the exclusion of his or her own or a third party's interest …'.

[53] *Arklow Investments Ltd v Maclean* [2000] 1 WLR 594, 598G (Henry J); *Onzm v Watson* [2018] EWHC 2016 (Ch) [131].

[54] *Tulip Trading Ltd v Bitcoin Association For BSV* [2023] EWCA Civ 83, [2023] 4 WLR 16 [70]–[79].

[55] [2020] UKSC 33, [2022] AC 155 [48].

[56] The alternative reading is that the 'reasonable expectation' test is simply one of the tests that could be applied, without primacy being accorded to any one test. Even on this reading, it suggests that there is no single test and the court decide on the appropriate test to apply to find that fiduciary duties arise in a given set of circumstances.

[57] In *Grimaldi v Chameleon Mining NL (No 2)* (2012) 287 ALR 22 [177], Finn J observed that 'there is no generally agreed and unexceptionable definition' for who is a 'fiduciary'.

[58] *Medsted Associates Ltd v Canaccord Genuity Wealth (International) Ltd* [2019] EWCA Civ 83, [2019] 1 WLR 4481 [32].

[59] *Johnson v FirstRand Bank Ltd* [2024] EWCA Civ 1282 [100] (NB the UK Supreme Court heard the appeal in April 2025).

switching to the reasonable/legitimate expectation test and what the test entails are also unclear,[60] although what is clear is that it is the court, and not party autonomy, that will decide the application of a different test.

Crucially, in the commercial context, the legitimate expectation test could potentially support finding actors who do not fall within established categories of fiduciaries, to owe *prescriptive* fiduciary duties[61] – a development that would change the English fiduciary landscape.[62] In *Tulip Trading v Bitcoin Association For BSV*,[63] the Court of Appeal held, in the context of a jurisdictional application, that it was arguable that the defendant developers of bitcoin networks owed a *fiduciary duty* to the claimant bitcoin owner to implement a software patch to enable the claimant to regain access to its lost bitcoins. Whilst acknowledging that the 'legitimate expectation' test is not able to explain every case,[64] the court commented that 'it is realistic' to say that the Bitcoin owners, who entrusted their property in the care of the developers, 'have legitimate expectation that the developers will not exercise their authority in their own self-interest' to the owners' detriment and further owe a duty to fix bugs brought to their attention, because they have the 'practical ability' to do so.[65]

Whilst *Tulip Trading* has endorsed a more controversial test, in respect of other commercial actors such as agents, the courts continue to apply more traditional tests to determine if fiduciary duties arise on the facts.[66] Although the label 'default rule' has not been used to describe the more traditional tests, the judicial endorsement of the 'legitimate expectation' test as an *additional* test that could be used to explain the results in some cases indicates a leaning towards default rules and alternatives.[67] The outcome in *Tulip Trading*, albeit not amounting to a settled point of law, is significant and may be explicated as stemming from the court's concern to ensure stronger protection for digital assets and foster greater accountability in innovative technological applications that impact society at large.[68] The deployment of the 'legitimate expectation' test in the *Tulip*

[60] For discussion of the 'basket of views' approach (as applied by Lady Arden in *Lehtimäki v Cooper* [2020] UKSC 33, [2022] AC 155) versus the 'basket of characteristics' approach (as applied by Birss LJ in *Tulip Trading* [2023] EWCA Civ 83, [2023] 4 WLR 16): Tan W, 'Directors, Concurrent Fiduciary Duties, and Ad Hoc Fiduciary Relationships' (2024) *Conveyancer* 76, 82.

[61] The term 'prescriptive duties' is used in contradistinction to 'proscriptive duties'. In England and Australia, fiduciary duties are conventionally perceived to be exhausted by proscriptive duties (that is, the duty *not* to put oneself in a position of conflict and the duty *not* to take unauthorised profits). On Conaglen's account of fiduciary loyalty based on prophylaxis, for instance, it is not necessary to have prescriptive fiduciary duties because fiduciary duties are 'concerned with preventing the fiduciary from acting in a way that might cause the fiduciary to breach his non-fiduciary duties': M Conaglen, *Fiduciary Loyalty: Protecting the Due Performance of Non-fiduciary Duties* (Oxford, Hart Publishing, 2010) 202–03.

[62] Worthington (n 39) 663. *cf* L Smith, 'Prescriptive Fiduciary Duties' (2018) *University of Queensland Law Journal* 261.

[63] [2023] EWCA Civ 83, [2023] 4 WLR 16.

[64] *Tulip Trading Ltd* [2023] EWCA Civ 83, [2023] 4 WLR 16 [46].

[65] ibid [78]–[79].

[66] *Eze v Conway* [2019] EWCA Civ 88 [55]; *Medsted Associates Ltd v Canaccord Genuity Wealth (International) Ltd* [2019] EWCA Civ 83, [2019] 1 WLR 4481 [33]; *Wood v Commercial First Business Ltd* [2021] EWCA Civ 471, [2022] Ch 123 [118]; *Kew Green Group Ltd v Lamb* [2023] EWHC 1289 [148].

[67] Notably, the 'legitimate expectation' test was not presented as an *exception* to the other tests.

[68] M Yip, 'Equity and Society' in A Robertson and J Neyers (eds), *Private Law and the State* (Oxford, Hart Publishing, 2024) ch 14. On my analysis, the approach taken by the Court of Appeal in *Tulip Trading* is aligned with Lady Arden's explanation in *Lehtimäki* [2020] UKSC 33, [2022] AC 155 as to why the members of a charitable company limited by guarantee without shares owe fiduciary duties. The 'legitimate expectation' test

Trading case is aimed at strengthening the justification for finding a non-traditional commercial fiduciary to owe prescriptive fiduciary obligations – an outcome that is not readily justifiable or apparent by applying the traditional tests alone.[69] However, the lack of certainty in the criteria for switching to the alternative 'legitimate expectation' test, coupled with the inherent uncertainty in the application of traditional tests in commercial relationships to find actors owing fiduciary duties on an ad hoc basis, contributes to a jagged frontier of commercial fiduciary accountability. Whilst fiduciary duties are imposed by law, should the onerous accountability be imposed as somewhat of a surprise to commercial parties? Where the establishment of relationships is concerned, certainty ought to be paramount.

B. Fiduciary Duties

The main purposes of fiduciary regulation is deterring disloyalty and minimising the costs of monitoring fiduciaries.[70] That (some) fiduciary rules are characterised as 'default rules' is not inconsistent with standard-setting, although their status as 'defaults' acknowledges that such (ie modifiable) rules do not constitute the irreducible core of fiduciary regulation.[71] However, it leaves open the possibility that other duties may constitute an irreducible minimum that operates as *mandatory* rules.[72] Crucially, the conditions for disapplying the default rule should be calibrated in a way to ensure that the purpose for imposing fiduciary duties is not undermined. In the modern commercial world, principals are dependent on agents with the relevant expertise 'to undertake imperfectly observable discretionary actions that affect the wealth of the principal'.[73] It is the very discretionary authority of the agent that the principal relies on to advance their interests in changing and/or uncertain environments.[74] The fiduciary regulation strategy is three-fold. First, to deter disloyalty, to formulate proscriptive duties as open-textured standards which a fiduciary cannot easily side-step in practice. Second, to provide a panoply of remedies to deter the breach of those proscriptive standards, from rescission to compensation to disgorgement. Third, to introduce mechanisms to

is used as a judicial tool to justify a non-traditional category of actors as owing fiduciary duties with the aim of enhancing governance and accountability in that sector.

[69] In *Tulip Trading* [2023] EWCA Civ 83, [2023] 4 WLR 16 [70]–[71], Birss LJ observed that finding that the developers 'have undertaken a role which at least bears some relationship to the interests of other people' was 'not sufficient' to fix them with fiduciary duties; the facts of the case were 'new and quite a long way from factual circumstances' that the courts have had examined before.

[70] Frankel (n 39) 1223.

[71] Worthington (n 39) 639.

[72] Sitkoff (n 24) 1046–48. In *Lehtimäki v Cooper* [2020] UKSC 33, [2022] AC 155 [83], Lady Arden declined to comment whether the reduction would be ineffective if the duties were reduced below the irreducible minimum. It is suggested that the duty to act honestly and in good faith in the interests of the principal is an irreducible core fiduciary duty. This corresponds to the formulation of the irreducible core of trusteeship (*cf* *Armitage v Nurse* [1998] Ch 241 (CA)). As the trustee is the paradigmatic fiduciary, it takes only a small and uncontroversial step to extend the same to other fiduciaries. Further, it is hard to imagine a principal would ever want to waive this duty.

[73] Sitkoff (n 24) 1040.

[74] ibid 1040–41.

disapply the relevant duty where concerns of disloyalty and high costs of monitoring fiduciaries are adequately addressed.

Writing from a law and economics perspective and focusing on US fiduciary law, Sitkoff argues that fiduciary duties (as defined under US law),[75] as default rules, enable courts to fill in the gaps left in the parties' contract, so that parties can focus on 'contingencies that are important and likely enough to warrant the transaction costs of express provision'.[76] This gap-filling account may be less appealing to English equity because English courts, in continuing to insist that fiduciary duties are imposed, does not adopt a fully contractarian account of fiduciary regulation. Nevertheless, English and Australian scholars embrace prudential arguments to justify the default nature of fiduciary duties. For instance, Harding argues that fiduciary law uses the 'distinctive strategy' of 'general default rules' to guarantee conduct consistent with the requirements of trustworthiness because it is more economically efficient than the alternative strategy of 'specifically contracted undertakings and monitoring systems'.[77] In a similar vein, in respect of controlling company directors' conflicts of interest, Nolan argues that adopting the 'general default rules' strategy is more efficient and practicable.[78]

i. *Informed Consent*

It is well established that the no-conflict rule and the no-profit rule are default rules which can be disapplied – most notably by the mechanism of informed consent in respect of specific transactions – without reducing the relationship to a non-fiduciary one.[79] Lady Arden observed in *Lehtimäki* that 'there must be some fiduciary duty which the court can enforce but it need not extend to the full range of fiduciary duties which a fiduciary might owe'.[80] Informed consent, which can only be sought from a principal of majority age and full capacity and on the disclosure of all material facts, might be sought *ex ante* as an authorisation or ex post as a waiver of the breach of duty. In the commercial setting, *ex ante* informed consent is conventionally obtained via the contractual agreement,[81] or in the case of company directors, via the articles of association or by a shareholders' resolution at a general meeting.[82] Given that fiduciary duties arise for the protection and benefit of the principal, there can hardly be any objection to the principal being the appropriate party to decide to switch out of the default position, as long as they do so on an informed basis.[83]

[75] In English law, the equitable duty of care owed by a fiduciary is not considered a *fiduciary* duty.
[76] Sitkoff (n 24) 1044.
[77] M Harding, 'Trust and Fiduciary Law' (2013) 33 *OJLS* 81, 96–98.
[78] R Nolan, 'The Legal Control of Directors' Conflicts of Interest in the United Kingdom: Non-Executive Directors Following the Higgs Report' (2005) 6 *Theoretical Inquiries in Law* 413, 422–23.
[79] *Barnsley v Noble* [2016] EWCA Civ 799, [2017] Ch 191; *Lehtimäki v Cooper* [2020] UKSC 33, [2022] AC 155 [82] (Lady Arden). 'Disapplication' here is concerned with limiting the fiduciary duties' scope, instead of excluding *all* fiduciary duties.
[80] [2020] UKSC 33, [2022] AC 155 [83].
[81] *Citibank NA v MBIA Assurance SA* [2007] EWCA Civ 11, [2007] 1 All ER (Comm) 475.
[82] See generally *BTI 2014 LLC v Sequana SA* [2022] UKSC 25, [2024] AC 211 [23]–[24].
[83] *cf* Frankel (n 39) (disagreeing with the use of surrogate consenters in corporate law).

In fact, the law allows the principal to use the informed consent mechanism to decide whether to tolerate a potential conflict till its maturation into an actual conflict or whether to enter a relationship that is founded on arrangements involving pre-existing actual conflicts (ie, an 'inherent actual conflict' scenario).[84] Underlining the concept of informed consent is the acknowledgement that 'not all conflicts are necessarily harmful or fatal' and in commercial life, 'conflicts are normal, intended and even helpful in the pursuit of mutual advantage'.[85]

Similarly, in respect of the no-profit rule, the default position is that all profits generated in connection with the fiduciary relationship would go to the principal, unless the fiduciary has obtained the principal's informed consent to obtain these profits for herself. The court, in exercise of its inherent jurisdiction, could also allow remuneration to fiduciaries in appropriate circumstances.[86]

ii. Context-specific Implementing Rules

Sitkoff has emphasised the fiduciary governance strategy's flexibility: the open-textured general duties operate in tandem with context-specific implementing rules that 'fit the particulars of the agency problem at issue'.[87] As Sitkoff points out:[88]

> Because the fiduciary obligation operates as an after-the-fact compliance review of the fiduciary's conduct, and because the agency problem varies across fiduciary contexts, the precise contours of the fiduciary obligation vary across the fiduciary fields. For example, the fiduciary obligation in trust law is generally stricter than the fiduciary obligation in corporate law. But those differences reflect the different contexts. The agency problem in a family trust in which the beneficiaries have no exit option and that is managed by a corporate fiduciary that cannot easily be replaced differs significantly from the agency problem in a large, publicly-traded corporation from which a shareholder can separate easily by selling his shares in a thick securities market …

Given the different actors and the myriad circumstances that fiduciary law covers, common law fiduciary duties are cast as open-ended, general standards which are applicable to all fiduciaries. Courts and statutes could adapt these default duties (in the sense of 'prima facie' rules) in respect of specific actors and specific scenarios to 'fit the particulars of the agency problem at issue'.[89] Their default nature enables more context-specific implementing rules to be applied. Given that these context-specific implementing rules concern the regulation of a specific sector or specific professionals, it is fitting that their

[84] M Yip and K Low, 'Reconceptualising Fiduciary Regulation in Actual Conflicts' (2021) 45 *Melbourne University Law Review* 323, in particular discussion at 339–41 of *Re Colorado Products Pty Ltd (in prov liq)* (2014) 101 ACSR 233. See further JH Langbein, 'Questioning the Trust Law Duty of Loyalty' (2005) 114 *Yale Law Journal* 929, 959–60 (not tolerating any conflicts in the corporate context would prevent the pursuit of many mutually beneficial transactions).

[85] Yip and Low (n 84) 358.

[86] M Conaglen, 'Identifying the profits for which a fiduciary must account' [2020] *CLJ* 36, 42. We look more closely at the court's exercise to award an allowance to a defaulting fiduciary below.

[87] Sitkoff (n 24) 1045.

[88] ibid.

[89] ibid.

application is generally to be decided by the legislature or courts, even though in some cases the parties' contractual terms may form part of the background context.

By way of example, section 961J of the Australian Corporations Act 2001 provides that the provider of financial advice 'must give priority to the client's interests when giving the advice' if the provider 'knows, or reasonably ought to know, that there is a conflict between the interests of the client and the [provider's] interests'. It has been noted that this requirement to 'prioritise' the client's interests is 'an alternative to, and seems to be a less demanding standard' than what the no-conflict rule requires.[90] The statutory concept, contrary to the common law conception of single-minded loyalty, contemplates the 'co-existence of two interests, that of the client and another interests, and to be satisfied by preferencing the client's interest while still having regard to the other interest'.[91]

Another example would be partners who owe fiduciary duties to each other in respect of the management of the affairs of the partnership,[92] but at the same time share in the partnerships' gains and losses. In other words, a partner is both a fiduciary and a stakeholder. Thus, unlike the traditional fiduciary roles, a partner's role is not based on an abnegation of self-interest because they have a personal financial interest in the partnership. Criddle labels partners in American law an example of 'stakeholder fiduciaries', arguing that a partner's role is one of 'solidarity' – ie, 'to exercise fiduciary power in a manner that respects all partners (including herself) as rightful co-beneficiaries'.[93] The mere fact that a partner profits from their fiduciary role does not establish a breach of duty, unless the partner in question did so at the expense of the interests of the other partners.[94] Therefore, whilst partners are still subject to the no-profit and no-conflict rules, these rules apply somewhat differently to such 'stakeholder fiduciaries'.[95] The position is no different in English law. In respect of the members of an LLP board, Sales J made very similar observations when setting out their fiduciary duties in *F&C Alternative Investments*.[96] He also acknowledged difficulty in determining the precise content of a stakeholder fiduciary's fiduciary duties:[97]

> It is in relation to this requirement that I have found the practical working through of the accommodation to be achieved between the defendants' self-interest and the interests of the LLP, on the one hand, and the F & C representatives' role to promote and protect the interests of F & C and the interests of the LLP, on the other, more difficult …

[90] Justice Ashley Black, 'Equitable and Statutory Regulation of Conflicts of Interests and Duty' (Speech, The University of New South Wales Law School, May 2016), available at supremecourt.nsw.gov.au/documents/Publications/Speeches/2016-Speeches/Black_20160510.pdf.

[91] ibid.

[92] *F&C Alternative Investments (Holding) Ltd v Barthelemy* [2011] EWHC 1731 (Ch), [2012] Ch 613 [208].

[93] EJ Criddle, 'Stakeholder Fiduciaries' in M Harding and PB Miller (eds), *Fiduciaries and Trust: Ethics, Politics, Economics, and Law* (Cambridge, Cambridge University Press, 2020).

[94] ibid (giving examples of diverting business opportunities from the partnership or paying to themselves a disproportionate share of partnership profits).

[95] In choosing partnership as the organisational structure for business, it may be argued that the parties have impliedly consented to the modification of the fiduciary duties on an informed basis *ex ante*.

[96] *F&C Alternative Investments (Holding) Ltd v Barthelemy* [2011] EWHC 1731 (Ch), [2012] Ch 613 [227].

[97] ibid [227(iii)] and [237].

> … the difficulty lies in identifying the degree to which it was legitimate for the LLP board members to have regard either to their own self-interest (in the case of the defendants) or interests (in the case of the F & C representatives). This is highly dependent on the particular factual circumstances in which the question what to do might arise. Whilst not being able to specify precisely in advance what they could or could not do is somewhat frustrating, that is simply a function of the blurring of roles which the parties intended should occur within the LLP and the usual flexibility of equitable standards of conscionable behaviour once one moves away from the clear paradigm fiduciary relationships, especially where those standards fall to be applied in relation to the management of a business in a relationship which was intended to continue over a substantial period of time and which would have to adapt to meeting a wide range of often unforeseen business situations.

These context-specific implementing rules are not only required to properly regulate commercial fiduciary actors in different sectors based on the nature of their dealings with the principals, but may also be necessary to ensure that the relevant fiduciary could properly discharge their duties when circumstances have changed. Where directors are concerned, it has been well established that when the company is financially stable, the director's duty to act in good faith in the company's best interests requires them to act in the best interests of the *shareholders*. It is not necessary to consider the creditors' interests separately, in that context. However, when the company descends into financial difficulties, the directors' duty to act in the best interests of the company is adjusted in that the company's interests would be understood to include its *creditors*' interests. This rule is generally attributed to *West Mercia Safetywear Ltd (in liq) v Dodd*,[98] and has been affirmed and clarified in subsequent cases,[99] and is also said to be preserved in section 172(3) of the Companies Act 2006.[100] More recently, in *BTI 2014 LLC v Sequana SA*, Lord Reed described the *West Mercia* doctrine as a 'modifying rule'[101] and explains its operation as follows:[102]

> [I]t seems to me that the effect of the rule in *West Mercia* is to preserve the directors' duty to act in the interests of the company, but to modify the sense of the latter expression so that, where the rule applies, the interests of the company are no longer regarded as solely those of its shareholders but are understood as including those of its creditors as a whole …
>
> … as a general rule that the more parlous the state of the company, the more the interests of the creditors will predominate, and the greater the weight which should therefore be given to their interests as against those of the shareholders. That is most clearly the position where an insolvent liquidation or administration is inevitable, and the shareholders consequently cease to retain any valuable interest in the company.

In other words, the traditional equiparation of the company's interests with its shareholders' interests is the default position, displaced when the company faces financial difficulties resulting in a change of its economic interests and consequently the understanding of the company's interests. In such circumstances, the creditors' interests are

[98] [1988] BCLC 250.

[99] See, eg, *Kinsela v Russell Kinsela Pty Ltd (in liq)* (1986) 4 NSWLR 722; *Bilta (UK) Ltd (in liq) v Nazir* [2015] UKSC 23, [2016] AC 1.

[100] *BTI 2014 LLC v Sequana SA* [2022] UKSC 25, [2024] AC 211 [69] (Lord Reed).

[101] ibid [11].

[102] ibid [79] and [81].

no longer aligned with the shareholders' interests because the former would desire the repayment of their debts, but the latter might wish to pursue commercial risks which would ultimately be borne by the creditors.[103] Unlike the examples discussed above, the formulation of the 'best interests' duty does not change. Instead, it is the understanding of a constituent element of the duty – the company's interests – which changes, depending on the financial health of the company.

More broadly, as alternative rules to the default, the context-specific implementing rules designed by the legislature/courts operate differently from the informed consent mechanism. The distinction depends on who is doing the choosing. The former's objective is for the legislature/courts to redefine what disloyalty means in a specific context: they are context-specific fiduciary duties. Whilst commercial parties could choose to modify their fiduciary duties through the informed consent mechanism to achieve a similar effect, the modified duties would only apply to those parties *inter se* and not affect fiduciary actors across the same sector.

C. Account of Profits and Equitable Allowance

Where unauthorised profits have been earned by a defaulting fiduciary, the starting position is that the fiduciary must account to their principal for all the unauthorised profits that fall within the scope of their duty.[104] As Lord Russell famously said in *Regal (Hastings) Ltd v Gulliver*, the liability to account arises 'from the mere fact of a profit having … been made' and does not depend on the fiduciary's fraud, absence of bona fides, or questions as to whether the secret profit would or should have gone to the principal.[105] The oft-cited justification for this 'inflexible rule'[106] is deterrence.[107] There is also a pragmatic reason underlining the rule: undertaking an investigation of the hypothetical situations of what might have happened if the fiduciary had not acted in breach of duty is difficult, speculative and uncertain.[108]

The harshness of the remedy to account may however be mitigated by the discretionary jurisdiction to award an 'equitable allowance' to an honest fiduciary to recompense their skill, undertaking of risk, and labour in generating the profit,[109] though the jurisdiction is sparingly exercised. The burden falls on the defaulting fiduciary to prove they are deserving of an allowance. In this way, the rigid rule of accounting

[103] ibid [59].

[104] *Gray v Global Energy Horizons Corp; Global Energy Horizons Corp v Gray* [2021] EWCA Civ, 1668 [2021] 1 WLR 2264 [126].

[105] [1967] 2 AC 134 (Note) 144–45.

[106] *Murad v Al Saraj* [2005] EWCA Civ 959 [101] (Jonathan Parker LJ).

[107] *Rukhadze v Recovery Partners GP Ltd* [2025] UKSC 10, [2025] 2 WLR 529 [47] and [52] (Lord Briggs, with whom Lords Reed, Hodge and Richards agreeing). The majority therefore declined to water down the strictness of the no-profit rule by introducing a 'but-for' causation test in determining whether the errant fiduciary should be ordered to account for the profits. *cf* L Smith, 'Deterrence, prophylaxis and punishment in fiduciary obligations' (2013) 7 *Journal of Equity* 87; JE Penner, 'Distinguishing Trust, Fiduciary and Accounting Relationships' (2014) 8 *Journal of Equity* 202; L Ho, 'Deemed Performance in Account of Profits' in P Devonshire and R Havelock (eds), *The Impact of Equity and Restitution in Commerce* (Oxford, Hart Publishing, 2019) 183.

[108] *Regal Hastings v Gulliver* [1967] 2 AC 134, 154G.

[109] *Boardman v Phipps* [1967] 2 AC 46 (HL).

for *all* unauthorised profits that fall within the scope of the fiduciary's duty may be characterised as the default rule that can be disapplied by the court, when the appropriate exceptional conditions are met.[110] The interplay between an account of profits and the discretionary award of allowance thus ensures that the rigour of the duty of loyalty, which is 'one of those foundation stones which separates business life from the jungle', is maintained.[111]

The trouble is that the law is not entirely clear as to what the conditions for switching out of the default position are. This is because historically, the account of profits was a process 'conducted safely away from the eyes of law reports and posterity in Masters' chambers',[112] and authority is thus 'scant'.[113] Modern courts are expected to demystify the process and articulate clear principles. According to the Court of Appeal's decision in *Recovery Partners GP Ltd v Rukhadze*, an important consideration in the court's exercise of discretion is the fiduciary's degree of culpability and whether allowing an allowance of the full or part of the remuneration in the circumstances would defeat the goal of deterrence.[114] A fiduciary who has committed a breach of duty in good faith (ie, a judicious breach of duty) is not disqualified from being considered for an allowance.[115] A fiduciary who had acted dishonestly or committed breaches in a sufficiently egregious manner, on the other hand, is not entitled to any allowance because these are cases where strong deterrence is required.[116] In *Rukhadze*, the defendants had not breached their fiduciary duties dishonestly,[117] but neither had they acted in good faith. They fell somewhere in the middle on the continuum of culpability, between good faith and dishonesty. The Court of Appeal upheld the trial court's order for an allowance of 25 per cent of the profits falling within the scope of the equitable duty to account, as remuneration for the defendants' skill, labour and undertaking of risk. The Court of Appeal noted that 'it is very probable' that the trial judge, in reaching this conclusion, had in mind that the fiduciaries would have expected to share the profits on a 50/50 basis[118] with the principal, had there been no breach of duty.[119] In other words, the disapplication of the prima facie position of accounting for all unauthorised profits made in connection with the fiduciary office is determined and calibrated by reference to the goal of deterrence.

On appeal in *Rukhadze* the Supreme Court did not have opportunity to examine the discretionary jurisdiction to award allowance in any great detail, as the defendants

[110] The inquiry, phrased more conventionally, is this: when is an equitable allowance – which has the effect of reducing the quantum of profits to be accounted to the principal – available to the defaulting fiduciary?

[111] Lord Briggs (n 22) 113. See *Rukhadze v Recovery Partners GP Ltd* [2025] UKSC 10, [2025] 2 WLR 529 [58] (Lord Briggs).

[112] Lord Briggs (n 22) 109.

[113] M Conaglen, 'Identifying the profits for which a fiduciary must account' (2020) *CLJ* 36, 42.

[114] *Rukhadze v Recovery Partners GP Ltd* [2023] EWCA Civ 305, [2023] Bus LR 646, [117]–[119].

[115] See, for example, *Boardman v Phipps* [1967] 2 AC 46 (the fiduciary was awarded equitable allowance on a 'liberal scale').

[116] *Rukhadze v Recovery Partners GP Ltd* [2023] EWCA Civ 305, [2023] Bus LR 646 [117].

[117] ibid [125].

[118] The 50/50 profit sharing arrangement was based on a non-binding common understanding between the parties.

[119] *Rukhadze v Recovery Partners GP Ltd* [2023] EWCA Civ 305, [2023] Bus LR 646 [145]–[146]. The court observed that the trial judge had said that 25% was 'not at all as much' as what would have been their remuneration.

were denied permission to appeal against the equitable allowance of 25 per cent. Nevertheless, Lord Briggs, delivering the majority judgment, highlighted that the uncertainty in the quantification of the allowance, together with the discretionary nature of the award, bolsters the deterrent effect of the no-profit rule.[120]

IV. Conclusion

Through my analysis of default rules in fiduciary law, I have shown that the default rule strategy (encompassing both the broad, presumptive sense and the narrow, contractual sense of 'default rule') has great utility for equity in the commercial context. First, equitable default rules embodied in the fiduciary duties are more economically efficient in regulating commercial fiduciary actors' conduct as it does away with the need for detailed contracting and constant monitoring. Second, in view of the range of commercial actors that are subjected to fiduciary regulation and the diversity of dealings they are engaged in, default rules (and alternatives) provide flexibility for equity to respond to different commercial contexts, as well as changing circumstances.

Importantly, the law allows a role for party autonomy in deciding whether the default position should be disapplied, but this is only appropriate in circumstances where the principal is in a position to decide, on an informed basis, that they do not require the rigorous level of equitable protection guaranteed through the application of the fiduciary duties. The legislature and the courts also play an involved role in setting the conditions for disapplying the default position, deciding whether these conditions are met, as well as prescribing what the alternative position is. Their involvement ensures adequate oversight that the goals of fiduciary regulation – which includes ensuring responsible commercial conduct – are not undermined in the process.

The default rule design is one of the ways which equity utilises in formulating its principles to ensure flexibility and equitability. This rule design strategy is particularly suitable for fiduciary law because it is an institution to govern the relationships between different actors in the commercial arena where contexts and considerations vary considerably, but a reasonable degree of certainty and simplicity is nonetheless expected to enable forward planning.

Postscript: Part III.A must be read in light of the Supreme Court decision in *Hopcraft v Close Brothers Ltd; Johnson v FirstRand Bank Ltd; Wrench v FirstRand Bank Ltd* [2025] UKSC 33 where the court authoritatively clarified that fiduciary duties arise pursuant to an objectively assessed undertaking of single-minded loyalty. The court further held that trust and confidence, the duty to act disinterestedly, and vulnerability are not indicia of fiduciary duties arising in a relationship that fall outside the relationships in which it is well recognised that fiduciary duties arise. There is no doubt that the Supreme Court's mission was to simplify and provide greater certainty to the test for relationship establishment but the formulation is not free from problems.

[120] ibid [58].

14

From Mandatory to Default Rules: Trusts in the 'Commercial' Context

YING KHAI LIEW

I. Introduction

Few would doubt that the flexibility of the trust is one of its greatest strengths. Its adaptability ranges from facilitating the achievement of settlors' aims, to providing an analytical framework for the holding of securities; from providing for needy beneficiaries, to protecting investors' investments. One emerging method of categorising this wide range of circumstances is to distinguish between the 'commercial' context and the 'traditional' context. Given this polarisation, there has been increasing debate as to whether there remains a unitary body of 'trusts law' rules or whether the time has now come to recognise that trusts law operates differently in the two contexts. On the former view, trusts law rules do not change depending on the context they are called upon to serve. On the latter view, in contrast, some of those rules have adapted, moulded and ultimately morphed depending on context, resulting in discernible core differences.

In this chapter I begin by observing that there is a detectable shift from *mandatory* trusts rules, as traditionally developed in the domestic context, to *default* rules in the 'commercial' context. I go on to argue, contrary to popular belief, that the explanation or justification for that shift does not lie in the context in which a trust arises, because what counts as 'commercial' or 'traditional' does not have a stable meaning. Neither does the presence of a contract or the view that trusts law is 'contractualised' fully explain the shift. Instead, I argue that the rationale underlying the shift is beneficiary-focused: the law affords special treatment to trusts where their beneficiaries consist solely of 'bargaining beneficiaries'. An important lesson, therefore, is that it may be more fruitful for judges and commentators to focus on whether all the beneficiaries under a trust were involved in the bargain of the trust terms at the outset (and focus less on the context in which a trust arises).

II. Shifts

'[V]irtually all trust law is default law – rules that the parties can reject.'[1] So wrote John Langbein in his discussion of American trusts law. Whether this accurately reflects trusts law in the Anglo-Australian context is debatable; but it is at least true that the *majority* of rules concerning express trust are 'default' in nature. This is hardly surprising, for default rules are what enable the express trust to serve as a facilitative device, allowing owners to realise their wishes concerning the use of their own property.[2] Moreover, default rules are what maintain the analytical distinctiveness of the trust within the law, while also saving transaction costs.[3]

On the other hand, it is undeniable that trusts law also contains 'mandatory' rules – rules which the parties cannot alter or exclude. In certain jurisdictions, such as those in the United States (US) which have enacted a version of the Uniform Trust Code, and New Zealand, those rules are codified in the relevant statutes.[4] But in Anglo-Australian law, most mandatory rules are found in case law. For that reason, the precise scope of their applicability is inherently ambiguous; also for that reason, their applicability is mouldable and evolves through case law development over time.

In this section, I discuss five areas of trusts law where a noticeable shift from mandatory to default rules can be detected. This discussion presupposes, for the moment, that the terms 'commercial' and 'traditional' have stable meanings. This is perhaps uncontroversial since I aim specifically to discuss situations which fall within what is generally understood as core examples of the 'commercial' context. However, later in the chapter I will make the argument that the term 'commercial' does not have a stable meaning.

A. Intention

According to orthodoxy, an intention to create a trust is a mandatory requirement for a trust to exist. Intention is objectively assessed; subjective intentions are irrelevant.[5] The intention need not be expressed by any particular words: equity looks to intent and not to form. Thus, the word 'trust' need not be used. Instead, there must be an intention to impose obligations[6] on the putative trustee in relation to the trust property, with a beneficiary or beneficiaries having correlative rights[7] against the

[1] JH Langbein, 'The Contractarian Basis of the Law of Trusts' (1995) 105 *Yale Law Journal* 625, 650.

[2] YK Liew, 'Justifying Anglo-American Trusts Law' (2021) 12 *William & Mary Business Law Review* 685, 697–700.

[3] Philip Sales, 'Default Rules in the Common Law: Substantive Rules and Precedent' in B Häcker and J Ungerer (eds), *Default Rules in Private Law* (Oxford, Hart Publishing, 2025).

[4] See Uniform Trust Code (USA), s 105(b); Trusts Act 2019 (New Zealand), ss 22–27.

[5] *Byrnes v Kendle* [2011] HCA 26, 243 CLR 253; *National Stadium Project (Grenada) Corporation v NH International (Caribbean) Ltd* [2020] UKPC 25, 194 Con LR 1 [39].

[6] *Re Endacott* [1960] Ch 232, 241; *Hilton v Cosnier* [2018] EWHC 2728 (Ch) [27].

[7] Rights and duties are correlative: Wesley Newcomb Hohfeld (Walter Wheeler Cook ed), *Fundamental Legal Conceptions as Applied in Judicial Reasoning* (New Haven, Yale University Press, 1964) 36, 38.

trustee.[8] Courts will be hesitant to find an intention to create a trust where the relevant parties are in a contractual relationship which provides for personal rights and duties between them.[9]

In two areas of trusts law, however, this mandatory requirement of intention appears to have transformed into a default requirement which can be overridden by the parties in particular circumstances.

i. Quistclose *Trusts*

Consider the '*Quistclose* trust', a doctrine which has almost exclusively featured in the commercial context.[10] In *Barclays Bank Ltd v Quistclose Investments Ltd*, A loaned money to B for B to pay off dividends which B had declared and was unable to meet. It was a contractual term that the money 'will only be used to meet the dividend'.[11] The dividend was not paid when B entered voluntary liquidation. Lord Wilberforce, with whom the other judges in the House of Lords agreed, decided that B held the money on trust for A, and therefore A was entitled to the return of the money. Key to this conclusion was the interpretive technique applied by Lord Wilberforce to the 'exclusive purpose' clause in question: 'by process simply of interpretation … the money was to be returned to the respondents: the word "only" or "exclusively" can have no other meaning or effect'.[12] It is this possibility of reinterpreting an 'exclusive purpose' clause which makes the *Quistclose* trust a unique doctrine: as Lord Millett summarised the point in *Twinsectra Ltd v Yardley*, 'an arrangement that the money shall be used *exclusively* for the stated purpose' 'necessarily' leads to a *Quistclose* trust.[13]

There is some debate as to the precise nature of the *Quistclose* trust, namely whether B holds the money for A under an express trust or a resulting trust.[14] Lord Millett's analysis in *Twinsectra* provides authority, at least formally, for the resulting trust analysis in English law, based on negative intention – that B holds on resulting trust for A because the money was not intended to be at B's free disposal.[15] However, lower courts have insisted that the *Quistclose* trust reflects a positive intention to create a trust instead, which is, in substance, an express trust analysis.[16] The express trust analysis is also the preferred approach in Australia.[17] What all this tells us is that the *Quistclose* doctrine

[8] See, eg, *Vandenberg v Palmer* (1858) 4 K & J 204, 70 ER 85. An intention that the trustee be subjected to the relevant duty, combined with an intention that the correlative right should not vest in any particular person, may lead to the imposition of a resulting, rather than an express, trust: see, eg, *Vandervell v IRC* [1967] 2 AC 291.

[9] *Hilton* (n 6).

[10] Although *cf* YK Liew, 'The Wider Ambit of the *Quistclose* Doctrine' (2015) 9 *Journal of Equity* 66.

[11] *Barclays Bank Ltd v Quistclose Investments Ltd* [1970] AC 567, 579.

[12] ibid, 580.

[13] [2002] UKHL 12, [2002] 2 AC 164 [74] (emphasis in original).

[14] See, eg, J Penner, 'Lord Millett's Analysis' in W Swadling (ed), *The Quistclose Trust: Critical Essays* (Oxford, Hart Publishing, 2004).

[15] *Twinsectra Ltd v Yardley* [2002] UKHL 12, [2002] 2 AC 164 [100].

[16] See, eg, *Challinor v Juliet Bellis & Co* [2015] EWCA Civ 59 [56]; *Re Holiday Promotions (Europe) Ltd* [1996] BCC 671, 674.

[17] See eg *Re Australian Elizabethan Theatre Trust* (1991) 30 FCR 491, 500; *Walsh Bay Developments Pty Ltd v Federal Commissioner of Taxation* (1995) 130 ALR 415, 425; *Roxborough v Rothmans of Pall Mall Australia Ltd* [1999] FCA 1535, 167 ALR 326 [71]; *Legal Services Board v Gillespie-Jones* [2013] HCA 35, 249 CLR 493 [115]. Cf *Salvo v New Tel Ltd* [2005] NSWCA 281 [47]; *Raulfs v Fishy Bite Pte Ltd* [2012] NSWCA 135 [43].

functions to enable courts to interpret an 'exclusive purpose' clause in a way which is consistent with a *positive* intention on the part of the parties, in substance, to create an express trust.

Furthermore, this interpretive technique characterises the *Quistclose* trust; it is the doctrine's unique contribution to trusts law. Unfortunately this point has, in recent times, been lost on some judges. For example, in *Prickly Bay Waterside Ltd v British American Insurance Company Ltd (Grenada)*, the Privy Council suggested that a '*Quistclose* trust' could also describe a loan arrangement which does not include an 'exclusive purpose' clause: 'the term *Quistclose* trust may commonly be used whenever a person provides assets to another for the purpose of paying debts under arrangements which create a[n express or resulting] trust'.[18] Certainly, an express trust would arise if a contractual loan arrangement includes an express declaration of trust to the effect that B will hold the money on trust for A. Alternatively, a court could hold B to be a trustee under a resulting trust of loan monies for A's benefit by drawing on evidence at the time of the transfer that A did not intend for B to take the beneficial interest in the monies. But in both these instances the *Quistclose* doctrine is functionally otiose, for it adds nothing to the analysis or the outcome. As mentioned, the doctrine's key function is to allow for a liberal interpretation of an 'exclusive purpose' clause consistent with the existence of a trust.

This interpretive technique is clearly radical. There is no doubt that parties to a loan are in a contractual relationship. The inclusion of an 'exclusive purpose' clause in the contractual document, all things equal, would not – and should not – ordinary alter that relationship: it would indicate no more than a contractual agreement on the borrower's part to undertake a contractual obligation, the breach of which will allow the lender to sue for breach of contract. The *Quistclose* doctrine alters this status quo by allowing for the interpretation of an 'exclusive purpose' clause as itself sufficient to imply an intention to create a trust. It is therefore radical. But more to the point of this chapter, this radical technique also reflects a shift from a mandatory to a default rule. It is difficult to see how, *simply* by virtue of an 'exclusive purpose' clause, the parties to a loan agreement can be said to have intended to impose binding trust obligations on B with A having correlative rights: after all, as just observed, that clause more naturally represents a contractual term of the loan agreement. Therefore, we can conclude that the traditionally mandatory requirement of certainty of intention transforms into a default rule in the *Quistclose* context, such that the parties can, by virtue of an 'exclusive purpose' clause, disapply that strict requirement, leading to the imposition of a trust in circumstances which would not ordinarily do so.

ii. Advanced Payments

In three important English decisions, *Re Kayford Ltd*,[19] *Re Lewis's of Leicester Ltd*,[20] and *Re Chelsea Cloisters Ltd (In Liquidation)*,[21] money had been sent to a company as advanced payment for the supply of goods in the future (or, in the last-mentioned case,

[18] [2022] UKPC 8, [2022] 1 WLR 2087 [32].
[19] *Re Kayford Ltd* [1975] 1 WLR 279.
[20] *Re Lewis's of Leicester Ltd* [1995] BCC 514.
[21] *Re Chelsea Cloisters Ltd (In Liquidation)* (1980) 41 P & CR 98.

as tenant deposits to be returned in the future, less deductibles). In all three cases, the judges found on their respective facts that the payee company had validly declared itself as trustee of the advanced payments for the benefit of the payors, and therefore that the payors took priority in the company's insolvency.

These cases are usually discussed in the insolvency context where it has been argued that because the companies were nearing insolvency when the trusts were established, the courts were wrong to allow a voidable preference being given to the relevant payors.[22] Quite separately, however, the judgments also suggest a shift from mandatory to default rules in two respects, namely the objectivity of intention to create a trust, and the importance of segregation for the finding of such intention.

It is first necessary to point out three factual similarities among the cases. As mentioned, when the trusts were found to have been created, all three companies were in financial difficulty, with insolvency on the horizon. In all three cases the companies unilaterally decided to place the received monies into a segregated bank account. And in all three instances, apart from this segregation, the singular evidence the courts relied upon was affidavits from the companies' managing directors (or, in the case of *Chelsea Cloisters*, the affidavit of the supervising accountant who was also running the company), concerning their motives in segregating the monies (they being influenced by and having acted upon the advice of their accountants).

In all three cases the courts took a strikingly similar approach towards the evidence leading to the conclusion that that the companies had validly declared trusts for the payors. In none of the cases was the impecuniosity of the company taken to be a relevant factor.[23] In none of them was segregation said to be itself enough to demonstrate an intention to create a trust: it 'is a useful (though by no means conclusive) indication of an intention to create a trust'.[24] But crucially, in all three cases the courts placed greatest weight on the intentions of those running the companies, as revealed in their affidavits.[25]

This last-mentioned point is highly surprising. In general, and subject to exceptions which did not affect any of these cases, the intention of managing directors (or those who run a company) are taken to be the intention of the company.[26] Such a director's subjective intention is likewise taken to be the company's subjective intention.[27] And, as is the case with natural persons,[28] the motive or aim for which an act is carried out – especially one which remains internal to the person and not otherwise communicated to others – is considered to be subjective intention.[29] The inevitable conclusion, then, is that all three courts found the trusts to be validly declared on the

[22] See, eg, W Goodhart and GH Jones, 'The Infiltration of Equitable Doctrine into English Commercial Law' (1980) 43 *MLR* 489, 496–98. *cf* M Yip, 'The Commercial Context in Trust Law' (2016) *Conveyancer* 347, 351.

[23] *cf* Yip (n 22) 351.

[24] *Re Kayford Ltd* [1975] 1 WLR 279, 282.

[25] ibid, 281–82; *Re Lewis's of Leicester Ltd* [1995] BCC 514, 519–20; *Re Chelsea Cloisters Ltd (In Liquidation)* (1980) 41 P & CR 98, 102, 103, 104–05.

[26] *Lennards Carrying Co Ltd v Asiatic Petroleum Co Ltd* [1915] AC 705, 713; *El Ajou v Dollar Land Holdings plc* [1993] 3 All ER 717, 740; *Bilta (UK) Ltd (In Liquidation) v Nazir* [2013] EWCA Civ 968, [2014] Ch 52 [29].

[27] *Iliffe News & Media Ltd v Revenue and Customs Commissioners* [2012] UKFTT 696 (TC), [2013] SFTD 309 [271].

[28] See, eg, *Byrnes v Kendle* [2011] HCA 26, 243 CLR 253.

[29] *Euromoney Institutional Investor Plc v The Commissioners for Her Majesty's Revenue and Customs* [2021] UKFTT 61 (TC), [2021] SFTD 891 [111]–[112].

basis of the *subjective* intentions of the companies. This reflects a shift from the mandatory rule requiring *objectivity* of intention to a default rule which can be overridden by the subjective intention of a company's managing director who intends unilaterally to create a trust over advanced payments received.

An alternative analysis may also be possible. If we maintain that subjective intentions are irrelevant to the creation of trusts, then we must likewise conclude that the directors' intentions in the cases were likewise irrelevant to the outcomes. This leaves the act of segregation to do all the heavy lifting in the cases. However, orthodoxy suggests that segregation does not itself indicate an intention to impose binding obligations on the putative trustee or confer rights in favour of putative beneficiaries.[30] Therefore, on this alternative analysis, the mandatory rule requiring an intention to create a trust to be properly manifested is treated instead as a default rule which can be overridden by the act of segregation in the context of trusts over advanced payments.

B. Subject Matter

According to orthodoxy, a trust can only validly be created if there is certainty of subject matter, by which is meant that the identity of the assets to be held on trust must be ascertainable at the outset.[31] This mandatory rule sees a shift to default rules in the case of unit trusts.

A 'unit trust' describes circumstances where, 'according to the trust deed, the beneficial interest in the trust fund is divided into units'.[32] A unit is

> an aliquot share or interest in the undivided assets of a trust that are held for investment or profit by the trustee for the benefit of the unit holders or beneficiaries of that unit trust. For convenience those shares are identified, and their ownership and transfer facilitated, by a system of private registration or recording in the books of the trustee.[33]

The phrase 'unit trust' is descriptive rather than definitive: it 'does not have a constant, fixed normative meaning'.[34] This is particularly so because the courts treat the effects of a unit trust as the product not of a stable concept inherent in the label but of the terms of the trust deed establishing the trust.[35] It follows that it is well possible for a trust deed to establish a 'unit trust' which nevertheless conforms entirely with orthodox trusts rules. However, this is not necessarily so, and indeed, is not so in the case of the typical unit trust. Typically, the terms of a unit trust will have the effect of conferring only a right to the 'net income' of the trust fund.[36] The fact that courts

[30] Unless, of course, the segregated bank account is named a 'trust' account.

[31] *Re Goldcorp Exchange Ltd* [1995] 1 AC 74, 90.

[32] *ElecNet (Aust) Pty Ltd v Commissioner of Taxation of the Commonwealth of Australia* [2016] HCA 51, 259 CLR 73 [56].

[33] *Reef & Rainforest Travel Pty Ltd v Commissioner of Stamp Duties* [2001] QCA 249, [2002] 1 Qd R 683 [50].

[34] *CPT Custodian Pty Ltd v Commissioner of State Revenue of the State of Victoria* [2005] HCA 53, 224 CLR 98 [15]. See too AH Slater, 'Unit Trusts: Law and Lore' (2006) 35 *Australian Tax Review* 185, 188–89.

[35] *CPT Custodian Pty Ltd* (ibid) [15].

[36] See, eg, *MSP Nominees Pty Ltd v Commissioner of Stamps* [1999] HCA 51, 198 CLR 494 [3].

recognise and give effect to this term signifies a shift from a mandatory to a default rule in relation to the conception of a trust's subject matter.

In *Karingal (No 2) Pty Ltd v Commissioner of State Revenue*,[37] Nettle J drew a distinction between the concepts of an 'amount' of income and the 'nature' of income. The former describes the usual case encountered in trusts law, where a trust can (rightly) be created over 'income' generated by certain assets or funds. The validity of 'income' as the subject matter of the trust here is unaffected by any power of the trustee to apply part of the income in defined ways, the exercise of which affects only the *amount* of income distributable to the beneficiary. Nor is it affected by the fact that the actual *amount* reflecting that income can only be determined in the future, after relevant trust investments have materialised. In contrast, in the case of typical unit trust, the trustee's power to apply receipts

> informs the *nature* of the income that the unit holders have a right to receive: not a total of all of the receipts derived from each asset the subject of the fund but rather such if any income as may be derived from the product of the application of gross receipts in various ways.[38]

The distinction between the two uses of 'income' is a matter of fundamental importance. 'Income', as used in traditional trusts, refers to the 'fruit' borne by the capital 'tree'.[39] Although not a liquidated amount at the time the trust is executed, 'income' here reflects a certain enough and ascertainable concept to form the subject matter of a trust. By contrast, the concept of 'income' in the typical unit trust aligns better with the concept of 'profits'. Indeed, 'profits' is more to the point, for what the typical unit trust is referring to is not *simply* the idea of 'receipts minus applications', which is what the last quoted sentence of the preceding paragraph states; rather, it 'implies a comparison between the state of a business at two specific dates … This can only be ascertained by a comparison of the assets of the business at the two dates.'[40] That 'profits' is in fact the contemplated subject matter of the trust is also reflected in the fact that typical unit trust deeds provide for the distribution of net income to unit holders at specified intervals, usually every quarter year.[41] It is clear that, on a traditional understanding, it is a mandatory rule that 'profits' is an uncertain concept and cannot be the subject matter of a trust.[42] This 'mandatory' rule therefore transforms into a default rule which can be overridden by the parties to a unit trust deed.

A riposte might be that, in fact, no uncertainty arises because the subject matter of the trust is simply a chose in action – the contractual right represented by the unit trust deed which includes the right of individual unit holders to their proportionate share of

[37] *Karingal (No 2) Pty Ltd v Commissioner of State Revenue* [2002] VSC 431, 51 ATR 190 [63]; affirmed by *CPT Custodian Pty Ltd v Commissioner of State Revenue of the State of Victoria* [2005] HCA 53, 224 CLR 98 [37].

[38] *Karingal (No 2) Pty Ltd v Commissioner of State Revenue* [2002] VSC 431, 51 ATR 190 [63] (emphasis added).

[39] P Matthews et al, *Underhill and Hayton: Law Relating to Trusts and Trustees*, 20th edn (London, LexisNexis Butterworths, 2022) [47.7].

[40] *Re The Spanish Prospecting Co Ltd* [1911] 1 Ch 92, 98; *Commissioner of Taxation (Cth) v Slater Holdings Pty Ltd* (1984) 156 CLR 447, 460.

[41] Slater (n 34) 190.

[42] *Ultraframe (UK) Ltd v Fielding* [2005] EWHC 1638 (Ch), [2006] FSR 17 [1533]–[1547]. See too Slater (n 34) 195.

the net value of the trust fund.[43] There are two short responses to this. The first is the practical point that such a conception would completely remove the benefits of structuring the investment scheme as a unit trust in the first place, since the ring-fencing advantage so central to the trust structure would disappear: on this conception, only the chose in action, and not the investment monies, is insolvency-remote. The second response is that courts have not adopted the chose in action analysis: for example, it would not have been possible for White J in *Jonsue Investments Pty Ltd v Balweb Pty Ltd*[44] to have held that the unit holders had an 'equitable interest' allowing them the statutory right to extend a caveat. It is clear that what is contemplated, in practice and in the courts, is that the subject matter of unit trusts is 'net income', ie, 'profits'. Thus, the shift from a mandatory to a default rule is detected.

C. Beneficiary's Interests

Unit trusts also reflect a shift of another mandatory trust rule, relating to the law's conceptualisation of a beneficiary's interest under a trust. According to orthodoxy, a beneficiary with a vested interest is recognised as having 'a proprietary interest in the trust property'.[45] One expression of this is the rule in *Saunders v Vautier*,[46] which provides that a beneficiary who is (or beneficiaries who together are) *sui juris* and absolutely entitled to the beneficial interest under a trust may terminate the trust and compel the trustee to convey the trust property to the beneficiary, even if the trust instrument attempts to postpone distribution of the property. A typical feature of unit trust deeds, however, is that they preclude unit holders from having an interest in any particular part of the trust fund; that is, a unit holder is given no more than a discrete bundle of rights instead of a joint interest with the all the issued units in the trust property.[47] The fact that courts faithfully recognise this signifies a shift from the mandatory rule concerning beneficiaries' proprietary interests to a default rule which can be overridden by a unit trust deed.

It must first be noted that in many of the leading cases, the discussion concerning a unit holder's interest as a beneficiary under the trust arises in a statutory context. For example, a unit holder's interest has been held not to constitute an 'ownership' interest for the purposes of the Land Act 1958 (Vic)[48] or a 'proprietary' interest for the purposes

[43] KF Sin, *The Legal Nature of the Unit Trust* (Oxford, Oxford University Press, 1998) 264.

[44] *Jonsue Investments Pty Ltd v Balweb Pty Ltd* [2013] NSWSC 325, 9 ASTLR 460.

[45] *Westdeutsche Landesbank Girozentrale v Islington LBC* [1996] AC 669, 705. See too *Foskett v McKeown* [2001] 1 AC 102, 108–09; *Akers v Samba Financial Group* [2017] UKSC 6, [2017] AC 424 [17]. The point is much less certain in relation to discretionary trusts: see, eg, J Palmer and C Rickett, 'The Revolution and Legacy of the Discretionary Trust' (2017) 11 *Journal of Equity* 157; but *cf* C Mitchell, '*Commissioner of Stamp Duties (Queensland) v Livingston* (1964): Rights of Estate Beneficiaries and Trust Beneficiaries Compared' in B Sloan (ed), *Landmark Cases in Succession Law* (Oxford, Hart Publishing, 2019), where it is argued that the 'proprietary' label is unhelpful in either case.

[46] (1841) 4 Beav 115, 49 ER 282.

[47] See, eg, *CPT Custodian Pty Ltd v Commissioner of State Revenue of the State of Victoria* [2005] HCA 53, 224 CLR 98 [20], [39].

[48] *CPT Custodian Pty Ltd v Commissioner of State Revenue of the State of Victoria* [2005] HCA 53, 224 CLR 98.

of the Transfer of Land Act 1958 (Vic),[49] but an 'equitable interest' for the purposes of the Real Property Act 1900 (NSW).[50] Therefore, in large part, it might be said that these discussions are exclusively a matter of statutory interpretation and do not have general application.

However, the courts' discussions often put the point in general terms. Most significantly, in *CPT Custodian Pty Ltd v Commissioner of State Revenue of the State of Victoria* the High Court of Australia held that a unit holder's interest under a typical unit trust is 'discrete' such that, even where all the units under a trust are held by one unit holder, he does not have a proprietary interest in the trust assets and does not have the benefit of the exercise of *Saunders v Vautier* rights.[51] This signifies a shift from the mandatory rule that a beneficiary's vested interest is proprietary in nature to a default rule which can be overridden by agreement in the form of a unit trust. The now-default nature of the rule is made crystal-clear by examining how the High Court in *CPT* justified its conclusion. Essentially, two related reasons were given: first, that the terms 'interest' and 'property' have no stable meaning and can only be understood within the context in which they arise;[52] and secondly, that the relevant context is the unit trust deed, and since its terms so provide for the restriction to the beneficiary's interest, courts must give effect to it.[53] These two reasons send one simple message: because the unit trust deed so provides, so its effect must be.

One might doubt this analysis on the basis of an alternative explanation: that even a sole unit holder does not have a *vested* interest, but simply an interest conditional upon a unit trustee's 'powers of appointment, to diminish the interests of present unitholders or (by "redemption") to exclude them from the class of beneficiaries, and to include new members in the class of unitholder beneficiaries'.[54] However, this is not what the cases say; the only relevant 'power' which the courts have concerned themselves with in their analysis is the trustee's power of investment,[55] but this hardly entails that the beneficiary's right is conditional or non-vested.[56] The clear conclusion, therefore, is that the courts have effected a shift from a mandatory to a default rule in relation to the nature of a beneficiary's interest in the unit trust context.

D. Core Content

It is well-known that in *Armitage v Nurse* Millett LJ held that 'The duty of the trustees to perform the trusts honestly and in good faith for the benefit of the beneficiaries is the minimum necessary to give substance to [a trust]'.[57] This statement of the irreducible

[49] *Re S&D International Pty Ltd (in liquidation) (No 4)* [2010] VSC 388, 79 ACSR 595 [148].

[50] *Jonsue Investments Pty Ltd v Balweb Pty Ltd* [2013] NSWSC 325, 9 ASTLR 460.

[51] *CPT Custodian Pty Ltd v Commissioner of State Revenue of the State of Victoria* [2005] HCA 53, 224 CLR 98 [39], [41]–[52]. This decision overrules older authorities to the contrary, eg, *Arjon Pty Ltd v Commissioner of State Revenue* [2003] VSCA 213, 8 VR 502.

[52] ibid [31].

[53] ibid [46], [47], [49].

[54] Slater (n 34) 192.

[55] *CPT Custodian Pty Ltd v Commissioner of State Revenue of the State of Victoria* [2005] HCA 53, 224 CLR 98 [37].

[56] *Underhill and Hayton* (n 39) [5.6].

[57] [1998] Ch 241, 253–54.

core content of a trust has since attracted extensive academic debate, both as to what the core content really is – Does it refer to fiduciary duties or something else? Are the constituent elements conjunctive or disjunctive? – and as to what it ought to be – Is it too wide, too narrow, or just right?[58] But case law since that decision has spoken with one voice, overwhelmingly approving Millett LJ's statement, both in England[59] and Australia.[60]

It would be difficult to disagree that this statement represents a mandatory rule of trusts law. Certain offshore decisions bear out this fact. For example, in *Re An Application for Information About a Trust*[61] and *Centre Trustees (CI) Ltd v Pabst*,[62] the Court of Appeal of Bermuda and the Royal Court of Jersey respectively had to consider the liability of 'protectors' whose powers were expressly stated in the trust deeds to be non-fiduciary. Both decisions held that the powers nevertheless had to be exercised for the benefit of the trust and the beneficiaries. Although the latter, and not the former, expressly cited *Armitage*, the decisions were in substance the same.[63]

The English Court of Appeal's decision in *Citibank NA v QVT Financial LP*,[64] however, demonstrates a shift of that rule to a default rule. *Citibank* concerned a securitisation arrangement under which Citibank was the trustee and MBI Assurance SA (MBIA) was the guarantor of the noteholders' rights. MBIA was given the power to direct Citibank in relation to its exercise of many of its trustee powers, and a clause in the trust deed provided that Citibank was not required to have regard to the noteholders' interests when acting on such instructions. In holding that clause to be valid, Arden LJ (with the agreement of the other judges in the Court of Appeal) held that it did not

> reduce the trustee's obligations below the irreducible minimum identified by Millett LJ in *Armitage v Nurse* … The trustee continues at all times to have an obligation of good faith, and in addition … there are other clauses in the trust deed where the trustee has a real discretion to exercise, for example … a discretion on the trustee to give authorisations or waivers … That point has not been reached [ie where the powers of the trustee were so reduced that it ceases to be a trustee at all] in the present case and therefore there is no risk of recharacterising the office of trustee as something else.[65]

Despite Arden LJ's claim that the outcome is consistent with *Armitage*, it is with respect clear that it is not. In the first place, Millett LJ's statement of the core content was intended to be of general application. Indeed, his Lordship's statement is inconsistent with allowing discrete terms of a trust deed to infiltrate that core, for it would then raise the question of how far the terms could go before a 'trust' is no longer a trust – the very

[58] A majority of these authors' views are noted and summarised in A Hofri-Winogradow, 'The Irreducible Cores of Trustee Obligations' (2023) 139 *LQR* 311.

[59] See, eg. *Lehtimäki v Cooper* [2020] UKSC 33, [2022] AC 155 [82]; *Spread Trustee Co Ltd v Hutcheson* [2011] UKPC 13, [2012] 2 AC 194 [52].

[60] See, eg, *Segelov v Ernst & Young Services Pty Ltd* [2015] NSWCA 156, 89 NSWLR 431 [145]; *Scaffidi v Montevento Holdings Pty Ltd* [2011] WASCA 146 [149].

[61] *Re An Application for Information About a Trust* [2013] CA (Bda) 8 Civ.

[62] *Centre Trustees (CI) Ltd v Pabst* [2009] JRC 109.

[63] See too, in the bonds trust context, P Rawlings, 'The Changing Role of the Trustee in International Bond Issues' (2007) *Journal of Business Law* 43, 52–55.

[64] [2007] EWCA Civ 11, [2007] 1 All ER (Comm) 475.

[65] ibid [82].

question Millett LJ intended conclusively to answer in *Armitage*. To allow digression is to open a can of worms, raising questions such as: How many digressing clauses can we tolerate? What proportion of digressing clauses should we allow? How do we weigh the clauses to come to a conclusion? These do not yield any principled answer.

The conclusion to be drawn, therefore, is that *Citibank* is not an application of *Armitage*, nor does it explain, expound or qualify Millett LJ's statement as it applies to trusts law generally. Rather, *Citibank* represents a specific occasion where the mandatory core content of a trust was treated as a default rule which could be overridden by the parties to a note issuance in relation to specific clauses in the trust deed.

E. Equitable Compensation

Trustees are stewards of trust property, which implies that unless the trust deed or statute provides otherwise, a trustee has a duty to keep the trust property safe and to distribute or disburse such property only in an authorised manner.

According to orthodoxy, a trustee commits a breach of trust where trust property is disbursed without authority. Such a breach does not, however, alter the nature of the trustee's continuing stewardship duty. Following an order of account, a beneficiary will be allowed to falsify an unauthorised disbursement, with the effect that the trustee will be liable to produce the trust property *in specie*. But this may not be possible, for example where the property (and its traceable proceeds) ceases to exist or has been paid out to a bona fide purchaser for value without notice. The next best thing that can be demanded of the trustee, then, is to require him to pay the monetary equivalent of the misappropriated trust property as a substitute for the trustee's ongoing duty to perform the trust. Although commonly labelled a claim for 'equitable compensation,' the beneficiary's claim is better described as a 'substitutive performance' claim, for the monetary compensation acts as a substitute for the trustee's ongoing stewardship duty. The claim focuses on the value of the property misappropriated and not on the loss of value which the breach causes to the trust fund; therefore, 'but for' causation and remoteness of loss are irrelevant to the claim.

A substitutive performance claim is to be distinguished from another imprecisely labelled 'equitable compensation' claim, which is better described as a 'reparation claim'. Where a trustee in breach of trust causes a loss to the trust fund, for example through a defective exercise of his investment powers, a beneficiary is allowed to surcharge the trust account with an amount reflecting the damage caused by the breach. This is a claim against the trustee for the payment of money to repair harm caused to the trust fund; therefore, the amount to be surcharged must be showed to reflect the loss caused by the trustee, usually on a 'but for' basis, and must not be too remote.[66]

The applicability of this body of rules concerning equitable compensation is no doubt mandatory in nature. However, as a result of the House of Lords' and Supreme Court's decision in, respectively, *Target Holdings Ltd v Redferns (a firm)*[67] and *AIB Group (UK)*

[66] *Head v Gould* [1898] 2 Ch 250 (Ch) 266; *Libertarian Investments Ltd v Hall* [2013] HKCFA 93 [167]–[170]; C Mitchell, 'Equitable Rights and Wrongs' (2006) 59 *Current Legal Problems* 267; Sir P Millett, 'Equity's Place in the Law of Commerce' (1998) 114 *LQR* 214; *Underhill and Hayton* (n 39) Art 91.

[67] [1996] AC 421.

plc v Mark Redler & Co Solicitors,[68] in a particular set of circumstances English law now treats this as a default rule which the parties can 'override'. What those circumstances are, and relatedly the breadth of the shift, are, however, matters which requires close examination.

i. Target Holdings

In *Target Holdings*, a firm of solicitors held £1.525m on bare trust for a finance company pursuant to an arrangement for the provision of a loan to a mortgagor. The solicitors were instructed to transfer the money to the mortgagor after the mortgagor had purchased the property and a charge in favour of the finance company had been registered; but in breach of trust the solicitors paid out £1.49m before a charge was received, although a month later the property was duly charged. When it was later discovered that the collateral was worth far less than represented by the mortgagor, the finance company sued the solicitors for breach of trust in paying the money without authority, claiming reconstitution of the full misapplied sum following what can be described as a falsification claim. In the House of Lords, Lord Browne-Wilkinson, with whom the other judges agreed, described the case as concerning a bare trust arising 'as but one incident of a wider commercial transaction involving agency'.[69] His Lordship held:

> The purpose of that transaction is to achieve the commercial objective of the client, be it the acquisition of property or the lending of money on security … until the underlying commercial transaction has been completed, the solicitor can be required to restore to client account moneys wrongly paid away. But to import into such trust an obligation to restore the trust fund once the transaction has been completed would be entirely artificial … once a conveyancing transaction has been completed the client has no right to have the solicitor's client account reconstituted as a 'trust fund.'[70]

What applied instead was 'the basic equitable principle applicable to breach of trust … that the beneficiary is entitled to be compensated for any loss he would not have suffered but for the breach'.[71] His Lordship held that the finance company was not entitled to any compensation for breach: it had 'obtained exactly what it would have obtained had no breach occurred, i.e. a valid security for the sum advanced. Therefore, [it] has suffered no compensatable loss.'[72]

ii. AIB

In *AIB*, a firm of solicitors held £3.3m on bare trust for a bank (AIB) pursuant to a mortgage arrangement. The mortgagor had an existing legal charge with a different bank (X) on the property valued at £4.25m. The solicitors were instructed to transfer the money

[68] [2014] UKSC 58, [2015] AC 1503.
[69] *Target Holdings Ltd v Redferns (a firm)* [1996] AC 421, 436.
[70] ibid.
[71] ibid.
[72] ibid.

to the mortgagor only after that charge was fully redeemed. Through the solicitors' mistake the relevant money was transferred to the mortgagor even though the redemption was not complete, leaving an outstanding loan of £309,000 under a first charge to X, with AIB having to settle for a second charge. Following default, the property was sold for only £1.2m, with AIB receiving a balance of £867,697 after the first charge was paid out. AIB sued the solicitors claiming reconstitution of £2.5m following falsification, ie the full amount paid out in breach of trust minus the sum already received.

Two judgments were handed down by Lords Toulson and Reed, with the remaining members of the bench concurring with both their Lordships. Both held that AIB was entitled to no more than the amount paid out to X under the first charge. Both also approved of Lord Browne-Wilkinson's speech in *Target Holdings*, and the non-applicability of the orthodox mandatory approach towards equitable compensation in the circumstances. However, the judgments reflected subtle but important differences, which will be discussed below.

iii. Discussion

It is sometimes suggested that the combined effect of *Target Holdings* and *AIB* on the present state of the law is that unauthorised disbursements in breach of trust no longer attract substitutive performance claims, but fall to be treated as reparation claims.[73] Support for this analysis can be found in Lord Toulson's judgment in *AIB*. There, his Lordship interpreted Lord Browne-Wilkinson in *Target Holdings* to mean that the aim of equitable compensation, whichever the particular claim involved, requires '[p]lacing the beneficiary in the same position as he would have been in but for the breach'.[74] This statement may of course mean one of two things. The first is that the law will act as if no breach has occurred, thus requiring the trustee substitutively to restore the trust fund with the value of the property misappropriated. The second meaning is that the remedy is concerned with the value of loss suffered by the trust fund, that is, the trustee is liable only for losses caused, measured on a 'but for' basis. While the first meaning is consistent with the orthodox approach to substitutive performance claims, Lord Toulson clearly had the second in mind, conceiving of equitable compensation as 'a monetary award which reflect[s] … loss caused'.[75] Thus, whether the court is concerned with a 'traditional trust' which 'typically govern[s] the ownership-management of property for a group of potential beneficiaries over a lengthy number of years'[76] or a 'commercial trust' which 'arises out of a contract',[77] Lord Toulson thought that the question was always what was the loss caused by the trustee's breach on a 'but for' basis.[78]

[73] eg PG Turner, 'Want of Causation as a Defence to Liability for Misapplication of Trust Assets' in PS Davies, Douglas, and J Goudkamp (eds), *Defences in Equity* (Oxford, Hart Publishing, 2018); A Chan, 'In Defence of *AIB v Mark Redler*' (2021) 27 *Trusts & Trustees* 725.

[74] *AIB Group (UK) plc v Mark Redler & Co Solicitors* [2014] UKSC 58, [2015] AC 1503 [64].

[75] ibid.

[76] ibid [67].

[77] ibid [70].

[78] The same view seems to be reflected in Lord Leggatt's judgment in *Rukhadze v Recovery Partners GP Ltd* [2025] UKSC 10 [169], [197].

If it is true that substitutive performance claims can no longer be brought in any circumstances, then the shift from mandatory to default rule would affect all of trusts law, rather than 'commercial' trusts only. But a different approach is detected in Lord Reed's judgment. In contrast to Lord Toulson's loss-based approach, Lord Reed thought that the aim of the remedy in the case of unauthorised disbursements, consistent with orthodoxy, was 'to restore the trust fund to the position it would have been in but for the default'.[79] His Lordship understood Lord Browne-Wilkinson in *Target Holdings* to hold that a modification is necessary, however, 'in a case where a bare trust had come into being for the purpose of a commercial transaction which had in practical terms been completed, leaving no active obligations for the trustee to perform'.[80] The trustee 'can be required to restore moneys paid away until the commercial transaction has been completed, but not after that point, since it would be artificial to impose the same obligation once the transaction has been completed'.[81] This view modifies the general rules affecting substitutive performance claims[82] by placing a 'completed commercial transaction' qualification on the extent of the trustee's liability: once the intended transaction is 'complete', the full amount of any prior unauthorised disbursement of trust money is no longer treated as loss 'flow[ing] directly from [the breach of trust]', and a more nuanced approach towards assessing the extent of the trustee's liability is required.[83]

A third view, taken by the authors of *Underhill and Hayton*, is that *Target Holdings* and *AIB*

> create an exception [which] requires claims for the reconstitution of depleted trust funds to be treated as though they were not substitutive performance claims but reparation claims in cases where the trust has been exhausted and the trust fund has become absolutely vested in possession and/or where money has been paid out of a bare trust arising as an incident of a wider commercial transaction.[84]

Although not found in so many words, Lord Browne-Wilkinson's speech in *Target Holdings* appears to support such an analysis. In particular, his Lordship held that:

> The obligation to reconstitute the trust fund applicable in the case of traditional trusts … has no application to a case such as the present … once a conveyancing transaction has been completed the client has no right to have the solicitor's client account reconstituted as a 'trust fund'.[85]

This suggests that a substitutive performance claim is inapplicable in a relevant commercial case, and instead only a reparation claim can be brought.

As Lord Leggatt said in the recent Supreme Court decision in *Rukhadze v Recovery Partners GP Ltd*,[86] *Target Holdings* and *AIB* are 'pathbreaking cases, whose ramifications are still being worked out'. Nevertheless, it is immediately obvious that Lord Toulson's view does not reflect the present state of law: cases post-*AIB* continue to treat

[79] *AIB Group (UK) plc v Mark Redler & Co Solicitors* [2014] UKSC 58, [2015] AC 1503 [105].
[80] ibid [106].
[81] ibid.
[82] See ibid [115]–[116].
[83] ibid [135].
[84] *Underhill and Hayton* (n 39) [91.32].
[85] *Target Holdings Ltd v Redferns (a firm)* [1996] AC 421, 436.
[86] *Rukhadze v Recovery Partners GP Ltd* [2025] UKSC 10 [151].

substitutive performance claims as of relevance.[87] As between the second and third views above, for present purposes it is not necessary for us to settle on a preferred view. Whether by modifying substitutive performance claims or by jettisoning such claims in favour of reparation claims, the two views represent a shift from the mandatory equitable compensation rules to default rules in the context of bare trusts arising within a wider commercial transaction, which can be overridden by the parties to the bare trust in the appropriate circumstances.

III. Explanations

This chapter has so far sought to demonstrate that there has been a trend of treating mandatory rules as default in nature in the context of trusts arising in a 'commercial' context. A critical question to ask next is: why so? One reason this question is critical is that it allows us to understand and evaluate the appropriateness of the underlying justifications for this trend. Another reason is that it can facilitate a rational development of the law by informing judges as to the precise ambit of circumstances within which mandatory trusts rules might be treated as default in the future.

As will be seen below, judges and commentators commonly rely on two explanations: the 'commercial' nature of the trust, and the 'contractual' underpinning of the arrangements. As Man Yip observes in her chapter in this collection,

> fierce disagreement persists in two main areas: first, whether the commercial context warrants the application of a different set of a principles from those that are applied in the domestic setting; and, secondly, the role of contract or contractarian thinking in shaping equitable principles in the commercial setting.[88]

I hope to show that these explanations are respectively unhelpful and misleading. Instead, I will suggest that a better explanation lies in the phenomenon of 'bargaining beneficiaries'. This provides the best guide as to the law's future development.

A. 'Commercial'?

When used in a purely descriptive sense, it is unobjectionable to describe all the circumstances discussed in section II above as involving trusts arising in the 'commercial' context. It is at least clear, for example, that they do not involve a settlor setting up a trust in a 'donative' sense, whereby the property is 'essentially a gift, projected on the plane of time and so subjected to a management regime'.[89] But the use of the 'commercial' label goes beyond its descriptive value.

It is clear that in each of those circumstances discussed, courts and commentators have relied on the distinctiveness of the 'commercial' context, in contrast to the

[87] See eg *Main v Giambrone & Law (a firm)* [2017] EWCA Civ 1193, [2018] PNLR 2; *Auden McKenzie (Pharma Division) Ltd v Patel* [2019] EWCA Civ 2291, [2020] BCC 316.

[88] M Yip, 'Equity in Commerce: Why Do We Need Default Rules?', this volume, ch 13, p 250.

[89] B Rudden, 'Book Review' (1981) 44 *MLR* 610.

'traditional' or 'domestic' context, in order to explain the shift from mandatory to default rules. There are numerous examples, and a selection of them will suffice. Perhaps the best known of all is Lord Browne-Wilkinson's speech in *Target Holdings* where modification of the orthodox approach to equitable compensation was justified on the basis that

> it is important, if the trust is not to be rendered commercially useless, to distinguish between the basic principles of trust law and those specialist rules developed in relation to traditional trusts which are applicable only to such trusts and the rationale of which has no application to trusts of quite a different kind.[90]

To cite another example, the modification of the mandatory approach towards the core content of a trust in *Citibank* has been justified on the basis that 'a security trustee is a gatekeeper to balance the interests of the note issuer and the note-holder, and not a traditional trustee who acts for the sole interests of the beneficiaries'.[91] This reflects one of the explanations relied upon by Mann J at first instance in the *Citibank* case, that the surrender of the trustee's decision-making powers to the guarantor 'was done as a matter of commerce'.[92] A third example concerns trusts arising in the context of advanced payments, which has been explained as 'explicable by reference to the companies' duties in times of impecuniosity', where they owe 'fiduciary duties to [their] creditors and must therefore act in their interests, which include ensuring the repayment of their debts'.[93]

The central difficulty with relying on the 'commercial' context as an explanation is that the term 'commercial' does not yield a stable definition. Its definitional instability has been noted on multiple occasions.[94] For example, Bathurst CJ has astutely observed:[95]

> On one end of the spectrum, a married couple may use a discretionary trust in their small family-owned business to benefit themselves and their children. On the other end of the spectrum, trusts are frequently used in superannuation funds or managed investment schemes. Furthermore, commercial trusts vary significantly in their lifespan. Some commercial trusts are established merely to facilitate a commercial objective and then abandoned, whilst other trusts are more enduring.

It is unclear that anyone would confidently label all the trusts referred to by Bathurst CJ as 'commercial' in nature. Furthermore, as Man Yip has observed, 'Even within the

[90] *Target Holdings Ltd v Redferns (a firm)* [1996] AC 421, 435.

[91] M Yip, 'Equity in Commerce: Too Much and Too Little?' in B McFarlane and S Elliott (eds), *Equity Today: 150 Years after the Judicature Reforms* (Oxford, Hart Publishing, 2023) 397.

[92] *Citibank NA v MBIA Assurance SA* [2006] EWHC 3215 (Ch) [48]. See too A Trukhtanov, 'The Irreducible Core of Trust Obligations' (2007) 123 *LQR* 342; Hofri-Winogradow (n 58) 320.

[93] Yip (n 22) 351.

[94] See, eg, *Underhill and Hayton* (n 39) [7.3]; *Chan Yuen Lan v See Fong Mun* [2014] SGCA 36 [155]; M Bryan, 'Reflections on Some Commercial Applications of the Trust' in I Ramsay (ed), *Key Developments In Corporate Law and Trusts Law: Essays in Honour of Professor Harold Ford* (London, LexisNexis Butterworths, 2002) 205, 207; J Morgan, *Contract Law Minimalism* (Cambridge, Cambridge University Press, 2013) 111. See too HW Disney, *The Elements of Commercial Law*, 4th edn (London, Macdonald, 1931) 1: '"Commercial law" is an expression incapable of strict definition.'

[95] TF Bathurst, 'Commercial Trusts and the Liability of Beneficiaries: Are Commercial Trusts a Satisfactory Vehicle to be Used in Modern Day Commerce?' (2021 Harold Ford Memorial Lecture) 10, available at law.unimelb.edu.au/__data/assets/pdf_file/0006/3932034/CJ-Bathurst-Paper-2021-Harold-Ford-Memorial-Lecture-Commercial-Trusts.pdf.

range of commercial transactions, every case is different and merits consideration of its unique circumstances'.[96]

Certainly, attempts have been made to define what counts as 'commercial' trusts. Perhaps the most significant of them is found in the New Zealand Trusts Act 2019, where 'specified commercial trusts' attract modified rules. Schedule 3 provides as follows:

> **1 Meaning of specified commercial trust**
>
> (1) A specified commercial trust means—
>
> (a) an express trust … —
>
> (i) that is created for the purpose of facilitating 1 or more commercial transactions; and
>
> (ii) every beneficiary of which is a beneficiary as a result of entering into the commercial transaction that the trust is created to facilitate, or as a result of entering into a commercial transaction of the type that the trust is created to facilitate
>
> …
>
> (3) In this clause,—
>
> **commercial transaction** is a transaction that all parties enter into in trade
>
> …
>
> **trade** means any trade, business, industry, profession, activity of commerce, or undertaking relating to the supply or acquisition of goods or services or to the disposition or acquisition of any interest in land.

This definition undeniably covers much of the terrain which we might consider to be the 'commercial' context. However, as a *general definition* of 'commercial' trusts,[97] it remains problematic in two important respects. First, under section 1(1)(a)(i), the 'commercial' label would be attracted in many instances where trusts would not usually be so labelled, for example, where the commercial transaction facilitated is but a small aspect of an otherwise domestic 'family office'. Secondly, the 'definition' is circular: a 'specified commercial trust' facilitates 'commercial transactions', which are transactions entered into in 'trade', which include activities 'of commerce'. A stable definition remains elusive.

In the end, we can only conclude that explaining the shifts from mandatory to default rules on the basis of the 'commercial' context is unhelpful. Due to the impossibility of defining what counts as 'commercial', the purported explanation lacks precision. This leads to the further problem that the purported explanation fails accurately to delineate the ambit of circumstances in which future courts might consider transforming mandatory rules to default rules. While it may be that, in theory, a case-by-case evolution of what counts as 'commercial' could provide a sharp enough definition, the present state of the law provides no comfort that case law is on such a trajectory. If anything, the cases themselves have caused more confusion than clarity.

[96] Yip (n 22) 364. She makes the same point in 'Equity in Commerce: Why Do We Need Default Rules', this volume, ch 13, 250: 'the label "commercial context" is not a monolithic concept'.

[97] It is acknowledged that Sch 3 does not purport to define 'commercial trusts' generally, but only for statutory purposes.

B. 'Contracts'?

It is trite that trusts are analytically distinct from contracts in Anglo-Australian law. It may be for this obvious reason that it is rare to find the contractual arrangement between the parties being cited as a direct *reason* for the shift from mandatory trust rules to default rules. But that reasoning often arises indirectly through two different channels.

The first channel is related to the 'commercial' context. Jurists often expressly or impliedly consider that a contract between the parties to the trust relationship is what makes 'commercial' trusts distinct and that it is the underlying contractual relationship which justifies according those trusts separate treatment. The two judgments in *AIB* are representative examples. In the course of explaining the reasoning in *Target Holdings*, Lord Toulson held that, while 'A traditional trust will typically govern the ownership-management of property for a group of potential beneficiaries over a lengthy number of years',[98]

> a commercial trust differs from a typical traditional trust in that it arises out of a contract rather than the transfer of property by way of gift. The contract defines the parameters of the trust … the trustee's duties are likely to be closely defined and may be of limited duration.[99]

Similarly, Lord Reed explained that 'commercial trusts, usually arising out of contractual relationships rather than the transfer of property by way of gift, differ in a number of respects from the more traditional trust'.[100] In a similar vein is The Financial Markets Law Committee Report of 2004, which states that, in contrast to domestic trusts, 'the commercial trust arises out of contract rather than the traditional transfer of property by way of gift'.[101]

The second channel through which the 'contract' explanation arises relates to the mandatory/default rules methodology. In the past 40 years or so, various American scholars have analysed discrete areas of law such as corporate[102] and contract[103] law through the lens of mandatory/default rules in order to discover the functions and implications of legal rules, as well as to provide normative guidelines for how the law ought to develop. These scholars generally view default rules as reflecting a 'contractarian' approach (or 'majoritarian' defaults): that is, they reflect, and should reflect, contracting terms which parties to it, bargaining to achieve private wealth maximisation, would normally reach if bargaining were costless.[104] Moreover, default rules are said to protect freedom of contract by allowing parties to agree, through contracting, to

[98] *AIB Group (UK) plc v Mark Redler & Co Solicitors* [2014] UKSC 58, [2015] AC 1503 [67].
[99] ibid [70].
[100] ibid [102].
[101] Financial Markets Law Committee, *Trustee Exemption Clauses Report* (Issue 62, May 2004) 1.
[102] JN Gordon, 'The Mandatory Structure of Corporate Law' (1989) 89 *Columbia Law Review* 1549; JC Coffee Jr, 'The Mandatory/Enabling Balance in Corporate Law: An Essay on the Judicial Role' (1989) 89 *Columbia Law Review* 1618.
[103] I Ayres and R Gertner, 'Filling Gaps in Incomplete Contracts: An Economic Theory of Default Rules Filling Gaps in Incomplete Contracts: An Economic Theory of Default Rules' (1989) 99 *Yale Law Journal* 87; T Baker and KD Logue, 'Mandatory Rules and Default Rules in Insurance Contracts' in D Schwarcz and P Siegelman (eds), *Research Handbook on the Economics of Insurance Law* (Cheltenham, Edward Elgar, 2015).
[104] Gordon (n 102) 1550–51.

disapply those rules.[105] Mandatory rules, on the other hand, are 'anti-contractarian': they are intent-defeating,[106] justified only by important reasons of public policy, or where there would typically be information asymmetry between the parties,[107] or a need to protect the contracting parties or those external to the contract.[108] Applying these analyses, the shift from mandatory to default trusts rules might be thought to find its explanation in the facilitation of the underlying contract between the parties.

It is undeniable that a contract underlies the trusts in all the circumstances discussed in section II above. Yet, to explain trusts law rules by reference to the contract gives rise to three fundamental problems.

First, the fundamental conceptual distinction between contracts and trusts cannot be ignored. The contractarian view presupposes that trusts are consensual devices which arise due to a 'contract' between the settlor and trustee, and that the protection of that bilateral autonomy is an overarching concern of trusts law.[109] But as Michael Bryan has convincingly demonstrated, trusts respond to the *unilateral* intention of the settlor, even if that intention may be shared by a trustee who is his counter-contracting party.[110] Therefore, unless we are prepared to say that instances where mandatory trusts rules have become default rules are instances where trusts are no longer trusts but contracts, there is considerable difficulty in explaining that phenomenon on the basis of the contract. This point is well made in the Law Commission Report, *Trustee Exemption Clauses*.[111] In that report the Law Commission considers the view advanced by the Financial Markets Law Committee, referred to earlier,[112] that 'commercial' trusts are those arising out of contracts and not gifts. It notes that the Committee argues that 'the trustee/beneficiary relationship in such arrangements is in many ways closer in substance to contracts between sophisticated parties with the freedom to contract, than to a traditional trust relationship'.[113] But the Law Commission's response is on point: 'This argument can only be taken so far, as obviously the relationship is more than a contractual one (else the market would feel no need to make use of trusts at all).'[114]

The second fundamental problem is that the contractarian explanation is not descriptively accurate. The contractarian explanation conceives of the deal 'between settlor and trustee'[115] as the key to explaining trusts rules. However, not all the contracts in the circumstances discussed in section II above are between settlor and trustee: in the

[105] Ayres and Gertner (n 103) 88.
[106] TP Gallanis, 'The Trustee's Duty to Inform' (2007) 85 *North Carolina Law Review* 1595, 1620. *cf* JH Langbein, 'Mandatory Rules in the Law of Trusts' (2004) 98 *Northwestern University Law Review* 1105, 1125–26.
[107] Baker and Logue (n 103).
[108] Ayres and Gertner (n 103).
[109] See Langbein (n 1) 627.
[110] M Bryan, 'The Inferred Trust: An Unhappy Marriage of Contract and Trust?' (2016) 69 *Current Legal Problems* 377. See also YK Liew, 'Trusts: Modern Taxonomy and Autonomy' (2021) 35 *Trust Law International* 27, 29–30.
[111] Law Commission, *Trustee Exemption Clauses* (Law Com No 301, 2006, Cm 6874).
[112] See main text to n 101 above.
[113] *Trustee Exemption Clauses* (n 111) [C.37].
[114] ibid [C.38].
[115] Langbein (n 1) 627.

case of unit trusts, the relevant contract is that between a unit holder and the trustee;[116] but it has been held that unit holders are not 'settlors'.[117] Moreover, in the case of trusts declared over advanced payments, the settlor and the trustee are the same individual – the company who declares itself trustee for the customer – and it is trite that one cannot contract with oneself.

Thirdly, the contractarian explanation unduly overreaches. In the modern day it is becoming increasingly rare to find trusts being established in the absence of a contract between the settlor and the trustee, even in the domestic context. And yet, no one ever treats those instances as warranting a shift from mandatory to default rules.

In sum, therefore, it is misleading to rest the requisite explanation on the underlying contract between the parties.

C. Bargaining Beneficiaries

In recent times, a number of academics have advanced the argument that it is crucial for a proper understanding of the law to focus on the basal aim of trusts, which is the provision of benefits to the trust beneficiaries. For example, drawing on Millett LJ's key statement in *Armitage v Nurse* that the irreducible core content of trusts involves performing a trust 'for the benefit of the beneficiaries',[118] Derwent Coshott has argued that express trusts can be theorised as having the purpose of 'ensur[ing] that enforceable benefits are conferred on people'.[119] Lusina Ho and Richard Nolan, addressing express trusts from the remedial perspective, argue the same:

> The obligations of a trustee give primacy to the 'performance interest' of beneficiaries of that trust: that is, the interest of those beneficiaries in actual execution of the trust rather than compensation for loss resulting from the trustee's failure to execute the trust.[120]

The shifts we see from mandatory to default trusts can be explained from a similar beneficiary-focused perspective: those shifts occur when the beneficiaries of the trusts consist solely of 'bargaining beneficiaries', that is, beneficiaries with an unconditional entitlement who had all bargained for the trust terms at the outset. Indeed, trusts whose beneficiaries consist solely of bargaining beneficiaries defines the proper ambit of circumstances where courts might consider shifting mandatory to default rules in the future.

It is certainly trite that the beneficiaries' positive consent or acceptance of terms is not essential for the creation of a trust; the highest the point can be put is that beneficiaries

[116] Although there is the initial contract between the manager, *qua* settlor, and trustee when setting up the unit trust, that contract is not relevant to explaining the trusts law rules applicable to unit holders because the doctrine of privity of contract precludes (at a minimum) burdens being imposed on unit holders as 'third parties'.

[117] *Re AEG Unit Trust (Managers) Ltd's Deed* [1957] Ch 415, 420.

[118] [1998] Ch 241, 253.

[119] D Coshott, 'To Benefit Another: A Theory of the Express Trust' (2020) 136 *LQR* 221, 244.

[120] L Ho and RC Nolan, 'The Performance Interest in the Law of Trusts' (2020) 136 *LQR* 402, 402.

must 'accept' their role through non-disclaimer.[121] But the present argument does not concern the prerequisites for creation of trusts: the discussion is situated not at the minimal end of the consent spectrum but at the maximal end where we find 'bargaining beneficiaries'. A 'bargaining beneficiary' may not have 'bargained' in the sense of having negotiated the trust terms, but they would have positively and fully assented to them in agreeing to be a beneficiary under the trust. Often such a beneficiary will be the settlor, for example in the case of a bare trust, where the settlor is in fact usually the initiator of the arrangement and constitutes himself a beneficiary according to terms they propose. However, as noted above, the unit trust arrangement indicates that it is not vital for a bargaining beneficiary also to have been the settlor.

As explained earlier, a 'bargaining beneficiary' refers to a beneficiary whose entitlement is unconditional. Two key points of clarification are required here.

First, if the trust contemplates that discretionary powers may be exercised in a way which affects a beneficiary's entitlement, for example, a trustee having distributive discretion under a discretionary trust or a protector having a power to appoint or remove beneficiaries, then even if the beneficiary or beneficiaries under the trust are involved in a 'bargaining' process, this does not make them 'bargaining beneficiaries' for the purposes of the present argument. This is because in these situations the trust would not *solely* be concerned with the interests of bargaining beneficiaries, but potentially others whose legal position ought not to be affected by any other individual beneficiary's actions. More importantly, it can also be observed that trusts which are typically considered to be within the 'domestic' context more often than not involve beneficiaries with a conditional interest (in the sense employed in this paragraph), whereas 'commercial' trusts typically concern trusts which solely involve 'bargaining beneficiaries'.

Secondly, the language of 'unconditional' as opposed to 'vested interest' is deliberate. This is not simply to take into account the nature of a unit holder's right under unit trusts, which is unconditional but certainly not 'vested' in the *Saunders v Vautier* sense. The more fundamental reason for the conception is that the explanation I proffer here does not hinge on the *nature* of the beneficiary's interest, but is intended to emphasise the beneficiary's involvement in the trust 'bargaining' process and the *sphere of effect* which that involvement can have. The point is that such involvement might only be significant where the beneficiary's interest is unconditional.

The reasons for which trusts whose beneficiaries solely include bargaining beneficiaries might attract a shift from mandatory to default rules are simple. As the earlier-mentioned works of Coshott, and Ho and Nolan, indicate, one important function of trusts law in general is the protection of the beneficiaries, for whose benefit express trusts exist in the first place. Hence the use of mandatory rules, which, by definition, have a protective function.[122] But bargaining beneficiaries are a distinct class: they are beneficiaries with an unconditional interest, who consciously choose to enter into the relevant trust relationship, positively and fully assenting to its terms. If all the beneficiaries of a trust solely consist of bargaining beneficiaries, then the need for the trust

[121] *Hardoon v Belilios* [1901] AC 118, 123. See too YK Liew and C Mitchell, 'The Creation of Express Trusts' (2017) 11 *Journal of Equity* 133, 152–55.

[122] See main text to nn 108 above.

structure to have a freestanding protective function is greatly reduced. Thus, mandatory rules are potentially less required. Instead, the primary concern is for the trust structure to preserve its integrity; that is, to reflect characteristics sufficient for the arrangement to count as a trust rather than, say, a contract. As one would expect, those characteristics are less stringent than those required under orthodox trusts law rules, since the law is here primarily concerned with a structural, rather than a substantive or protective, matter.

The fit of all the circumstances discussed in section II above with this explanation is obvious: the beneficiaries of all those trusts consisted solely of bargaining beneficiaries. Judicial statements as to the relevance of the parties' 'mutual'[123] or 'contractual'[124] intention can be understood in line with this explanation: they hint at the role the beneficiaries play in positively assenting to the trust terms at the outset. And the explanation is also in line with Arden LJ's judgment in *Citibank*, which indicates that courts in these situations are only concerned with the structural integrity of the trust: they will be enforced so long as 'the powers of the trustee [are not] so reduced that it ceases to be a trustee at all' and so long as 'there is no risk of recharacterising the office of trustee as something else'.[125] Less obvious, perhaps, are the advanced payments cases, where the trust appears to arise due to the company's unilateral decision to constitute itself trustee for its customers. However, even here, the cases treat the customers/beneficiaries as 'bargaining beneficiaries'. Thus, in *Lewis's of Leicester*, Robert Walker J in describing the company's actions of segregating the customers' money said that the company had aimed 'to ensure that future receipts …, *believed to be already subject to a trust under the standard-form agreements*, were kept separate and identifiable'.[126] And in *Re Kayford*, Megarry J said that the result would have been different had the monies been paid to the company not by 'members of the public' but by 'trade creditors',[127] implying that what different payors accepted at the outset mattered to the outcome.

Given the explanatory force of the 'bargaining beneficiaries' rationale, it is but a small step further to suggest that it can provide useful guidance to future courts in deciding the appropriate circumstances for potentially shifting mandatory trusts rules to default ones. The point is most conveniently put in the reverse: if a trust does not solely consist of bargaining beneficiaries, then there is probably no justification in departing from mandatory rules, since an important aspect of those rules is the protection of the actual and potential beneficiaries under the trust. Conversely, no unintended damage can be caused to any beneficiary if the beneficiaries of the trust consist solely of bargaining beneficiaries. The basal concern in such cases is to ensure that the trust device remains distinctive; beyond that minimal criterion, it might be possible for the court to transform mandatory rules to default ones.

[123] See, eg, *Barclays Bank Ltd v Quistclose Investments Ltd* [1970] AC 567, 580.

[124] See, eg, *Newby v Enron Corp (Re Enron Corporation Securities, Derivative & 'ERISA' Litigation)*, 70 Fed R Serv 3d 113, [8] (SD Tex, 2008) (unit trusts); *Target Holdings Ltd v Redferns (a firm)* [1996] AC 421, 436.

[125] [2007] EWCA Civ 11 [82].

[126] [1995] BCC 514, 520.

[127] [1975] 1 WLR 279, 282.

IV. Addendum

In the workshop at which this chapter was presented, some participants[128] raised the concern that conceptualising the trusts rules in this chapter as 'default' rules in the circumstances discussed may be both wrong and misleading. It may be wrong because they are unlike what typical default rules resemble in contract law, where parties are free to specify the content of the rule they wish to apply; it may be misleading because trusts, unlike contracts generally, have third-party effects, and therefore understanding those rules as 'default' rules mistakenly suggests that the law allows parties freely to bargain out of core trusts rules while obtaining the ring-fencing advantage which trusts afford. The suggestion is that, rather than 'default' rules, perhaps the circumstances discussed in this chapter demonstrate simply that the relevant trusts rules are mandatory rules with exceptions.

To this, four points can be made.

First, 'default' rules are rules which allow the relevant party or parties to 'alter or negate'[129] their application. Certainly, they come in various shapes and forms, some of which provide more latitude for customisation. However, even a rule which simply allows for the negation of its content can rightly be termed 'default'. It is this 'thinner' sense of 'default' to which this chapter refers.

Secondly, some analytical confusion occurs if we reject the language of 'default' rules and adopt instead the conception of 'mandatory rules with exceptions'. Mandatory trusts law rules, by their very nature, ought to apply universally to all trusts, without exception. To speak of those rules as inapplicable – or having limits – in certain types of trust arrangements is a contradiction of terms.

Thirdly, and linked to the previous point, identifying those trusts law rules as 'default' rules in the relevant circumstances provides the all-important message that it is something which the parties intended, acted on, agreed or bargained for which leads to the rules' disapplication. To conceive of those circumstances as being simply 'limits' to the application of mandatory rules fails to explain when and why those limits apply. Even more worrisome is the fact that it may suggest that the courts, at their discretion, are disapplying those otherwise mandatory rules. This detracts from the certainty which is so crucial in (at least the core) commercial contexts, but also deprives future courts of guidance as to when those limits ought to apply.

Finally, this chapter does not suggest that *all* trusts rules ought to be considered to be default rules whenever bargaining beneficiaries are involved. It simply makes the argument that it is because there are bargaining beneficiaries that some trusts rules are taken to be default rather than mandatory in nature. There remains an extant – and fundamentally critical – question of which mandatory trusts rules ought never to be understood as default rules, even in the context of a trust solely consisting of bargaining beneficiaries. The answer to that question will provide us clarity as to the absolute core content of what makes a trust a trust. As discussed earlier, it may be that the absolute

[128] I thank, in particular, Louise Gullifer, Rory Gregson and Jonathan Morgan for pressing me on the point.
[129] Langbein (n 1) 1105.

irreducible core content of a trust is concerned primarily with the structural integrity of a trust rather than with a substantive protective function.[130] Normatively, that answer ought also to identify the boundary between when it and is not legitimate for bargaining beneficiaries to intend, act, agree, or bargain out of those rules while benefiting from the asset protection function of trusts law.

[130] See main text from n 122 above.

INDEX

www.ingramcontent.com/pod-product-compliance
Ingram Content Group UK Ltd.
Pitfield, Milton Keynes, MK11 3LW, UK
UKHW020238290926
15470UKWH00002B/605

9 781509 971206